EYEWITNESS TRAVEL

ISTANBUL

EYEWITNESS TRAVEL

ISTANBUL

DK Penguin Random House

Project Editor Nick Inman
Art Editor Kate Poole
Editors Claire Folkard, Jane Oliver, Christine Stroyan
Designers Jo Doran, Paul Jackson
Visualizer Joy Fitzsimmons

Main Contributors Rosie Ayliffe, Rose Baring,
Barnaby Rogerson, Canan Silay

Maps Paul Bates, Anne Rayski, Glyn Rozier (Esr Cartography Ltd); Neil Cook,
Maria Donnelly, Ewan Watson (Colourmap Scanning Ltd)

Photographers Anthony Souter, Linda Whitwam, Francesca Yorke

Illustrators Richard Bonson, Stephen Conlin, Gary Cross,
Richard Draper, Paul Guest, Maltings Partnership,
Chris Orr & Associates, Paul Weston, John Woodcock

Printed and bound in China

First American Edition, 1998
16 17 18 19 10 9 8 7 6 5 4 3 2 1

Published in the United States by Dorling Kindersley Limited,
345 Hudson Street, New York, New York 10014

**Reprinted with revisions 1999, 2000, 2001, 2002,
2004, 2007, 2009, 2011, 2013, 2014, 2016**

Copyright 1998, 2016 © Dorling Kindersley Limited, London
A Penguin Random House Company

Published in the UK by Dorling Kindersley Limited.

A catalog record for this book is available from the Library of Congress.

ISSN 1542-1554
ISBN 978-1-4654-4063-1

Throughout this book, floors are referred to in accordance with
European usage; i.e., the "first floor" is the floor above ground level.

MIX
Paper from
responsible sources
FSC FSC™ C018179
www.fsc.org

Front cover main image: The Blue Mosque, Istanbul's most famous religious building

◀ The stunning interior of the Blue Mosque in Sultanahmet Square

Contents

How to Use this Guide **6**

Madonna mosaic in the Church of
St Saviour in Chora

Introducing Istanbul

Great Days in Istanbul **10**

Putting Istanbul on the Map **14**

The History of Istanbul **20**

Istanbul at a Glance **36**

Tile panel in the Paired Pavilions of Topkapı
Palace's Harem

The great 6th-century
Byzantine church of Haghia
Sophia *(see pp74–7)*

Travellers' Needs

Men smoking bubble pipes in Çorlulu Ali
Paşa Courtyard

Beyond Istanbul

Simit seller

Ferry passing the busy Karaköy waterfront
below the Galata Tower

Survival Guide

Dolmabahçe Mosque with the skyline of Sultanahmet in the distance

HOW TO USE THIS GUIDE

This guide helps you to get the most from your stay in Istanbul. It provides both expert recommendations and detailed practical advice. *Introducing Istanbul* locates the city geographically, sets Istanbul in its historical and cultural context and gives an overview of the main attractions. *Istanbul Area by Area* is the main sightseeing section, giving detailed information on all the major sights plus three recommended walks, with photographs,

maps and illustrations throughout. *Greater Istanbul* looks at sights outside the city centre. *The Bosphorus* guides you through a trip up the straits, and *Excursions from Istanbul* explores other places within easy reach of the city. Tips for restaurants, hotels, entertainment and shopping are found in *Travellers' Needs*, while the *Survival Guide* contains useful advice on everything from personal security to public transport.

Finding your way around Istanbul

The centre of Istanbul has been divided into four sightseeing areas, each with its own chapter, colour-coded for easy reference. All sights are numbered and plotted on an area map for each chapter. The major sights are covered in more detail.

The area shaded pink is shown in greater detail on the Street-by-Street map on the following pages.

2 **Street-by-Street Map** This gives a bird's-eye view of the heart of each sightseeing area. Interesting features are labelled. There is also a list of "star sights" that no visitor should miss.

1 **Area Introduction** This describes the history and character of the area and has a map on which the sights have been plotted. Other key information is also given.

Each area has colour-coded thumb tabs.

Locator Map

A suggested route takes in the most interesting and attractive streets in the area.

3 **Detailed Information** All the important sights are described individually. They are listed in order, following the numbering on the area map, with practical information about each.

Istanbul Area Map

The coloured areas shown on this map *(see inside front cover)* are the four main sightseeing areas used in this guide. Each is covered in a full chapter in *Istanbul Area by Area (pp50–109)*. They are highlighted on other maps throughout the book. In *Istanbul at a Glance (see pp36–45)*, they help you to locate the top sights. The introduction to the *Street Finder (see pp246–263)* shows on which detailed street map you will find each area.

4 **Introduction to Greater Istanbul** Greater Istanbul has its own introduction, outlining what the city suburbs have to offer the sightseer. It is divided into five districts, shown on a map.

Introductory text gives an overview of the main sights in the Greater Istanbul area.

A map of the city shows Greater Istanbul and the areas covered in the chapter's sub-divisions.

5 **Introduction to Greater Istanbul areas** An introduction places the area in its historical context and provides a map showing the numbered sights.

Practical information is provided in an information block. The key to the symbols used is on the back flap.

The Visitors' Checklist provides detailed practical information.

6 **Istanbul's Major Sights** These are given two or more full pages. Historic buildings are dissected to reveal their interiors. Where necessary, sights are colour-coded to help you locate the most interesting areas.

INTRODUCING
ISTANBUL

GREAT DAYS IN ISTANBUL

Istanbul is a frenetic city with a wealth of culture, history and nightlife. Split in two by the Bosphorous Strait, it is the only city in the world to straddle two continents, Europe and Asia, and thus has two contrasting atmospheres. These itineraries are designed to provide a flavour of the city as a whole.

Some of the city's best attractions are arranged first thematically and then by duration of stay. All the sights are cross-referenced to the rest of the guide, so it is possible to look up more information and tailor the day to suit your needs. Price guides include meals, transport and admission fees.

A range of exotic spices for sale in the Spice Bazaar

Shopping and Seafood

Two Adults allow at least $105

- Refresh your senses in the Spice Bazaar
- Shop for antiques in Çukurcuma
- Haggle in the unmissable Grand Bazaar
- Enjoy the buzz on Nevizade Sokak

Morning

Start the day with a riot of colour, stalls and smells at the **Spice Bazaar** *(see p90)*. Shop for exotic food items, including handmade Turkish delight and creamy goats' cheese here. Next, head up to the bustling **Grand Bazaar** *(see pp100–101)*, a labyrinthine Ottoman shopping complex housing thousands of leather, rug, ceramics and jewellery shops. Be sure to bargain as prices are mostly inflated and price tags are often absent altogether. All this shopping is bound to whet your appetite, so head for the waterfront district of

Kumpkapı. Savour delicious seafood from any of the 50 fish restaurants located here. Again, many outlets do not display prices, so inquire before placing your order.

Afternoon

After lunch, take a taxi to the Galata Bridge. Stroll across the bustling bridge to Karaköy, then ride the Tünel antique funicular up to **Beyoğlu** *(see pp102–109)*, before making your way up **İstiklâl Caddesi** *(see pp104–5)* to shop for clothes, shoes, books and music. Further up is the district of **Çukurcuma** *(see p109)*, which is famous as a hunting ground for antique furniture and ornaments. Nevizade Sokak, just off İstiklâl Caddesi, is a narrow street lined with dozens of traditional *meyhanes* or taverns *(see p191)*. The area comes alive at night, when hundreds of locals flock here and passers-by are serenaded by traditional musicians playing *fasil*, a local form of gypsy music.

A Family Day Out

Family of four allow $120

- See Istanbul in miniature
- Take a boat trip to Büyükada
- Admire Büyükad from a horse-drawn carriage

Morning

Catch a bus or taxi from Taksim Square to **Miniatürk** *(see pp222–3)* in Sütlüce on the northern shore of the **Golden Horn** *(see p91)*. The park displays miniatures of the city's most famous sights, such as **Haghia Sophia** *(see pp74–7)*, as well as other treasures from around the country that reflect Turkey's rich heritage. There is also a children's park and a museum showcasing photographs of Atatürk, the great Turkish leader of the early 20th century, and the battles at Gallipoli. After such a busy morning, head to **Miniatürk's** attractive café-restaurant overlooking the Golden Horn.

The busy, bustling dock at Eminönü

◀ Mosaic depicting the infancy of the Virgin Mary, Church of St Saviour in Chora

Afternoon

Head back to Istanbul after lunch and hop on a ferry bound for Büyükada, one of the nine islands that make up the **Princes' Islands** *(see p161)*. It is a one-and-a-half-hour trip from Kabataş pier (one hour and ten minutes from Kadıköy pier), so there is plenty of time to admire the pretty view and watch as Istanbul recedes on the horizon. On arrival, stroll around the main square of Saat Meydanı or take a horse-drawn carriage ride around the island. Climb the hill to St George's Monastery for panoramic views and enjoy a meal at the hilltop restaurant.

The Fortress of Europe overlooking the Bosphorus

Mosques, Museums and Hamams

Two Adults allow at least $140

- **Byzantine iconography at Haghia Sophia**
- **Get a glimpse of the past at the Museum of Turkish and Islamic Arts**
- **An awe-inspiring visit to Topkapı Palace**

Morning

Begin the day with a visit to the iconic **Blue Mosque** *(see pp80–81)*, famous for its slender minarets and blue Iznik tiles. Stroll through the well-tended garden at the front before making your way to the imposing **Haghia Sophia** *(see pp74–7)*, once the largest and most famous church in the city, later a mosque and today a museum. Inside is a marvellous array of Byzantine mosaics, marble tile panels and beautifully incised capitals, as well as a huge domed ceiling. Next, head to the nearby **Museum of Turkish and Islamic Arts** *(see p79)*, which has a wonderful collection of glass and metalwork, carpets and manuscripts from down the centuries, as well as modern art from Turkey and overseas. For lunch, head to Divanyolu Caddesi, which is dotted with traditional restaurants offering prices to suit all budgets.

Afternoon

Devote at least three hours to exploring **Topkapı Palace** *(see pp56–61)*, a sprawling complex of courtyards, gardens, fountains, a harem and a collection of priceless antiques. Then, at the end of a long day, indulge in that most Turkish of pleasures, a visit to a Turkish bath *(see p69)*. **Çemberlitaş Baths** *(see p83)* in Sultanahmet is one of the finest.

Golden mosaic of Virgin Mary with baby Jesus, at Haghia Sophia

---

Up the Bosphorus

Two Adults allow at least $95

- **Experience the European shore of the Bosphorus**
- **Soak up the views at the Fortress of Europe**
- **Stroll through the pretty village of Bebek**

Morning

Catch a bus from Taksim Square or Eminönü bus terminus to Sarıyer or Emirgan and get off at Arnavutköy on the Bosphorus. There are some lovingly restored Ottoman houses and mansions to admire here, most of them painted in pastel shades and trimmed with intricate wooden fretwork. Cafés line the backstreets, so relax and unwind over a coffee and a pastry. From Arnavutköy, continue walking northwards, past the fishing boats and pleasure cruisers bobbing on the water, until you reach **Bebek** *(see p140 & p148)*, one of Istanbul's most affluent villages. Dine in style at the well-reviewed **Poseidon** *(see p206)*. Sip an aperitif and enjoy the splendid view here before savouring the menu of fresh fish.

Afternoon

Delve into history at the imposing **Fortress of Europe** *(see pp142–3)*, built in the 15th century as part of the Ottoman Turkish conquest of Constantinople. There is also a fantastic view of the Bosphorus from here. Afterwards, walk up the Bosphorus to the **Sakıp Sabancı Museum** *(see p143)*, set in a restored 1920s villa with fine views across the strait. The museum hosts remarkable art and culture exhibitions and has a beautiful calligraphy display. Continue north to the delightful 19th-century pavilions of nearby **Emirgan Park** *(see p143)* with its many pine, fir and cypress trees and an ornamental lake. This attractive setting is the venue for the Tulip Festival, which is held in April every year.

2 days in Istanbul

- Gaze in awe at the soaring dome of the Haghia Sophia
- Enjoy a steamed bath in the Ottoman Çemberlitaş Baths
- Cruise the Bosphorus, the ribbon of water separating Europe and Asia

Day 1
Morning
Start at the monumental **Haghia Sophia** *(see pp74–7)*, one of the world's truly iconic buildings. Cross the tram line to the **Milion** *(see p73)*, a marble fragment once part of a mighty triumphal arch. Beneath your feet lies the atmospherically lit **Basilica Cistern** *(see p78)*. Resurface onto Divanyolu Caddesi, an historic thoroughfare lined with traditional Turkish lunch spots.

Afternoon
Cross Divanyolu to the **Blue Mosque** *(see pp80–81)*, a cascade of tumbling domes and slender minarets. Exit onto the **Hippodrome** *(see p82)*, the central barrier of the chariot-racing track marked by the Egyptian Obelisk. Then ride the tram to the **Grand Bazaar** *(see pp100–101)*, a centuries old mall selling everything from fake Louis Vuitton bags to antique Turkish rugs. Exit to **Constantine's Column** *(see p83)* before crossing an alley to relax in the steam of Ottoman-era **Çemberlitaş Baths** *(see p83)*.

Day 2
Morning
Begin the day with a trip to the 15th-century **Topkapı Palace** *(see pp56–61)*, which stands in splendid isolation on a hilltop overlooking the Bosphorus and Sea of Marmara. Don't miss the labyrinthine **Harem** *(see pp60–61)* before catching the tram to the peaceful grounds of the Süleymaniye Mosque complex.

Afternoon
Explore the **Süleymaniye Mosque** *(see pp92–93)* complex which presides majestically over the third of Istanbul's seven hills.

Then walk down to **Rüstem Paşa Mosque** *(see pp90–91)*, famed for its İznik tiles, before wandering through the exotically scented **Spice Bazaar** *(see p90)*. Exit onto the Eminönü waterfront, clustered around the historic **Galata Bridge** *(see p91)*, before finishing with the **Bosphorus Cruise** *(see pp146–51)* up the famous strait.

3 days in Istanbul

- Delve into the eerie underground world of the Basilica Cistern
- Haggle for a Turkish carpet in the Grand Bazaar
- Follow in the footsteps of Ottoman sultans through the Topkapı Palace

Day 1
Morning
Get to know Istanbul's history at the maze-like **Archaeological Museums** *(see pp64–7)* before strolling through **Gülhane Park** *(see p63)* to tea gardens overlooking the Bosphorus. Exit the park and head up pretty **Soğukçeşme Sokaği** *(see p63)*, lined with period houses, to lunch in **Cafer Ağa Courtyard** *(see p63)*.

Afternoon
Explore the city's Byzantine past in the sunken **Basilica Cistern** *(see p78)*, famed for its Medusa-head carvings. Emerge at street level by the **Milion** *(see p73)*, a scrap of a once magnificent triumphal arch, before crossing the tramway to **Haghia Sophia** *(see pp74–7)*, with its soaring dome and glittering mosaics.

Day 2
Morning
Visit the **Blue Mosque** *(see pp80–81)*, its vast interior spangled with predominantly blue İznik tiles. Head out onto the **Hippodrome**, a pleasant square once a chariot-racing circuit rivalling Rome's Circus Maximus. Flanking it is the **Museum of Turkish and Islamic Arts** *(see p79)*, which is home to superb carpets. Tread downhill to the beautiful **Sokullu Mehmet Paşa Mosque** *(see p84)* and the nearby Byzantine **SS Sergius and Bacchus' Church** *(see pp84–5)*.

Afternoon
Weave through the crowds to explore the wonderful **Topkapı Palace** *(see pp56–61)*, home to artifacts as varied as the 86 carat Spoonmaker's diamond and the mantle of the Prophet Mohammed. After exiting the intriguing suite of rooms that comprise the palace's women's quarters, the **Harem** *(see pp60–61)*, catch a tram to the **Cemberlitaş Baths** *(see p83)* and ease those aching limbs. Opposite the baths rises **Constantine's Column** *(see p83)*, erected in AD 330.

Day 3
Morning
Start with the short version of the **Bosphorus Cruise** *(see pp146–51)*, which takes visitors up to the first continent-spanning bridge and back again. Cross the square to the Ottoman **Spice Bazaar** *(see p90)* and try your hand at haggling. Head back to the vibrant Eminönü waterfront for a fish sandwich and watch the anglers massed on the **Galata Bridge** *(see p91)*.

The majestic Haghia Sophia, Istanbul's most famous monument

Afternoon
After lunch, head to the **Rüstem Paşa Mosque** *(see pp90–91)*, an intimate place of worship in the heart of the bazaar, before visiting the **Süleymaniye Mosque** *(see pp92–93)* complex to soak up fine views from its grounds. Next, stop at the **Grand Bazaar** *(see pp100–101)*, where a cornucopia of wares awaits eager buyers.

5 days in Istanbul

- **Get to grips with Turkey's fascinating history in the Archaeological Museums**
- **Enjoy impressive views of the Old City from the landmark Galata Tower**
- **Admire the glittering Byzantine mosaics at the Church of St Saviour**

The colourful Grand Bazaar teeming with shoppers

Day 1
Morning
The sprawling administrative heart of the Ottoman Empire and the opulent residence of its sultans, the **Topkapı Palace** *(see pp56–61)*, makes for an engrossing start to the day, especially when combined with the "forbidden" women's quarters, the **Harem** *(see pp60–61)*.

Afternoon
Catch the tram to the **Grand Bazaar** *(see pp100–101)*, a 500-year-old mall, and lunch in one of its myriad tradesmen's cafés before exploring its maze of alleys and thousands of shops. Exit by the Nuruosmaniye Gate and head to **Constantine's Column** *(see p83)*, a late Roman marvel. Opposite is the **Çemberlitaş Baths** *(see p83)*, ideal for relaxing after a day's sightseeing.

Day 2
Morning
Take the tram to the city's imposing land walls, walk to the **Church of St Saviour in Chora** *(see pp120–21)* and admire its splendid mosaics. Stroll north alongside the walls, past the remnants of the Byzantine **Palace of the Porphyrogenitus** *(see p119)* and drop down to the Golden Horn and catch a ferry to Eminönü.

Afternoon
Head uphill to the **Archaeological Museums** *(see pp64–7)* and immerse yourself in Turkey's long history before relaxing with tea in **Gülhane Park** *(see p63)* and enjoying the views to Asia. Finish with a short stroll up period **Soğukçeşme Sokaği** *(see p62)*.

Day 3
Morning
Weave your way down to the Sea of Marmara to view the **SS Sergius and Bacchus' Church** *(see pp84–5)*, then up to Istanbul's finest small mosque, **Sokullu Mehmet Paşa** *(see p84)*. Housed in a former Grand Vizier's residence above is the engaging **Museum of Turkish and Islamic Arts** *(see p79)*. Outside the museum is the **Hippodrome** *(see p82)*, where chariots once raced. Walk across it to the spectacular **Blue Mosque** *(see pp80–81)*.

Afternoon
Spare a quick glance for the sole surviving piece of a monumental triumphal arch, the **Milion** *(see p73)*, then head down into the beautiful **Basilica Cistern** *(see p78)*. Emerge from its depths and cross the tramway to explore

Detail on a mosaic in the Church of St Saviour in Chora

Istanbul's signature building, **Haghia Sophia** *(see pp74–7)*.

Day 4
Morning
Begin atop the city's third hill and explore its "crown", the wonderful **Süleymaniye Mosque** *(see pp92–93)* complex. Wind down through a bustling bazaar to **Rüstem Paşa Mosque** *(see pp90–91)*, an Ottoman gem, then stroll to the domed splendours of the **Spice Bazaar** *(see p90)*. Weave through the Eminönü waterfront crowds, cross the **Galata Bridge** *(see p91)* to the Tünel underground funicular and ride up to İstiklâl Caddesi.

Afternoon
Start the afternoon at the **Mevlevi Lodge** *(see pp106–107)*, home of the mystical Whirling Dervishes, then wander along Istanbul's main shopping street, **İstiklâl Caddesi** *(see pp104–105)*. Walk down cobbled lanes to the Genoese **Galata Tower** *(see p107)* for panoramic views of the Old City.

Day 5
Escape the inevitable foot-slogging around the sites and relax on the full-day **Bosphorus Cruise** *(see pp146–51)*, starting near the Galata Bridge. The cruise passes two suspension bridges, various waterfront mansions and palaces and a couple of Ottoman fortresses – and there's a lunch stop in a fishing village. Alternatively, take a ferry from Kabataş to explore one or more of the picturesque, traffic-free **Princes' Islands** *(see p161)* in the Sea of Marmara, where you can explore on foot, hire a bicycle or opt for a horse-drawn carriage.

Putting Istanbul on the Map

Istanbul stands astride the straits of the Bosphorus, straddling the European and Asian parts of Turkey and bordered to the south by the Sea of Marmara. The city is divided not only by the Bosphorus but also by the Golden Horn, an inlet forming a natural harbour. Although no longer the capital of Turkey *(see p33)*, Istanbul continues to be the country's largest and most fascinating city.

Odessa

BULGARIA

Svilengrad

Lambúh

Edirne

Kırklareli

Demirköy

Arda

Meriç Nehri

Uzunköprü

Ergene Nehri

Babaeski

Lüleburgaz

Saray

Çerkezköy

GREECE

İpsala

Keşan

Malkara

Çorlu

Tekirdağ

See inset map above

ISTANBUL

Alexandroupolis

Korukőy

Şarköy

Marmara

Sea of Marmara

Princes' Islands

Yalova

Gelibolu

Gökçeada

Eceabat

Çanakkale

Biga

Erdek

Bandırma

Gemlik

Mudanya

Bursa

Çan

Gönen

Kuş Gölü

Ulubat Gölü

Göne n Çayı

Koca Çayı

TURKEY

Gülpınar

Ayvacık

Edremit

Balya

Balıkesir

Kepsut

Harmancık

Tavşan

Lésvos

Burhaniye

Ayvalık

Bakır Çayı

Sındırgı

Emet

Mytilíni

Bergama

Akhisar

Simav

Gediz

Aegean Sea

Venice

Karaburun

Gölmarmara

Marmara Gölü

Tekstil Osb

Uş

Chíos

Manisa

Gediz Nehri

Kula

Çeşme

İzmir

Turgutlu

Salihli

Alaşehir

Kusadası

Ödemiş

Key

- Motorway
- Major road
- Other main road
- Railway
- Ferry route
- International border

0 kilometres 40
0 miles 40

Greater Istanbul and Environs

Black Sea

Arnavutköy
Bahçeköy
Sarıyer
Alibahadır
Cumhuriyet
Beykoz
Emirgan
Polonez
Başakşehir
Esenyurt
Bağcılar
Beyoğlu
Küçükçekmece
Fatih
Üsküdar
Sultanbeyli
Atatürk Airport
See next page
Sabiha Gökçen Airport
Maltepe
Sea of Marmara
Pendik
Princes Islands

020
02
03
03
100
O2
O4
020
100

0 kilometres 7
0 miles 4

Samsun, Trabzon ↑

Black Sea

Meydan
Bartın
Zonguldak
010
Kayabaşı
755
Gökçebey
Safranbolu
Ereğli
Devrek
Karabük
Yenice Irmağı
Şile
020
Kandıra
Karasu
010
Akçakoca
656
Kocaeli (İzmit)
Sakarya (Adapazarı)
Düzce
750
Gerede Çayı
Gölcük
Sapanca Gölü
Akyazı
100
Bolu
100
Gerede
İznik
650
140
160
Mudurnu
750
Yenişehir
150
160
Göynük
Sarılar
Bilecik
140
Nallıhan
Beypazarı
Kirmir Çayı
Kazan
Sakarya Nehri
Bozüyük
Sarıyar Barajı
140
O4
İnönü
200
Milhallıçcık
Ankara
200
Eskişehir
200
650
Kütahya
vdarhisar
Altıntaş
nlupınar
300
Afyonkarahisar
Çivril

Europe and the Mediterranean Region

North Sea
SWEDEN
ESTONIA
LATVIA
DENMARK
LITHUANIA
REP. OF IRELAND
UNITED KINGDOM
RUSSIAN FEDERATION
NETH.
GERMANY
POLAND
BELARUS
BELGIUM
CZECH REPUBLIC
UKRAINE
Atlantic Ocean
FRANCE
AUSTRIA
SLOVAKIA
SWITZ.
HUNGARY
MOLDOVA
SLOV.
ROMANIA
CROATIA
BOSNIA HERZ.
SERBIA
Black Sea
ITALY
MONTEN.
BULGARIA
GEORGIA
SPAIN
MAC.
ALBANIA
Istanbul
ARMENIA
PORTUGAL
GREECE
TURKEY
Mediterranean Sea
CYPRUS
SYRIA
IRAQ
LEBANON
MOROCCO
TUNISIA
ISRAEL
JORDAN
SAUDI ARABIA
ALGERIA
LIBYA
EGYPT

For map symbols *see back flap*

Greater Istanbul

The expanding metropolis of Istanbul spreads along the Bosphorus to the north, beyond the airport to the west, and inland from the Asian shore in the east. Its official population is just over 14 million but the actual population is probably much higher. Transport improvements are being made to make getting around this vast urban area easier. Most visitors, however, stay in the historical central parts where the major sights are located.

Sea of Marmara

0 kilometres 2
0 miles 2

For map symbols see back flap

Marmara, Bandirma, Bursa

Sarıyer

Beykoz

Beykoz

Yeniköy

Yeniköy

İstinye

Çubuklu

ŞİŞLİ İSTİNYE CADDESİ

M2

Kanlıca

Kanlıca

Emirgan

EMİRGAN CADDESİ

O2

TEM YOLU

Alibeyköy

BÜYÜKDERE ŞİŞLİ CADDESİ

Levent

Anadolu
Hisarı

NİSPETİYE CADDESİ

M2

RUMELİHİSARI CADDESİ

Küçüksu

İSMET PAŞA CADDESİ

Kağıthane

Etiler

Bebek

Kandili

O1

Arnavutköy

VANİKÖY CADDESİ

HALİÇ KÖPRÜSÜ ÇEVRE YOLU

Şişli

Bosphorus

NATO YOLU

MAÇKA
PARKI

Ortaköy

Çengelköy

Ümraniye

M2

ÇIRAĞAN CADDESİ

Beşiktaş

Ortaköy

Beylerbeyi

Beşiktaş

Kuzguncuk

BİRİNCİ ÇEVRE YOLU

...paşa

Beyoğlu

Kabataş

Üsküdar

Bulgurlu

T1

Karaköy

Üsküdar

O1

Çamlıca

Eminönü

Üsküdar

STANBUL

Harem

SAHİL YOLU

AÇIBADEM CAD

ANADOLU OTOYOLU

O4

T1

Batı
Ataşehir

M4

D100

ANKARA İZMİT DEVLET YOLU

Sabiha Gökcen Airport ✈

Ayrılık Çeşmesi

*Kocaeli (İzmit),
Ankara*

Kadıköy

Söğütlüçeşme

Kadıköy

O2

M4

Kızıltoprak

KAYIŞDAĞI CADDESİ

D100

Feneryolu

Kozyatağı

Göztepe

BAĞDAT CADDESİ

Erenköy

Suadiye

YENİ SAHİL YOLU

Bostancı

Bostancı

Key

- ▢ Central Istanbul
- ▢ Greater Istanbul
- ▬ Motorway
- ▬ Main road
- ═ Other road
- — Railway
- - - Ferry route
- –O– Metro / light rail station
- –O– Tram station

↓ *Princes' Islands,
Yalova, Çınarcık, Gemlik*

Central Istanbul

This guide divides central Istanbul into four distinct areas, each with its own chapter. Three areas lie on the southern side of the Golden Horn. Seraglio Point is a raised promontory on which stands the sumptuous Topkapı Palace. Two architectural masterpieces, Haghia Sophia and the Blue Mosque, dominate the area of Sultanahmet. The pace of life is quite different in the Bazaar Quarter, a maze of narrow streets filled with frenetic commerce. North of the Golden Horn is Beyoğlu, which for centuries was the preferred place of residence of Istanbul's foreign communities, and is still markedly cosmopolitan in atmosphere.

İstiklâl Caddesi, Beyoğlu
Old-fashioned trams shuttle up and down the pedestrianized street that forms the backbone of this area
(see pp102–109).

The Grand Bazaar, Bazaar Quarter
This quaint former coffee house stands at a junction in the labyrinthine old shopping complex at the heart of the city's Bazaar Quarter *(see pp86–101).*

Key

▨ Major Sight

```
0 metres        500
0 yards         500
```

Topkapı Palace, Seraglio Point
This 18th-century marble pavilion, the Library of Ahmet III, stands in one of the courtyards of Topkapı Palace. The walls of the palace grounds now enclose Gülhane Park *(see p63)* as well as many other historic buildings.

View across Sultanahmet
The six slender minarets of the Mosque of Sultan Ahmet I, better known as the Blue Mosque, soar above the spacious square in the middle of Sultanahmet *(see pp70–85)*, Istanbul's most historical district.

THE HISTORY OF ISTANBUL

Istanbul was founded in the 7th century BC on a naturally defensive site from which trade along the Bosphorus could be controlled. For 16 centuries it was a great imperial capital, first of the Byzantine Empire and then of the Ottoman sultans. Some knowledge of the histories of these two civilizations will help the visitor to appreciate the magnificent monuments found throughout the city.

The topography of Istanbul was formed at the end of the last Ice Age, when meltwaters created the Bosphorus. The Stone Age cultures in the area were replaced by Copper Age villages and walled Bronze Age towns (notably Troy, see p173). The Bosphorus was an important trade route in the ancient world along which ships carried wine and olive oil north from the Mediterranean, and grain, skins, wool, timber, wax, honey, salted meat and salted fish south from regions around the Black Sea.

The area around the Bosphorus was subjugated by a series of peoples, starting with the Mycenaeans (1400–1200 BC). Between 800 and 680 BC the region was controlled by the kingdom of Phrygia. Later, in 676 BC, Greek expeditionaries founded the city of Chalcedon (on the site where modern Kadıköy now stands).

The Foundation of Byzantion

The foundation of Istanbul is usually dated to 667 BC when, according to legend, a Greek colonist, Byzas, led an expedition from the overcrowded cities of Athens and Megara to establish a colony on the European side of the Bosphorus. This colony, known as Byzantion, grew to be a successful independent city-state, or polis, one of the 40 most important such states throughout the ancient Greek world. During the next few centuries, Byzantion worked in partnership with Chalcedon, using the same coinage and sharing the tolls exacted from passing sea trade.

But Byzantion had to struggle to maintain its independence in the mercurial politics of the ancient world. It endured Lydian (560–546 BC), Persian (546–478 BC), Athenian (478–411 BC) and Macedonian (334–281 BC) rule before briefly regaining its autonomy. In 64 BC it was subsumed into the Roman Empire as Byzantium. The city was almost destroyed in AD 195 by Septimius Severus because of its support for his rival for the imperial throne, Pescennius Niger. It survived the Goths' devastation of Chalcedon in AD 258 but trade in the region dramatically declined in the following years.

c.676 BC Chalcedon, a Greek settlement, founded on the Asian shore	340 BC Philip II of Macedonia unsuccessfully besieges city	Alexander the Great	AD 195 Roman emperor Septimius Severus destroys Byzantium but later rebuilds it and creates the Hippodrome	
600 BC	**400 BC**	**200 BC**	**AD 1**	**AD 200**
c.667 BC Byzantion reputedly founded by Greek colonists from Athens and Megara, led by Byzas	334 BC Alexander the Great crosses the Hellespont (Dardanelles) and conquers Anatolia	64 BC Pompey brings Byzantion into the Roman Empire, renaming it Byzantium	AD 258 Goths destroy Chalcedon	

◀ The Byzantine emperor Justinian the Great shown with one of his prefects in a mosaic

Constantine the Great

In AD 324, after defeating his co-emperor Licinius, Constantine the Great (324–37) became sole ruler of the Roman Empire. One of his greatest achievements was to move the capital of the empire from Rome to Byzantium. Initially, Constantine preferred the site of Troy (see p173) for his capital, but was persuaded by advisers that Byzantium held a superior position for both defence and trade.

Gold aureus of Constantine

Constantine's city was officially styled the "New Rome" but became widely known as Constantinople. The emperor quickly started on an ambitious programme of construction work, which included the Great Palace (see pp84–5) and various public buildings.

Constantine was also instrumental in the spread of Christianity. According to legend, he saw a vision of the cross before a battle in 312. Although not actually baptized until just before his death, he worked hard to create a coherent system of Christian belief out of the variant practices of the day. All the early church councils took place in the city or nearby, the first being held in Nicaea (modern-day İznik, see p162), and the second in Constantinople itself.

A successor of Constantine, Theodosius I (379–95), divided the empire between his two sons, Honorius and Arcadius. When the Latin-speaking Western Empire fell to barbarian armies during the 5th century, the Greek-speaking Eastern Empire, which we know today as the Byzantine Empire, survived.

The Age of Justinian

The 6th century was dominated by the extraordinary genius of Justinian (527–65), who developed Constantinople into a thriving city and almost succeeded in reconquering the lost provinces of the Western Empire from the barbarians. At the time of his death the empire had expanded to its greatest size, and covered Syria, Palestine, Asia Minor, Greece, the Balkans, Italy, southern Spain and many territories in northern Africa, including Egypt.

Empress Theodora, wife of Justinian

Justinian's formidable wife, the ex-courtesan Theodora, had a great deal of influence over him. In 532 she persuaded the emperor to use mercenaries to put down an angry mob in the most notorious event of his reign, the Nika Revolt. In the carnage that followed, 30,000 were killed inside the Hippodrome (see p82).

Justinian was also responsible for much of the city's great architecture, including Haghia Sophia (see pp74–7), Haghia Eirene (see p62) and parts of the Great Palace.

Relief from the Egyptian Obelisk (see p82), showing Theodosius I and his courtiers

The Byzantines at War

The Byzantine Empire never again attained the splendour of the reign of Justinian, but throughout the first millennium it remained rich and powerful. During the early Middle Ages, Constantinople was an oasis of learning, law, art and culture at a time when Europe was plunged into a dark age of ignorance and illiteracy. Considering themselves to be the leaders of Christianity, the Byzantine rulers dispatched missionaries to spread their religion and culture among the Slavic nations, especially Russia.

"Greek fire", used by the Byzantines against the Arabs

During this period, Constantinople produced some capable emperors, in particular Heraclius (610–41), Basil the Macedonian (867–86), Leo the Wise (886–912) and Basil the Bulgar-Slayer (976–1025). Between them these rulers contributed a number of buildings to the city and recaptured lost provinces.

Never without enemies greedy for a share of the prodigious riches that had been amassed in the city, Constantinople was besieged by Slavs, Arabs, Avars, Bulgars, Persians and Russians, all without success because of the protection of the land walls. The surrounding seas, meanwhile, were under the control of Constantinople's powerful navy. Its main ship was the dromon, an oared vessel which could ram another ship but above all deliver the dreaded "Greek fire", an early form of napalm.

A 6th-century ivory carving of a Byzantine emperor, possibly Anastasius I (491–518)

In 1059 Constantine X, the first of the Dukas dynasty of emperors, ascended to the throne. The state over which the dynasty presided was a weakened one, divided between the over-privileged bureaucracy in the capital and the feudal landlords of the provinces. At the same time increasing dependency on foreign mercenaries placed the empire's defence in the hands of its most aggressive neighbours. These included the Normans from southern Italy, the Venetians, and Turkic nomads from the east. The Byzantine imperial army was totally destroyed at the Battle of Manzikert (1071) and again, a century later, at the Battle of Myriocephalon (1176) by the Seljuk Turks from the east. These losses effectively ended Byzantine rule of Anatolia, which had for so long been the backbone of the empire. The remarkable Comnenus dynasty (1081–1185) ruled for a century after the Dukas emperors, between these two defeats. Their main achievement was to succeed in holding the rest of the empire together.

843 Icons are permitted again by seventh church council at Haghia Sophia

1071 The Byzantine army is destroyed by the Seljuk Turks at the Battle of Manzikert. Emperor Romanus Diogenes is disgraced and deposed

1138 John II Comnenus recovers Serbia

1176 The Seljuk Turks defeat the Byzantine forces at the Battle of Myriocephalon

| 800 | 900 | 1000 | 1100 | 1200 |

Haghia Sophia mosaic

1054 The Orthodox and Catholic churches break away from each other because of differences over dogma

1096 The armies of the First Crusade pass through Constantinople and assist Alexius I Comnenus to retake the Anatolian seaboard from the Seljuk Turks

The City of Constantinople

For almost a thousand years Constantinople was the richest city in Christendom. It radiated out from three great buildings: the church of Haghia Sophia (see pp74–7), the Hippodrome (see p82) and the Great Palace (see pp84–5). The city also had a great many other fine churches and palaces, filled with exquisite works of art. Daily life for the populace centred on the four market squares, or *fora*. Meanwhile, their need for fresh water was met by an advanced network of aqueducts and underground water cisterns.

Walls of Theodosius
Theodosius II's great chain of land walls (see p116) withstood countless sieges until the Ottoman conquest of the city in 1453 (see p28).

The City in 1200

At its height, the magnificent city of Constantinople probably had about 400,000 inhabitants. The population density was relatively low however, and there was space within the city walls for fields and orchards.

Mocius Cistern

The Golden Gate
was a ceremonial gate through the city's ramparts.

Church of St John of Studius (see p118)

Walls of Constantine (now totally destroyed)

Forum of Arcadius

Harbour of Theodosius

Byzantine Church Architecture

Early Byzantine churches were either basilical (like St John of Studius) or built to a centralized plan (as in SS Sergius and Bacchus). From the 9th century, churches, like the typical example shown here, were built around four corner piers, or columns. Exteriors were mostly unadorned brickwork, but interiors were lavishly decorated with golden mosaics. Although the Ottomans converted Constantinople's churches into mosques after their conquest of the city, many original features are clearly discernible today.

Typical Late Byzantine Church

A central apse is flanked by two smaller side apses.

Four columns support the dome.

Brickwork may alternate with layers of stone.

The narthex, a covered porch, forms the entrance to the church.

Golden mosaics cover the ceilings and upper walls.

Church of the Holy Apostles
The domes of what was one of the city's most important churches *(see p115)* are shown in this 12th-century image of the Ascension.

Valens Aqueduct
Water from the Belgrade Forest *(see p160)* and the mountains west of the city was brought into Constantinople on this great structure *(see p91)*.

Aetius Cistern

St Saviour in Chora
(see pp120–21)

Blachernae Palace
(see p119)

Monastery of the
Pantocrator *(see p115)*

Forum of Theodosius
(see p95)

Forum of
Constantine *(see p83)*

Basilica Cistern
This cavernous cistern *(see p78)* represented a great feat of engineering when it was built in the 6th century.

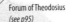

Chain across Golden
Horn *(see p91)*

Church of
SS Sergius
and Bacchus
(see p84)

Hippodrome
(see p82)

Great Palace
(see pp84–5)

Haghia Eirene
(see p62)

Milion
This stone pillar *(see p73)* is all that remains of a Byzantine triumphal arch from which road distances to all corners of the empire were once measured.

Haghia Sophia
The great church of Constantinople *(see pp74–7)* was filled with mosaics, including this one showing the Virgin and Child with the emperors Constantine and Justinian.

The capture of Constantinople during the Fourth Crusade of 1202–4

The Fourth Crusade

In 1202, an army of 34,000 responded to an appeal from Pope Innocent III for a new crusade to the Holy Land. This unruly force of Christians lacked the funds to get beyond Venice, where it needed to hire ships. It consequently fell under the influence of Enrico Dandolo, the manipulative Doge of Venice. With his backing, the crusaders were soon diverted to Constantinople, where they helped the young Alexius IV take the throne.

However, six months later, when they realized they were unlikely to receive their promised financial reward from the emperor, the crusaders lost patience and launched a new attack, ousting Alexius in favour of one their own, Baldwin I,

Icon of St Michael, now in Venice, an example of the fine Byzantine art plundered by the Venetians during the Fourth Crusade

Count of Flanders. Through the dark years that followed, known as the Latin Empire, the once great city was reduced by pillage, misrule and emigration to a scattering of disconnected villages grouped behind the city walls. Outside Constantinople, the exiled Byzantine emperors survived the turmoil, biding their time as the rulers of the Empire of Nicaea, just to the south, which included modern-day İznik (see p162).

Constantinople in Decline

In 1261, Constantinople was recaptured for Byzantium by Michael VIII Palaeologus (1258–82), who met almost no resistance in the process. He did this with the aid of the Italian city of Genoa,

1202 An army assembles in Venice to launch the Fourth Crusade

1204 Alexius IV is deposed and Baldwin I is crowned emperor of a new Latin Empire

1261 Michael VIII Palaeologus recaptures Constantinople from the Venetians

1331 Ottomans capture Nicaea (modern İznik)

1326 Prusa (Bursa) is taken and becomes the Ottoman capital

1200	1225	1250	1275	1300	1325

1203 Dandolo, Doge of Venice, diverts the Fourth Crusade to Constantinople. He cuts the chain across the Golden Horn (see p91) and storms the city

1299 Osman I founds the Ottoman Empire

Bronze horses taken by Dandolo from the Hippodrome (see p82) to Venice

1321 Outbreak of the disastrous 33-year-long Byzantine civil war which was naturally disposed to fight against her rival Venice. Yet she still exacted a crippling price for her assistance. The Genoese established the colony of Pera across the Golden Horn from Constantinople, and effectively took control of the city's trade.

Constantinople's recapture and reconstruction caused a flowering of scholarship and artistic activity, known as the Palaeologue Renaissance after the family of emperors. An example of the many beautiful buildings dating from this period is the Church of St Saviour in Chora (*see pp120–21*).

During this period the double-headed eagle was adopted as the imperial crest, with the two heads symbolizing the western and eastern halves of the empire. Yet, within a few decades there was further discord in Constantinople, when a quarrel arose between Andronicus II (1282–1328) and his grandson Andronicus III

Two-headed Byzantine eagle

(1328–41) over the succession. This led to the disastrous civil war of 1321–54.

The Rise of the Ottomans

The Ottoman state was born in 1299 when Osman I, a leader of warriors who were fighting for the Muslim faith on the eastern frontier of the Byzantine Empire, declared his independence. The new state quickly expanded and in 1326 captured Prusa (modern-day Bursa, *see pp164–70*), which became its capital. The judicious piety of the Ottomans soon won them the support of the general population of their territories, and even of some Christian brotherhoods. Meanwhile, a professional core of Janissaries (*see p129*) was created to add stability to an army which was otherwise too dependent on Turkic and renegade volunteer cavalry.

By 1362, with the Ottoman capture of Adrianople (Edirne, *see pp156–9*), Byzantium had been reduced to the city-state of Constantinople and a few minor outposts, isolated within Ottoman domains. In 1391 the Ottoman army made its first attack on the city's colossal land walls. Only a Mongol incursion in 1402 delayed the invasion of Constantinople itself. As the threat increased, the Byzantine emperor made a last-ditch effort to win the support of the Latin West in 1439. The Hungarians alone answered his call for help, forming a 25,000-strong crusade. However, in 1444 they were defeated en route by the Ottomans at the Battle of Varna on the Black Sea.

Mosaic of the Virgin Mother and Child in St Saviour in Chora

1362 Murat I conquers Adrianople (Edirne), which then becomes the Ottoman capital. Byzantium is reduced to the city of Constantinople

1451 Mehmet II succeeds to the Ottoman throne and orders the construction of the Fortress of Europe (*see p142*) to seal the Bosphorus

1350	1375	1400	1425	1450

1348 The Galata Tower is built by the Genoese inhabitants of the city as a watchtower over the Pera quarter

Galata Tower

1391 First Ottoman siege of Constantinople by Yıldırım Beyazıt (Beyazıt I)

1444 A Hungarian army on its way to help Constantinople is destroyed by the Ottomans at Varna on the Black Sea. Constantinople's last hope of survival is lost

The Conquest of Constantinople

On 29 May 1453 Sultan Mehmet II (1432–81), known as "the Conqueror", entered Constantinople after a 54-day siege during which his cannon had torn a huge hole in the Walls of Theodosius II *(see p116)*. Mehmet's first task was to rebuild the wrecked city,

Sultan Mehmet II, "the Conqueror"

which would later become known as Istanbul. The Grand Bazaar *(see pp100–101)* and Topkapı Palace *(see pp56–9)* were erected in the years following the Muslim conquest. Religious foundations were endowed to fund the building of mosques such as the Fatih *(see p115)* and their associated schools and baths *(see pp40–41)*. The city had to be repopulated by a mixture of force and encouragement. People from all over the empire moved to Istanbul, and Jews, Christians and Muslims lived together in a cosmopolitan society.

Mehmet and his successors pushed the frontiers of the empire across the Middle East and into Europe. In the early 16th century, Selim I (1512–20) conquered Egypt and assumed the title of caliph *(see p31)*, as well as establishing the Ottomans as a sea power. He is also notorious for killing all his male relatives bar one son, to ensure that there were no rivals for the succession.

Süleyman the Magnificent

Selim's one surviving son was Süleyman I, "the Magnificent" (1520–66), under whose rule the Ottoman Empire reached its maximum extent. At the time of his death the empire stretched from Algiers to the Caspian Sea and from Hungary to the Persian Gulf.

Ottoman Empire
Maximum extent (1683)

Much of western Europe only just escaped conquest when an Ottoman army was driven back from the gates of Vienna in 1529. Süleyman's reign was a time of great artistic and architectural achievements. The architect Sinan *(see p93)* designed many mosques and other great buildings in the city, while the Ottoman arts of ceramics *(see p163)* and calligraphy *(see p97)* also flourished.

Depiction of the unsuccessful siege of Vienna by the Ottomans

1453 Mehmet the Conqueror enters Constantinople on 29 May

1458 The Ottomans conquer Athens

1461 Trebizond on the Black Sea, the last part of the Byzantine Empire, is conquered

1536 Grand Vizier İbrahim Paşa is killed on the orders of Süleyman's wife, Roxelana *(see p78)*

1561 Süleyman executes his son Beyazıt on suspicion of treason

1571 Defeat of the Ottoman navy at the Battle of Lepanto

1450 | **1475** | **1500** | **1525** | **1550**

1455 Yedikule Castle *(see p117)* is built and work begins on the Grand Bazaar

1478 Topkapı Palace completed

1470 Fatih Mosque is built over the Church of the Holy Apostles

1533 Hayrettin Paşa, better known as Barbarossa, is appointed grand admiral

1556 Inauguration of Sinan's Süleymaniye Mosque *(see pp92–3)*

Süleyman I

THE HISTORY OF ISTANBUL | 29

The Sultanate of Women

Süleyman's son Selim II (1566–74), "the Sot", was not such a capable ruler, although he added Cyprus to the empire. The defeat of his navy by the Venetians at the Battle of Lepanto was a heavy blow to Ottoman ambitions to be a seafaring power. This era was also the start of the so-called "Sultanate of Women", when

The Battle of Lepanto, a defeat for the Ottoman navy

Selim's mother (the valide sultana, *see pp30–31*) and Nur Banu, his principal wife (the first *kadın*), effectively took over power and exercised it for their own ends. Corruption and intrigue became endemic, and after Selim's death Nur Banu kept her son, Murat III (1574–95), distracted by the women of the harem so that she could maintain her control over imperial affairs.

Osman II (1618–22) was the first sultan to try to reverse the decline of the empire. But when the Janissaries (*see p129*) learnt of his plans to abolish their corps, they started a revolt which eventually led to his assassination. Murat IV (1623–40) enjoyed more success in his attempts at reform and significantly reduced corruption during his stable period of rule.

The late 17th century saw many years of capable government by a succession of grand viziers from the Albanian Köprülü family. Yet their efforts were not sufficient to stem the decline in imperial fortunes, symbolized by a failed

Osman II, who failed to halt Ottoman decline

attempt to capture Vienna in 1683. The Treaty of Karlowitz in 1699 marked the start of the Ottoman withdrawal from Europe.

The Tulip Period

Ahmet III (1703–30), on his succession to the throne, left power in the hands of his capable grand vizier, İbrahim Paşa. The sultan preferred pleasure to politics. During his reign, beautiful Baroque palaces, such as Aynalı Kavak Palace (*see p129*), fountains, mosques and yalıs (*see p141*) were built. Formal gardens were laid out and filled with tulips, Ahmet's favourite flower, which lent their name to the period of his rule. The sultan even ordered tulips to be scattered over the floor at the lavish festivals and entertainments that he staged for the Ottoman elite. He also sent an ambassador, Mehmet Çelebi, to France to investigate Western civilization and culture. On his return, Western clothes and costumes became not only acceptable for the first time, but fashionable.

1616 The Blue Mosque (*see pp80–81*) is finished after eight years of construction work by the architect Mehmet Ağa

1699 The loss of Hungary under the Treaty of Karlowitz marks the Ottomans' retreat from Europe

| 00 | 1625 | 1650 | 1700 | 1725 |

1622 Revolt of the Janissaries. They murder Osman II in Yedikule Castle, the Prison of the Seven Towers

Domes of the Blue Mosque

1729 The first Ottoman printing press is set up in Istanbul and begins to print texts in Turkish

Ottoman Society

Beneath the sultan, Ottoman society was divided into a privileged ruling class (the *askeri*, which included the religious hierarchy, or *ulema*) and a tax-paying subject population (*reaya*). Rank and honour, however, were not hereditary but could be gained through education or service in the army or administration. This social structure was modified during the reforms of the 19th century *(see p32)*, but Ottoman titles were only finally abolished in 1922 after the Turkish Republic was created *(see p33)*.

The grand vizier, the prime minister, was the sultan's right-hand man.

The sultan was at the apex of the social order and everyone owed allegiance to him. He lived a life of ease and luxury, as seen in this portrait of Selim III (1789–1807). The Ottoman (Osmanlı in Turkish) sultans were always succeeded by one of their sons, but not automatically by the eldest.

Bayram Reception (c.1800)

In this painting by Konstantin Kapidagi, Selim III (1789–1807, see p32) presides over a parade of high-ranking officials during the celebration of a religious festival (see p49) at Topkapı Palace.

Ağa of the Janissaries

Minister of the Interior

Şeyhülislam (Grand Mufti)

Chief executioner

Men of high rank could be recognized by their different uniforms, above all their large and distinctive headgear, as seen in this portrait of four Ottoman officials. The turban was abolished by Mahmut II *(see p32)* in 1829 in favour of the more egalitarian fez.

The Women of the Harem

Like all other Ottoman institutions the harem was hierarchical. It was presided over by the sultan's mother, the valide sultana. Next in order of importance came the sultan's daughters. Immediately below them were the four *kadıns*, the official wives or favourites. Then came the *gözdes* (girls who had recently caught the sultan's eye), and the *ikbals* (women with whom he had already slept). Apart from the sultan's family members, all these women had entered the harem as slaves. They were kept under a watchful eye by a powerful stewardess, the *kahya kadın*.

One of the sultan's favourites (*kadıns*) as depicted in a 19th-century engraving

Black eunuchs

Sword bearer to the sultan

The Gate of Felicity
(see p56), in the second courtyard of Topkapı Palace, was used for such ceremonial occasions.

Chief lackey (footman)

The sultan is surrounded by his courtiers. He is the only seated figure.

Şeyhülislam (Grand Mufti)

Chief of the sultan's bodyguard

Black eunuchs

Dancing women

Valide sultana

Dwarf

The valide sultana, the most powerful woman in the harem, is the centre of attention in this festive scene. The picture was commissioned c.1689 by Madame Giradin, wife of the French ambassador.

Ottoman Titles

Ağa: leader of an organization. The most influential *ağas* were the commander of the Janissary corps, the sultan's elite troops *(see p129)*, and the Ağa of the Abode of Felicity, or chief black eunuch, who was in charge of the harem *(see pp60–61)*.

Chief black eunuch

Bey: governor of a district or province. The word is now used simply to mean "Mr".

Caliph: spiritual ruler of the Islamic world. The title was assumed by the Ottoman sultans, beginning with Selim the Grim in 1517.

Gazi: honorary title given to a victorious Islamic warrior.

Kadi: judge charged with interpreting Islamic law and Ottoman administrative codes.

Khedive: viceroy of Egypt under Ottoman rule (1867–1914). The autonomous khedives acknowledged the religious leadership of the Ottoman Empire.

Paşa: title bestowed on a senior civil servant or high-ranking army officer. According to his rank, a *paşa* was entitled to display one, two or three horsetails on his standard *(see p58)*.

Sultan: political and religious ruler of the empire.

Şeyhülislam (Grand Mufti): head of the *ulema*, a religious institution which was made up of "learned men" responsible for interpreting and enforcing Islamic law *(sharia)*.

Valide sultana: mother of the ruling sultan.

Vizier: minister of state. The four most senior ministers were called "viziers of the dome" because they attended cabinet meetings in the domed hall of the divan in Topkapı Palace *(see pp56–61)*. From the 16th century, the divan was presided over by the immensely powerful grand vizier (the prime minister).

Grand vizier

A Janissary leaps to his death in a German painting
of the Auspicious Event of 1826

The Reforming Sultans

Abdül Hamit I (1774–89) resumed the work
of reform and was succeeded by Selim III,
who instituted a wide range of changes to
the military and to Ottoman society. He was
deposed by a Janissary mutiny in 1807.
Mahmut II (1808–39) realized that the
Janissary corps *(see p129)* could not be
reformed, so he established a modern
army alongside them, but the Janissaries
rebelled and were massacred on 15 June
1826 in the "Auspicious Event". Soon after,
in 1829, the sultan introduced further
modernizing measures including
changes in the dress code.

Later in his reign Mahmut reorganized
central government so that a regulated
bureaucracy replaced the old system of
rule by military and religious powers. By
doing this he paved the way for his sons
Abdül Mecit (1839–61) and Abdül Aziz (1861–
76) to oversee the Tanzimat (Reordering), a
series of legislative reforms. Functionaries
were given higher salaries to deter them
from taking bribes, and the grand vizier's
post was replaced by that of prime minister.

A constitution was declared in 1876,
creating parliamentary government.
However, the Russian-Turkish War of 1877–8
led to Abdül Hamit II suspending it and ruling
alone for the next 30 years. In 1908 a bloodless
revolution by a collection of educated men –
the so-called Young Turks – finally forced
the sultan to recall parliament.

Atatürk and Westernization

Throughout the 19th- and early 20th-
centuries, the Ottoman Empire steadily
lost territory through wars with Russia and
Austria, and to emerging Balkan nation-states
such as Serbia, Greece and Bulgaria. Then, in
World War I, despite famously winning the
battle for Gallipoli in a valiant defence of the
Dardanelles *(see p172)*, the Ottoman Empire
found itself on the losing side. Istanbul was
occupied by victorious French and British

Artillery in action at Gallipoli

1807 Much of the city
is destroyed during
a Janissary revolt
against Mahmut II

Dolmabahçe clock tower

1845 First (wooden)
Galata Bridge is built
over the Golden Horn

1870 Schliemann
begins excavation of
Troy *(see p173)*

1888 Rail link
with Paris leads to
first run of the
Orient Express
(see p68)

1800 1825 1850 1875 1900

1826 Mahmut II
finally destroys the
Janissaries in their
own barracks in the
"Auspicious Event"

1856 Abdül Mecit I abandons
Topkapı Palace for the new
Dolmabahçe Palace *(see pp130–31)*

1875 The Tünel underground railway system, the third
built in the world, opens in Galata

*Orient
Express
poster*

troops, and much of Western Anatolia by Greek forces. The peace treaties that followed rewarded the victors with Ottoman territory and as a result stimulated Turkish nationalists to take over power from the sultan.

The history of modern Turkey is dominated by the figure of Mustafa Kemal Paşa (1881–1938), a military hero turned politician, universally known as Atatürk, or "Father of the Turks". It was at his instigation that the Turkish War of Independence was fought to regain land lost to the Allies and, in particular, Greece. At the end of this war, the present territorial limits of Turkey were established. Atatürk then started a programme of political and social change. The sultanate was abolished in 1922, and religion and state were formally separated a year later, when the country was declared a secular republic. His reforms included replacing the Arabic alphabet with a Roman one, allowing women greater social and political rights, encouraging Western dress (the fez was banned) and obliging all Turks to choose a surname.

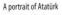
A portrait of Atatürk

Modern Istanbul

Another part of this process was to move the institutions of state from the old Ottoman city of Istanbul to the more centrally located Ankara, which became the capital of Turkey in 1923. Since then, Istanbul has gone through a dramatic transformation into a modern city. As migrants from Anatolia have poured in, the population has increased, and although small communities of Jews and Armenian and Greek Orthodox Christians remain within the city, they are now vastly outnumbered by Turks.

A booming economy has led to an overhaul in the city's transport infrastructure. Several metro lines have been built, new trams run through the city and high-speed catamarans make use of the seas around Istanbul. A third Bosphorus road bridge is under construction, along with a third international airport. The beautifully restored historic buildings, an array of hotels and restaurants and the vibrant nightlife have led to a major increase in the number of visitors.

But, like Turkey as a whole, Istanbul is forever wrestling with a divided half-Asian, half-European identity. The influences of these contrasting cultures remain widely evident today and create the city's unique atmosphere.

The suspension bridge spanning the Bosphorus, which opened in October 1973

1919–22 British and French occupy Istanbul	**1938** Atatürk dies in Dolmabahçe Palace at 9:05am on 10 November (*see p131*)	*Turkish flag*	**2014** Recep Tayyip Erdoğan elected president of Turkey	
1922 Sultanate finally ends			**1993** The Islamicist Welfare Party takes control of the Greater Istanbul Municipality	**2010** Istanbul becomes European Capital of Culture
1925	**1950**		**1975**	**2000**
1915 Allied forces land at Gallipoli but are repulsed by Turkish troops	**1936** Haghia Sophia becomes a museum. Restoration starts	**1973** A suspension bridge is built across the Bosphorus (*see p140*), linking east and west Turkey	**1996** The UN Conference on Human Settlement (Habitat II) is held in Istanbul	**2013** Erdoğan's AKP (Justice and Development Party) win record third election
	1928 Istanbul becomes the city's official name		**2002** Recep Tayyip Erdoğan is elected Prime Minister	

The Ottoman Sultans

The first Ottomans were the leaders of warlike tribes living on the borders of the Byzantine Empire. From the 13th century, however, the dynasty established itself at the head of a large empire. In their heyday, having captured Istanbul in 1453 *(see p28)*, the Ottoman sultans were admired and feared for their military strength and ruthlessness towards opponents and rival pretenders to the throne. Later sultans often led a decadent lifestyle while power was exercised by their viziers *(see p31)*.

Murat III (1574–95), whose *tuğra (see p97)* is shown above, fathers over 100 children

Selim II, "the Sot" (1566–74), prefers drinking and harem life to the affairs of state

Selim I, "the Grim" (1512–20), seen here at his coronation, assumes the title of caliph after his conquest of Egypt

Osman Gazi (1299–1326), a tribal chieftain, establishes the Ottoman dynasty

Murat I (1359–89)

Mehmet I (1413–21)

Beyazıt II (1481–1512)

1250	1300	1350	1400	1450	1500	1550
1250	1300	1350	1400	1450	1500	1550

Orhan Gazi (1326–59) is the first Ottoman to bear the title of sultan

Beyazıt I (1389–1402) is nicknamed "the Thunderbolt" because of the speed at which he takes strategic decisions and moves his troops from one place to another

Süleyman I, "the Magnificent" (1520–66), expands the empire and fosters a golden age of artistic achievement

Period of Interregnum (1402–13) while Beyazıt's sons fight each other over the succession

Murat II (1421–51), the greatest of the warrior sultans, gains notable victories against the Crusaders

Mehmet II, "the Conqueror" (1451–81), captures Constantinople in 1453. He then rebuilds the city, transforming it into the new capital of the empire

Mehmet III (1595–1603) succeeds to the throne after his mother has all but one of his 19 brothers strangled

Mustafa I (1617–18 and 1622–3), a weak and incompetent ruler, reigns for two short periods and is deposed twice

Abdül Mecit I (1839–61) presides over the reforms of the Tanzimat *(see p32)*

Mehmet VI (1918–22), the last Ottoman sultan, is forced into exile by the declaration of the Turkish Republic *(see p33)*

İbrahim, "the Mad" (1640–48), much despised, goes insane at the end of his short but disastrous reign

Mahmut II, "the Reformer" (1808–39), finally defeats the Janissaries *(see p129)*

Mehmet V (1909–18)

Süleyman II (1687–91)

Mustafa II (1695–1703)

Mahmut I (1730–54)

Mustafa III (1757–74)

Murat V (1876)

1650	1700	1750	1800	1850	1900

1650	1700	1750	1800	1850	1900

Ahmet II (1691–5)

Osman III (1754–7)

Abdül Aziz (1861–76)

Abdül Mecit II (1922–3) is caliph only, the sultanate having been abolished in 1922 *(see p33)*

Mehmet IV (1648–87)

Abdül Hamit I (1774–89)

Murat IV (1623–40)

Mustafa IV 1807–8

Ahmet III (1703–30) presides over a cultural flowering known as the Tulip Period *(see p29)*

Osman II (1618–22)

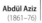

Abdül Hamit II (1876–1909) suspends parliament for 30 years and rules an auto-cratic police state until toppled from power by the Young Turk movement

Ahmet I (1603–17) has the Blue Mosque *(see pp80–81)* constructed in the centre of Istanbul

Selim III (1789–1807) attempts Western-style reforms but is over-thrown by a revolt of the Janissaries

ISTANBUL AT A GLANCE

More than 100 places worth visiting in Istanbul are described in the *Area by Area* section of this book, which covers the sights of central Istanbul as well as those a short way out of the city centre. They range from mosques, churches, palaces and museums to bazaars, Turkish baths and parks. For a breathtaking view across Istanbul, you can climb the Galata Tower *(see p107)*, or take a ride on a ferry *(see pp242–3)* to the city's Asian shore. A selection of the sights you should not miss is given below. If you are short of time, you will probably want to concentrate on the most famous monuments, namely Topkapı Palace, Haghia Sophia and the Blue Mosque, which are all located conveniently close to each other.

Istanbul's Top Ten Sights

Topkapı Palace
See pp56–9

Dolmabahçe Palace
See pp130–31

Basilica Cistern
See p78

Archaeological Museums
See pp64–7

Süleymaniye Mosque
See pp92–3

Blue Mosque
See pp80–81

Haghia Sophia
See pp74–7

The Bosphorus Trip
See pp146–51

Grand Bazaar
See pp100–101

Church of St Saviour in Chora
See pp120–21

◀ İznik tiles in the Harem of the Topkapı Palace

Istanbul's Best: Mosques and Churches

Most visitors to Istanbul will immediately be struck by the quantity of mosques, from the imposing domed buildings dominating the skyline to the small neighbourhood mosques which would pass unnoticed were it not for their minarets. Several mosques were built as churches, but converted for Islamic worship after the Ottoman conquest *(see p28)*. Some of the most outstanding of them have since become national monuments, but no longer serve a religious function.

Eyüp Mosque
The holiest mosque in Istanbul stands beside the tomb of Eyüp Ensari, a companion of the Prophet Mohammed *(see p122)*.

Rüstem Paşa Mosque

St Saviour in Chora
The Dormition of the Virgin is one of many beautiful mosaics that fill this Byzantine church *(see pp120–21)*.

Church of the Pammakaristos
An image of Christ Pantocrator gazes down from the main dome of what was one of the most important churches in the city *(see p112)*.

Golden H
ABÜLEZEL PAŞA
VATAN CADDESİ
ATATÜRK BULVARI
ORDU CADD

Fatih Mosque
Rebuilt after an earthquake, this mosque was founded by Mehmet the Conqueror after his conquest of the city *(see p28)*. The inner courtyard is especially fine *(see p115)*.

Süleymaniye Mosque
Sinan, the greatest Ottoman imperial architect, built this mosque in honour of his patron, Süleyman the Magnificent *(see p28)*. He placed ablution taps in the side arches of the mosque to serve a large number of worshippers *(see pp92–3)*.

Rüstem Paşa Mosque
The fine tiles decorating this mosque date from the mid-16th century, the greatest period of İznik tile *(see p163)* production *(see p90)*.

Haghia Sophia
One of the world's greatest feats of architecture, Haghia Sophia dates from AD 537. The calligraphic roundels were added in the 19th century *(see pp74–7)*.

Atik Valide Mosque
The last major work of Sinan *(see p93)*, this mosque was built in 1583 for the wife of Selim II. Its mihrab (niche indicating the direction of Mecca) is surrounded by İznik tiles *(see p133)*.

İSTİKLAL CAD

NECATİ BEY CADDESİ

Bosphorus

PAŞA LİMANI CADDESİ

SEL MANİPAK CAD

ÜSKÜDAR-HAREM SAHİL YOLU

GÜNDOĞUMU CAD

ÇAVUŞDERE CAD

KENNEDY CAD

Sea of Marmara

Blue Mosque
Istanbul's most famous landmark was built by some of the same stonemasons who later helped construct the Taj Mahal in India *(see pp80–81)*.

Church of SS Sergius and Bacchus
An intricate frieze with a Greek inscription honouring the two dedicatees of this former church has survived for 1,400 years *(see p84)*.

0 kilometres   1
0 miles   1

Exploring Mosques

Five times a day throughout Istanbul a chant is broadcast over loudspeakers set high in the city's minarets to call the faithful to prayer. Over 99 per cent of the population is Muslim, though the Turkish state is officially secular. Most belong to the Sunni branch of Islam, but there are also a few Shiites. Both follow the teachings of the Koran, the sacred book of Islam, and the Prophet Mohammed (c.570–632), but Shiites accept, in addition, the authority of a line of 12 imams directly descended from Mohammed. Islamic mystics are known as Sufis *(see p106).*

Overview of the Süleymaniye Mosque complex

The ablutions fountain *(şadırvan)* was used by worshippers for ritual washing.

The caravanserai or *han (see p98)* provided accommodation for travellers.

The kitchen *(imaret)* catered for mosque officials, students, the sick and the poor.

Hospital *(darüşşifa)*

Colleges *(medreses)* for general and theological education were built adjacent to the mosque. Most now serve other uses.

Turkish baths *(hamam)*

Courtyard *(avlu)*

Prayer hall *(cami)*

A mausoleum *(türbe)* was built for the founder of the mosque.

Plan of a Typical Mosque Complex (Külliye)

A large complex such as the Süleymaniye Mosque *(see pp92–3),* shown here, was built as a charitable foundation as well as a place of worship. It would typically include a hospital, school, Islamic study halls, caravanserai (lodgings for travellers), public kitchen for the poor, and bathhouse. Today most such buildings no longer fulfil their original functions.

Inside a Mosque

Visitors will experience a soaring sense of space on entering the prayer hall of one of Istanbul's great mosques. Islam forbids images of living things (human or animal) inside a mosque, so there are never any statues or figurative paintings; but the geometric and abstract architectural details of the interior can be exquisite. Men and women pray separately. Women often use a screened-off area or a balcony.

The müezzin mahfili is a raised platform found in large mosques. The muezzin (mosque official) stands on this when chanting responses to the prayers of the imam (head of the mosque).

The mihrab, an ornate niche in the wall, marks the direction of Mecca. The prayer hall is laid out so that most people can see it.

The minbar is a lofty pulpit to the right of the mihrab. This is used by the imam when he delivers the Friday sermon *(khutba).*

Muslim Beliefs and Practices

Muslims believe in God (Allah), and the Koran shares many prophets and stories with the Bible. However, whereas for Christians Jesus is the son of God, Muslims hold that he was just one in a line of prophets – the last being Mohammed, who brought the final revelation of God's truth to mankind. Muslims believe that Allah communicated the sacred texts of the Koran to Mohammed, via the archangel Gabriel. There are five basic duties for Muslims. The first of these is the profession of faith: "There is no God but God, and Mohammed is his Prophet". Muslims are also enjoined to pray five times a day, give alms to the poor, and fast during the month of Ramazan *(see p49)*. Once in their lifetime, if they can afford it, they should make the pilgrimage (hajj) to Mecca (in Saudi Arabia), the site of the Kaaba, a sacred shrine built by Abraham, and also the birthplace of the Prophet.

The call to prayer used to be given by the muezzin from the balcony of the minaret. Nowadays loudspeakers broadcast the call across the city. Only imperial mosques have more than one minaret.

Ritual ablutions must be under- taken before prayer. Worshippers wash their head, hands and feet either at the fountain in the courtyard or, more usually, at taps set in a discreet wall of the mosque.

When praying, Muslims always face the Kaaba in the holy city of Mecca, even if they are not in a mosque, where the mihrab indicates the right direction. Kneeling and lowering the head to the ground are gestures of humility and respect for Allah.

Prayer Times

The five daily prayer times are calculated according to the times of sunrise and sunset, and so change throughout the year. Exact times will be posted up on boards outside large mosques. Those given here are a guide.

Prayer	Summer	Winter
Sabah	5am	7am
öğle	1pm	1pm
İkindi	6pm	4pm
Akşam	8pm	6pm
Yatsı	9:30pm	8pm

Visiting a Mosque

Visitors are welcome at any mosque in Istanbul, but non-Muslims should try to avoid prayer times, especially the main weekly congregation and sermon on Fridays at 1pm. Take off your shoes before entering the prayer hall. Shoulders and knees should be covered. Some mosques require women to cover their hair; scarves can usually be borrowed. Do not eat, take photographs with a flash or stand close to worshippers. A contribution to a donation box or mosque official is courteous.

Board outside a mosque giving times of prayer

The loge *(hünkar mahfili)* provided the sultan with a screened- off balcony where he could pray, safe from would-be assassins.

The kürsü, seen in some mosques, is a chair or throne used by the imam while he reads extracts from the Koran.

Istanbul's Best: Palaces and Museums

As the former capital of an empire that spanned from Algeria to Iraq and from Arabia to Hungary, Istanbul is home to a huge and diverse collection of treasures. Some, from musical instruments to priceless jewels, are housed in the beautiful former imperial palaces of the Ottoman sultans, which are worth visiting in any case for their architecture and opulent interiors. Topkapı and Dolmabahçe are the most famous palaces in Istanbul. The Archaeological Museums should also be on any itinerary of the city. This map points out these and other palaces and museums which are worth visiting for their splendid buildings or the exceptional collections they contain.

Aynalı Kavak Palace
This reclusive palace, with its airy feel and intimate proportions, shows subtler aspects of Ottoman taste. It houses a collection of Turkish musical instruments.

Archaeological Museums
Purpose-built in 1896, these superb museums have exhibits ranging from prehistory to the Byzantine era. They include this classical sculpture of the 2nd-century Roman Emperor Hadrian.

Museum of Calligraphy
Some of the texts in Istanbul's collection of Ottoman calligraphy (see p97) are by sultans, such as this panel by Ahmet III (1703–30).

Museum of Turkish and Islamic Arts
This Seljuk example is one of the many carpets (see pp218–19) included in this museum's display of Turkish heritage. Other collections include glassware and ceramics.

DOLAPDERE CADDESİ
İSTİKLAL CAD
SIRASELVİLER
Golden Horn
ABDÜLEZELPAŞA CAD
NECAT
MACAR KARDEŞLER CAD
VATAN CADDESİ
MİLLET CADDESİ
ATATÜRK BULVARI
ORDU CADDESİ
KENNEDY CADDESİ
KENNE

Mosaic Museum
Gladiators fighting a lion are shown in one of the floors from the Great Palace (see pp84–5) displayed in this small museum.

Topkapı Palace

Beylerbeyi Palace
Adorning one of the principal atriums of this 19th-century imperial summer palace is this elegant marble fountain. The palace was built to entertain visiting foreign dignitaries.

Military Museum
A highlight of this museum is the famous Mehter Band, which gives regular outdoor concerts of Ottoman military music.

Şale Pavilion
One of a group of pavilions built in leafy Yıldız Park by 19th-century sultans, the Şale Pavilion has around 50 splendid rooms, including the Mother-of-Pearl Hall.

BARBAROS BULVARI

ÇIRAĞAN CADDESİ

PAŞA LİMANI CADDESİ

SELMANİPAK CADDESİ

ÜSKÜDAR-HAREM SAHİL YOLU

GÜNDOĞUMU CADDESİ

Bosphorus

Sea of Marmara

Dolmabahçe Palace
This opulent 19th-century palace is home to such marvels as 2 m (7 ft) high vases, a crystal staircase and an alabaster bathroom.

Topkapı Palace
This huge palace was used as the official royal residence for 400 years. The treasury contains a myriad of precious objects including the Kasikci Diamond and this ornate ceremonial canteen.

0 kilometres   1

0 miles   1

Exploring Istanbul's Collections

Each museum in Istanbul contributes a piece to the vast cultural jigsaw of this cosmopolitan city. From ancient Greek remains and early Chinese ceramics, which arrived in the city along the Silk Route, to 16th-century tiles commissioned for the great mosques and modern industrial machinery, each has its place in the history of Istanbul. Many of the larger museums have a wide range of exhibits and therefore feature under several of the headings below.

The Sarcophagus of the Mourning Women, Archaeological Museum

Archaeology

The archaeological fruits of the expansive Ottoman Empire are displayed in the **Archaeological Museums**, where the exhibits range from monumental 6th-century BC Babylonian friezes to exquisite classical sarcophagi and statues. Classical sculpture fills the ground floor.

Upstairs there is a gallery for the archaeology of Syria and Cyprus. Ancient oriental finds are housed in the Ancient Orient Museum, located in the same complex. The **Museum of Turkish and Islamic Arts** features specifically Muslim artifacts, including early Iraqi and Iranian ceramics as well as beautiful displays of glassware, metalwork and woodwork.

Byzantine Antiquities

Although Constantinople was the capital of the Byzantine Empire (see pp22–27) for over 1,000 years, it can be hard to get a full picture of the city in that period. The best place to start is the **Archaeological Museums**, which have displays illustrating the city's Byzantine history. Its courtyard contains the purple sarcophagi of the Byzantine emperors.

For Byzantine church mosaics, visit the **Church of St Saviour in Chora** near the city walls which has some particularly fine examples vividly depicting the lives of Christ and the Virgin Mary. The impressive **Haghia Sophia** has a few brilliant gold mosaics remaining, some dating back to the reign of Justinian (see p22). The galleries and upper walls of the funerary chapel of the **Church of the Pammakaristos** are covered with mosaics. Today, the former side chapel has been converted into a museum.

The **Mosaic Museum** houses mosaic floors and murals from the now-vanished Byzantine Great Palace (see pp84–5), which were discovered by archaeologists in 1938. The **Sadberk Hanım Museum** also houses several Byzantine antiquities, including icons, ceramics and jewellery.

Byzantine mosaic floor in the Mosaic Museum

Calligraphy

In the days before the printed word, Ottoman calligraphy (see p97) developed into a highly skilled art form, widely used both to ornament religious texts and legal documents and decrees. The **Museum of Calligraphy** mounts a continuous series of temporary exhibitions. Early Koranic calligraphy can be viewed in **Topkapı Palace**, the **Museum of Turkish and Islamic Arts** and the **Sakıp Sabancı Museum** (see p143).

Ceramics

Experts and amateurs come from all over the world to view the collection of Chinese ceramics and porcelain on display in the kitchens of **Topkapı Palace**. The earliest examples provided the inspiration for Turkey's indigenous ceramic production at İznik (see p163). Examples of İznik tiles can be seen on the walls of Topkapı Palace and in the city's mosques. İznik tiles and also pottery are on display in the Tiled Kiosk Museum, in the **Archaeological Museums** complex, and at the **Sadberk Hanım Museum**. A wider selection of ceramics from all over the Islamic world can be found in the **Museum of Turkish and Islamic Arts**.

Mosque lamp from the Archaeological Museum

Ottoman Interiors

The interiors that can be visited in Istanbul run the gamut from the classical Ottoman styling of the older parts of **Topkapı Palace** to extravagant European-inspired 19th-century decor. In the latter category, the huge **Dolmabahçe Palace** set the style. It was decorated with Bohemian glass and Hereke carpets and has an ornate central stairway

The opulent Süfera Salon in Dolmabahçe Palace

fashioned of crystal and brass. The **Pavilion of the Linden Tree** and the Rococo **Küçüksu Palace**, although more intimate in scale, are equally lavish in their interior style.

Textiles

The Ottomans were justifiably proud of their textile tradition, which can be admired in the huge imperial costume collection at **Topkapı Palace**, begun in 1850. The palace collection houses older materials, including kaftans dating back to the 15th century. The **Sadberk Hanım Museum** houses magnificent, mostly 19th-century pieces on the top floor and some fine examples of delicate Turkish embroidery.

On a larger scale, there are huge imperial campaign tents in the **Military Museum**, which also has a collection of miniature Janissary (see p129) costumes. Uniforms, nomadic tents and a renowned selection of fine carpets are on display in the **Museum of Turkish and Islamic Arts**. The collection includes rug fragments dating back to the 13th century, as well as palatial silks on a larger scale.

Kaftan from Topkapı Palace

Musical Instruments

Examples of typical Turkish instruments, such as the *saz* (lute), can be found in a museum devoted to them at **Aynalı Kavak Palace**. Those played by the Whirling Dervishes are on display at the **Mevlevi Lodge**. Instruments can also be seen, and bought, in two shops situated near the entrance to Gülhane Park (see p63). Traditional Turkish military instruments can be heard being played at the **Military Museum**.

Militaria

The beautiful barges in which the Ottoman sultans were rowed around the Golden Horn and the Bosphorus are part of the **Naval Museum** collection. Naval uniforms and paintings of military scenes also feature. Weapons and armour from the 12th to the 20th centuries can be found in the **Military Museum**, along with a cannon, captured by the Turks during their European campaigns. There is a smaller selection of weaponry in the armoury of **Topkapı Palace**. The **Florence Nightingale Museum** (located in the Selimiye Barracks on the Asian Side) commemorates

the work of the nurse during the Crimean War. It also has some interesting military exhibits on display.

Painting

Close to Dolmabahçe Palace is Istanbul's **National Palaces Painting Museum**, which offers a collection of largely late 19th- and early 20th-century Turkish paintings. Another place to see paintings from a similar period is the Pera Museum in Beyoğlu. Those interested in more contemporary works should visit the impressive **Istanbul Modern** on the Bosphorus waterfront in Tophane.

Science and Technology

Located in a converted warehouse in the heart of Istanbul's docks is the **Rahmi M Koç Museum**. It is home to a selection of mechanical and scientific instruments dating from the early years of the Industrial Revolution, as well as an entire reconstructed bridge taken from an early 20th-century ship.

ISTANBUL THROUGH THE YEAR

Istanbul is at its best in late May and early September, when temperatures are mild and sunshine is plentiful. High season, from June to August, is the most expensive, crowded and hottest time to visit, but the summer arts and music festivals are highlights in the city's cultural calendar. Late November until March or April can be damp and dreary. However, Istanbul is still mild in autumn and winter and, with fewer tour parties around, you can enjoy the sights in peace. As well as arts and sporting events, several public holidays and religious festivals punctuate the year. It is wise to be aware of these when planning an itinerary as some sights may be closed or else crammed with locals enjoying a day out. Some of these celebrations are also fascinating spectacles in their own right.

Tulips growing in Emirgan Park, scene of the spring Tulip Festival

Spring

As the winter smog fades and sunshine increases, cafés and restaurants prepare for the first wave of alfresco dining. After a winter's diet of apples and oranges, a welcome crop of spring fruits, including fresh figs, strawberries and tart green plums, arrives in the shops. Toasted sweetcorn is sold from carts (see p208), and a spring catch of sea bream, sea bass and turbot is on the menu. Tulips, hyacinths, daffodils and pansies fill parks and gardens, and the distinctive pink buds of the Judas tree are seen along the Bosphorus. Monuments and museums are generally uncrowded in spring, and discounts are available at many hotels. In May the popular son et lumière shows outside the Blue Mosque (see pp80–81) begin and continue until September.

Events

Easter (March or April). Pilgrimage to the Monastery of St George on Büyükada in the Princes' Islands (see p161).

International Istanbul Film Festival (late March–mid-April), selected cinemas. Screening of Turkish and foreign films and related events.

Tulip Festival (April), Emirgan Park (see p143) and around the city. Displays of spring-time blooms.

National Sovereignty Day (23 April). Public holiday marking the inauguration of the Turkish Republic in 1923 (see pp32–3). Children take to the streets in folk costume.

Commemoration of the Anzac Landings (25 April), Gallipoli. Britons, Australians and New Zealanders gather at the location of the Anzac landings at Gallipoli during World War I (see pp172–3).

Work and Solidarity Day (1 May). Official public holiday when workers usually attend union-organized rallies.

Kakava Festival (early May), Edirne. A celebration of gypsy music and dance.

Youth and Sports Day (19 May). Public holiday in commemoration of the start of the War of Independence (see p33) in 1919, with sporting events and other activities held throughout the city in stadiums and on the streets.

International Istanbul Theatre Festival (May–June, every two years), various venues. European and Turkish productions.

Conquest of Istanbul (29 May), between Tophane and Karaköy and on the shores of the upper Bosphorus. Mehmet the Conqueror's taking of the city in 1453 (see p28) is re-enacted in street parades and mock battles.

Colourful evening son et lumière show at the Blue Mosque

Average daily hours of sunshine

Hours

Sunshine Chart
One of Istanbul's attractions is its summer sunshine – there are about 2,500 hours each year. From May to October the city is bathed in light well into the evening; bursts of heavy rain, however, are common in high summer. Winter, by contrast, is notoriously deprived of sun.

Summer

In contrast to an all-too-brief spring, the warm weather and clear skies of summer can linger on in Istanbul until November. In July and August temperatures soar. Rooftop and street dining options can be considered during this time. Popular sights are packed with tourists throughout the high season. Picturesque locations outside Istanbul may, on the other hand, be overrun by locals. At weekends, city dwellers trek out to the Belgrade Forest and Black Sea beaches (see p160) or to health clubs along the Bosphorus. Those who can afford it flee to their Aegean homes until autumn.

For those who stay behind there is a strong summer culture. This includes a wild nightlife in hundreds of bars and night spots (see p209), and enthusiastic support for many arts festivals, which attract world-famous performers. Look out, too, for events taking place in historical buildings. You may be able to listen to classical music in Haghia Eirene (see p62) or enjoy a pop concert in the Fortress of Europe on the Bosphorus (see pp142–3). This is also the best time of year for outdoor sports such as hiking, horse riding, water sports, golf and parachuting.

In summer, the menu focuses more on meat than fish, but vegetables and fresh fruit – such as honeydew melons,

Silk Market in Bursa, which operates all year round

cherries, mulberries, peaches and apricots – are widely available. In July and August many shops have summer sales (see p211).

Events

Silk Market (June–July), Bursa. Special market for the sale of silk cocoons (see pp166–7).
International Istanbul Music Festival (mid-June–July). Classical music, opera and dance performed in historic locations. Mozart's Abduction from the Seraglio is staged annually in Topkapı Palace (see pp56–61).

Scene from Abduction from the Seraglio, Topkapı Palace

Bursa Festival (June–July), Bursa Park. Music, folk dancing, plays, opera and shadow puppetry.
Navy Day (1 July). Parades of old and new boats along the Bosphorus.
International Istanbul Jazz Festival (July), various venues. International event with a devoted following.
International Sailing Races (July). Regatta held at the Marmara Islands (see p171).
Grease Wrestling (July), Kırkpınar, Edirne. Wrestlers smeared in olive oil grapple with each other (see p156).
Hunting Festival (3 days, late July), Edirne. Music, art and fishing displays.
Folklore and Music Festival (late July), Bursa. Ethnic dances and crafts displays.
Festival of Troy (August), Çanakkale. Re-enactment of the tale of Troy (see p173).
Victory Day (30 August). Public holiday commemorating victory over Greece in 1922.

Average monthly rainfall

Rainfall Chart
Winter is the wettest season in Istanbul. Heavy showers of rain can sometimes continue into April and May, making spring seem shorter. Sudden snowstorms are not uncommon in winter, but these are short-lived and snowfalls will usually melt away as quickly as they come.

Autumn

Residents of Istanbul often consider their city to be at its best in autumn. As the summer heat loses its grip, chestnut sellers appear on the streets (see p208), pumpkins are sold in the markets, and fresh figs are eaten in abundance. In the surrounding countryside, cotton, wheat and sunflowers are harvested. Migratory grouper and bonito are among the tastiest types of fish which are caught at this time of year.

A popular beauty spot for its array of autumn colours is Lake Abant, 200 km (125 miles) east of Istanbul. Meanwhile, bird-watchers converge on the hills overlooking the Bosphorus to view great flocks of migratory birds heading for their warm wintering grounds in Africa (see p143).

On the cultural agenda is a world-class arts biennial and an antiques fair which blends Turkish and Western aesthetics. Several public holidays reaffirm Turkey's commitment to secularism, including Republic Day in late October, during which flags are hung from balconies. The bridges over the Bosphorus (see p140) are hung with particularly huge flags.

Street-side roasting of seasonal chestnuts

Events

Art International (September), Haliç Congress Center on the Golden Horn (see p91). This event symbolizes Istanbul's newly acquired status in the international art circuit.

Republic Day (29 October). Public holiday commemorating Atatürk's proclamation of the Republic in 1923 (see p33). The Turkish flag adorns buildings in the city.

Akbank Jazz Festival (October), various venues. Jazz music (see p221).

International Istanbul Fine Arts Biennial (October–November every two years, 2017, 2019). International and local avant-garde artists exhibit work in historic locations such as Haghia Eirene and the Imperial Mint (see p62), and the Basilica Cistern (see p78).

Anniversary of Death (10 November). A minute's silence is observed at 9:05am, the precise time of Atatürk's death in Dolmabahçe Palace (see pp130–31) in 1938.

Istanbul Marathon (November), provides participants the oppor-tunity to run from Asia to Europe across the Bosphorus Bridge.

Tüyap Book Fair (October), Tüyap Fair and Congress Centre. Istanbul's premier publishing event showcases prominent writers.

Efes Pilsen Blues Festival (early November), selected venues. Foreign and local blues bands play in popular music venues across the city.

Interior Design Fair (first week of November), Çırağan Palace Hotel Kempinski (see p125). Interior designers and antique dealers display upmarket wares in this popular annual show.

Contemporary Istanbul (November), Lütfi Kirdar Convention Centre. Works by domestic and international artists are showcased here.

Crowds gathering to celebrate Republic Day on 29 October

Average monthly temperature

Temperature Chart
The temperature of the city rarely drops below freezing in winter, and even very cold snaps seldom last longer than three days. The heat of the long, humid summer is intensified by the lodos wind, which blows in from the Sea of Marmara. However, the northerly *poyraz* occasionally provides a cooling breeze.

Winter

There are distinct bonuses to visiting Istanbul in the winter, when even major sights are uncrowded, but be prepared for rain, fog and, sometimes, snow. Shops in the Akmerkez, Galleria, Capitol and Carousel malls *(see p223)* hold sales, making the city a shopper's paradise for leather, woollens and fashion.

Outside Istanbul, when enough snow has fallen on the mountains, the ski season begins in Uludağ *(see p171)*, one of Turkey's most important winter sports resorts. Meanwhile baklava and cream cakes are consumed in the cosy cafés along the Bosphorus and in the old quarter of Beyoğlu *(see pp102–109)*.

View of Bebek on the Bosphorus *(see p140)* in winter

founder of the famous Whirling Dervishes or the Mevlevi.
Christmas *(late December)*. Though Christmas Day is not a public holiday, major hotels organize seasonal festivities.
New Year's Day *(1 January)*. Public holiday incorporating European Christmas traditions including eating turkey, decorating trees and partying. Strings of lights adorn the main roads.
Karadam Ski Festival *(second half of February)*, Uludağ Mountain. Competitions organized by local radio stations and the Uludağ Ski Instructors' Association.

Multitude of lights to welcome in the New Year in Beyoğlu

Events

Mevlâna Festival *(17–24 December)*, Mevlevi Lodge *(see p106)*. Enthusiastic Istanbul devotees perform special dances in honour of the

Muslim Holidays

The dates of Muslim holidays vary according to the phases of the moon and therefore change from year to year. In the holy month of **Ramazan**, Muslims refrain from eating and drinking between dawn and dusk. Some restaurants are closed during the day, and tourists should be discreet when eating in public. Straight after this is the three-day **Şeker Bayramı** (Sugar Festival), when sweetmeats are prepared. Two months later the four-day **Kurban Bayramı** (Feast of the Sacrifice) commemorates the Koranic version of Abraham's sacrifice. This is the main annual public holiday in Turkey, and hotels, trains and roads are packed. Strict Muslims also observe the festivals of **Regaip Kandili, Miraç Kandili, Berat Kandili** and **Mevlid-i-Nebi**.

Festivities during Şeker Bayramı

ISTANBUL AREA BY AREA

SERAGLIO POINT

The hilly, wooded promontory that marks the meeting point of the Golden Horn, the Sea of Marmara and the Bosphorus occupies a natural strategic position. In the Byzantine era, monasteries and public buildings stood on this site. Today it is dominated by the grandiose complex of buildings forming Topkapı Palace, the residence of the Ottoman sultans and the women of the harem for 400 years. The palace is now open to the public as a rambling museum, with lavish apartments and glittering collections of jewels and other treasures. Originally, the palace covered almost the whole of the area with its gardens and pavilions. Part of the grounds have now been turned into a public park. Adjacent to it is the Archaeological Museums, a renowned collection of finds from Turkey and the Near East.

Sights at a Glance

Museums and Palaces
1. Topkapı Palace pp56–61
2. Archaeological Museums pp64–7
8. Istanbul History of Science and Technology in Islam Museum

Churches
3. Haghia Eirene

Historic Buildings and Monuments
4. Fountain of Ahmet III
9. Sublime Porte
11. Sirkeci Station

Streets and Courtyards
5. Soğukçeşme Sokağı
6. Cafer Ağa Courtyard

Parks
7. Gülhane Park

Turkish Baths
10. Cağaloğlu Baths

☐ **Restaurants** p196
1. Café Mese
2. Can Oba
3. Hocapaşa Pidecisi
4. Imbat
5. Karakol
6. Konyalı
7. Neyzade
8. Olive Restaurant
9. Orient Express Restaurant
10. Paşazade
11. Sarnıç
12. Şehzade Erzurum Cağ Kebabı

See also Street Finder maps 2, 3, 4 & 5

0 metres 400
0 yards 400

◀ Interior of the Harem, Topkapı Palace

For map symbols see back flap

Street-by-Street: The First Courtyard of Topkapı

The juxtaposition of Ottoman palace walls, intimately proportioned wooden houses and a soaring Byzantine church lends plenty of drama to the First Courtyard, the outer part of Topkapı Palace. This was once a service area, housing the mint, a hospital, college and a bakery. It was also the mustering point of the Janissaries *(see p129)*. Nowadays, the Cafer Ağa Courtyard and Büfe, just outside the courtyard wall, offer unusual settings for refreshments. Gülhane Park, meanwhile, is one of the few shady open spaces in a city of monuments.

❼ Gülhane Park
Once a rose garden in the outer grounds of Topkapı Palace, the wooded Gülhane Park provides welcome shade in which to escape from the heat of the city.

Istanbul History of Science and Technology in Islam Museum

Ancient Orient Museum

❺ Soğukçeşme Sokağı
Traditional, painted wooden houses line this narrow street.

❾ Sublime Porte
A Rococo gate stands in place of the old Sublime Porte, once the entrance to (and symbol of) the Ottoman government.

Entrance to Gülhane Park

Alay Pavilion

ALEMDAR CAD

0 metres 75
0 yards 75

Gülhane tram stop

Key

— Suggested route

SOĞUKÇEŞME SO

Büfes, tiny ornate kiosks, sell drinks and snacks.

Zeynep Sultan Mosque
Resembling a Byzantine church, this mosque was built in 1769 by the daughter of Ahmet III, Princess Zeynep.

❻ Cafer Ağa Courtyard
The cells of this former college, ranged round a tranquil courtyard café, are now occupied by jewellers, calligraphers and other artisans selling their wares.

❷ ★ Archaeological Museums
Classical statues, dazzling carved sarcophagi, Turkish ceramics and other treasures from all over the former Ottoman Empire make this complex one of the world's great collections of antiquities.

Locator Map
See Street Finder maps 2, 3, 4 & 5

Tiled Kiosk Museum
(see p67)

The Executioner's Fountain
is so named because the executioner washed his hands and sword here after a public beheading.

❶ ★ Topkapı Palace
For 400 years the Ottoman sultans ruled their empire from this vast palace. Its fine art collections, opulent rooms and leafy courtyards are among the highlights of a visit to Istanbul.

Entrance to Topkapı Palace

Topkapı Palace ticket office

Imperial Mint
produced coins from the Ottoman era until 1967.

❸ Haghia Eirene
The Byzantine church of Haghia Eirene dates from the 6th century. Unusually, it has never been converted into a mosque.

Imperial Gate

❹ Fountain of Ahmet III
Built in the early 18th century, the finest of Istanbul's Rococo fountains is inscribed with poetry likening it to the fountains of paradise.

❶ Topkapı Palace

Between 1459 and 1465, shortly after his conquest of Constantinople (see p28), Mehmet II built Topkapı Palace as his main residence. Rather than a single building, it was conceived as a series of pavilions contained by four enormous courtyards, a stone version of the tented encampments from which the nomadic Ottomans had emerged. Initially, the palace served as the seat of government and housed a school in which civil servants and soldiers were trained. In the 18th century, however, the government was moved to the Sublime Porte (see p63). Sultan Abdül Mecit I abandoned Topkapı in 1853 in favour of Dolmabahçe Palace (see pp130–31). In 1924 Topkapı was opened to the public as a museum.

★ Harem
The labyrinth of exquisite rooms where the sultan's wives and concubines lived is open to visitors (see pp60–61).

KEY

① **The kitchens** contain an exhibition of ceramics, glass and silverware (see p58).

② **Second courtyard**

③ **Harem ticket office**

④ **Exhibition of arms and armour** (see p58)

⑤ **The Gate of Felicity** is also called the Gate of the White Eunuchs.

⑥ **Throne Room**

⑦ **Exhibition of imperial costumes** (see p58)

⑧ **Third courtyard**

⑨ **Exhibition of clocks** (see p59)

⑩ **Pavilion of the Holy Mantle** (see p59)

⑪ **Circumcision Pavilion**

⑫ **The fourth courtyard** is a series of gardens dotted with pavilions.

⑬ **Konyalı Restaurant** (see p196)

Entrance to Harem

Divan
The viziers of the imperial council met in this chamber, sometimes watched covertly by the sultan.

Gate of Salutations: entrance to the palace

İftariye Pavilion
Standing between the Baghdad and Circumcision pavilions, this canopied balcony provides views down to the Golden Horn.

VISITORS' CHECKLIST

Practical Information
Babıhümayun Cad. **Map** 3 F3.
Tel (0212) 512 04 80. **Open** Apr–Oct: 9am–7pm; Nov–Mar: 9am–5pm Wed–Mon.
Harem: **Open** 10am–4pm Wed–Mon. (book early).
w topkapisarayi.gov.tr

Transport
Sultanahmet.

Baghdad Pavilion
In 1639 Murat IV built this pavilion to celebrate his capture of Baghdad. It has exquisite blue-and-white tilework.

Library of Ahmet III
Erected in 1719, the library is an elegant marble building. This ornamental fountain is set into the wall below its main entrance.

★ Treasury
This 17th-century jewel-encrusted jug is one of the precious objects exhibited in the former treasury (see p59).

Exploring the Palace's Collections

During their 470-year reign, the Ottoman sultans amassed a glittering collection of treasures. After the foundation of the Turkish Republic in 1923 *(see p33)*, this was nationalized and the bulk of it put on display in Topkapı Palace. As well as diplomatic gifts and articles commissioned from the craftsmen of the palace workshops, a large number of items in the collection were brought back as booty from successful military campaigns. Many such trophies date from the massive expansion of the Ottoman Empire during the reign of Selim the Grim (1512–20), when Syria, Arabia and Egypt were conquered.

Ceramics, Glass and Silverware

The kitchens contain the palace's collection of glass, ceramics and silverware. The silverware section is currently closed for renovation.

Turkish and European pieces are overshadowed by the vast display of Chinese and, to a lesser extent, Japanese porcelain. This was brought to Turkey along the Silk Route, the overland trading link between the Far East and Europe. Topkapı's collection of Chinese porcelain is the world's second best after China itself.

The Chinese porcelain on display spans four dynasties: the Sung (10–13th centuries), followed by the Yüan (13–14th centuries), the Ming (14–17th centuries) and the Ching (17–20th centuries). Celadon, the earliest form of Chinese porcelain collected by the sultans, was made to look like jade, a stone believed by the Chinese to be lucky. The Ottomans prized it because it was said to neutralize poison in food. There are also several exquisite blue-and-white pieces, mostly of the Ming era.

Chinese aesthetics were an important influence on Ottoman craftsmen, particularly in the creation of designs for their fledgling ceramics industry at İznik *(see p163)*. Although there are no İznik pieces in the Topkapı collection, many of the tiles on the palace walls originated there. These clearly show the influence of designs used for Chinese blue-and-white porcelain, such as cloud scrolls and stylized flowers. Much of the later porcelain, particularly the Japanese Imari ware, was made specifically for the export market. The most obvious examples of this are some plates decorated with quotations from the Koran. A part of the kitchens, the old confectioners' pantry, has been preserved as it would have been when in use. On display are huge cauldrons and other utensils wielded by the palace's chefs to feed its 12,000 residents and guests.

Japanese porcelain plate

Arms and Armour

Taxes and tributes from all over the empire were once stored in this chamber, which was known as the Inner Treasury. Straight ahead as you enter is a series of horse-tail standards. Carried in processions or displayed outside tents, these proclaimed the rank of their owners. Viziers *(see p31)*, for example, merited three standards; the grand vizier, five; and the sultan's banner, nine.

The weaponry includes ornately embellished swords and several bows made by sultans themselves (Beyazıt II was a particularly masterful craftsman). The bulky iron weaponry used by European crusaders look rudimentary by comparison. Also on view are examples of 15th-century Ottoman chain mail and colourful shields. The shields have metal centres surrounded by closely woven straw painted with flowers.

Imperial Costumes

A collection of imperial costumes is displayed in the Hall of the Campaign Pages, whose task was to look after the royal wardrobe. It was a palace tradition that on the death of a sultan his clothes were carefully folded and placed in sealed bags. As a result, it is possible to see a perfectly preserved kaftan once worn by Mehmet the Conqueror *(see p28)*. The reforms of Sultan Mahmut II included a revolution in the dress code *(see p32)*. The end of an era came as plain grey serge replaced the earlier luxurious silken textiles.

Sumptuous silk kaftan once worn by Mehmet the Conqueror

Treasury

Of all the exhibitions in the palace, the Treasury's collection is the easiest to appreciate, glittering as it does with thousands of precious and semi-precious stones. The only surprise is that there are so few women's jewels here. Whereas the treasures of the sultans and viziers were owned by the state and reverted to the palace on their deaths, those belonging to the women of the court did not.

In the first hall stands a full, diamond-encrusted suit of chain mail, designed for Mustafa III (1757–74) for ceremonial use.

Diplomatic gifts include a fine pearl statuette of a prince seated beneath a canopy, which was sent to Sultan Abdül Aziz (1861–76) from India.

The Topkapı dagger

The greatest pieces are in the second hall. Foremost among these is the Topkapı dagger (1741). This splendid object was commissioned by the sultan from his own jewellers. It was intended as a present for the Shah of Persia, but he died before it reached him. Among other exhibits here are a selection of the bejewelled aigrettes (plumes) which added splendour to imperial turbans.

In the third hall, the 86-carat Spoonmaker's diamond is said to have been discovered in a rubbish heap in Istanbul in the 17th century, and bought from a scrap merchant for three spoons. The gold-plated Bayram throne was given to Murat III *(see p34)* by the Governor of Egypt in 1574 and used for state ceremonies until early this century.

It was the throne in the fourth hall, given by the Shah of Persia, which was to have been acknowledged by the equally magnificent gift of the Topkapı dagger. In a cabinet near the throne is an unusual relic: a case containing bones said to be from the hand of St John the Baptist.

Miniatures and Manuscripts

It is possible to display only a tiny fraction of Topkapı's total collection of over 13,000 miniatures and manuscripts at any one time. This section, which has been closed for some time, includes highlights such as the depictions of warriors and fearsome creatures known as *Demons and Monsters in the Life of Nomads*, painted by Mohammed Siyah Qalem, possibly as early as the 12th century. It is from this Eastern tradition of miniature painting, which was also prevalent in Mogul India and Persia, that the ebullient Ottoman style of miniatures developed.

Also on show are some fine examples of calligraphy *(see p97)*, including texts of the Koran, manuscripts in Turkish, Arabic, Persian, Latin, Hebrew and Greek, along with several firmans, or imperial decrees.

Cover of a Koran, decorated in gold filigree work

Clocks

European clocks given to, or bought by, various sultans form the majority of this collection, despite the fact that there were makers of clocks and watches in Istanbul from the 17th century.

A 17th-century watch made of gold, enamel and precious stones

The clocks range from simple, weight-driven 16th-century examples to an exquisite 18th-century English mechanism encased in mother-of-pearl and featuring a German organ which played tunes on the hour to the delight of the harem.

Interestingly, the only male European eyewitness accounts of life in the harem were written by the mechanics sent to service these instruments.

Pavilion of the Holy Mantle

Some of the holiest relics of Islam are displayed in these five domed rooms, which are a place of pilgrimage for Muslims. Most of the relics found their way to Istanbul as a result of the conquest by Selim "the Grim" *(see p28)* of Egypt and Arabia, and his assumption of the caliphate (the leadership of Islam) in 1517.

The most sacred treasure is the mantle once worn by the Prophet Mohammed. Visitors cannot actually enter the room in which it is stored; instead they look into it from an antechamber through an open doorway. Night and day, holy men continuously chant passages from the Koran over the gold chest in which the mantle is stored. A stand in front of the chest holds two of Mohammed's swords.

A glass cabinet in the anteroom contains hairs from the beard of the Prophet, a letter written by him and an impression of his footprint.

In the other rooms you can see some of the ornate locks and keys for the Kaaba *(see p41)* which were sent to Mecca by successive sultans.

Topkapı Palace: The Harem

The word Harem derives from the Arabic for "forbidden". A Harem was the residence of the sultan's wives, concubines and children, who were guarded by black slave eunuchs. The sultan and his sons were the only other men allowed access to the Harem, which also included the Cage, a set of rooms where the sultan's brothers were confined to avoid destabilizing succession contests. Topkapı's Harem was laid out by Sultan Murat III in the late 16th century and is a labyrinth of brilliantly tiled corridors and chambers.

Locator Map
See main illustration of the palace on pp56–7

★ **Paired Pavilions**
These twin apartments, built in the 17th century for the crown prince, boast superb İznik tiles *(see p163)* and a dome lined with gilded canvas.

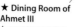

★ **Dining Room of Ahmet III**
A sumptuous array of fruit and flowers is painted on to the walls of this 18th-century chamber, which is also known as the Fruit Room.

Imperial Hall
The largest room in the Harem, this hall was used for entertainments. Against one wall stands a large throne, from which the sultan would view the proceedings.

Life in the Harem

The women of the Harem were slaves, gathered from the furthest corners of the Ottoman Empire and beyond. Their dream was to become a favourite of the sultan *(see p30)* and bear him a son, which on some occasions led to marriage. Competition was stiff, however, for at its height the Harem contained over 1,000 concubines, many of whom never rose beyond the service of their fellow captives. The last women eventually left in 1909.

A Western view of Harem life in a 19th-century engraving

Salon of the Valide Sultana
The sultan's mother, the valide sultana *(see p31)*, was the most powerful woman in the Harem and had some of the best rooms.

Key

☐ Rooms open to the public
☐ Areas closed to the public

Exit

Entrance

Courtyard of the Black Eunuchs
Marble columns line this courtyard, which still has some old-fashioned, wrought-iron lamps.

KEY

① **The Salon of Murat III**, built by Sinan *(see p93)*, has fine tiled walls, a handsome fountain and a large hearth.

② **The Library of Ahmet I** is pleasantly light and airy, with ivory-faced shutters.

③ **Apartments and courtyard of the favourites**

④ **Sultan's bathroom**

⑤ **Courtyard of the valide sultana**

⑥ **The Golden Way** is so called because new sultans reputedly threw gold coins to their concubines here.

⑦ **The Tower of Justice** offers a superb view of Topkapı's rooftops and beyond.

⑧ **Barracks of the black eunuchs**

⑨ **The Harem baths** were where the concubines bathed and relaxed.

⑩ **Courtyard of the concubines**

⑪ **Valide sultana's bedchamber**

⑫ **Valide sultana's prayer room**

❷ Archaeological Museums

See pp64–7.

❸ Haghia Eirene
Aya İrini Kilisesi

First courtyard of Topkapı Palace. **Map** 3 E4 (5 F3). **Tel** (0212) 522 17 50. 🚊 Gülhane or Sultanahmet. **Open** 9am–4pm Wed–Mon.

Though the present church dates only from the 6th century, it is at least the third building to be erected on what is thought to be the oldest site of Christian worship in Istanbul. Within a decade of the Muslim conquest of the city in 1453 (*see p28*) it had been included within the Topkapı Palace complex for use as an arsenal. Today the building, with its good acoustics, hosts concerts during the Istanbul Music Festival (*see p47*).

Inside are three fascinating features that have not survived in any other Byzantine church in the city. The *synthronon*, the five rows of built-in seats hugging the apse, were occupied by clergymen officiating during services. Above this looms a simple black mosaic cross on a gold background, which dates from the iconoclastic period (*see p22*), when figurative images were forbidden. At the back of the church is a cloister-like courtyard where deceased

One of the four elaborately decorated sides of the Fountain of Ahmet III

Byzantine emperors once lay in their porphyry sarcophagi. Most have been moved to the Archaeological Museums.

❹ Fountain of Ahmet III
Ahmet III Çeşmesi

Junction of İshak Paşa Cad & Babıhümayun Cad. **Map** 3 E4 (5 F4). 🚊 Gülhane or Sultanahmet.

Built in 1729, the most beautiful of Istanbul's countless fountains survived the violent deposition of Sultan Ahmet III two years later. Many of the other monuments constructed by the sultan during his reign, which has become known as the Tulip Period (*see p29*), were destroyed. The fountain is in

the delicate Turkish Rococo style, with five small domes, mihrab-shaped niches and dizzying floral reliefs.

Ottoman "fountains" do not spout jets of water, but are more like ornate public taps. They sometimes incorporated a counter, or *sebil*, from which refreshments would be served.

In this case, each of the fountain's four walls is equipped with a tap, or *çeşme*, above a carved marble basin. Over each tap is an elaborate calligraphic inscription by the 18th-century poet Seyit Vehbi Efendi. The inscription, in gold on a blue-green background, is in honour of the fountain and its founder. At each of the four corners there is a *sebil* backed by three windows covered by ornate marble grilles. Instead of the customary iced water, passers-by at this fountain would have been offered sherbets and flavoured waters in silver goblets.

❺ Soğukçeşme Sokağı

Map 3 E4 (5 F3). 🚊 Gülhane.

Charming old wooden houses line this narrow, sloping cobbled lane ("the street of the cold fountain"), which squeezes between the outer walls of Topkapı Palace and the towering minarets of Haghia Sophia. Traditional houses like these were built in the city from the late 18th century onwards.

The apse of Haghia Eirene, with its imposing black-on-gold cross

The buildings in the lane were renovated by the Turkish Touring and Automobile Club (TTOK, *see p245*) in the 1980s. Of these, nine buildings form the Ayasofya Konakları (*see p187*), a series of attractive pastel-painted guesthouses popular with tourists. Another building has been converted by the TTOK into a library of historical writings on Istanbul, and archive of engravings and photographs of the city. A Roman cistern towards the bottom of the lane has been converted into the Sarnıç restaurant (*see p196*).

Restored Ottoman house on Soğukçeşme Sokağı

Ottoman Houses

The typical, smart town house of 19th-century Istanbul had a stone ground floor above which were one or two wooden storeys. The building invariably sported a *çıkma*, a section projecting out over the street. This developed from the traditional Turkish balcony, which was enclosed in the northern part of the country because of the colder climate. Wooden lattice covers, or *kafesler*, over the windows on the upper storeys ensured that the women of the house were able to watch life on the street below without being seen themselves. Few wooden houses have survived. Those that remain usually owe their existence to tourism and many have been restored as hotels. While the law forbids their demolition, it is extremely hard to obtain insurance for them in a city that has experienced many devastating fires.

Traditional calligraphy on sale in Cafer Ağa Courtyard

❻ Cafer Ağa Courtyard

Cafer Ağa Medresesi

Caferiye Sok. **Map** 5 E3. **Tel** (0212) 513 18 43. 🚋 Gülhane or Sultanahmet. **Open** 8:30am–8pm daily.

This peaceful courtyard at the end of an alley was built in 1559 by Sinan (*see p93*) for the chief black eunuch (*see p31*) as a *medrese* (theological college, *see p40*). Sinan's bust presides over the café tables in the courtyard. The former students' lodgings are now used to display a variety of craft goods typically including jewellery, silk prints, ceramics and calligraphy.

❼ Gülhane Park

Gülhane Parkı

Alemdar Cad. **Map** 3 E3 (5 F2). 🚋 Gülhane. **Open** daily. Museum: **Open** 9am–4:30pm Wed–Mon. 🎟 Library: **Open** 10am–7pm Mon–Sat.

Gülhane Park occupies what was the lower grounds of Topkapı Palace. Today it has a neglected air but it is still a shady place to stroll and it includes a couple of interesting landmarks.

The Alay Köşkü (Procession Kiosk), built into the Topkapı Palace complex, enabled sultans to keep an eye on who was coming out of and going into the Sublime Porte. At the far end of the park is the Goths' Column, a well-preserved 3rd-century victory monument, surrounded by clapboard teahouses. Its name comes from the Latin inscription on it which reads: "Fortune is restored to us because of victory over the Goths".

Across Kennedy Caddesi, the main road running along the northeast side of the park, there is a viewpoint over the busy waters where the Golden Horn meets the Bosphorus.

❽ Istanbul History of Science and Technology in Islam Museum

Istanbul Islam ve Teknoloji Tarihi Müzesi

Gülhane Park. **Map** 3 3E. 🚋 Gülhane. **Open** 9am–5pm Wed–Mon.

Housed in the former Topkapı Palace stables, this fine museum is home to scale models of some of the greatest inventions in the Islamic world, between the 8th and 16th centuries. The intricate models, which include a planetarium and water clock, were built in Frankfurt's Johann Wolfgang Goethe University.

❾ Sublime Porte

Bab-ı Ali

Alemdar Cad. **Map** 3 E3 (5 E2). 🚋 Gülhane.

Foreign ambassadors to Ottoman Turkey were known as Ambassadors to the Sublime Porte, after this monumental gateway which once led into the offices and palace of the grand vizier. The institution of the Sublime Porte filled an important role in Ottoman society because it could often provide an effective counter-balance to the whims of sultans.

The Rococo gateway you see today was built in the 1840s. Its guarded entrance now shields the offices of Istanbul's provincial government.

Rococo decoration on the roof of the Sublime Porte

❷ Archaeological Museums
Arkeoloji Müzeleri

Although this collection of antiquities was begun only in the mid-19th century, provincial governors were soon sending in objects from the length and breadth of the Ottoman Empire. Today the complex includes three different museums – the Archaeological Museum (Arkeoloji Müzesi), the Ancient Orient Museum (Eski Şark Eserleri Müzesi) and Tiled Kiosk Museum (Çinili Köşk Müzesi). It has one of the world's richest collections of classical artifacts, and also includes treasures from the pre-classical world. The main building was erected under the directorship of Osman Hamdi Bey (1881–1910), to house his finds. This archaeologist, painter and polymath discovered the exquisite sarcophagi in the royal necropolis at Sidon in present-day Lebanon.

★ **Alexander Sarcophagus**
This fabulously carved marble tomb from the late 4th century BC is thought to have been built for King Abdalonymos of Sidon. It is called the Alexander Sarcophagus because Alexander the Great is depicted on it winning a victory over the Persians.

Key to Floorplan

- ☐ Classical Archaeology
- ☐ Children's Museum
- ☐ Thracian, Bithynian and Byzantine Collections
- ☐ Istanbul Through the Ages
- ☐ Anatolia and Troy
- ☐ Anatolia's Neighbouring Cultures
- ☐ Tiled Kiosk Museum
- ☐ Ancient Orient Museum
- ☐ Non-exhibition space

The porticoes of the museum take their design from the 4th-century BC Sarcophagus of the Mourning Women.

Sarcophagus of the Mourning Women

Outdoor café

★ **Karaman Mihrab**
This blue, richly tiled mihrab (see p40) comes from the city of Karaman in southeast Turkey, which was the capital of the Karamanid state from 1256–1483. It is the most important artistic relic of that culture.

Gallery Guide

The 20 galleries of the main building house the Archaeological Museum's important collection of classical antiquities. The four-storey wing has displays on the archaeology of Istanbul and nearby regions, and includes the Children's Museum. There are two other museums within the grounds: the Tiled Kiosk Museum, the oldest building in the complex showcasing Turkish tiles and ceramics, and the Ancient Orient Museum.

Geometric Period Cypriot Jug
Stylized fish decorate this jug, in a design typical of the Geometric Period (1050 –750 BC), when a vibrant ceramics culture flourished on Cyprus.

Stairs to main building

Third floor

Second floor

First floor

Ground floor

Statue of Marsyas

Statue and bust of Alexander the Great

Entrance

Mosaic Icon of the Presentation
Dating from the 6th–7th centuries AD, this battered panel from Kalenderhane Mosque (see p94) is the only religious figurative mosaic to have survived Byzantium's iconoclastic period (see p22).

Porphyry Sarcophagi
These monumental purple sarcophagi (4th–5th centuries AD) are thought to have held the bodies of some of the early Byzantine emperors.

★ Treaty of Kadesh
This tablet constitutes the world's earliest surviving peace treaty, agreed between the Egyptians and Hittites in 1269 BC. Among its many clauses are provisions for the return of political refugees.

Exploring the Archaeological Museums

This collection spans over 5,000 years, from figurines of the Mother Goddess modelled in the 3rd millennium BC to Turkish pottery thrown in the 19th century. To cover everything in one visit is impossible. Visitors with little time should not miss the breathtaking sarcophagi from the royal necropolis at Sidon. To learn more about the history of Istanbul itself you should head for the gallery on the first floor of the New Building wing. Youngsters may enjoy the displays in the Children's Museum. Some of the galleries are, however, closed for renovations.

Classical Archaeology

Monumental Bes, the ancient Egyptian god, greets visitors at the door to the main building. Hugely popular in the 1st–3rd centuries, Bes' comically grotesque appearance was an effective deterrent for evil spirits. Rooms 8 and 9 contain the highlights of the museum's entire collection: a group of sarcophagi unearthed in 1887 at Sidon (in present-day Lebanon).

Marble bust of Emperor Augustus

These are thought to have been made for a line of Phoenician kings who ruled in the 6th–4th centuries BC. Their decoration vividly shows the transition from Egyptian to Greek influence in the art of the Near East at that time.

The latest and finest of them is the so-called Alexander Sarcophagus (late 4th century BC). Alexander the Great features in two decorative, high-relief friezes on the longest sides. These show a battle scene and a hunting scene. The friezes survive in almost perfect condition, showing traces of their original colouring, though the metal weapons of the soldiers and hunters have been lost.

The Sarcophagus of the Mourning Women is thought to have been made for King Straton (374–358 BC), who was known for his fondness for women. The grief-stricken females may have been members of his harem.

Rooms 14–20 contain some remarkable statues. Among them is a Roman copy of a 3rd-century BC statue of Marsyas, depicting the satyr about to be flayed after daring to challenge Apollo's musical ability. A statue and bust of Alexander the Great (3rd–2nd centuries BC) show the conqueror as the perfect hero, with a meditative expression on his face. Room 18 contains realistic busts of Roman emperors.

Children's Museum

Special low cabinets are used in this part of the museum, which is designed for visiting schoolchildren. Paper and coloured crayons are to hand in a bid to stimulate future archaeologists.

Thracian, Bithynian and Byzantine Collections

This interesting gallery on the ground floor of the New Building wing displays religious and other artifacts from the ancient civilizations of Thrace and Bithynia, and from Byzantium (see pp22–27) – including a statue of Byzantine Emperor Valens. This section of the musuem also covers the architecture of the ancient world.

Bronze head of a snake from the Serpentine Column

Istanbul through the Ages

With a series of well-chosen pieces and explanatory texts in Turkish and English, this gallery brilliantly chronicles Istanbul's archaeological past from the Neolithic to the Byzantine period.

The rare Mosaic Icon of the Presentation (c.AD 600) originally adorned the Kalenderhane Mosque (see p94). One of the three snakes' heads from the Serpentine Column, which has stood headless in the Hippodrome (see p82) since the 18th century, is also displayed here. Look out too for a section of the iron chains that the Byzantines hung across the Golden Horn to stop hostile ships (see p25).

Frieze showing the battle of Issus (333 BC), on the side panel of the Alexander Sarcophagus

Reconstruction of a mausoleum discovered at Palmyra in Syria

Anatolia and Troy

One side of this narrow, long hall chronicles the history of Anatolia (the Asiatic part of modern Turkey) from the Palaeolithic era to the Iron Age. It culminates with a room devoted to the Phrygian culture, which centred on the city of Gordion. The highlight is a recreation of an 8th-century BC royal tomb, which was housed beneath a tumulus in a juniper-wood chamber. As well as cooking utensils, the king was buried with furniture made of oak, box, yew and juniper.

The other side of the gallery traces the excavations of nine different civilizations at Troy *(see p173)*, from 3000 BC to the time of Christ. On display are a few pieces of the gold hoard known as the Schliemann treasure, after the archaeologist who first discovered it in the late 19th century. Most of the pieces were smuggled out of Turkey, however, and are now in museums around the world.

Anatolia's Neighbouring Cultures

This long gallery is also divided in two, with one side devoted to Cyprus and the other to Syria-Palestine. The Cypriot collection was assembled by the joint American and Russian consul to Cyprus, Luigi Palma di Cesnola, who systematically looted its tombs from 1865–73. Apart from some beautiful pots, the most interesting objects are the figures of plump, naked temple boys (3rd century BC). They are thought to represent boy prostitutes at temples to Aphrodite, the Greek goddess of love.

Among the Syrian exhibits are funerary reliefs, the Gezer Calendar (925 BC) – a limestone tablet bearing the oldest known Hebrew inscription – and a reconstruction of a 1st–3rd-century mausoleum from the trading oasis of Palmyra.

16th-century İznik tiled lunette in the Çinili Pavilion

Tiled Kiosk Museum

Apart from carpets, the most distinctive Turkish art form is ceramics. This is particularly seen in the sheets of tiles used to decorate the walls of mosques and pavilions such as the Çinili Pavilion in which the Tiled Kiosk Museum is located, where the entrance archway is plastered with geometric and calligraphic tiles.

In the main room there is an exquisite early 15th-century tiled mihrab from central Anatolia. Rooms 3 and 4 contain tiles and mosque lamps from the famed İznik potteries, the hub of Turkish ceramics production *(see p163)*. With the decline in quality of İznik ceramics in the late 16th century, other centres took over. One of these, Kütahya, also produced pieces of beauty and high quality (rooms 5 and 6).

Ancient Orient Museum

Although this collection contains antiquities of great rarity and beauty from the Egyptian and Hittite cultures, pride of place goes to the artifacts from the early civilizations of Mesopotamia (present-day Iraq).

The monumental glazed brick friezes from Babylon's main entrance, the Ishtar Gate, (rooms 3 and 9) date from the reign of Nebuchadnezzar II (605–562 BC), when the capital of Babylon experienced its final flowering. The elegant, 30 kg (65 lb) duck-shaped weight in room 4 comes from a much earlier Babylonian temple (c.2000 BC).

Room 5 contains some of the earliest known examples of writing, in the form of cuneiform inscriptions on clay tablets, dating from 2700 BC. The famous Treaty of Kadesh (room 7), concluded around 1269 BC between the Egyptian and Hittite empires, was originally written on a sheet of silver. The one in this collection is a Hittite copy. The treaty includes many sophisticated clauses, including one providing for the return of a political refugee, who was "not to be charged with his crime, nor his house and wives and his children be harmed".

Glazed frieze of a bull from Ishtar Gate, Babylon

❿ Cağaloğlu Baths
Cağaloğlu Hamamı

Prof Kazım İsmail Gürkan Cad 34, Cağaloğlu. **Map** 3 E4 (5 D3). **Tel** (0212) 522 24 24. 🚊 Sultanahmet. **Open** 8am–10pm daily. Ⓦ cagalogluhamami.com.tr

Among the city's more sumptuous Turkish baths, the ones in Cağaloğlu were built by Sultan Mahmut I in 1741. The income from them was designated for the maintenance of Mahmut's library in Haghia Sophia (see pp74–7).

The city's smaller baths have different times at which men and women can use the same facilities. But in larger baths, such as this one, there are

Corridor leading into the Cağaloğlu Baths, built by Mahmut I

entirely separate sections. In the Cağaloğlu Baths the men's and women's sections are at right angles to one another and entered from different streets. Each consists of three parts: a *camekan*, a *soğukluk* and the main bath chamber or *hararet*, which centres on a massive octagonal massage slab.

The Cağaloğlu Baths are popular with foreign visitors because the staff are happy to explain the procedure. Even if you do not want to sweat it out, you can still take a look inside the entrance corridor and *camekan* of the men's section. Here you will find a small display of Ottoman bathing regalia, including precarious wooden clogs once worn by women on what would frequently be their only outing from the confines of the home. You can also sit and have a drink by the fountain in the peaceful *camekan*.

⓫ Sirkeci Station
Sirkeci Garı

Sirkeci İstasyon Cad, Sirkeci. **Map** 3 E3 (5 E1). **Tel** (0212) 527 00 50 or 520 65 75. 🚊 Sirkeci. **Open** daily.

This magnificent railway station was built to receive the long-anticipated Orient Express from Europe. It was officially opened in 1890, even though the luxurious train had been

Sirkeci Station, final destination of the historic Orient Express

running into Istanbul for a year by then. The design, by the German architect Jasmund, successfully incorporates features from the many different architectural traditions of Istanbul. Byzantine alternating stone and brick courses are combined with a Seljuk-style monumental recessed portal and Muslim horseshoe arches around the windows.

The station is now closed to trains but is still a stop on the Marmaray Metro line, which links Europe with Asia via the Bosphorus tunnel. The station building houses the Orient Express Restaurant (see p196), as well as a small, free railway museum (open 9am–5pm Tue–Sat).

The World-Famous Orient Express

The Orient Express made its first run from Paris to Istanbul in 1889, covering the 2,900-km (1,800-mile) journey in three days. Both Sirkeci Station and the Pera Palas Hotel (see p106) in Istanbul were built especially to receive its passengers. The wealthy and often distinguished passengers of "The Train of Kings, the King of Trains" did indeed include kings among the many presidents, politicians, aristocrats and actresses. King Boris III of Bulgaria even made a habit of taking over from the driver of the train when he travelled on it through his own country.

A byword for exoticism and romance, the train was associated with the orientalist view of Istanbul as a treacherous melting pot of diplomats and arms dealers. It inspired no fewer than 19 books – *Murder on the Orient Express* by Agatha Christie and *Stamboul Train* by Graham Greene foremost among them – six films and one piece of music. During the Cold War standards of luxury crashed, though a service of sorts, without even a restaurant car, continued twice weekly to Istanbul until 1977.

A 1920s poster for the Orient Express, showing a romantic view of Istanbul

Turkish Baths

No trip to Istanbul is complete without an hour or two spent in a Turkish bath *(hamam)*, which will leave your whole body feeling rejuvenated. Turkish baths differ little from the baths of ancient Rome, from which they derive, except there is no pool of cold water to plunge into at the end.

A full service will entail a period of relaxation in the steam-filled hot room, punctuated by bouts of vigorous soaping and massaging. There is no time limit, but allow at least an hour and a half. Towels and soap will be provided, but you can take toiletries with you. Four historic baths located in the Old City – Çemberlitaş *(see p83)*, Hürrem Sultan Hamamı *(see p78)*, Cağaloğlu (illustrated below) and the Süleymaniye Hamamı – are used to catering for tourists. Most luxury hotels have their own baths *(see pp182)*.

Choosing a Service
Services, detailed in a price list at the entrance, range from a self-service option to a luxury body scrub, shampoo and massage.

The *camekan* (entrance hall) is a peaceful internal courtyard near the entrance of the building. Bathers change clothes in cubicles surrounding it. The *camekan* is also the place to relax with a cup of tea after bathing.

Changing Clothes
Before changing you will be given a cloth *(peştemal)*, to wrap around you, and a pair of slippers for walking on the hot, wet floor.

Corridor from street

Basin and tap for washing

Small, star-like windows piercing the domes

Cağaloğlu Baths
The opulent, 18th-century Turkish baths at Cağaloğlu have separate, identical sections for men and women. The men's section is shown here.

The *soğukluk* (intermediate room) is a temperate passage between the changing room and the *hararet*. You will be given dry towels here on your way back to the *camekan*.

In the *hararet* (hot room), the main room of the Turkish bath, you are permitted to sit and sweat in the steam for as long as you like.

The Exfoliating Body Scrub
In between steaming, you (or the staff at the baths) scrub your body briskly with a coarse, soapy mitt *(kese)*.

The Body Massage
A marble plinth *(göbek taşı)* occupies the centre of the hot room. This is where you will have your pummelling full-body massage.

SULTANAHMET

Istanbul's two principal monuments face each other across an area of gardens known informally as Sultanahmet Square. This part of the city gets its name from Sultan Ahmet I, who built the Blue Mosque. Opposite is Haghia Sophia, an outstanding example of early Byzantine architecture, and still one of the world's most remarkable churches. A neat oblong square next to the Blue Mosque marks the site of the Hippodrome, a chariot-racing stadium built by the Romans in around AD 200. On the other side of the Blue Mosque, Sultanahmet slopes down to the Sea of Marmara in a jumble of alleyways. Here, traditional-style Ottoman wooden houses have been built over the remains of the Great Palace of the Byzantine emperors.

Sights at a Glance

Mosques and Churches
1 Haghia Sophia pp74–7
7 Blue Mosque pp80–81
14 Sokollu Mehmet Paşa Mosque
15 SS Sergius and Bacchus' Church

Museums
2 Carpet Museum
6 Mosaic Museum
8 Museum of Turkish and Islamic Arts
10 Marmara University Museum of the Republic

Squares and Courtyards
4 Istanbul Handicrafts Centre
9 Hippodrome

Historic Buildings and Monuments
3 Basilica Cistern
5 Baths of Roxelana
11 Cistern of 1001 Columns
12 Tomb of Sultan Mahmut II
13 Constantine's Column
16 Bucoleon Palace

☐ Restaurants pp197–8
1 Ahırkapı Balıkçısı
2 Albura Kathisma
3 Aloran Café & Restaurant
4 Amedros
5 Balıkçı Sabahattin
6 Doy Doy
7 Dubb
8 Faros Hotel Restaurant
9 Fuego Restaurant
10 Giritli Restaurant
11 Karışma Sen Meyhane
12 Khorasani
13 Köfteci Ramiz
14 Mozaik Restaurant
15 Patara Restaurant
16 Port Shield
17 Seasons Restaurant
18 Sultanahmet Fish House
19 Tarihi Sultanahmet Köftecisi
20 Tria Elegance
21 Vonalı Celal

See also Street Finder maps 3 & 5

0 metres 250
0 yards 250

◀ The Blue Mosque in the luminescent glow of the setting sun

For map symbols see back flap

Street-by-Street: Sultanahmet Square

Two of Istanbul's most venerable monuments, the Blue
Mosque and Haghia Sophia, face each other across a
leafy square, informally known as Sultanahmet Square
(Sultanahmet Meydanı), next to the Hippodrome of
Byzantium. Also in this fascinating historic quarter are a
few museums, including the Mosaic Museum, built over
part of the old Byzantine Great Palace (see pp84–5), and
the Museum of Turkish and Islamic Arts. No less divert-
ing than the cultural sights of this pedestrianized area
are the cries of the simit (bagel) hawkers and carpet
sellers, and the chatter of children selling postcards.

Tomb of Sultan Ahmet I
Stunning 17th-century İznik tiles
(see p163) adorn the inside of this
tomb, which is part of the outer
complex of the Blue Mosque.

Sultanahmet
tram stop

❼ ★ Blue Mosque
Towering above
Sultanahmet Square are the
six beautiful minarets of this
world-famous mosque. It
was built in the early 17th
century for Ahmet I.

Firuz Ağa
Mosque

Fountain
of Kaiser
Wilhelm II

Egyptian
Obelisk

**❽ Museum of Turkish and
Islamic Arts**
Yurts, used by Turkey's nomadic
peoples, and rugs are included in
this impressive collection.

Key
— Suggested route

Brazen Column

ATMEYDANI SOK

TAVUKHANE SOK

TORUN SO

Serpentine
Column

❾ Hippodrome
This stadium was the city's
focus for more than 1,000 years
before it fell into ruin. Only a few
sections, such as the central line
of monuments, remain.

❻ Mosaic Museum
Hunting scenes are one
of the common subjects
that can be seen in some
of the mosaics from the
Great Palace.

❸ ★ Basilica Cistern
This marble Medusa head is one of two classical column bases found in the Basilica Cistern. The cavernous cistern dates from the reign of Justinian (see p22) in the 6th century.

A stone pilaster next to the remains of an Ottoman water tower is all that survives of the Milion (see p85), a triumphal gateway.

Locator Map
See Street Finder maps 3 & 5

❷ Carpet Museum
Housed in the soup kitchens of Haghia Sophia, this museum displays fine carpets woven between the 14th and 20th centuries.

❶ ★ Haghia Sophia
The supreme church of Byzantium is over 1,400 years old but has survived in a remarkably good state. Inside it are several glorious figurative mosaics.

❺ Baths of Roxelana
Sinan (see p93) designed these baths in the mid-16th century. In the past, the building has housed a carpet shop, but it has been restored, and reopened in 2012 as the Hürrem Sultan Hamamı.

Yeşil Ev Hotel
(see p186)

❹ Istanbul Handicrafts Centre
Visitors have a rare opportunity here to observe Turkish craftsmen practising a range of skills.

Arasta Bazaar
Quality carpets, ceramics and other handicraft items are a major draw in this upmarket bazaar. With two long rows of shops on either side of a lane, the bazaar was once a stable yard.

0 metres 75
0 yards 75

❶ Haghia Sophia
Ayasofya

The "church of holy wisdom," Haghia Sophia is among the world's greatest architectural achievements. More than 1,400 years old, it stands as a testament to the sophistication of the 6th-century Byzantine capital. The vast edifice was built over two earlier churches and inaugurated by Emperor Justinian in 537. In the 15th century the Ottomans converted it into a mosque: the minarets, tombs and fountains date from this period. To help support the structure's great weight, the exterior has been buttressed on numerous occasions, which has partly obscured its original shape. Three mausoleums at the site are also open to the public.

Print of Haghia Sophia from the mid-19th century

Byzantine Frieze
Among the ruins of the monumental entrance to the earlier Haghia Sophia (dedicated in AD 415) is this frieze of sheep, symbolizing the apostles.

Historical Plan of Haghia Sophia

Nothing remains of the first 4th-century church on this spot, but there are traces of the second one from the 5th century, which burnt down in AD 532. Earthquakes have taken their toll on the third structure, which has been strengthened and added to many times.

Entrance

Key

☐ 5th-century church
☐ 6th-century church
☐ Ottoman additions

★ **Nave**
Visitors cannot fail to be staggered by this vast space which is covered by a huge dome reaching to a height of 56 m (184 ft).

VISITORS' CHECKLIST

Practical Information
Ayasofya Sultanahmet Meydanı 1.
Map 3 E4 (5 F3). **Tel** (0212) 528 45 00. **Open** 9am–7pm (5pm Nov–Mar). 🐾 🎫 ♿ ground floor only.

Transport
🚊 Sultanahmet.

★ **The Mosaics**
The church's splendid Byzantine mosaics include this one at the end of the south gallery. It depicts Christ flanked by Emperor Constantine IX and his wife, the Empress Zoe.

KEY

① **Outer Narthex**

② **Buttresses**

③ **Inner Narthex**

④ **Imperial Gate**

⑤ **The galleries** were originally used by women during services.

⑥ **Kürsü** *(see p41)*

⑦ **Calligraphic roundel**

⑧ **Seraphims** adorn the pendentives at the base of the dome.

⑨ **Sultan's loge**

⑩ **Brick minaret**

⑪ **Müezzin mahfili** *(see p40)*

⑫ **The Coronation Square** served for the crowning of emperors.

⑬ **Library of Sultan Mahmut I**

⑭ **The Baptistry**, part of the 6th-century church, now serves as the tomb of two sultans.

⑮ **The mausoleum of Murat III** was used for his burial in 1599. Murat had by that time sired 102 children.

⑯ **Mausoleum of Selim II**
The oldest of the three mausoleums was completed in 1577 to the plans of Sinan *(see p93)*. Its interior is entirely decorated with İznik tiles *(see p163)*.

⑰ **Mausoleum of Mehmet III**

Exit →

★ **Ablutions Fountain**
Built around 1740, this fountain is an exquisite example of Turkish Rococo style. Its projecting roof is painted with floral reliefs.

Exploring Haghia Sophia

Designed as an earthly mirror of the heavens, the interior of Haghia Sophia succeeds in imparting a truly celestial feel. The artistic highlights are a number of glistening figurative mosaics – remains of the decoration that once covered the upper walls but which has otherwise mostly disappeared. These remarkable works of Byzantine art date from the 9th century or later, after the iconoclastic era (see p22). Some of the patterned mosaic ceilings, however, particularly those adorning the narthex and the neighbouring Vestibule of the Warriors, are part of the cathedral's original 6th-century decoration.

Interior as it looked after restoration in the 19th century

Ground Floor

The first of the surviving Byzantine mosaics can be seen over the Imperial Gate. This is now the public entrance into the church, although previously only the emperor and his entourage were allowed to pass through it. The mosaic shows **Christ on a throne with an emperor kneeling beside him** ① and has been dated to between 886 and 912. The emperor is thought to be Leo VI, the Wise (see p23).

The most conspicuous features at ground level in the nave are those added by the Ottoman sultans after the conquest of Istanbul in 1453, when the church was converted into a mosque.

The **mihrab** ②, the niche indicating the direction of Mecca, was installed in the apse of the church directly opposite the entrance. The **sultan's loge** ③, on the left of the mihrab as you face it, was built by the Fossati brothers. These Italian-Swiss architects undertook a major restoration of Haghia Sophia for Sultan Abdül Mecit in 1847–9.

To the right of the mihrab is the **minbar** ④, or pulpit, which was installed by Murat III (1574–95). He also erected the four **müezzin mahfilis** ⑤, marble platforms for readers of the Koran (see p40). The largest of these is adjacent to the minbar. The patterned marble **coronation square** ⑥ next to it marks the supposed site of the Byzantine emperor's throne, or omphalos (centre of the world). Nearby, in the south aisle, is the **library of Mahmut I** ⑦, which was built in 1739 and is entered by a decorative bronze door.

Across the nave, between two columns, is the 17th-century marble **preacher's throne** ⑧, the contribution of Murat IV (1623–40). Behind it is one of several **maqsuras** ⑨. These low, fenced platforms were placed beside walls and pillars to provide places for elders to sit, listen and read the Koran.

In the northwestern and western corners of the church are two **marble urns** ⑩, thought to date from the Hellenistic or early Byzantine period. A rectangular pillar behind one of the urns, the **pillar of St Gregory the Miracle-Worker** ⑪, is believed to have healing powers. As you leave the church you pass through the Vestibule of the Warriors, so called because the emperor's bodyguards would wait here for him when he came to worship. Look behind you as you enter it at the wonderful mosaic of the **Virgin with Constantine and Justinian** ⑫ above the door. It shows Mary seated on a throne holding the infant Jesus and flanked by two of the

Floorplan of Haghia Sophia

- Upper walls and domes
- Galleries
- Ground floor

Apse

North gallery

West gallery

Ramp to gallery

South gallery

Upper walls and domes

Apse

Nave

Entrance

Outer narthex

Narthex

Vestibule of the Warriors

greatest emperors of the city. Constantine, on her left, presents her with the city of Constantinople, while Justinian offers her Haghia Sophia. This was made long after either of these two emperors lived, probably in the 10th century, during the reign of Basil II *(see p23)*. Visitors exit the church by the door that was once reserved for the emperor due to its proximity to the Great Palace *(see pp84–5)*.

Figure of Christ, detail from the Deësis Mosaic in the south gallery

Galleries

A ramp leads from the ground floor to the north gallery. Here, on the eastern side of the great northwest pier, you will find the 10th-century mosaic of **Emperor Alexander holding a skull** ⑬. On the west face of the same pier is a medieval drawing of a galleon in full sail. The only point of interest in the western gallery is a green marble disk marking the location of the Byzantine **Empress's throne** ⑭.

There is much more to see in the south gallery. You begin by passing through the so-called **Gates of Heaven and Hell** ⑮, a marble doorway of which little is known except that it predates the Ottoman conquest *(see p28)*.

Around the corner to the right after passing through this doorway is the **Deësis Mosaic** ⑯ showing the Virgin Mary and John the Baptist with Christ Pantocrator (the All-Powerful). Set into the floor opposite it is the tomb of Enrico Dandalo, the Doge of Venice responsible for the sacking of Constantinople in 1204 *(see p26)*.

In the last bay of the southern gallery there are two more mosaics. The right-hand one of these is the **Virgin holding Christ, flanked by Emperor John II Comnenus and Empress Irene** ⑰. The other shows **Christ with Emperor Constantine IX Monomachus and Empress Zoe** ⑱. The faces of the emperor and empress have been altered.

Eight great **wooden plaques** ⑲ bearing calligraphic inscriptions hang over the nave at the level of the gallery. An addition of the Fossati brothers, they bear the names of Allah, the Prophet Mohammed, the first four caliphs and Hasan and Hussein, two of the Prophet's grandsons who are revered as martyrs.

Mosaic depicting Gabriel, on the lower wall of the apse

Upper Walls and Domes

The apse is dominated by a large and striking mosaic showing the **Virgin with the infant Jesus on her lap** ⑳. Two other mosaics in the apse show the archangels **Gabriel** ㉑ and, opposite him, Michael, but only fragments of the latter now remain. The unveiling of these mosaics on Easter Sunday 867 was a triumphal event celebrating victory over the iconoclasts *(see p23)*.

Three mosaic portraits of **saints** ㉒ adorn niches in the north tympanum and are visible from the south gallery and the nave. From left to right they depict: St Ignatius the Younger, St John Chrysostom and St Ignatius Theophorus.

In the four pendentives (the triangular, concave areas at the base of the dome) are mosaics of six-winged **seraphim** ㉓. The ones in the eastern pendentives date from 1346–55, but may be copies of much older ones. Those on the western side are 19th-century imitations that were added by the Fossati brothers.

The great **dome** ㉔ itself is decorated with Koranic inscriptions. It was once covered in golden mosaic and the tinkling sound of pieces dropping to the ground was familiar to visitors until the building's 19th-century restoration.

Mosaic of the Virgin with Emperor John II Comnenus and Empress Irene

The cavernous interior of the Byzantine Basilica Cistern

❷ Carpet Museum
Halı Müzesi

Babıhümayan Cad. **Map** 3 E5 (5 E5)
Open 9am–noon, 1–5pm
Mon–Fri. 🆆 halimuzesi.com

This beautifully constructed museum is housed in the soup kitchens built around 300 years back, following the conversion of the Haghia Sophia into the Aya Sofya Mosque. It has displays of fine carpets, mainly Turkish, woven between the 14th and 20th centuries. The exhibits are well labelled. There is also plenty of useful information available on weaving processes and the symbolism of the motifs featured on the rugs.

❸ Basilica Cistern
Yerebatan Sarayı

13 Yerebatan Cad, Sultanahmet.
Map 3 E4 (5 E4). **Tel** (0212) 522 12 59. 🚇 Sultanahmet. **Open** 9am–7pm daily.

This vast underground water cistern, a beautiful piece of Byzantine engineering, is the most unusual tourist attraction in the city. Although there may have been an earlier, smaller cistern here, this cavernous vault was laid out under Justinian in 532, mainly to satisfy the growing demands of the Great Palace (see pp84–5)

on the other side of the Hippodrome (see p82). For a century after the conquest (see p26), the Ottomans did not know of the cistern's existence. It was rediscovered after people were found to be collecting water, and even fish, by lowering buckets through holes in their basements.

Visitors tread walkways to the mixed sounds of classical music and dripping water. The cistern's roof is held up by 336 columns, each over 8 m (26ft) high. The original structure covered a total area of 9,800 sq m (105,000 sq ft) but today only about two thirds of it is visible, the rest having been bricked up in the 19th century. Water reached the cistern, which held about 100 million litres (22 million gal), from the Belgrade Forest, 20 km (12 miles) north of Istanbul, via the Valens Aqueduct (see p91).

❹ Istanbul Handicrafts Centre
Mehmet Efendi Medresesi

Kabasakal Cad 5, Sultanahmet.
Map 3 E4 (5 E4). **Tel** (0212) 517 67 82.
🚇 Sultanahmet. **Open** 9:30am–5:30pm daily.

If you are interested in Turkish craftwork, this former Koranic college is worth a visit. You can watch skilled artisans at work: they may be binding a book, executing an elegant piece of calligraphy or painting glaze onto ceramics. Items produced here are all for sale.

❺ Baths of Roxelana
Hürrem Sultan Hamamı

Ayasofya Meydanı, Sultanahmet.
Map 3 E4 (5 E4). **Tel** (0212) 517 35 35.
🚇 Sultanahmet. **Open** 8am–10pm daily. 🆆 ayasofyahamami.com

These baths were built in 1556 for Süleyman the Magnificent

Roxelana

Süleyman the Magnificent's power-hungry wife Roxelana (1500–58, Hürrem Sultan in Turkish), rose from being a concubine in the imperial harem to become his chief wife, or first kadın (see p30). Thought to be of Russian origin, she was also the first consort permitted to reside within the walls of Topkapı Palace (see pp56–61).

Roxelana would stop at nothing to get her own way. When Süleyman's grand vizier and friend from youth, İbrahim Paşa, became a threat to her position, she persuaded the sultan to have him strangled. Much later, Roxelana performed her *coup de grâce*. In 1553 she persuaded Süleyman to have his handsome and popular heir, Mustafa, murdered by deaf mutes to clear the way for her own son Selim (see p28) to inherit the throne.

Red-and-white brick exterior of the Baths of Roxelana

❻ Mosaic Museum
Mozaik Müzesi

Arasta Çarşısı, Sultanahmet.
Map 3 E5 (5 E5). **Tel** (0212)
518 12 05. Sultanahmet.
Open Apr–Oct: 9am–7pm;
Nov–Mar: 9am–4pm.

Located near Arasta Bazaar, among a warren of small shops, this museum was created simply by roofing over a part of the Great Palace of the Byzantine Emperors (see pp84–5), which was discovered by archaeologists in the 1930s. In its heyday the palace boasted hundreds of rooms, many of them glittering with gold mosaics.

The surviving mosaic has a surface area of 1,872 sq m (1,969 sq ft), making it one of the largest preserved mosaics in Europe. It is thought to have been created by an imperial workshop that employed the best craftsmen from across the empire under the guidance of a master artist. In terms of imagery, the mosaic is particularly diverse, with many different landscapes depicted, including domestic and pastoral episodes, such as herdsmen with their grazing animals, as well as hunting and fighting scenes. It portrays over 150 different human and animal figures, including wild and domestic beasts. There are also scenes from mythology, with fantastical creatures featuring on the design. The mosaic is thought to have adorned the colonnade leading from the royal apartments to the imperial enclosure beside the Hippodrome, and dates from the late 5th century AD.

Detail of a 5th-century mosaic in the Mosaic Museum

❼ Blue Mosque
See pp80–81.

(see p28) by Sinan (see p93), and are named after Roxelana, the sultan's scheming wife. They were designated for the use of the congregation of Haghia Sophia (see pp74–7) when it was used as a mosque. With the women's entrance at one end of the building and the men's at the other, their absolute symmetry makes them perhaps the most handsome baths in the city. The men's section of the baths faces Haghia Sophia and has a fine colonnaded portico.

Each end of the baths starts with a *camekan*, a massive domed hall which would originally have been centred on a fountain. Next is a small *soğukluk*, or intermediate room, which opens into a *hararet*, or steam room. The hexagonal massage slab in each *hararet*, the *göbek taşı*, is inlaid with coloured marbles, indicating that the baths are of imperial origin.

The baths functioned as a public bathhouse for over 350 years until 1910. After being used for other purposes over several decades, the bathhouse underwent major restoration and reopened for public use in 2012.

❽ Museum of Turkish and Islamic Arts
Türk ve İslam Eserleri Müzesi

Atmeydanı Sok, Sultanahmet.
Map 3 D4 (5 D4). **Tel** (0212) 518 18 05.
Sultanahmet. **Open** Apr–Oct:
9am–7pm Tue–Sun; Nov–Mar:
9am–5pm Tue–Sun. **W tiem.gov.tr**

Over 40,000 items are on display in the former palace of İbrahim Paşa (c.1493–1536), the most gifted of Süleyman's many grand viziers. Paşa married Süleyman's sister when the sultan came to the throne. The collection was begun in the 19th century and ranges from the earliest period of Islam, under the Omayyad caliphate (661–750), through to modern times.

Each room concentrates on a different chronological period or geographical area of the Islamic world, with detailed explanations in both Turkish and English. The museum is particularly renowned for its collection of rugs. These range from 13th-century Seljuk fragments to the palatial Persian silks that cover the walls from floor to ceiling in the palace's great hall.

On the ground floor, an ethnographic section focuses on the lifestyles of different Turkish peoples, particularly the nomads of central and eastern Anatolia. The exhibits include recreations of a round felt yurt (Turkic nomadic tent) and a traditional brown tent.

Recreated yurt interior, Museum of Turkish and Islamic Arts

● Blue Mosque

Sultan Ahmet Camii

The blue mosque, which takes its name from the mainly blue İznik tilework *(see p163)* decorating its interior, is one of the most famous religious buildings in the world. Serene at any time, it is at its most magical when floodlit at night, its minarets circled by keening seagulls. Sultan Ahmet I *(see p35)* commissioned the mosque during a period of declining Ottoman fortunes, and it was built between 1609–16 by Mehmet Ağa, the imperial architect. The splendour of the plans provoked great hostility at the time, especially because a mosque with six minarets was considered a sacrilegious attempt to rival the architecture of Mecca itself.

A 19th-century engraving showing the Blue Mosque viewed from the Hippodrome *(see p82)*

KEY

① **Exit for tourists**

② **Prayer hall**

③ **The Imperial Pavilion**

④ **The loge** *(see p41)* accommodated the sultan and his entourage during mosque services.

⑤ **Mihrab**

⑥ **The 17th-century minbar** is intricately carved in white marble. It is used by the imam during prayers on Friday *(see p40)*.

⑦ **Thick piers** support the weight of the dome.

⑧ **Müezzin mahfili** *(see p40)*.

⑨ **Over 250 windows** allow light to flood into the mosque.

⑩ **The courtyard** covers the same area as the prayer hall, balancing the whole building.

⑪ **Exit to Hippodrome**

⑫ **Each minaret** has two or three balconies.

Entrance to courtyard

★ İznik Tiles
No cost was spared in the decoration of the mosque. The tiles were made at the peak of tile production in İznik *(see p163)*.

★ **Inside of the Dome**
Mesmeric designs, employing flowing arabesques, are painted onto the interior of the mosque's domes and semidomes. The windows which pierce the domes no longer have their original 17th-century stained glass.

Entrance

★ **View of the Domes**
The graceful cascade of domes and semidomes makes a striking sight when viewed from the courtyard below.

Ablutions Fountain
The hexagonal şadırvan is now purely ornamental since ritual ablutions are no longer carried out at this fountain.

Washing the Feet
The Muslim's ritual ablutions conclude with the washing of the feet (see p41). Taps outside the mosque are used by the faithful for this purpose.

Egyptian Obelisk and the Column of Constantine Porphyrogenitus

❾ Hippodrome
At Meydanı

Sultanahmet. **Map** 3 E4 (5 D4). 🚊 Sultanahmet.

Little is left of the gigantic chariot-racing arena which once stood at the heart of the Byzantine city of Constantinople *(see pp24–5)*. It was originally laid out by Emperor Septimus Severus during his rebuilding of the city in the 3rd century AD *(see p21)*. Emperor Constantine *(see p22)* enlarged the Hippodrome and connected its *kathisma*, or royal box, to the nearby Great Palace *(see pp84–5)*. It is thought that the arena held up to 100,000 people. The site is now an elongated public garden, At Meydanı, Cavalry Square. There are, however, enough remains of the Hippodrome to get a sense of its scale and importance.

The road running around the square almost directly follows the line of the chariot-racing track. You can also make out some of the arches of the *sphendrome* (the curved end of the Hippodrome) by walking a few steps down Nakilbent Sok. Constantine adorned the *spina*, the central line of the stadium, with obelisks and columns from ancient Egypt and Greece. The four bronze horses that stood on the long-vanished starting gate were pillaged during the Fourth Crusade *(see p26)* and taken to St Mark's in Venice. Three ancient monuments remain, however. The **Egyptian Obelisk**, which was built in 1500 BC, stood outside Luxor until Constantine had it brought to his city. This carved monument is probably only one third of its original height. Next to it is the **Serpentine Column**, dating back to 479 BC, which was shipped here from Delphi.

Another obelisk still standing, but of unknown date, is usually referred to as the **Column of Constantine Porphyrogenitus**, after the emperor who restored

Relief carved on the base of the Egyptian Obelisk

it in the 10th century AD. Its dilapidated state owes much to the young Janissaries *(see p129)* who routinely scaled it as a test of their bravery.

The only other structure in the Hippodrome is a domed fountain which commemorates the visit of Kaiser Wilhelm II to Istanbul in 1898.

The Hippodrome was the scene of one of the bloodiest events in Istanbul's history. In 532 a brawl between rival chariot-racing teams developed into the Nika Revolt, during which much of the city was destroyed. The end of the revolt came when an army of mercenaries, under the command of Justinian's general Belisarius, massacred an estimated 30,000 people trapped in the Hippodrome.

❿ Marmara University Museum of the Republic
Cumhuriyet Müzesi

Sultanahmet. **Map** 3 D5 (5 D5). 🚊 Sultanahmet. **Open** 10am–6pm Tue–Sun.

This fine art collection run by Marmara University is comprised of works by more than 85 artists, both from Turkey and around the world. The museum was initiated in 1973 as an etching exhibition held to celebrate 50 years of Turkey as a Republic. Today, visitors can see prints, paintings, calligraphy and other traditional Turkish art forms.

⓫ Cistern of 1001 Columns
Binbirdirek Sarnıcı

Imran Okten Sok 4, Sultanahmet. **Map** 3 D4 (5 D4). **Tel** (0212) 518 10 01. 🚊 Çemberlitaş. **Open** 9am–6pm daily.

This cistern, dating back to the 4th century AD, is the second-largest underground Byzantine cistern in Istanbul after the Basilica Cistern *(see p78)*. Spanning an area of 64 m

Ceremonies in the Hippodrome

Beginning with the inauguration of Constantinople on 11 May 330 (see p22), the Hippodrome formed the stage for the city's greatest public events for the next 1,300 years. The Byzantines' most popular pastime was watching chariot racing in the stadium. Even after the Hippodrome fell into ruins following the Ottoman conquest of Istanbul (see p28), it continued to be used for great public occasions. This 16th-century illustration depicts Murat III watching the 52-day-long festivities staged for the circumcision of his son Mehmet. All the guilds of Istanbul paraded before the sultan displaying their crafts.

Sultan Murat III

Palace of İbrahim Paşa (Museum of Turkish and Islamic Arts, see p79)

Column of Constantine Porphyrogenitus

Serpentine Column

Egyptian Obelisk

(210 ft) by 56 m (185 ft), the herring-bone brick roof vaults are held up by 264 marble columns – the 1,001 columns of its name is poetic exaggeration. Until not long ago, the cistern was filled with rubble and only explored by adventurous visitors, but it has been transformed into an atmospheric shopping complex specializing in jewellery, carpets and tiles and other merchandise inspired by Ottoman culture.

⑫ Tomb of Sultan Mahmut II

Mahmut II Türbesi

Divanyolu Cad, Çemberlitaş.
Map 3 D4 (4 C3). 🚊 Çemberlitaş.
Open 9:30am–4:30pm daily.

This large octagonal mausoleum is in the Empire style (modelled on Roman architecture), made popular by Napoleon. It was built in 1838, the year before Sultan Mahmut II's death and is shared by sultans Mahmut II, Abdül Aziz and Abdül Hamit II (see pp34–5). Within, Corinthian pilasters divide up walls which groan with symbols of victory and prosperity. The huge tomb dominates a cemetery that has beautiful headstones, a fountain and a good café.

⑬ Constantine's Column

Çemberlitaş

Yeniçeriler Cad, Çemberlitaş.
Map 3 D4 (4 C3). 🚊 Çemberlitaş.
Çemberlitaş Baths: Vezirhani Cad 8.
Tel (0212) 511 25 35.

A survivor of both storm and fire, this 35-m (115-ft) high column was constructed in AD 330 as part of the celebrations to inaugurate the new Byzantine capital (see p22). It once dominated the magnificent Forum of Constantine (see p25). Made of porphyry brought from Heliopolis in Egypt, it was surmounted by a Corinthian capital bearing a statue of Emperor Constantine dressed as Apollo. This was brought down in a storm in 1106. Although what is left is relatively unimpressive, it has been carefully preserved. In the year 416 the 10 stone drums making up the column were reinforced with metal rings. These were renewed in 1701 by Sultan Mustafa II, and consequently the column is known as Çemberlitaş (the Hooped Column) in Turkish. In English it is sometimes referred

Constantine's Column

to as the Burnt Column because it was damaged by several fires, especially one in 1779 which decimated the Grand Bazaar (see pp100–101).

A variety of fantastical holy relics were supposedly entombed in the base of the column, which has since been encased in stone to strengthen it. These included the axe which Noah used to build the ark, Mary Magdalen's flask of anointing oil, and remains of the loaves of bread with which Christ fed the multitude.

Next to Constantine's Column, on the corner of Divanyolu Caddesi, stand the Çemberlitaş Baths. This splendid *hamam* complex (see p69) was commissioned by Nur Banu, wife of Sultan Selim II, and built in 1584 to a plan by the great Sinan (see p93). Although the original women's section no longer survives, the baths still have separate facilities for men and women.

The staff are used to foreign visitors, so this is a good place for your first experience of a Turkish bath.

⓪ Sokollu Mehmet Paşa Mosque

Sokollu Mehmet Paşa Camii

Şehit Çeşmesi Sok, Sultanahmet.
Map 3 D5 (4 C5). 🚊 Çemberlitaş or
Sultanahmet. **Open** daily.

Built by the architect Sinan (see p93) in 1571–2, this mosque was commissioned by Sokollu Mehmet Paşa, grand vizier to Selim II (see p34). The simplicity of Sinan's design solution for the mosque's sloping site has been widely admired. A steep entrance stairway leads up to the mosque courtyard from the street, passing beneath the teaching hall of its medrese (see p40), which still functions as a college. Only the tiled lunettes above the windows in the portico give a hint of the jewelled mosque interior to come.

Inside, the far wall around the carved mihrab is entirely covered in İznik tiles (see p163) of a sumptuous green-blue hue. This tile panel, designed specifically for the space, is complemented by six stained-glass windows. The "hat" of the minbar is covered with the same tiles. Most of the mosque's other walls are of plain stone, but they are enlivened by a few more tile panels. Set into the wall over the entrance there is a small piece of greenish stone which is supposedly from the Kaaba, the holy stone at the centre of Mecca.

The Byzantine Church of SS Sergius and Bacchus, now a mosque

⓯ SS Sergius and Bacchus' Church

Küçük Ayasofya Camii

Küçük Ayasofya Cad. **Map** 3 D5 (4 C5).
🚊 Çemberlitaş or Sultanahmet.
Open daily. ♿

Commonly referred to as "Little Haghia Sophia", this church was built in 527, a few years before its namesake (see pp74–7). It too was founded by Emperor Justinian (see p22), together with his empress, Theodora, at the beginning of his long reign. Ingenious and highly decorative, the church gives a somewhat higgledy-piggledy impression both inside and out and is one of the most charming of all the city's architectural treasures.

Inside, an irregular octagon of columns on two floors supports a broad central dome composed of 16 vaults. The mosaic

Reconstruction of the Great Palace

In Byzantine times, present-day Sultanahmet was the site of the Great Palace, which, in its heyday, had no equal in Europe and dazzled medieval visitors with its opulence. This great complex of buildings – including royal apartments, state rooms, churches, courtyards and gardens – extended over a sloping, terraced site from the Hippodrome to the imperial harbour on the shore of the Sea of Marmara. The palace was built in stages, be-ginning under Constantine in the 4th century. It was enlarged by Justinian following the fire caused by the Nika Revolt in 532 (see p82). Later emperors, especially the 9th-century Basil I (see p23), extended it further. After several hundred years of occupation, it was finally abandoned in the second half of the 13th century in favour of Blachernae Palace (see p119).

The Mese was a colonnaded street lined with shops and statuary.

Hippodrome (see p82)

Hormisdas Palace

Church of SS Peter and Paul

Church of SS Sergius and Bacchus

Interior of the 16th-century Sokollu Mehmet Paşa Mosque

decoration which once adorned some of the walls has long since crumbled away. However, the green and red marble columns, the delicate tracery of the capitals and the carved frieze running above the columns are original features of the church.

The inscription on this frieze, in boldly carved Greek script, mentions the founders of the church and St Sergius, but not St Bacchus. The two saints were Roman centurions who converted to Christianity and were martyred. Justinian credited them with saving his life when, as a young man, he was implicated in a plot to kill his uncle, Justin I. The saints supposedly appeared to Justin in a dream and told him to release his nephew.

The Church of SS Sergius and Bacchus was built between two important edifices to which it was connected, the Palace of Hormisdas and the Church of SS Peter and Paul, but has outlived them both. After the conquest of Istanbul in 1453 *(see p28)* it was converted into a mosque.

⑯ Bucoleon Palace
Bukoleon Sarayı

Kennedy Cad, Sultanahmet. **Map** 3 E5. 🚋 Sultanahmet.

Finding the site of what remains of the Great Palace of the Byzantine emperors requires precision. It is not advisable to visit the ruins alone as they are sometimes occupied by vagrants.

Take the path under the disused railway from the Church of SS Sergius and Bacchus, turn left and walk beside Kennedy Caddesi, the main road along the shore of the Sea of Marmara for about 400 m (450 yards). This will bring you to a stretch of the ancient sea walls, constructed to protect the city from a naval assault. Within these walls you will find a creeper-clad section of stonework pierced by three vast windows framed in marble. This

is all that now survives of the Bucoleon Palace, a maritime residence that formed part of the sprawling Great Palace. The waters of a small private harbour lapped right up to the palace and a private flight of steps led down into the water, allowing the emperor to board imperial caïques. The ruined tower just east of the palace was a lighthouse, called the Pharos, in Byzantine times.

Fragment of the Bucoleon Palace wall that remains intact

The Kathisma was the imperial box of the Hippodrome.

The Milion was the point from which road distances were measured *(see p73)*.

Haghia Sophia *(see pp74–7)*

The Augusteum was a porticoed public square.

Chalke Gate was the main entrance to the palace.

Daphne Palace

Hall of Gold (site of Mosaic Museum, *see p79*)

The Bucoleon Palace had a magnificent façade looking out over the sea.

Lighthouse

Magnaura Palace

The Nea Ekklesia, erected by Basil I, set the style for all subsequent Byzantine churches.

THE BAZAAR QUARTER

Trade has always been important in a city that straddles the continents of Asia and Europe. Nowhere is this more evident than in the warren of streets lying between the Grand Bazaar and Galata Bridge. Everywhere, goods tumble out of shops onto the pavement. Look through any of the archways in between shops and you will discover hidden courtyards or hans (see p98) containing feverishly industrious workshops.

With its seemingly limitless range of goods, the labyrinthine Grand Bazaar is at the centre of all this commercial activity. The Spice Bazaar is equally colourful but smaller and more manageable.

Up on the hill, next to the university, is Süleymaniye Mosque, a glorious expression of 16th-century Ottoman culture. It is just one of numerous beautiful mosques in this area.

Sights at a Glance

Mosques and Churches
1. New Mosque
3. Rüstem Paşa Mosque
5. *Süleymaniye Mosque pp92–3*
6. Church of St Theodore
9. Prince's Mosque
10. Kalenderhane Mosque
11. Tulip Mosque
12. Bodrum Mosque
20. Atik Ali Paşa Mosque
21. Nuruosmaniye Mosque
22. Mahmut Paşa Mosque

Bazaars, Hans and Shops
2. Spice Bazaar

8. Vefa Bozacısı
16. Book Bazaar
17. Valide Han
18. *Grand Bazaar pp100–101*

Museums and Monuments
7. Valens Aqueduct
13. Forum of Theodosius
14. Museum of Calligraphy

Squares and Courtyards
15. Beyazıt Square
19. Çorlulu Ali Paşa Courtyard

Waterways
4. Golden Horn

Restaurants pp198–9
1. Aslan Restaurant
2. Aynen Dürüm
3. Bizim Mutfak
4. Borsa
5. Can Restaurant
6. Çiğ Köfteci Ali Usta
7. Darüzziyafe
8. Doyuran Lokantası
9. Fes Café
10. Gaziantep Burç Ocakbaşı
11. Hamdi
12. Havuzlu
13. Imren Lokantası
14. Kahve Dünyası
15. Kardeşler Pilav Evi
16. Kral Kokoreç
17. Nar Lokanta
18. Nuruosmaniye Köftecisi
19. Ocakbaşı Dürüm Ve Kebap Salonu
20. Şark Kahvesi
21. Siirt Şeref Büryan
22. Surplus

See also Street Finder maps 2, 3, 4 & 5

| 0 metres | 500 |
| 0 yards | 500 |

◀ Shop selling porcelain and other colourful wares in the Grand Bazaar

For map symbols *see back flap*

Street-by-Street: Around the Spice Bazaar

The narrow streets around the Spice Bazaar encapsulate the
spirit of old Istanbul. From here buses, taxis and trams head
off across the Galata Bridge and into the interior of the city.
The blast of ships' horns signals the departure of ferries from
Eminönü to Asian Istanbul. It is the quarter's shops and markets,
though, that are the focus of attention for the eager shoppers
who crowd the Spice Bazaar and the streets around it, sometimes
breaking for a leisurely tea beneath the trees in its courtyard.
Across the way, and entirely aloof from the bustle, rise the
domes of the New Mosque. On one of the commercial alleyways
which radiate out from the mosque, an inconspicuous doorway
leads up stairs to the terrace of the serene, tile-covered Rüstem
Paşa Mosque.

❸ ★ Rüstem Paşa Mosque
The interior of this secluded
mosque is a brilliant pattern-
book made of İznik tiles *(see
p163)* of the finest quality.

| 0 metres | 75 |
| 0 yards | 75 |

**Tahtakale Hamamı
Çarşısı**, now a bazaar,
was formerly a
Turkish bath.

**Kurukahveci
Mehmet Efendi** is
one of Istanbul's oldest
and most popular
coffee shops. You can
drink coffee on the
premises or buy a
packet to take away
with you *(see p213)*.

Stall holders and street
traders, such as this man
selling garlic cloves, ply
their wares in Sabuncuhanı
Sokağı and the other
narrow streets around the
Spice Bazaar.

Eminönü is the port from which ferries depart to many destinations (*see p242*) and for trips along the Bosphorus (*see pp146–51*). It bustles with activity as traders compete to sell drinks and snacks.

Locator Map
See Street Finder map 2, 3, 4, & 5

Galata Bridge

The royal pavilion, a suite of beautifully tiled private rooms, is linked by a passage to the sultan's loge inside the New Mosque.

Eminönü sea bus boarding point

Eminönü bus terminal

Eminönü tram stop

REŞADİYE CAD

MIS CAD

CAMI MEYDANI SOK

YENİ CAMİ CAD

EK PAZARI SOK

❶ ★**New Mosque** This mosque, which dominates the Eminönü waterfront, was completed in the 17th century by the mother of Sultan Mehmet IV (*see p35*).

Tea Gardens

Mausoleum of Turhan Hatice Valide Sultana, mother of Mehmet IV

❷ ★**Spice Bazaar** This market was built in 1660 as part of the New Mosque complex, and it has always been associated with the sale of spices, though today there is much more on offer.

Pet market and garden centre

Key

— Suggested route

❶ New Mosque
Yeni Cami

Yeni Cami Meydanı, Eminönü.
Map 3 D2. 🚊 Eminönü. **Open** daily.

Situated at the southern end of Galata Bridge, the New Mosque is one of the most prominent mosques in the city. It dates from the time when a few women from the harem became powerful enough to dictate the policies of the Ottoman sultans (see p29). The mosque was started in 1597 by Safiye, mother of Mehmet III, but building was suspended on the sultan's death as his mother then lost her position. It was not completed until 1663, after Turhan Hatice, mother of Mehmet IV, took up the project.

Though the mosque was built after the classical period of Ottoman architecture, it shares many traits with earlier imperial foundations, including a monumental courtyard. The mosque once had a hospital, school and public baths.

The turquoise, blue and white floral tiles decorating the interior are from İznik (see p163) and date from the mid-17th century, though by this time the quality of the tiles produced there was already in decline. More striking are the tiled lunettes and bold Koranic frieze decorating the porch between the courtyard and the prayer hall.

At the far left-hand corner of the upper gallery is the sultan's loge (see p41), which is linked to his personal suite of rooms (see p89).

A selection of nuts and seeds for sale in the Spice Bazaar

❷ Spice Bazaar
Mısır Çarşısı

Cami Meydanı Sok. **Map** 3 D2 (4 C1). 🚊 Eminönü. **Open** 8am–7pm Mon–Sat.

This cavernous, L-shaped market was built in the early 17th century as an extension of the New Mosque complex. Its revenues once helped maintain the mosque's philanthropic institutions.

In Turkish the market is named the Mısır Çarşısı – the Egyptian Bazaar – because it was built with money paid as duty on Egyptian imports. In English it is usually known as the Spice Bazaar. From medieval times spices were a vital and expensive part of cooking and they became the market's main produce. The bazaar came to specialize in spices from the orient, taking advantage of Istanbul's site on the trade route between the East (where most spices were grown) and Europe.

Stalls in the bazaar stock spices, herbs and other foods such as honey, nuts, sweetmeats and pastirma (cured beef). Today's expensive Eastern commodity, caviar, is also available, the best variety being Iranian. Nowadays an eclectic range of other items can be found in the Spice Bazaar, including everything from household goods, toys and clothes to exotic aphrodisiacs. The square between the two arms of the bazaar is full of commercial activity, with cafés, and stalls selling plants and pets.

Floral İznik tiles adorning the interior of Rüstem Paşa Mosque

❸ Rüstem Paşa Mosque
Rüstem Paşa Camii

Hasırcılar Cad, Eminönü. **Map** 3 D2. 🚊 Eminönü. **Open** daily.

Raised above the busy shops and warehouses around the Spice Bazaar, this mosque was built in 1561 by the great architect Sinan (see p93) for Rüstem Paşa, son-in-law of and grand vizier to Süleyman I (see p28). Rents from the businesses in the bazaar were intended to pay for the upkeep of the mosque.

The staggering wealth of its decoration says something about the amount of money that the corrupt Rüstem managed to salt away during his career. Most of the interior is covered in İznik tiles of the very highest quality.

The New Mosque, a prominent feature on the Eminönü waterfront

The four piers are adorned with tiles of one design but the rest of the prayer hall is a riot of different patterns, from abstract to floral. Some of the finest tiles can be found on the galleries. All in all, there is no other mosque in the city adorned with such a magnificent blanket of tiles.

The mosque is also notable for its numerous windows: it was built with as many as the structure would allow.

❹ Golden Horn
Haliç

Map 3 D2. 🚋 Eminönü.
🚌 55T, 99A.

Often described as the world's greatest natural harbour, the Golden Horn is a flooded river valley which flows southwest into the Bosphorus. The estuary attracted settlers to its shores in the 7th century BC and later enabled Constantinople to become a rich and powerful port. According to legend, the Byzantines threw so many valuables into it during the Ottoman conquest (see p28), that the waters glistened with gold. Heavily polluted until recently, the waters today are clean enough to support fish and cormorants. There are plans to turn a part of it into a marina.

For hundreds of years the city's trade was conducted by ships that off-loaded their goods into warehouses lining the Golden Horn. Nowadays, though, the great container ships coming to Istanbul use ports on the Sea of Marmara. Spanning the mouth of the Horn is the Galata Bridge, which joins Eminönü to Galata. The bridge, built in 1994, opens in the middle to allow access for tall ships. It is a good place from which to appreciate the complex geography of the city and admire the minaret-filled skyline.

To the north of Galata Bridge lies the Haliç Bridge. It was opened in 2013 amid controversy as its prominent profile interrupts views of the Old City's famous skyline. The bridge carries the M2 Metro line across the Golden Horn, linking the Old City with Beyoğlu. Beyond it lies the Atatürk (Unkapanı) Bridge. There is also a motorway bridge across the estuary near the terminus of the Theodisian Walls, much further up the Horn.

❺ Süleymaniye Mosque

See pp92–3.

❻ Church of St Theodore
Vefa Kilise Camii

Vefa Cad, Cami Sok, Vefa. **Map** 2 B2.
🚌 28, 61B, 87.

The elaborate Byzantine Church of St Theodore was built in the 12th–14th centuries, the last great era of Byzantine construction. It was converted into a mosque following the Ottoman conquest of the city in 1453 (see p28). Today, it is known as Molla Gürani Mosque. The attractive brick exterior is admirable. The mosque is, however, currently closed and awaiting restoration.

The 4th-century Valens Aqueduct crossing Atatürk Bulvarı

❼ Valens Aqueduct
Bozdoğan Kemeri

Atatürk Bulvarı, Saraçhane.
Map 2 A3. 🚋 Laleli. 🚌 28, 61B, 87.
Ⓜ Vezneciler.

Emperor Valens built this mighty aqueduct, supported by two imposing rows of arches, in the late 4th century AD. Part of the elaborate water system feeding the palaces and fountains of the Byzantine capital, it brought water from the Belgrade Forest (see p160) and mountains over 200 km (125 miles) away to a vast cistern which stood in the vicinity of what is now Beyazıt Square (see p96).

The aqueduct supplied the city's water until the late 19th century, when it was made obsolete by a modern water distribution network. The original open channels, however, had by this stage already been replaced first by clay pipes and then by iron ones.

The structure was repaired many times during its history, latterly by sultans Mustafa II (1695–1703) and Ahmet III (see p29). It was originally 1,000 m (3,300 ft) long, of which 625 m (2,050 ft) remain.

Fisherman on the modern Galata Bridge spanning the Golden Horn

❺ Süleymaniye Mosque
Süleymaniye Camii

Istanbul's most important mosque is both a tribute to its architect, the great Sinan, and a fitting memorial to its founder, Süleyman the Magnificent (*see p28*). It was built above the Golden Horn in the grounds of the old palace, Eski Saray (*see p96*), between 1550–57. Like the city's other imperial mosques, the Süleymaniye Mosque was not only a place of worship, but also a charitable foundation, or *külliye* (*see p40*). The mosque is surrounded by its former hospital, soup kitchen, schools, caravanserai and bathhouse. This complex provided a welfare system which fed over 1,000 of the city's poor – Muslims, Christians and Jews alike – every day.

Courtyard
The ancient columns that surround the courtyard are said to have come originally from the *kathisma*, the Byzantine royal box in the Hippodrome (*see p82*).

KEY

① **Café in a sunken garden**

② **Muvakkithane Gateway**
The main courtyard entrance (now closed) contained the rooms of the mosque astronomer, who determined prayer times.

③ **İmaret Gate**

④ **The caravanserai** provided lodging and food for travellers and their animals.

⑤ **Tomb of Sinan**

⑥ **Minaret**

⑦ **The Tomb of Roxelana** contains Süleyman's beloved wife (*see p78*).

⑧ **Graveyard**

⑨ **These marble benches** were used to support coffins before burial.

⑩ **"Addicts Alley"** is so called because the cafés here once sold opium and hashish as well as coffee and tea.

⑪ **The medreses** (*see p40*) to the south of the mosque house a library containing 110,000 manuscripts.

⑫ **Former hospital and asylum**

İmaret
The kitchen – now a restaurant, Dârüzziyafe (*see p199*) – fed the city's poor as well as the mosque staff and their families. The size of the millstone in its courtyard gives an idea of the amount of grain needed to feed everyone.

★ Mosque Interior
A sense of soaring space and calm strikes you as you enter the mosque. The effect is enhanced by the fact that the height of the dome from the floor is exactly double its diameter.

Entrance

★ Tomb of Süleyman
Ceramic stars said to be set with emeralds sparkle above the coffins of Süleyman, his daughter Mihrimah and two of his successors, Süleyman II and Ahmet II.

Sinan, the Imperial Architect

Like many of his eminent contemporaries, Mimar Sinan (c.1490–1588) was brought from Anatolia to Istanbul in the *devşirme*, the annual roundup of talented Christian youths, and educated at one of the elite palace schools. He became a military engineer but won the eye of Süleyman I, who made him chief imperial architect in 1538. With the far-sighted patronage of the sultan, Sinan – the closest Turkey gets to a Renaissance architect – created masterpieces which demonstrated his master's status as the most magnificent of monarchs. Sinan died aged 98, having built 131 mosques and 200 other buildings.

Bust of the great architect Sinan

❽ Vefa Bozacısı

Katip Çelebi Cad 104/1, Vefa. **Map** 2 B2.
Tel (0212) 519 49 22. 🚌 61B, 90. 🚇
Vezneciler. **Open** 8am–midnight daily.

With its wood-and-tile interior
and glittering glass-mosaic
columns, this unusual shop and
bar has changed little since the
1930s. It was founded in 1876 to
sell *boza*, a popular winter drink,
often made from bulgur (cracked
wheat, *see p195*), although millet
is the grain of choice here. In
summer a fermented grape juice
known as *şıra* is sold. The shop's
main trade throughout the whole
year, however, is in wine vinegar.
    Inside the shop you will see a
glass from which Kemal Atatürk
(*see p33*) drank *boza* in 1937,
enshrined beneath a glass dome.

Bottles of *boza*, a wheat-based drink, in the
Vefa Bozacısı

❾ Prince's Mosque
Şehzade Camii

Şehzade Başı Cad 70, Saraçhane.
Map 2 B3. 🚋 Laleli/Üniversite.
🚇 Vezneciler. **Open** daily. Tombs:
Open 9am–5pm Tue–Sun.

This mosque complex was
erected by Süleyman the
Magnificent (*see p28*) in memory
of his eldest son by Roxelana
(*see p78*), Şehzade (Prince)
Mehmet, who died of smallpox
at the age of 21. The building
was Sinan's (*see p93*) first major
imperial commission and
was completed in 1548. The
architect used a delightful
decorative style in designing
this mosque before abandoning
it in favour of the classical
austerity that characterizes
his later work. The mosque is

Dome of the Prince's Mosque, Sinan's first
imperial mosque

approached through an elegant
porticoed inner courtyard, while
the other institutions making up
the mosque complex, including
a *medrese* (*see p40*), are enclosed
within an outer courtyard.
    The interior of the mosque is
unusual and was something of
an experiment in that it is
symmetrical, having a semidome on each of its four sides.
    The three tombs located to
the rear of the mosque,
belonging to Şehzade Mehmet
himself and grand viziers
İbrahim Paşa and Rüstem Paşa
(*see p90*), are the finest in the
city. Each has beautiful İznik tiles
(*see p163*) and lustrous original
stained glass. That of Şehzade
Mehmet also boasts the finest
painted dome in Istanbul.
    On Fridays you will notice
women flocking to another
tomb within the complex, that
of Helvacı Baba, as they have
done for over 400 years. Helvacı
Baba is said to miraculously cure

crippled children, solve fertility
problems and find husbands or
accommodation for those who
beseech him.

❿ Kalenderhane Mosque
Kalenderhane Camii

16 Mart Şehitleri Cad, Saraçhane.
Map 2 B3. 🚋 Laleli/Üniversite.
🚇 Vezneciler. **Open** prayer times only.

Sitting in the lee of the Valens
Aqueduct (*see p91*), this
Byzantine church has a che-
quered history. It was built and
rebuilt several times between
the 6th and 12th centuries,
before being converted into
a mosque shortly after the
conquest in 1453 (*see p28*). It
is named after the Kalender
brotherhood of dervishes,
who occupied it for some
years following the conquest.
    The building has the
cruciform layout characteristic
of Byzantine churches of the
period. Some of the decoration remaining from its last
incarnation, as the Church
of Theotokos Kyriotissa (her
Ladyship Mary, Mother of
God), also survives in the prayer
hall with its marble panelling
and in the fragments of fresco
in the narthex (entrance hall).
A series of frescoes depicting
the life of St Francis of Assisi
were removed in the 1970s.
Fragments can be seen in
the Archaeology Museum,
as can the only iconoclastic
figurative mosaic to have
survived in the city, the Icon
of the Presentation (*see p65*).

A shaft of light illuminating the interior of Kalenderhane Mosque

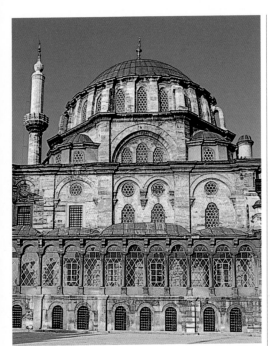

The Baroque Tulip Mosque, housing a marketplace in its basement

⓫ Tulip Mosque
Lâleli Camii

Ordu Cad, Lâleli. **Map** 2 B4. 🚋 Lâleli/
Üniversite Ⓜ Vezneciler. **Open** prayer
times only.

Built from 1760–64, this mosque
complex is the best example
in the city of the Baroque style,
of which its architect, Mehmet
Tahir Ağa, was the greatest
exponent. Inside the mosque,
a variety of gaudy, coloured
marble covers all of its surfaces.

More fascinating is the area
underneath the main body
of the mosque. This is a great
hall supported on eight piers,
with a fountain in the middle.
The hall is now used as a sub-
terranean marketplace and is
packed with Eastern Europeans
and Central Asians haggling
over items of clothing.

The nearby Büyük Taş Han (see
p98), or Big Stone Han, is likely to
have been part of the mosque's
original complex but now houses
a number of leather shops and a
restaurant. To get to it turn left
outside the mosque into Fethi
Bey Caddesi and then take the
second left into Çukur Çeşme

Sokağı. The main courtyard of
the han is at the end of a long
passage situated off this lane.

⓬ Bodrum Mosque
Bodrum Camii

Sait Efendi Sok, Laleli. **Map** 2 A4.
🚋 Laleli/Üniversite. **Open** prayer
times only.

Narrow courses of brick forming
the outside walls, and a window-
pierced dome, betray the early
origins of this mosque as a
Byzantine church. It was built
in the early 10th century by
co-Emperor Romanus I
Lacapenus (919–44) as part of
the Monastery of Myrelaion, and
it adjoined a small palace. The
palace was later converted into
a nunnery where the emperor's
widow, Theophano, lived out
her final years. She was eventually buried in a sanctuary
chapel beneath the church,
which is closed to the public.

In the late 15th century the
church was converted into a
mosque by Mesih Paşa, a
descendant of the Palaeologus
family, the last dynasty to rule

Byzantium. The building was
gutted by fire several times
and nothing remains of its
internal decoration. Today it is
still a working mosque and is
accessed via a stairway which
leads up to a raised piazza filled
with coat stalls.

⓭ Forum of Theodosius
Theodosius Forumu

Ordu Cad, Beyazıt. **Map** 2 C4 (4 A3).
🚋 Laleli/Üniversite or Beyazıt.

Constantinople (see pp24–5) was
built around several large public
squares or forums. The largest of
them stood on the site of
present-day Beyazıt Square. It
was originally known as the
Forum Tauri (the Forum of the
Bull) because of the huge bronze
bull in the middle of it in which
sacrificial animals, and sometimes
even criminals, were roasted.

After Theodosius the
Great enlarged it in the late 4th
century, the forum took his
name. Relics of the triumphal
arch and other structures can
be found on either side of the
tram tracks along Ordu Caddesi.
The huge columns, with a motif
reminiscent of a peacock's tail,
are particularly striking. Once
the forum had become derelict,
these columns were reused all
over the city. Some can be seen
in the Basilica Cistern (see p78).
Other fragments from the forum
were built into Beyazıt Hamamı,
a Turkish bath (see p69) further
west down Ordu Caddesi, now
a bazaar.

Peacock feather design on a column from
the Forum of Theodosius

⓮ Museum of Calligraphy
Türk Vakıf Hat Sanatları Müzesi

Beyazıt Meydanı, Beyazıt. **Map** 2 C4 (4 A3). **Tel** (0212) 527 58 51. 🚇 Laleli/ Üniversite. **Open** 9am–4pm Tue–Sat. 🐕 ♿ with assistance.

The pretty courtyard in which this museum has been installed was once a *medrese (see p40)* of Beyazıt Mosque, situated on the other side of the square.

Its changing displays are taken from the massive archive belonging to the Turkish Calligraphy Foundation. As well as some beautiful manuscripts, including some dating back to the 13th century, there are examples of calligraphy on stone and glass. There is also an exhibition of tools used in calligraphy. One of the cells in the *medrese* now contains a waxwork tableau of a master calligrapher with his pupils.

The museum is slated to reopen in 2016 after renovation.

Beyazıt Tower, within the wooded grounds of Istanbul University

⓯ Beyazıt Square
Beyazıt Meydanı

Ordu Cad, Beyazıt. **Map** 2 C4 (4 A3). 🚇 Beyazıt.

Always filled with crowds of people and huge flocks of pigeons, Beyazıt Square is the most vibrant space in the old part of the city. Throughout the week the square is the venue for a flea market, where everything from carpets *(see pp218–19)* and

The fortress-like entrance to Istanbul University, Beyazıt Square

Central Asian silks to general bric-a-brac can be purchased. When you have tired of rummaging, try one of the cafés.

On the northern side of the square is the Moorish-style gateway leading into Istanbul University. The university's main building dates from the 19th century and once served as the Ministry of War. Within the wooded grounds rises Beyazıt Tower. This marble fire-watching station was built in 1828 on the site of Eski Saray, the palace first inhabited by Mehmet the Conqueror *(see p28)* after Byzantium fell to the Ottomans. Two original timber towers were destroyed by fire. The tower is now illuminated, indicating weather conditions through the use of different lights.

On the square's eastern side is Beyazıt Mosque, which was commissioned by Beyazıt II and completed in 1506. It is the oldest surviving imperial mosque in the city. Behind the impressive outer portal is a harmonious courtyard with an elegant domed fountain at its centre. Around the courtyard are columns made of granite and green and red Egyptian porphyry, and a pavement of multicoloured marble. The layout of the mosque's interior, with its central dome and sur-rounding semidomes, is heavily inspired by the design of Haghia Sophia *(see pp74–7)*.

⓰ Book Bazaar
Sahaflar Çarşısı

Sahaflar Çarşısı Sok, Beyazıt. **Map** 2 C4 (4 A3). 🚇 Laleli/Üniversite. **Open** 8am–8pm daily. ♿

This charming booksellers' courtyard, on the site of the Byzantine book and paper market, can be entered either from Beyazıt Square or from inside the Grand Bazaar *(see pp100–101)*. Racks are laden with all sorts of books, from tourist guides to academic tomes.

During the early Ottoman period *(see pp27–9)*, printed books were seen as a corrupting European influence and were banned in Turkey. As a result the bazaar only sold manuscripts. Then on 31 January 1729 İbrahim Müteferrika (1674–1745) produced the first printed book in the Turkish language, an Arabic dictionary. His bust stands in the centre of the market today. Note that book prices are fixed and cannot be haggled over.

Customers browsing in the Book Bazaar

The Art of Ottoman Calligraphy

Calligraphy is one of the noblest of Islamic arts. Its skills were handed down from master to apprentice, with the aim of the pupil being to replicate perfectly the hand of his master. In Ottoman Turkey, calligraphy was used to ornament firmans (imperial decrees) as well as poetry and copies of the Koran. However, many examples are also to be found on buildings, carved in wood and applied to architectural ceramics. The art of the calligrapher in all cases was to go as far as possible in beautifying the writing without altering the sense of the text. It was particularly important that the text of the Koran should be accurately transcribed. With the text of a firman, made to impress as much as to be read, the calligrapher could afford to add more flourishes.

The great calligraphers of the Ottoman period were Şeyh Hamdullah (1436–1520), whose work is seen in this Koran, Hafiz Osman (1642–98) and Ahmet Karahisari (d.1556). Their pupils also achieved great renown.

Floral decorations

Ornamental loops

The sultan's *tuğra* was his personal monogram, used in place of his signature. It would either be drawn by a calligrapher or engraved on a wooden block and then stamped on documents. The *tuğra* incorporated the sultan's name and title, his patronymic and wishes for his success or victory – all highly stylized. This is the *tuğra* of Selim II (1566–74).

Calligraphy developed further in the 19th and early 20th centuries, when artists explored more creative forms and worked with new media. There was greater freedom to depict human faces and animal forms. Calligraphers also began to practise the technique of découpage (cutting out the letters) and, as seen here, wrote inscriptions on delicate leaf skeletons.

The later sultans were taught calligraphy as part of their education and became skilled artists. This panel, from the 19th century, is by Mahmut II (1808–39).

Breathing techniques were probably practised by some calligraphers in order to achieve the steadiness of hand required for their craft.

Burnisher

Knife for cutting pen nib

The calligrapher's tools and materials included a burnisher, usually made of agate, which was used to prepare the paper. A knife was used to slit the reed nib of the pen before writing.

⑰ Valide Han

Valide Han

Junction of Tarakçılar Sok and
Çakmakçılar Yokuşu, Beyazıt. **Map** 2 C3
(4 B2). 🚇 Beyazıt, then 10 mins walk.
Open 9:30am–5pm Mon–Sat.

If the Grand Bazaar *(see pp100–101)* seems large, it is sobering to realize that it is only the covered part of a huge area of seething commercial activity which reaches all the way to the Golden Horn *(see p91)*. As in the Grand Bazaar, most manufacturing and trade takes place in hans, courtyards hidden away from the street behind shaded gateways.

The largest han in Istanbul is Valide Han. It was built in 1651 by Kösem, the mother of Sultan Murat IV. You enter it from Çakmakçılar Yokuşu through a massive portal. After passing through an irregularly shaped forecourt, you come out into a large courtyard centring on a Shiite mosque. This was built when the han became the centre of Persian trade in the city. Today, the han throbs to the rhythm of hundreds of weaving looms.

A short walk further down Çakmakçılar Yokuşu is Büyük Yeni Han, hidden behind another impressive doorway. This Baroque han, built in 1764,

Carpet shops in Çorlulu Ali Paşa Courtyard

has three arcaded levels. The entrance is on the top level, where distinctive bird cages are among the wares.

In the labyrinth of narrow streets around these hans, artisans are grouped according to their wares: on Bakırcılar Caddesi, for instance, you will find metal workers, while the craftsmen of Uzunçarşı Caddesi make wooden items.

⑱ Grand Bazaar

See pp100–101.

Hans of Istanbul

The innumerable hans that dot the centre of Istanbul originally provided temporary accommodation for travellers, their pack animals and their wares. The typical han was built as part of a mosque complex *(see pp40–41)*. It consists of two- or three-storey buildings around a courtyard. This is entered via a large gateway which can be secured by a heavy wooden door at night. When vans and lorries replaced horses and mules, the city's hans lost their original function and most of them were converted into warrens of small factories and workshops. These working hans are frequently

Café in Büyük Taş Han, near the Tulip Mosque *(see p95)*

in bad repair, but they are places in which you can still sense the entrepreneurial, oriental atmosphere of bygone Istanbul.

⑲ Çorlulu Ali Paşa Courtyard

Çorlulu Ali Paşa Külliyesi

Yeniçeriler Cad, Beyazıt. **Map** 4 B3.
🚇 Beyazıt. **Open** daily.

Like many others in the city, the *medrese (see p40)* of this mosque complex outside the Grand Bazaar has become the setting for a tranquil outdoor café. It was built for Çorlulu Ali Paşa, son-in-law of Mustafa II, who served as grand vizier under Ahmet III *(see p29)*. Ahmet later exiled him to the island of Lésbos and had him executed there in 1711. Some years later his family smuggled his head back to Istanbul and interred it in the tomb built for him. The complex is entered from Yeniçeriler Caddesi by two alleyways. Several carpet shops now inhabit the *medrese* and rugs are hung and spread all around, waiting for prospective buyers. The carpet shops share the *medrese* with a *kahve*, a traditional café *(see p208)*, which is popular with locals and students from the nearby university. It advertises itself irresistibly as the "Traditional Mystic Water Pipe and Erenler Tea Garden". Here you can sit and drink tea, and perhaps smoke a nargile (bubble pipe), while deciding which carpet to buy *(see pp218–19)*.

Situated across Bıleycıler Sokak, an alleyway off Çorlulu Ali Paşa Courtyard, is the Koca Sinan Paşa tomb complex, the courtyard of which is another tea garden. The charming *medrese*, mausoleum and *sebil* (a fountain where water was handed out to passers-by) were built in 1593 by Davut Ağa, who succeeded Sinan *(see p93)* as chief architect of the empire. The tomb of Koca Sinan Paşa, grand vizier under Murat III and Mehmet III, is a striking 16-sided structure.

Just off the other side of Yeniçeriler Caddesi is Gedik Paşa Hamamı, thought to be the oldest working Turkish baths *(see p69)* in the city. T built around 1475 for Gedik Ahmet Paşa, grand vizier under Mehmet the Conqueror *(see p28).*

The dome and minaret of the mosque of Atik Ali Paşa

⑳ Atik Ali Paşa Mosque
Atik Ali Paşa Camii

Yeniçeriler Cad, Beyazıt. **Map** 3 D4 (4 C3). 🚈 Çemberlitaş.
Open daily. ✉

Secreted behind walls in the area south of the Grand Bazaar, this is one of the oldest mosques in the city. It was built in 1496 during the reign of Beyazıt II, the successor of Mehmet the Conqueror, by his eunuch grand vizier, Atik Ali Paşa. The mosque stands in a small garden. It is a simple rectangular structure entered through a deep stone porch.

In an unusual touch, its mihrab is contained in a kind of apse. The other buildings which formed part of the mosque complex – its kitchen (*imaret*), *medrese* and Sufi monastery (*tekke*) – have all but disappeared during the widening of the busy Yeniçeriler Caddesi.

㉑ Nuruosmaniye Mosque
Nuruosmaniye Camii

Vezirhanı Cad, Beyazıt. **Map** 3 D4 (4 C3). 🚈 Çemberlitaş.
Open daily. ✉

Nuruosmaniye caddesi, a street lined with carpet and antique shops, leads to the gateway of the mosque from which it gets its name. Mahmut I began the mosque in 1748, and it was finished by his brother, Osman III in 1755. It was the first in the city to exhibit the exaggerated traits of the Baroque, as seen in its massive cornices. Its most striking features, however, are the enormous unconcealed arches supporting the dome, each pierced by a mass of windows. Light floods into the plain square prayer hall, allowing you to see the finely carved wooden calligraphic frieze which runs around the walls above the gallery.

On the other side of the mosque complex is the Nuruosmaniye Gate. This leads into Kalpakçılar Caddesi, the Grand Bazaar's street of jewellery shops *(see p101).*

The tomb of Mahmut Paşa, behind the mosque named after him

㉒ Mahmut Paşa Mosque
Mahmut Paşa Camii

Vezirhanı Cad, Beyazıt. **Map** 3 D3 (4 C3). 🚈 Çemberlitaş. 🚌 61B.
Open daily. ✉

Built in 1462, just nine years after Istanbul's conquest by the Ottomans, this was the first large mosque to be erected within the city walls. Unfortunately, it has been over-restored and much of its original charm lost.

The mosque was funded by Mahmut Paşa, a Byzantine aristocrat who converted to Islam and became grand vizier under Mehmet the Conqueror. In 1474 his disastrous military leadership incurred the sultan's fury, and he was executed. His tomb, behind the mosque, is unique in Istanbul for its Moorish style of decoration, with small tiles in blue, black, turquoise and green set in swirling geometric patterns.

Rows of windows illuminating the prayer hall of Nuruosmaniye Mosque

⓲ Grand Bazaar

Kapalı Çarşı

Nothing can prepare you for the Grand Bazaar. This labyrinth of streets covered by painted vaults is lined with thousands of booth-like shops, whose wares spill out to tempt you and whose shopkeepers are relentless in their quest for a sale. The bazaar was established by Mehmet II shortly after his conquest of the city in 1453 (see p28). It can be entered by several gateways, two of the most useful being Çarşıkapı Gate (from Beyazıt tram stop) and Nuruosmaniye Gate (from Nuruosmaniye Mosque). It is easy to get lost in the bazaar in spite of the signposting. Most of the bazaar's goods were once manufactured and traded behind the scenes in a large area made up of secluded courtyards called hans (see p98).

Key

— Suggested route

The Rooftops of the Grand Bazaar
Cafés, restaurants, toilets, banks, a post office, a police station and a mosque serve those who work and shop inside the bazaar.

Örücüler Gate

Spice Bazaar Valide Han

YOLGEÇE HAN

ASTARCI HANI

ÇUKUR HAN

ÇEBECİ HANI

İÇ CEBECİ HAN

PERDAHÇILA

YORGANCILAR CAD

YAĞLIKÇILAR SOK

KAVAFLAR SO

HACI HASAN SOK

ZENNECİLER SOK

FERACECİLER SOK

BODRUM HANI

Beyazıt Gate

Çadırcılar Caddesi, Book Bazaar (see p96)

FESÇİLER CAD

KALPAKÇILAR

Havuzlu Lokanta
is the best restaurant in the bazaar (see p199).

Çarşıkapı Gate

Beyazıt tram stop

Şark Kahvesi
This traditional Turkish café is a popular choice with local bazaar traders.

Marble Fountain
Two copper and marble fountains once provided the bazaar with fresh water.

Zincirli Han
This is one of the prettiest hans in the bazaar. Here a piece of jewellery can be made to your own choice of design.

The İç Bedesten
is the oldest part of the bazaar. Once a locked warehouse, it also served as a place where jewellers could make and sell their wares.

The Oriental Kiosk
was built as a coffee house in the 17th century and is now a jewellery shop.

Rugs on Display
Carpets and kilims (see pp218–19) from all over Turkey and Central Asia are on sale in the bazaar.

Mahmut Paşa Gate

Money trading is conducted on mobile phones.

ZİNCİRLİ HAN

AYNACILAR SOK

ALICILAR ÇARŞISI CAD

AGA SOK

İÇ BEDESTEN

MUHAFAZACILAR SOK

TERZİ BAŞI SOK

SANDAL BEDESTENİ SOK

KESECİLER CAD

SANDAL BEDESTENİ

Gateway to the İç Bedesten
Though the eagle was a symbol of the Byzantine emperors (see p27), this eagle, like the bazaar itself, postdates the Byzantine era.

The Sandal Bedesteni
dates from the 16th century and is covered by 20 brick domes supported on piers.

Nuruosmaniye Mosque (see p99), Çemberlitaş tram stop

Nuruosmaniye Gate

0 metres 40
0 yards 40

Key
- Antiques and carpets
- Leather and denim
- Gold and silver
- Fabrics
- Souvenirs
- Household goods and workshops
- Boundary of the bazaar

Kalpakçılar Caddesi,
the widest of the streets in the bazaar, is lined with the glittering windows of countless jewellery shops.

Souvenirs
Traditionally crafted items, such as this brass coffee pot, are for sale in the bazaar.

BEYOĞLU

For centuries Beyoğlu, a steep hill north of the Golden Horn, was home to the city's foreign residents. First to arrive here were the Genoese. As a reward for their help in the reconquest of the city from the Latins in 1261 *(see p26)*, they were given the Galata area, which is now dominated by the Galata Tower. During the Ottoman period, Jews from Spain, Arabs,

Greeks and Armenians settled in communities here. From the 16th century the great European powers established embassies in the area to further their own interests within the lucrative territories of the Ottoman Empire. The district has not changed much in character over the centuries and is still a thriving commercial quarter today.

Sights at a Glance

Historic Buildings and Monuments
1 Pera Palas Hotel
3 Mevlevi Lodge
4 Galata Tower
11 Tophane Fountain

Mosques and Churches
5 Church of SS Peter and Paul
6 Arab Mosque
7 Azap Kapı Mosque
9 Yeraltı Mosque
10 Kılıç Ali Paşa Mosque
12 Nusretiye Mosque

Museums and Galleries
2 Pera Museum
8 Ottoman Bank Museum
13 Istanbul Modern

Quarters
14 Çukurcuma
15 Taksim

Selected Restaurants pp199–202
1 5 Kat
2 Ada Café & Bookstore
3 Ara Kafe
4 Cezayir
5 Çok Çok Thai
6 Date
7 Datli Maya
8 Hacıbaba
9 İsmail Kebab
10 Kahve6
11 Karaköy Lokantası
12 Kitchenette
13 Klemuri
14 Mandabatmaz
15 Meze by Lemon Tree
16 Münferit
17 Ninja
18 Solera
19 Yeni Lokanta
20 Van Kahvaltı Evi

See also Street Finder maps 3, 6 & 7

◀ Galata Tower, one of the city's most distinctive sights

For map symbols see back flap

Street-by-Street: İstiklâl Caddesi

The pedestrianized İstiklal Caddesi is Beyoğlu's main street. Once known as the Grande Rue de Pera, it is lined by late 19th-century apartment blocks and European embassy buildings whose grandiose gates and façades belie their use as mere consulates since Ankara became the Turkish capital in 1923 *(see p33)*. Hidden from view stand the churches which used to serve the foreign communities of Pera (as this area was formerly called), some still buzzing with worshippers, others just quiet echoes of a bygone era. The once seedy backstreets of Beyoğlu, off İstiklâl Caddesi, are now filled with trendy jazz bars, shops selling handcrafted jewellery, furniture and the like. Crowds are also drawn by the area's cinemas and numerous stylish restaurants. A red period tram rumbles up and down İstiklal Caddesi, linking Tünel Square with Taksim Square.

❶ ★ **Pera Palas Hotel** This hotel is an atmospheric period piece. Many famous guests, including Agatha Christie, Ernest Hemingway and Alfred Hitchcock, have stayed here since it opened in 1892.

St Mary Draperis is a Franciscan church dating from 1789. This small statue of the Virgin stands above the entrance from the street. The vaulted interior of the church is colourfully decorated. An icon of the Virgin, said to perform miracles, hangs over the altar.

Tünel underground funicular to Karaköy

Tünel Square

Galata Tower

Swedish Consulate

Russian Consulate

❸ ★ **Mevlevi Lodge** A peaceful garden surrounds this small museum of the Mevlevi Sufi sect *(see p106)*. On the last Sunday of every month visitors can see dervishes perform their famous swirling dance.

Galatasaray Fish Market
(Balık Pazarı) mainly sells fresh fish, but inside you will also discover numerous delicatessens offering everything from meats and cheeses through to delicious sweetmeats and pickles.

Locator Map
See Street Finder map 3, 6 & 7

British Consulate

Armenian church

Taksim →

Galatasaray High School

Çiçek Pasajı was originally a flower market. Its stalls have now been replaced by bars and restaurants, which are particularly lively in the evenings.

Dutch Consulate

❷ **Pera Museum**
Oriental paintings, Anatolian weights and measures and Kütahya tiles and ceramics are part of the collection.

The Church of the Panaghia
serves the now much-reduced Greek Orthodox population of Beyoğlu. Dedicated to the Virgin Mary, it contains this beautiful classical iconostasis.

Key

— Suggested route

0 metres	75
0 yards	75

For map symbols *see back flap*

The elegant Grand Orient bar in the Pera Palace Hotel

❶ Pera Palace Hotel
Pera Palas Oteli

Meşrutiyet Cad 98–100, Tepebaşı.
Map 7 D5. **Tel** (0212) 251 45 60.
🚇 Tünel Beyoğlu. ♿ by arrangement. 📷 by appointment only. 🅆 **perapalas.com**

The Pera Palace (see p188) has attained a legendary status. Relying on the hazy mystique of yesteryear, it has changed little since it opened in 1892, mainly to cater for travellers on the Orient Express (see p68). It still evokes images of uniformed porters and exotic onward destinations such as Baghdad. The Grand Orient bar serves cocktails beneath its original chandeliers, while the patisserie attracts customers with its irresistible cakes and genteel ambience.

Former guests who have contributed to the hotel's reputation include Mata Hari, Greta Garbo, Jackie Onassis, Sarah Bernhardt, Josephine Baker and Atatürk (see p33), whose favourite room is now a museum. A room used by the writer Agatha Christie can be visited on request.

Sufism and the Whirling Dervishes

Sufism is the mystical branch of Islam (see pp40–41). The name comes from *suf*, the Arabic for wool, for Sufis were originally associated with poverty and self-denial, and often wore rough woollen clothes next to the skin. Sufis aspire to a personal experience of the divine. This takes the form of meditative rituals, involving recitation, dance and music, to bring the practitioner into direct, ecstatic communion with Allah. There are several sects of Sufis, the most famous of which are the Mevlevi, better known as the Whirling Dervishes on account of their ritual spinning dance.

Painting of the Whirling Dervishes (1837) at the Mevlevi Lodge

❷ Pera Museum
Pera Müzesi

Meşrutiyet Cad 141, Tepebaşı.
Map 7 D4. **Tel** (0212) 334 99 00.
🚇 Tünel Beyoğlu. **Open** 10am–7pm Tue–Thu & Sat, 10am–10pm Fri, noon–6pm Sun. **Closed** 1 Jan, first day of Religious Holidays. ♿ 🎨 (disabled visitors enter free). 📷 📷
🅆 **peramuzesi.org.tr**

The Pera Museum was opened in June 2005 by the Suna and İnan Kıraç Foundation, with the aim of providing a cultural centre. It is housed in a historic building, formerly the Hotel Bristol. Notable collections include Ottoman weights and measures, over 400 examples of 18th-century Kütahya tiles and ceramics, and the Suna and İnan Kıraç Foundation's exhibition of Orientalist art. This collection brings together works by European artists inspired by the Ottoman world from the 17th century to the early 19th century. The most famous painting is the *Tortoise Trainer* by Osman Hamdi Bey, the late Ottoman noble who set up Istanbul's excellent Archaeology Museum. It also covers the last two centuries of the Ottoman Empire and provides an insight into upper-class lives, customs and dress. The Pera also provides spaces for modern art exhibitions. Past shows have included works by Warhol and Miro. There is also an in-house arts cinema.

❸ Mevlevi Lodge
Mevlevi Tekkesi

Galip Dede Cad 15, Beyoğlu.
Map 7 D5. **Tel** (0212) 245 41 41.
🚇 Tünel Beyoğlu. **Open** 9am–4pm Wed–Mon. 📷

This lodge, today a fine museum, belonged to the most famous sect of Sufis, who were known as

The peaceful courtyard of the Mevlevi Lodge

the Whirling Dervishes. The original dervishes were disciples of the mystical poet and great Sufi master "Mevlana" (Our Leader) Celaleddin Rumi, who died in Konya, in central Anatolia in 1273. Tucked away off a street named after one of the great poets of the sect, Galip Dede, the museum is housed in an 18th-century lodge. Downstairs are a series of rooms that display well-labelled objects used by the sect, from begging bowls to musical instruments and calligraphy pens. The *semahane*, or ritual dance floor, lies upstairs. Performances are held on many Sundays throughout the year, and information about them is displayed on the notice boards at the entry of the lodge. Outside, in the calm, terraced garden, stand the ornate tombstones of ordinary sect members and prominent sheikhs (leaders).

❹ Galata Tower
Galata Kulesi

Büyük Hendek Sok, Beyoğlu. **Map** 3 D1. **Tel** (0212) 293 81 80. 🚇 Tünel Beyoğlu. **Open** 9am–8pm daily. 🍴 Restaurant & show. **Open** 8pm–midnight daily. **w** galatatower.net

The most recognizable feature on the Golden Horn, the Galata Tower is 60 m- (196 ft-) high and topped by a conical tower. Its origins date from the 6th century

Doorway into the main courtyard of the Church of SS Peter and Paul

when it was used to monitor shipping. After the conquest of Istanbul in 1453, the Ottomans turned it into a prison and naval depot. In the 18th century, aviation pioneer, Hezarfen Ahmet Çelebi, attached wings to his arms and "flew" from the tower to Üsküdar. The building was subsequently used as a fire watchtower.

The tower has been renovated and on the ninth floor there is a restaurant with nightly shows of folk music and belly dancing. The unmissable view from the top encompasses the city's skyline and beyond as far as Princes' Islands (*see p160*).

❺ Church of SS Peter and Paul
Sen Piyer Kilisesi

Galata Kulesi Sok 44, Karaköy. **Map** 3 D1. **Tel** (0212) 249 23 85. 🚇 Tünel. **Open** 7am–5pm Mon–Sat & 10:30am–noon Sun.

When their original church was requisitioned as a mosque (to become the nearby Arab Mosque) in the early 16th century, the Dominican brothers of Galata moved to this site. The present building, dating from 1841, was built by the Fossati brothers, architects of Italian-Swiss origin who also worked on the restoration of Haghia Sophia (*see pp74–7*).

According to Ottoman regulations, the main façade of the building could not be directly on a road, so the church is reached through a courtyard, the entrance to which is via a tiny door on the street. Ring the bell to gain admittance.

The church is built in the style of a basilica, with four side altars. The cupola over the choir is sky blue, studded with gold stars. Mass is said here in Italian every morning.

❻ Arab Mosque
Arap Camii

Kalyon Sok 1, Galata. **Map** 3 D1. 🚇 Tünel. **Open** prayer times only.

The Arabs after whom this mosque was named were Moorish refugees from Spain. Many settled in Galata after their expulsion from Andalusia follo-wing the fall of Granada in 1492. The church of SS Paul and Domi-nic, built in the first half of the 14th century by Dominican monks, was given to the settlers for use as a mosque. It is an unusual building for Istanbul: a vast, strikingly rectangular Gothic church with a tall square belfry which now acts as a minaret. The building has been restored several times, but of all the converted churches in the city it makes the least convincing mosque.

The distinctive Galata Tower, as seen from across the Golden Horn

Azap Kapı Mosque, built by the great architect Sinan

7 Azap Kapı Mosque

Azap Kapı Camii

Tersane Cad, Azapkapı. **Map** 2 C1.
🚇 Tünel Karaköy. 🚌 46H, 61B.
Open prayer times only.

Delightful though they are, this little mosque complex and fountain are somewhat overshadowed by the stream of traffic thundering over the adjacent Atatürk Bridge on one side, and trains rumbling over the Haliç bridge on the other. It was built in 1577–8 by Sinan (see p93) for Grand Vizier Sokollu Mehmet Paşa and is one of Sinan's more attractive mosques. Unusually, the entrance is up a flight of internal steps.

8 Ottoman Bank Museum/SALT Galata

Osmanlı Bankası Müzesi

Bankalar Cad 35–37, Karaköy. **Map** 3 D1. **Tel** (0212) 334 22 70. 🚇 Tünel Karaköy. 🚌 25E, 56. **Open** 10am–6pm daily. 🅿️ 📷 🛍️ 🚻
🌐 obmuze.com

The Ottoman Bank Museum has the most interesting collection of state archives in Turkey. Exhibits include Ottoman banknotes, promissory notes from officials at the imperial palace and photos of the Empire's ornately crafted branches. Outstanding are the 6,000 photographs of the bank's employees –

a unique social registry. It is also home to one of Istanbul's leading art galleries, the SALT Galata.

9 Yeraltı Mosque

Yeraltı Camii

Karantina Sok, Karaköy. **Map** 3 E1.
🚇 Tünel. **Open** daily.

This mosque, literally "the underground mosque", contains the shrines of two Muslim saints, Abu Sufyan and Amiri Wahibi, who died during the first Arab siege of the city in the 7th century (see p23). It was the discovery of their bodies in the cellar of an ancient Byzantine fortification in 1640 that led to the creation of a shrine on the site and later, in 1757, a mosque.

10 Kılıç Ali Paşa Mosque

Kılıç Ali Paşa Camii

Necatibey Cad, Tophane.
Map 7 E5. 🚌 25E, 56.
🚋 Tophane. **Open** daily.

This mosque was built in 1580 by Sinan, who was by then in his 90s. The church of Haghia Sophia (see pp74–7) provided the architect with his inspiration. İznik tiles adorn the mihrab and there is a delightful deep porch before the main door. Above the entrance portal is an inscription giving the date when the mosque was established.

Kılıç Ali Paşa, who commissioned the mosque, had a colourful life. Born in Italy, he was captured by Muslim pirates and later converted to Islam in the service of Süleyman the Magnificent (1520–66). He served as a naval commander under

Koranic inscription in İznik tiles at the Kılıç Ali Paşa Mosque

three sultans and after retiring asked Murat III (see p29) where to build his mosque. The sultan is said to have replied "in the admiral's domain, the sea". Taking him at his word, Kılıç Ali Paşa re-claimed part of the Bosphorus for his complex.

The Turkish bath attached to the mosque has undergone restoration and provides a wonderful alternative to the bathhouses in the Old City, for visitors in search of an authentic *hamam* experience.

11 Tophane Fountain

Tophane Çeşmesi

Tophane İskele Cad, Tophane.
Map 7 E5. 🚌 25E, 56. 🚋 Tophane.

Detail of a carved panel on Tophane Fountain

Beside Kılıç Ali Paşa Mosque stands a beautiful but abandoned Baroque fountain, built in 1732 by Mahmut I. With its elegant roof and dome, it resembles the fountain of Ahmet III (see p62). Each of the four walls is entirely covered in low-relief floral carving.

The name, meaning "cannon foundry fountain", comes from the brick and stone foundry building on the hill nearby. Established in 1453 by Mehmet the Conqueror (see p28) and rebuilt several times, the foundry now hosts art and other exhibitions.

12 Nusretiye Mosque

Nusretiye Camii

Meclis-i Mebusan Cad, Tophane.
Map 7 E5. 🚌 25E, 56. **Open** daily.

The baroque "Mosque of Victory" was built in the 1820s by Kirkor Balyan (see p130), who went on to found a dynasty of architects.

Commissioned by Mahmut II to commemorate his abolition of the Janissary corps in 1826 (see p32), it faces the Selimiye Barracks (see p134), across the

The window-filled dome and arches of Nusretiye Mosque

Bosphorus, which housed the New Army that replaced the Janissaries. The Empire-style swags and embellishments celebrate the sultan's victory. The marble panel of calligraphy around the interior of the mosque is particularly fine, as is the pair of *sebils* (kiosks for serving drinks) outside.

🄫 Istanbul Modern
İstanbul Modern

Meclis-i Mebusan Cad, Liman İşletmeleri Sahası, Antrepo 4, Karaköy. **Map** 3 F1. **Tel** (0212) 334 73 00. 🚋 Tophane. 🚌 56. **Open** 10am–6pm Tue–Sun. ♿🅿️🛍️📷
📶 istanbulmodern.org

Istanbul Modern, a new building perched on the Golden Horn, opened in 2005 as the most upbeat and thoroughly contemporary museum in Turkey. It houses both permanent collections and temporary exhibitions, providing a showcase for many of the eccentric and talented personalities who have shaped modern art in Turkey from the early 20th century to the present day. Many of the works are from the private collection of the Eczacıbaşı family, who founded the museum. Exhibits include abstract art, landscapes and watercolours as well as a sculpture garden and a stunning display of black and white photography.

🄬 Çukurcuma

Map 7 E4. 🎭 Taksim. Museum of Innocence: Çukurcuma Cad, Dalgıç Çıkmazı, Beyoğlu. **Open** 10am–6pm Tue–Sun. 📶 masumiyetmuzesi.org

This charming old quarter has become an important centre for Istanbul's furnishings and antiques trades. The old warehouses and houses in this district have been converted into shops and showrooms, where modern upholstery materials are piled up in carved marble basins and antique cabinets. It is worth browsing here to discover hidden treasures, ranging from valuable paintings and prints and 19th-century Ottoman embroidery to 1950s biscuit boxes.

Suzani textiles (*see p212*) on sale in Çukurcuma

The district is also home to Nobel prize winner Orhan Pamuk's Masumiyet Müzesi (Museum of Innocence). Set in a 19th-century house, the museum celebrates Pamuk's novel of the same name. The exhibits relate to the items used and owned by the characters in the novel.

🄭 Taksim

Map 7 E3. 🚋 Taksim. 🎭 Taksim. Taksim Republic Art Gallery: İstiklâl Cad No. 2, Taksim. **Tel** (0212) 245 78 32. **Open** daily.

Taksim Square is the focal point of Republican Istanbul. In 2013, Gezi Park, located close to Taksim Square, became the centre of anti-government protests. Taksim means "water distribution centre"; from the early 1700s, it was from

this site that water from the Belgrade Forest (*see p160*) was distributed in the city. The original stone reservoir, built in 1732 by Mahmut I, still stands at the top of İstiklâl Caddesi. In the southwest of the square is the 1928 Monument of Independence, by the Italian artist Canonica. It shows Atatürk (*see pp32–3*) and the other founding fathers of the modern Turkish Republic.

Near the entrance to İstiklal Caddesi is Taksim Cumhuriyet Sanat Galerisi (Taksim Republic Art Gallery). As well as temporary exhibitions, the gallery has a permanent display of Istanbul landscapes by some of Turkey's most important 20th-century painters.

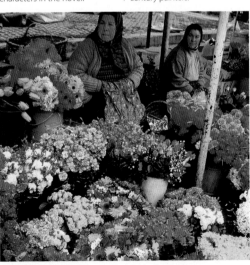

Flower sellers in Taksim Square

GREATER ISTANBUL

Away from the city centre there are many sights which repay the journey to visit them. Greater Istanbul has been divided into five areas shown on the map below; each also has its own map to help you get around. Closest to the centre are the mosques and churches of Fatih, Fener and Balat: most conspicuously the gigantic Fatih Mosque. Across the Golden Horn *(see p91)* from Balat are two sights worth seeing: Aynalı Kavak Palace and a fascinating industrial museum. The Theodosian Walls, stretching from the Golden Horn to the Sea of Marmara, are one of the city's most impressive monuments. Along these walls stand several ancient palaces and churches: particularly interesting is the Church of St Saviour in Chora, with its stunning Byzantine mosaics. Beyond the walls, up the Golden Horn, is

Eyüp, a focus of pilgrimage to Muslims, where you can visit a number of fine mausoleums and walk up the hill to the historic café associated with the French writer Pierre Loti. Following the Bosphorus northwards past Beyoğlu *(see pp102–109)* brings you to the Dolmabahçe Palace, one of the top sights of Istanbul. This opulent fantasy created in the 19th century by Sultan Abdül Mecit I requires a lengthy visit. Beyond it is peaceful Yıldız Park, containing yet more beautiful palaces and pavilions. Not all visitors to Istanbul make it to the Asian side, but if you have half a day to spare consider taking the short ferry trip from Eminönü *(see pp242–3)*. Its attractions include some splendid mosques, a handsome railway station and a small museum dedicated to British nurse, Florence Nightingale.

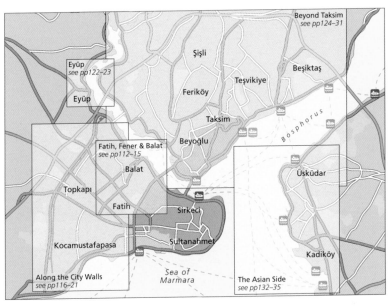

Key

- Central Istanbul
- Greater Istanbul
- Main road
- Motorway
- Other road
- City Walls
- Ferry route

0 kilometres 1

0 miles 1

◀ Modest interiors of the Church of St Saviour in Chora

For map symbols *see back flap*

Fatih, Fener and Balat

A visit to these neighbourhoods is a reminder that for centuries after the Muslim conquest (see p28), Jews and Christians made up around 40 per cent of Istanbul's population. Balat was home to Greek-speaking Jews from the Byzantine era onwards; Sephardic Jews from Spain joined them in the 15th century. Fener became a Greek enclave in the early 16th century and many wealthy residents rose to positions of prominence in the Ottoman Empire. Hilltop Fatih is linked to the city's radical Islamic tradition and you will see far more devout Muslims here than anywhere else in Istanbul. All three areas are residential, their maze of streets the preserve of washing lines and children playing.

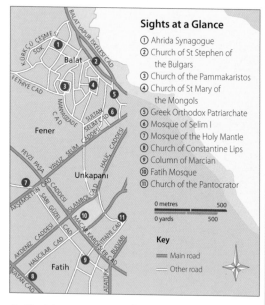

Sights at a Glance

① Ahrida Synagogue
② Church of St Stephen of the Bulgars
③ Church of the Pammakaristos
④ Church of St Mary of the Mongols
⑤ Greek Orthodox Patriarchate
⑥ Mosque of Selim I
⑦ Mosque of the Holy Mantle
⑧ Church of Constantine Lips
⑨ Column of Marcian
⑩ Fatih Mosque
⑪ Church of the Pantocrator

```
0 metres        500
0 yards         500
```

Key
━━ Main road
── Other road

❶ Ahrida Synagogue
Ahrida Sinagogu

Gevgili Sok, Balat. **Map** 1 C1. 🚌 55T, 99A. **Open** by appointment. 📷

The name of Istanbul's oldest and most beautiful synagogue is a corruption of Ohrid, a town in Macedonia from which its early congregation came. It was founded before the Muslim conquest of the city in 1453 and, with a capacity for up to 500 worshippers, has been in constant use ever since. However, tourists can only visit by prior arrangement with a guided tour company (see p227). The synagogue's painted walls and ceilings, dating from the late 17th century, have been restored to their Baroque glory. Pride of place, however, goes to the central Holy Ark, covered in rich tapestries, which contains rare holy scrolls.

During an explosion of fervour that swept the city's Jewish population in the 17th century, the religious leader Shabbetai Zevi (1629–76), a self-proclaimed messiah, started preaching at this synagogue. He was banished from the city and later converted to Islam. However, a significant number of Jews held that Zevi's conversion was a subterfuge and his followers, the Sabbatians, exist to this day.

❷ Church of St Stephen of the Bulgars
Bulgar Kilisesi

Mürsel Paşa Cad 85, Balat. **Map** 1 C1. 🚌 55T, 99A. **Closed** for renovation.

Astonishingly, this entire church was cast in iron, even the internal columns and galleries. It was created in Vienna in 1871, shipped all the way to the Golden Horn (see p91) and assembled on its shore. The church was needed for the Bulgarian community who had broken away from the authority of the Greek Orthodox Patriarchate just up the hill. Today, it is still used by this community, who keep the marble tombs of the first Bulgarian patriarchs permanently decorated with flowers. The church stands in a pretty little park that is dotted with trees and flowering shrubs and which runs down to the edge of the Golden Horn.

The Church of St Stephen of the Bulgars, wholly made of iron

❸ Church of the Pammakaristos
Fethiye Camii

Fethiye Cad, Draman. **Map** 1 C2. 🚌 90, 90B. **Open** 9am–4:30pm Thu–Tue. 📷

This Byzantine church is one of the hidden secrets of Istanbul. It is rarely visited despite the important role it has played in the history of the city, as well as its breathtaking series of mosaics.

Façade of the late Byzantine Church of the Pammakaristos

For over 100 years after the Ottoman conquest it housed the Greek Orthodox Patriarchate, but was converted into a mosque in the late 16th century by Murat III *(see p34)*. He named it the Mosque of Victory to commemorate his conquests of Georgia and Azerbaijan.

The charming exterior is obviously Byzantine, with its alternating stone and brick courses and finely carved marble details. The main body of the building is the working mosque, while the extraordinary mosaics are in a side chapel, which today is a museum with a small admission charge.

Dating from the 14th century, the great Byzantine renaissance *(see p27)*, the mosaics show holy figures isolated in a sea of gold, a reflection of the heavens. From the centre of the main dome, Christ Pantocrator ("the All-Powerful"), surrounded by the Old Testament prophets, stares solemnly down. In the apse another figure of Christ, seated on a jewel-encrusted throne, gives his benediction. On either side are portraits of the Virgin Mary and John the Baptist beseeching Christ. They are overlooked by the four archangels, while the side apses are filled with other saintly figures.

❹ Church of St Mary of the Mongols
Kanlı Kilise

Tevkii Cafer Mektebi Sok, Fener. **Map 1** C2. **Tel** (0212) 521 71 39. 🚌 55T, 99A. **Open** by appointment.

Consecrated in the late 13th century, the Church of St Mary of the Mongols is the only Greek Orthodox church in Istanbul to have remained continuously in the hands of the Greek community since the Byzantine era. Its immunity from conversion into a mosque was decreed in an order signed by Mehmet the Conqueror *(see p28)*. A copy of this is kept by the church to this day.

The church gets its name from the woman who founded it, Maria Palaeologina, an illegitimate Byzantine princess who was married off to a Mongol khan, Abagu, and lived piously with him in Persia for 15 years. On her husband's assassination, she returned to Constantinople, built this church and lived out her days in it as a nun.

Ring the bell of the compound to gain entry. The caretakers, a family from ancient Antioch in Turkey, are usually around. Donations are appreciated.

❺ Greek Orthodox Patriarchate
Ortodoks Patrikhanesi

Sadrazam Ali Paşa Cad 35, Fener. **Tel** (0212) 525 54 16. 🚌 55T, 99A. **Open** 9am–5pm daily. 🛈

This walled complex has been the seat of the patriarch of the Greek Orthodox Church since the early 17th century. Though nominally head of the whole church, the patriarch is now shepherd to a diminishing flock in and around Istanbul.

As you walk up the steps to enter the Patriarchate through a side door you will see that the main door has been welded shut. This was done in memory of Patriarch Gregory V, who was hanged here for treason in 1821 after encouraging the Greeks to overthrow Ottoman rule at the start of the Greek War of Independence (1821–32). Antagonism between the Turkish and Greek communities worsened with the Greek occupation of parts of Turkey in the 1920s *(see p33)*. There were anti-Greek riots in 1955, and in the mid-1960s many Greek residents were expelled. Today the clergy here is protected by a metal detector at the entrance.

The Patriarchate centres on the basilica-style Church of St George, which dates back to 1720. Yet the church contains much older relics and furniture. The patriarch's throne, the high structure to the right of the nave, is thought to be Byzantine, while the pulpit on the left is adorned with fine Middle Eastern wooden inlay and Orthodox icons.

Church of St George in the Greek Orthodox Patriarchate

İznik tile panel capping a window in the Mosque of Selim I

❻ Mosque of Selim I

Yavuz Sultan Selim Camii

Yavuz Selim Cad, Fener. **Map** 1 C2. 🚌 55T, 90, 90B, 99A. **Open** daily.

This much-admired mosque is also known locally as Yavuz Sultan Mosque: Yavuz, "the Grim", being the nickname the infamous Selim acquired *(see p28)*. It is one of the most beautiful mosques in Istanbul, seemingly at odds with the bar-baric reputation of the sultan.

The mosque, built between 1519 and 1522, sits alone on a hill beside a sunken car park, once the Byzantine Cistern of Aspar. It has been beautifully restored, but is rarely visited as it does not fall on the beaten track. At the centre of this lovely garden is an octagonal, domed fountain, surrounded by trees filled with chirruping birds.

The windows set into the porticoes in the courtyard are capped by early *İznik* tiles *(see p163)*. These were made by the *cuerda seca* technique, in which each colour is separated during the firing process, thus affording the patterns greater definition.

Similar tiles lend decorative effect to the impressive yet simple prayer hall, with its fine mosque furniture *(see pp40–41)* and stunning shallow dome.

❼ Mosque of the Holy Mantle

Hırka-i Şerif Camii

Keçeciler Cad, Karagümrük. **Map** 1 B3. 🚌 28, 87, 90, 91. **Open** daily.

Built in the Empire Style in 1850, this mosque was designed to house a cloak *(hırka)* in the imperial collection which once belonged to and was worn by the Prophet Moham-med. This resides in a sanctuary directly behind the mihrab. The mosque's minarets are in the form of Classical columns, and its balconies styled like Corinthian capitals. The interior of the octagonal prayer hall, meanwhile, has a plethora of decorative marble. Abdül Mecit I, the mosque's patron, was jointly responsible for the design of its calligraphic frieze.

Knocker, Mosque of the Holy Mantle

❽ Church of Constantine Lips

Fenari İsa Camii

Vatan Cad, Fatih. **Map** 1 B4. 🚌 90B. **Open** daily.

This 10th-century monastic church, dedicated to the Immaculate Mother of God, was founded by Constantine Lips Dungarios, a commander of the Byzantine fleet. Following the Byzantine reconquest

Byzantine brickwork exterior of the Church of Constantine Lips

of the city in 1261 *(see p26)*, Empress Theodora, wife of Michael VIII Palaeologus *(see pp26–7)*, added a second church. She also commissioned a funerary chapel, where she and her sons were buried.

This unusual history has given the structure its present rambling appearance. In an idiosyncratic touch, there are also four tiny chapels perched on the roof around the main dome. Another highlight is the building's eastern exterior wall. This is decorated with a *tour de force* of brick friezes, typical hallmarks of Byzantine churches of this period. When the church was con-verted into a mosque in 1496, it adopted the name Fenari İsa, or the Lamp of Jesus. This was in honour of İsa (Turkish for Jesus), the leader of a Sufi brotherhood *(see p106)* who worshipped here at that time. Inside the mosque, which is still in use today, are well-restored capitals and decorated cornices.

❾ Column of Marcian

Kız Taşı

İskender Paşa, Saraçhane. **Map** 1 C4 (2 A3). 🚌 28, 87, 90, 91.

Standing in a little square, this 5th-century Byzantine column was once surmounted by a statue of the Emperor Marcian (AD 450–57). On its base you can still see a pair of Nikes, Greek winged goddesses of victory, holding an inscribed medallion.

Interestingly, the column's Turkish name translates as the Maiden's Column, suggesting that it was mistaken for the famous Column of Venus. According to legend, this column was said to sway at the passing of an impure maid. It originally stood nearby and is thought to have been employed as one of the largest columns in the Süleymaniye Mosque *(see pp92–3)*.

Chandelier hanging in the light and airy interior of Fatih Mosque

⑩ Fatih Mosque

Fatih Camii

Macar Kardeşler Cad, Fatih. **Map** 1 C3. 28, 87, 90, 91. **Open** daily.

A spacious outer courtyard surrounds this vast Baroque mosque, which is the third major structure on this site. The first was the Church of the Holy Apostles *(see p25)*, the burial place of most of the Byzantine emperors. When Mehmet the Conqueror *(see p28)* came to construct a mosque here, the church's crumbling remains provided a symbolic location. But the first Fatih Mosque collapsed in an earthquake in 1766, and most of what you see today was the work of Mehmet Tahir Ağa, the chief imperial architect under Mustafa III. Many of the buildings he constructed around the prayer hall, including eight Koranic colleges *(medreses)* and a hospice, still stand.

The only parts of Mehmet the Conqueror's mosque to have survived are the three porticoes of the courtyard,

the ablutions fountain, the main gate into the prayer hall and, inside, the mihrab. Two exquisite forms of 15th-century decoration can be seen over the windows in the porticoes: İznik tiles made using the *cuerda seca* technique and lunettes adorned with calligraphic marble inlay.

Inside the prayer hall, stencilled patterns decorate the domes, while the lower level of the walls is revetted with yet more tiles – although these are inferior to those used in the porticoes.

The tomb of Mehmet the Conqueror stands behind the prayer hall, near that of his consort Gülbahar. His sarcophagus and turban are both appropriately large. It is a place of enormous gravity, always busy with supplicants.

If you pay a visit to the mosque on a Wednesday, you will also see the weekly market *(see p214)* which turns the streets around it into a circus of commerce. From tables piled high with fruit and vegetables to lorries loaded with unspun wool, this is a real spectacle, even if you don't buy anything.

⑪ Church of the Pantocrator

Zeyrek Camii

İbadethane Sok, Küçükpazar.
Map 2 B2. 28, 61B, 87.
Open prayer times daily.

Empress Irene, the wife of John II Comnenus *(see p21)*, founded the Church of the Pantocrator ("Christ the Almighty") during the 12th century. This hulk of Byzantine masonry was once the centrepiece of one of the city's most important religious foundations, the Monastery of the Pantocrator. As well as a monastery and church, the complex included a hospice for the elderly, an asylum and a hospital. In this respect it prefigured the social welfare system provided by the great imperial mosque complexes that the Ottomans later built in the city *(see p40)*.

The church, now a mosque, boasts a magnificent figurative marble floor. It is composed of three interlinked chapels. The one with the highest dome was built by Empress Irene. Emperor John II added another as a mortuary chapel when Irene died in 1124, and he later filled the area between with a third apsed chapel. The rest of the Comnenus dynasty and many of the Palaeologus imperial family were interred within these chapels.

Shortly after the Muslim conquest in 1453 *(see p28)*, the building was converted into a mosque. It has recently undergone major restoration work. A caretaker may let you in outside prayer times in the afternoons.

Church of the Pantocrator, built by Empress Irene in the 12th century

Along the City Walls

Istanbul's Theodosian Walls are one of the most impressive remains of the city's Byzantine past. Pierced by monumental gates and strengthened by towers, they encompass the city centre in a great arc, stretching all the way from Yedikule, on the Sea of Marmara, to Ayvansaray, on the Golden Horn (see p91). The suburbs that lie adjacent to the walls, particularly Edirnekapı and Topkapı, are mainly working-class, residential districts, interspersed with areas of wasteland which are unsafe to explore alone. Dotted around these suburbs, however, are important remnants of the city's past, particularly the Byzantine period. The outstanding sight here is the Church of St Saviour in Chora (see pp120–21), with its beautifully preserved mosaics and frescoes.

Silivrikapı, one of the gateways through the Theodosian Walls

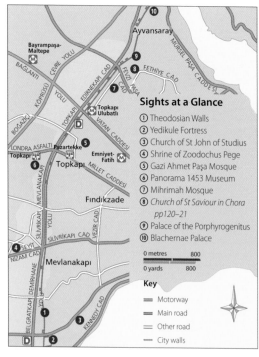

Sights at a Glance

1. Theodosian Walls
2. Yedikule Fortress
3. Church of St John of Studius
4. Shrine of Zoodochus Pege
5. Gazi Ahmet Paşa Mosque
6. Panorama 1453 Museum
7. Mihrimah Mosque
8. Church of St Saviour in Chora pp120–21
9. Palace of the Porphyrogenitus
10. Blachernae Palace

```
0 metres        800
0 yards         800
```

Key

▬ Motorway
▬ Main road
▬ Other road
▬ City walls

❶ Theodosian Walls

Teodos II Surları

From Yedikule to Ayvansaray.
Map 1 A1. 🚊 Topkapı, Ulubatlı.

With its 11 fortified gates and 192 towers, this great chain of double walls sealed Constantinople's landward side against invasion for more than a thousand years. Extending for a distance of 6.5 km (4 miles) from the Sea of Marmara to the Golden Horn, the walls are built in layers of red tile alternating with limestone blocks. Different sections can be reached by metro, tram, train or bus; but to see their whole length you will need to take a taxi or dolmuş (see p238) along the main road that runs outside them.

The walls were built in the period AD 412–22, during the reign of Theodosius II (408–50). In 447 an earthquake destroyed 54 of the towers but these were immediately rebuilt, under threat of the advancing Attila the Hun. Subsequently the walls resisted sieges by Arabs, Bulgarians, Russians and Turks. Even the determined armies of the Fourth Crusade (see p26) only managed to storm the ramparts along the Golden Horn, while the land walls stood firm.

Mehmet the Conqueror finally breached the walls in May 1453 (see p28).

Successive Ottoman sultans then kept the walls in good repair until the end of the 17th century.

Large stretches of the walls, particularly around Belgratkapı (Belgrade Gate) have been rebuilt. Byzantine scholars have criticized the restoration for insensitive use of modern building materials, but the new sections do give you an idea of how the walls used to look. Many, although not all, of the gateways are still in good repair.

Mehmet the Conqueror directed his heaviest cannon at the St Romanus and Charsius gates. Under the Ottomans, the former became known as Topkapı, the Gate of the Cannon (not to be confused with Topkapı Palace, see pp56–61). Unfortunately, a section of walls close to this gate was

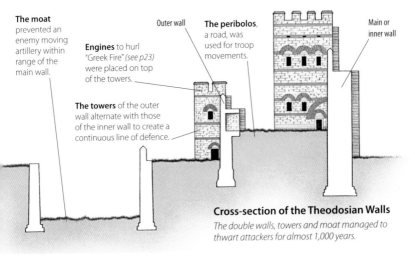

The moat prevented an enemy moving artillery within range of the main wall.

Outer wall

Engines to hurl "Greek Fire" *(see p23)* were placed on top of the towers.

The peribolos, a road, was used for troop movements.

Main or inner wall

The towers of the outer wall alternate with those of the inner wall to create a continuous line of defence.

Cross-section of the Theodosian Walls
The double walls, towers and moat managed to thwart attackers for almost 1,000 years.

demolished in the 1950s to make way for a road, Millet Caddesi. The Charsius Gate (now called Edirnekapı), Silivrikapı, Yeni Mevlanakapı and other original gates still give access to the city.

The Yedikule Gate (which stands beside the fortress of the same name) has an imperial Byzantine eagle *(see p27)* carved above its main archway.

❷ Yedikule Fortress
Yedikule Müzesi

Kule Meydanı 4, Yedikule.
Tel (0212) 585 89 33. 🚌 31, 80, 93T.
Open 9am–6pm daily.

Yedikule, the "Fortress of the Seven Towers", is built on to the southern section of the Theodosian Walls. Its seven towers are connected by thick walls to make a five-sided fortification. One of the sides, with four towers spaced along it, is formed by a stretch of the land walls themselves.

The fortress as it is today incorporates both Byzantine and Ottoman features. The two stout, square marble towers built into the land walls once flanked the Golden Gate (now blocked up), the triumphal entrance into medieval Byzantium *(see p24)* built by Theodosius II. Imperial processions would enter the city through this gate to mark the

investiture of a new emperor or in celebration of a successful military campaign. When it was first built, the gate was covered in gold plate and the façade decorated with sculptures, including a statue of a winged Victory, four bronze elephants and an image of Emperor Theodosius himself.

In the 15th century, Mehmet the Conqueror added the three tall, round towers that are not part of the land walls, and the connecting curtain walls, to complete the fortress.

After viewing the castle from the outside, you can enter through a doorway in the northeastern wall. The tower immediately to your left as you enter is known as the *yazılı kule*, "the tower with inscriptions". This was used as a prison for

foreign envoys and others who fell foul of the sultan. These hapless individuals carved their names, dates and other details on the walls and some of these inscriptions are still visible.

Executions were carried out in Yedikule Castle, in the northern of the two towers flanking the Golden Gate. Among those executed here was the 17-year-old Osman II *(see p35)*. In 1622 he was dragged to Yedikule by his own Janissaries *(see p129)*, after four years of misrule, which included, it is alleged, using his own pages as targets for archery practice.

The walkway around the ramparts is accessible via a steep flight of stone steps. It offers good views of the land walls and nearby suburbs, and also of the cemeteries.

Aerial view of Yedikule Fortress with the Sea of Marmara behind

❸ Church of St John of Studius

İmrahor Camii

İmam Aşir Sok, Yedikule. ▦ 80, 80B, 80T. Ⓜ Kazlıçeşme.

Istanbul's oldest surviving church, St John of Studius, is now a mere shell consisting only of its outer walls. It is locked and can only be viewed from the outside, though it may be rebuilt as a mosque in the future.

The church was completed in AD 463 by Studius, a Roman patrician who served as consul during the reign of Emperor Marcian (450–57). Originally connected to the most powerful monastery in the Byzantine Empire, in the late 8th century it was a spiritual and intellectual centre under the rule of Abbot Theodore, who was buried in the church's garden.

In the 15th century the church housed a university and was converted into a mosque. The building was abandoned in 1894 when it was severely damaged by an earthquake.

The church is a perfect basilica, with a single apse at the east end, preceded by a narthex and a courtyard. It has a magnificent entrance portal, with carved Corinthian capitals and a sculpted architrave and cornice.

❹ Shrine of Zoodochus Pege

Balıklı Kilise

Seyit Nizam Cad 3, Silivrikapı. **Tel** (0212) 582 30 81. Ⓜ Kazlıçeşme. ▦ 93T. **Open** 8am–4pm daily.

The Fountain of Zoodochus Pege ("Life-Giving Spring") is built over Istanbul's most famous sacred spring, which is believed to

Ruins of the Church of St John of Studius

The Shrine of Zoodochus Pege, founded on a sacred spring

have miraculous powers. The fish swimming in it are supposed to have arrived though a miracle which occurred shortly before the fall of Constantinople (see p28). They are said to have leapt into the spring from a monk's frying pan on hearing that declare that a Turkish invasion of Constantinople was as likely as fish coming back to life.

The spring was probably the site of an ancient sanctuary of Artemis. Later, with the arrival of Christianity, a church, dedicated to the Virgin Mary, was built around it. The spring was popular throughout the Byzantine era, especially on Ascension Day, when the emperor would visit it. The church was destroyed and rebuilt many times over the years by various Byzantine emperors, but the present one dates from 1833. The inner courtyard is filled with tombs of bishops and patriarchs of the Greek Orthodox Church.

❺ Gazi Ahmet Paşa Mosque

Gazi Ahmet Paşa Camii

Undeğirmeni Sok, Fatma Sultan. Ⓜ Ulubatlı. 🚆 Topkapı. ▦ 93T. **Open** Prayer times only.

One of the most worthwhile detours along the city walls is to the Gazi Ahmet Paşa Mosque, also known as Kara Ahmet Paşa. This lovely building, with its peaceful leafy courtyard and graceful proportions, is one of Sinan's (see p93) lesser-known achievements.

He built it in 1554 for Kara Ahmet Paşa, a grand vizier of Süleyman the Magnificent (see p28).

The courtyard is surrounded by the cells of a medrese and a dershane, or main classroom. Attractive apple-green and yellow İznik tiles (see p163) grace the porch, while blue-and-white ones are found on the east wall of the prayer hall. These tiles date from the mid-16th century. Of the three galleries, the wooden ceiling under the west one is elaborately painted in red, blue, gold and black.

Tilework over medrese doorway at Kara Ahmet Paşa Mosque

❻ Panorama 1453 History Museum

Panorama 1453 Tarihi Müzesi

Topkapı Kültür Parkı. **Tel** (0212) 415 14 53. 🚆 Topkapı. 🖥 **panoramik muze.com**

This museum recreates a vivid picture of the final day in the historic Ottoman siege of the city in 1453, through realistic sound effects, over 10,000 painted figures and numerous models forming a tableau vivant. In addition to this, there are Byzantine defenders manning the battlements, "Greek fire" erupting among Ottoman troops, cannonballs shattering previously impregnable walls, and scaling ladders being thrown into a ditch. Situated close to the Theodisian Walls where Mehmet the Conqueror concentrated his forces and weapons, the focus of the museum is a large dome depicting the entire length of the walls in a 360-degree panorama.

❼ Mihrimah Mosque
Mihrimah Camii

Sulukule Cad, Edirnekapı. **Map** 1 A2.
🚌 28, 87, 91. **Open** daily.

An imposing monument located just inside the city walls, the Mihrimah Mosque complex was built by Sinan between 1562 and 1565. Mihrimah, the daughter of Süleyman the Magnificent *(see p28)*, was then the recently widowed wife of Rüstem Paşa, a grand vizier who gave his name to the tiled mosque near the Spice Bazaar *(see pp90–91)*.

This mosque rests on a platform, occupying the highest point in the city.

The building is square in shape, with four strong turrets at its corners, and is surmounted by a 37-m (121-ft) high dome. The single minaret is tall and slender, so much so that it has twice been destroyed by earthquakes.

The interior is illuminated by numerous windows, some of which have stained glass. The supporting arches of the sultan's loge *(see p41)* have been skilfully painted to resemble green-and-white marble. The carved marble *minbar* is also impressive.

Stained-glass window in the Mihrimah Mosque

❽ Church of St Saviour in Chora

See pp120–21.

❾ Palace of the Porphyrogenitus
Tekfur Sarayı

Şişehane Cad, Edirnekapı. **Map** 1 B1.
Tel (0212) 522 175. 🚌 87, 90, 126.
Open daily.

This beautiful Byzantine palace, has a three-storey façade decorated with red brick and white marble and has undergone major renovations. Once a mere shell, it now has a roof and windows have been installed. It might eventually be turned into a conference centre.

The palace, also known as Tekfur Palace, dates from the late Byzantine era and is the only surviving palace from this period. Its exact age is debatable since the technique of alternating stone with three courses of brick is typical of the 10th century, whereas its geometrical designs were common in the 14th century. It was most likely constructed as an annexe of nearby Blachernae Palace. These two palaces became the main residences of the imperial sovereigns in the last two centuries before the fall of Byzantium in 1453 *(see p28)*.

During the reign of Ahmet III (1703–30, *see p29*) the last remaining İznik potters *(see p163)* moved to the palace. However, by this time their skills were in decline and the tiles made here never acquired the excellence of those created at the height of production in İznik. Cezri Kasım Paşa Mosque in Eyüp *(see p123)* has some fine examples of these tiles.

❿ Blachernae Palace
Anemas Zindanları

İvaz Ağa Cad, Ayvansaray.
🚌 55T, 99A. 🚋 Ayvansaray.

As the city walls approach the Golden Horn you come to the scant remains of Blachernae Palace. These consist of a tower in the city walls, known as the Prison of Anemas, a terrace to the east (the present site of the İvaz Efendi Mosque), and another tower to the south of the terrace, known as the Tower of Isaac Angelus.

The origins of the palace date as far back as AD 500, when it was an occasional residence for imperial visitors to the shrine of Blachernae. It was the great Comnenus emperors *(see p23)* who rebuilt the structure in the 12th century, transforming it into a magnificent palace.

The remains of the marble decoration and wall frescoes in the Anemas tower indicate that this was probably an imperial residence. Although you can walk around the site, you will be unable to gain access into the towers unless the caretaker is there.

Brick and marble façade in the Palace of the Porphyrogenitus

❽ Church of St Saviour in Chora
Kariye Müzesi

Some of the very finest Byzantine mosaics and frescoes can be found in the Church of St Saviour in Chora. Little is known of the early history of the church, although its name "in Chora", which means "in the country", suggests that the church originally stood in a rural setting. The present church dates from the 11th century. Between 1315 and 1321 it was remodelled and the mosaics and frescoes added by Theodore Metochites, a theologian, philosopher and one of the elite Byzantine officials of his day.

Exterior of the Church of St Saviour in Chora

The Genealogy of Christ

Theodore Metochites, who restored St Saviour, wrote that his mission was to relate how "the Lord himself became a mortal on our behalf". He takes the *Genealogy of Christ* as his starting point: the mosaics in the two domes of the inner narthex portray 66 of Christ's forebears.

The crown of the southern dome is occupied by a figure of Christ. In the dome's flutes are two rows of his ancestors: Adam to Jacob ranged above the 12 sons of Jacob. In the northern dome, there is a central image of the Virgin and Child, with the kings of the House of David in the upper row and lesser ancestors of Christ in the lower row.

The Life of the Virgin

All but one of the 20 mosaics in the inner narthex depicting the *Life of the Virgin* are well preserved. This cycle is based mainly on the apocryphal Gospel of St James, written in the 2nd century, which gives an account of the Virgin's life. This was popular in the Middle Ages and was a rich source of material for ecclesiastical artists.

Among the events shown are the first seven steps of the Virgin, the Virgin entrusted to Joseph and the Virgin receiving bread from an angel.

The Infancy of Christ

Scenes from the *Infancy of Christ*, based largely on the New Testament, occupy the semicircular panels of the outer narthex. They begin on the north wall of the outer

Mosaic showing Christ and his ancestors, in the southern dome of the inner narthex

Guide to the Mosaics and Frescoes

Outer narthex
Entrance
Nave
Inner narthex
Entrance to nave
Parecclesion

Key
- ☐ The Genealogy of Christ
- ☐ The Life of the Virgin
- ☐ The Infancy of Christ
- ☐ Christ's Ministry
- ☐ Other Mosaics
- ☐ The Frescoes

Outer narthex looking east

Outer narthex looking west

narthex with a scene of Joseph being visited by an angel in a dream. Subsequent panels include Mary and Joseph's *Journey to Bethlehem*, their *Enrolment for Taxation*, the *Nativity of Christ* and, finally, Herod ordering the *Massacre of the Innocents*.

The Enrolment for Taxation

Christ's Ministry

While many of the mosaics in this series are badly damaged, some beautiful panels remain. The cycle occupies the vaults of the seven bays of the outer narthex and some of the south bay of the inner narthex. The most striking mosaic is the portrayal of Christ's temptation in the wilderness, in the second bay of the outer narthex.

Theodore Metochites presents
St Saviour in Chora to Christ

Other Mosaics

There are three panels in the nave of the church, one of which, above the main door from the inner narthex, illustrates the *Dormition of the Virgin*. This mosaic, protected by a marble frame, is the best preserved in the church. The Virgin is depicted laid out on a bier, watched over by the Apostles, with Christ seated behind. Other devotional panels in the two narthexes include one, on the east wall of the south bay of the inner narthex, of the Deësis, depicting Christ with the Virgin Mary and, unusually, without St John. Another, in the inner narthex over the door into the nave, is of Theodore Metochites himself, shown wearing a large turban, and humbly presenting the restored church as an offering to Christ.

The Frescoes

The frescoes in the parecclesion (side chapel) are thought to have been painted just after the mosaics were completed, probably in around 1320. The most engaging of the frescoes – which reflect the purpose of the parecclesion as a place of burial – is the *Anastasis*, in the semidome above the apse. In it, the central figure of Christ, the vanquisher of death, is shown dragging Adam and Eve out of their tombs. Under Christ's feet are the gates of hell, while Satan lies before him. The fresco in the vault overhead depicts *The Last Judgment*, with the souls of the saved on the right and those of the damned to the left.

Figure of Christ from the *Anastasis* fresco in the parecclesion

VISITORS' CHECKLIST

Practical Information
Kariye Camii Sok, Edirnekapı.
Map 1 B1. **Tel** (0212) 631 92 41.
Open 9am–6pm Thu–Tue.

Transport
28, 86 or 90, then
5 minutes' walk

Inner narthex looking east

Parecclesion and outer narthex looking south

Inner narthex looking west

Parecclesion and outer narthex looking north

Eyüp

As the burial place of Eyüp Ensari, the standard bearer of the Prophet Mohammed, the village of Eyüp is a place of pilgrimage for Muslims from all over the world. Its sacrosanct status has kept it a peaceful place of contemplation, far removed from the squalid effects of industrialization elsewhere on the Golden Horn (see p91). The wealthy elite established mosques and street fountains in the village but, above all, they chose Eyüp as a place of burial. Their grand mausoleums line the streets surrounding Eyüp Sultan Mosque, while the cypress groves in the hills above the village are filled with the gravestones of ordinary people.

Gateway to the Baroque Complex of Valide Sultan Mihrişah

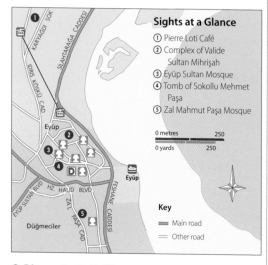

Sights at a Glance

① Pierre Loti Café
② Complex of Valide Sultan Mihrişah
③ Eyüp Sultan Mosque
④ Tomb of Sokollu Mehmet Paşa
⑤ Zal Mahmut Paşa Mosque

0 metres 250
0 yards 250

Key

▬ Main road
═ Other road

❷ Complex of Valide Sultan Mihrişah
Mihrişah Valide Sultan Külliyesi

Seyit Reşat Cad. 🚌 39, 55T, 99A.
Open 9am–6pm Tue–Sun.

Most of the northern side of the street leading from Eyüp Mosque's northern gate is occupied by the largest Baroque *külliye (see p40)* in Istanbul, although unusually it is not centred on a mosque. Built for Mihrişah, mother of Selim III *(see p35)*, the *külliye* was completed in 1791.

The complex includes the ornate marble tomb of Mihrişah and a soup kitchen, which is still in use today. There is also a beautiful grilled fountain *(sebil)*, from which an attendant once served water and refreshing drinks of sweet sherbet to passers-by.

❶ Pierre Loti Café
Piyer Loti Kahvehanesi

Gümüşsuyu Karyağdı Sok 5, Eyüp. **Tel** (0212) 581 26 96.
🚌 39, 55T, 99A. **Open** 8:30am–midnight daily.

This famous café stands at the top of the hill in Eyüp Cemetery, about 20 minutes' walk or short funicular ride up Karyağdı Sokağı from Eyüp Mosque, from where it commands sweeping views down over the Golden Horn. It is named after the French novelist and Turkophile Pierre Loti, who frequented a café in Eyüp – claimed to be this one – during his stay here in 1876. Loti, a French naval officer, fell in love with a married Turkish woman and wrote an autobiographical novel,

Aziyade, about their affair. The café is prettily decked out with 19th-century furniture and the waiters wear period clothing.

The path up to the café passes by a picturesque array of tombstones, most of which date from the Ottoman era. Just before the café on the right, a few tall, uninscribed tombstones mark the graves of executioners.

Period interior of the Pierre Loti Café *(see p208)*

❸ Eyüp Sultan Mosque
Eyüp Sultan Camii

Camii Kebir Sok. **Tel** (0212) 564 73 68.
🚌 39, 55T, 99A. **Open** daily.

Mehmet the Conqueror built the original mosque on this site in 1458, five years after his conquest of Istanbul *(see p28)*, in honour of Eyüp Ensari. That building fell into ruins, probably as a result of an earthquake, and the present mosque was completed in 1800, by Selim III *(see p35)*.

The mosque's delightful inner courtyard is a garden in which two huge plane trees grow on a platform. This platform was the setting for the Girding of the Sword of Osman, part of a sultan's inauguration from the days of Mehmet the Conqueror.

The mosque itself is predominantly covered in gleaming white marble.

Opposite the mosque is the tomb of Eyüp Ensari himself, believed to have been killed during the first Arab siege of Constantinople in the 7th century (see p23). The tomb dates from the same period as the mosque and most of its decoration is in the Ottoman Baroque style. Both the outer wall of the tomb facing the mosque, and most of its interior, have an impressive covering of tiles, some of them from İznik (see p162).

Zal Mahmut Paşa Mosque, as viewed from its tomb garden

Visitors at the tomb of Eyüp Ensari, Mohammed's standard bearer

❹ Tomb of Sokollu Mehmet Paşa
Sokollu Mehmet Paşa Türbesi

Camii Kebir Sok. 🚌 39, 55T, 99A.
Open 9:30am–4:30pm Tue–Sun.

Grand vizier (see p31) Sokollu Mehmet Paşa commissioned his tomb around 1574, five years before he was assassinated by a madman in Topkapı Palace (see pp56–61). Of Balkan royal blood, he started his career as falconer royal and steadily climbed the social order until he became grand vizier to Süleyman the Magnificent (see p28) in 1565. He held this position through the reign of Selim II (see p29) and into that of Murat III. The architect Sinan (see p93) built this elegantly proportioned

octagonal tomb. It is notable for its stained glass, some of which is original.

A roofed colonnade connects the tomb to what was formerly a Koranic school.

❺ Zal Mahmut Paşa Mosque
Zal Mahmut Paşa Camii

Zal Paşa Cad. 🚌 39, 55T, 99A.
Open daily.

Heading south from the centre of Eyüp, it is a short walk to Zal Mahmut Paşa Mosque. The complex was built by Sinan for the man who assassinated Mustafa, the first-born heir of Süleyman the Magnificent.

Probably erected some time in the 1560s, the mosque is notable for the lovely floral tiles around its mihrab, and for its carved marble *minbar* and *müezzin mahfili* (see p40). Proceeding down some stone steps to the north of the mosque you will come to a garden. In it stands the large tomb of Zal Mahmut Paşa and his wife, both of whom are said to have died on the same day.

On the same street is Cezri Kasım Paşa Mosque (1515), a small mosque with a pretty portal and a tiled mihrab. Most of the tiles were produced at the Palace of the Porphyrogenitus (see p119) in the first half of the 18th century.

Ottoman Gravestones

The Ottoman graveyard was a garden of the dead, where the living happily strolled without morbid inhibitions. The gravestones within it were often lavishly symbolic: from their decoration you can tell the sex, occupation, rank and even the number of children of the deceased. As the turban was banned in 1829 (see p32), only the fez appears on men's gravestones erected after that date.

Women's graves have a flower for each child.

A turban's size reflected a gentleman's status.

This hat indicates the grave of a member of a Sufi order.

A fez was worn by a paşa, or public servant (see p30).

Beyond Taksim

The area to the north of Taksim Square (see p109) became fashionable in the 19th century, when sultans built palaces along the Bosphorus and in the wooded hills above it. The extravagant Dolmabahçe Palace, built by Abdül Mecit I (see p32), started the trend. High-ranking court officials soon followed, and the area achieved a glamour that it retains to this day. Two other sights worth seeing are on the northern shore of the Golden Horn. Aynalı Kavak Palace is the last surviving trace of a grand palace built by Ahmet III (see p29), while the Rahmi M Koç Museum, in nearby Hasköy, is an interesting industrial museum. Hasköy became a royal park in the 15th century and later supported fruit orchards, before dockyards brought industrialization to the area in the 19th century.

Ortaköy's fashionable waterfront square and ferry landing

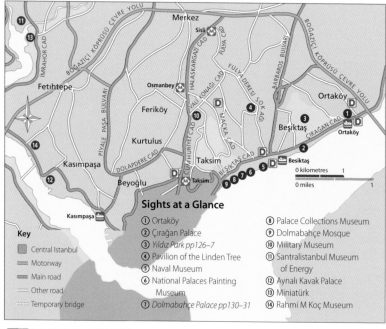

Sights at a Glance

1. Ortaköy
2. Çırağan Palace
3. Yıldız Park pp126–7
4. Pavilion of the Linden Tree
5. Naval Museum
6. National Palaces Painting Museum
7. Dolmabahçe Palace pp130–31
8. Palace Collections Museum
9. Dolmabahçe Mosque
10. Military Museum
11. Santralistanbul Museum of Energy
12. Aynalı Kavak Palace
13. Miniatürk
14. Rahmi M Koç Museum

Key
- Central Istanbul
- Motorway
- Main road
- Other road
- Temporary bridge

Cobbled Ortaköy side street lined with cafés and shops

❶ Ortaköy

Map 9 F3. 25E, 40.

Crouched at the foot of Bosphorus Bridge (see p140), the suburb of Ortaköy has retained a village feel. Life centres on İskele Meydanı, the quayside square, which used to be busy with fishermen unloading the day's catch. Nowadays, though, Ortaköy is better known for its lively Sunday market (see p215), which crowds out the square and surrounding streets, and its shops selling the wares of local artisans. It is also the location for a thriving bar and café scene, which in the summer especially is the hub of Istanbul's nightlife (see p221).

Mecidiye Mosque (or Ortaköy Camii), the suburb's impressive landmark, is on the waterfront. Built in 1855 by Nikoğos Balyan, who was responsible for Dolmabahçe Palace (see pp130–31), it has grace and originality, with window-filled tympanum arches and corner turrets.

Ortaköy also has a Greek Orthodox church, Haghios Phocas, and a synagogue, Etz Ahayim. The origins of both date from the Byzantine era.

❷ Çırağan Palace
Çırağan Sarayı

Dolmabahçe Cad, Beşiktaş. **Map** 9 D3.
Tel (0212) 236 90 00. 🚌 25E, 40.
W ciragan-palace.com

Sultan Abdül Mecit I started work on Çırağan Palace in 1864, but it was not completed until 1871, during the reign of Abdül Aziz (see p32). It replaced an earlier wooden palace where torchlit processions were held during the Tulip Period (see p29).

The palace was designed by Nikoğos Balyan. At the sultan's request he added Arabic touches from sketches of Moorish buildings such as the Alhambra in Granada in Spain. Externally this is reflected in the honeycomb capitals over its windows. The sultan entered Çırağan Palace directly from the Bosphorus, through the ornate ceremonial gates along its shoreline.

Çırağan Palace had a sad, short history as an imperial residence. Abdül Aziz died here in 1876, having supposedly committed suicide – although his friends believed he had been murdered. His successor, Murat V (see p35), was imprisoned in the palace for a year after a brief reign of only three months. He died in the Malta Pavilion (see p127) 27 years later, still a prisoner. The palace was eventually destroyed by fire in 1910. It remained a burnt-out shell for

Baroque-style staircase at the Pavilion of the Linden Tree

many years, before being restored in 1990 as the Çırağan Palace Kempinski (see p188).

❸ Yıldız Park
See pp126–7.

❹ Pavilion of the Linden Tree
Ihlamur Kasrı

Dolmabahçe Cad, Beşiktaş. **Map** 8 B2.
Tel (0212) 236 90 00. 🚌 26 (from Eminönü). **Open** 9am–5pm Tue–Wed & Fri–Sun. 📷 📹

This one-time residence of sultans, dating from the early 19th century, stands in beautiful, leafy gardens which are planted with magnolias and camellias, and decorated with ornamental fountains. Today, the gardens are a somewhat incongruous reminder of the city's Ottoman past, being situated in the midst of the modern suburbs of Teşvikiye and Ihlamur.

As the pavilion's name suggests, the area was once a grove of lime (linden) trees, and the gardens are all that remain of what was previously a vast wooded park. This park was a favourite retreat and hunting ground of the Ottoman sultans. In the early 19th century, Abdül

Mecit I (see p32) often came here and stayed in the original pavilion on this site. That building was so unassuming that the French poet Alphonse de Lamartine (1790–1869) expressed great surprise that a sultan should have entertained him in a humble cottage, with a gardener working in plain view through the windows.

In 1857 Abdül Mecit chose Nikoğos Balyan, who had by then finished Dolmabahçe Palace with his father, to design another residence here. Two separate pavilions were built, the grander of which is the Ceremonial Pavilion, or Mabeyn Köşkü, used by the sultan and his guests. The Entourage Pavilion, or Maiyet Köşkü, a short distance away, was reserved for the sultan's retinue, including the women of the harem. Both buildings are open to visitors – the Entourage Pavilion is currently a café and bookshop.

The pavilions are constructed mainly of sandstone and marble. Their façades are in the Baroque style, with double stairways, many decorative embellishments and hardly a single straight line to be seen. The ornate interiors of the buildings reflect 19th-century Ottoman taste, incorporating a mixture of European styles. With their mirrors, lavish furnishings and gilded details, they are similar to but less ostentatious than those of Dolmabahçe Palace.

Çırağan Palace, notable for the Moorish-style embellishments above its windows

❸ Yıldız Park

Yıldız Parkı

Yıldız Park was originally laid out as the garden of the first
Çırağan Palace (see p125). It later formed the grounds of
Yıldız Palace, an assortment of buildings from different eras
now enclosed behind a wall and entered separately from
Ihlamur-Yıldız Caddesi. Further pavilions dot Yıldız Park,
which, with its many ancient trees and exotic shrubs, is a
favourite spot for family picnics. The whole park is situated
on a steep hill and, as it is a fairly long climb, you may prefer
to take a taxi up to the Şale Pavilion and walk back down
past the other sights.

Bridge over the lake in the grounds
of Yıldız Palace

Yıldız Palace

The palace is a collection of
pavilions and villas built in the
19th and 20th centuries. Many of
them are the work of the eccentric Sultan Abdül Hamit II (1876–
1909, see p35), who made it his
principal residence as he feared a
seaborne attack on Dolmabahçe
Palace (see pp130–31).

The main building in the
entrance courtyard is the **State
Apartments** (Büyük Mabeyn),
which date from the reign of
Sultan Selim III (1789–1807, see
p35); they are not presently
open to the public. Around the
corner, the **City Museum** (Şehir
Müzesi) has a display of Yıldız
porcelain. The Italianate
building opposite it is the
former armoury, or Silahhane.
Next door to the City Museum is
the **Yıldız Palace Museum**,
housed in what was once the
Marangozhane, Abdül Hamit's
carpentry workshop. This has a
changing collection of art and
objects from the palace.

A monumental arch leads
from the first courtyard to the
harem section of the palace.
On the left beside the arch
is a pretty greenhouse, the

The Italianate Silahhane, the former armoury of Yıldız Palace

Limonluk Serası (Lemon House).

Further on is the **Yıldız Palace Theatre**, now a museum. It was completed in 1889 by Abdül Hamit, who encouraged all forms of Western art. The decor of the theatre's restored interior is mainly blue and gold. The stars on the domed ceiling are a reference to the name of the palace: *yıldız* means "star" in Turkish.

Abdül Hamit sat alone in a box over the entrance. Since no one was allowed to sit with his back to the sultan, the stalls were not used. Backstage, the former dressing rooms are given over to displays on the theatre, including costumes and playbills.

The lake in the palace grounds is shaped like Abdül Hamit's *tuğra (see p97)*. A menagerie was kept on the islands in the lake, where 30 keepers tended tigers, lions, giraffes and zebras.

Salon in the lavish Şale Pavilion

Şale Pavilion

The single most impressive building in the park, the Şale Pavilion (Şale Köşkü) was among those erected by Abdül Hamit II. Although its façade appears as a whole, it was in fact built in three stages.

The first, left-hand section of the buildling was designed to resemble a Swiss chalet. It probably dates from the 1870s. Winston Churchill, Charles de Gaulle and Nicolae Ceauşescu have all stayed in its rooms.

The second section was added in 1889, to accommodate Kaiser Wilhelm II on the first ever state visit of a foreign monarch to the Ottoman capital. The 14-room suite includes a dining room known as the Mother-of-Pearl Salon (Sedefli Salon) after the delicate inlay that covers almost all of its surfaces.

The third section was also built for a visit by Kaiser Wilhelm II, this time in 1898. Its reception chamber is the grandest room in the whole pavilion. The vast silk Hereke carpet *(see p218)* covering its floor was painstakingly hand-knotted by 60 weavers.

Malta and Çadır Pavilions

These two lovely pavilions were built in the reign of Abdül Aziz (1861–76, *see p32*). Both formerly served as prisons but are now open as cafés. Malta Pavilion, also a restaurant, has a superb view and on Sunday

VISITORS' CHECKLIST

Practical Information
Çırağan Cad, Beşiktaş. **Map** 9 D2.
Yıldız Palace: **Tel** (0212) 258 30 80.
Open 9:30am–4pm Wed–Sun.
Şale Pavilion: **Tel** (0212) 259 45 70. **Open** 9:30am–4:30pm.
Closed Mon & Thu. Malta & Çadır Pavilions: **Tel** (0212) 258 94 53. **Open** 9am–9pm daily. (Malta Pavilion until 10:30pm). Imperial Porcelain Factory: **Tel** (0212) 260 23 70. **Open** 9am–noon, 1–4:30pm Mon–Fri.

Transport
25E, 40, 56.

is a haunt for locals wanting to relax and read the newspapers.

Mithat Paşa, reformist and architect of the constitution, was among those imprisoned in Çadır Pavilion, for instigating the murder of Abdül Aziz. Meanwhile, Murat V and his mother were locked away in Malta Pavilion for 27 years after a brief incarceration in Çırağan Palace *(see p125)*.

Façade of Çadır Pavilion, which has now been refurbished as a café

Imperial Porcelain Factory

In 1895 this factory opened to feed the demand of the upper classes for European-style ceramics, with which to decorate their homes. The unusual building was designed to look like a stylized European medieval castle, complete with turrets and portcullis windows.

The original sugar bowls, vases and plates produced here depict idealized scenes of the Bosphorus and other local beauty spots; they can be seen in museums and palaces all over Istanbul. The factory is normally not open to visitors but the mass-produced china of today is on sale in its shop.

Park entrance

PALANGA CADDESİ

...AĞAN CADDESİ

0 metres 250
0 yards 250

Key

Buildings of palace

Park wall/Palace wall

⑤ Naval Museum
Deniz Müzesi

Hayrettin Paşa İskelesi Sok, Beşiktaş.
Map 8 B4. **Tel** (0212) 261 00 40. 🚌 25E,
28, 40, 56. **Open** 9am–5pm Tue–Sun.
📷 🅿 🌐 denizmuzeleri.tsk.tr

The Naval Museum, reopened
in 2013 in a new, state-of-the-
art building, is well worth a visit.
The main exhibition space is
devoted to a series of beautifully restored caïques, the
elegant imperial rowing boats
used to take the sultans and
their entourages up and down
the Bosphorus. The largest, at 40
m (130 ft), was used by Mehmet
IV and required 144 oarsmen.
The floor below has wood-
carving in the
Ottoman navy as
its theme, with
stunning
examples
of ships'
figureheads
gleaming with
gilt. There is a
small kids' section,
a café and fine
Bosphorus views
from the large
plate-glass windows.

**Rowing boat
used by Atatürk**

⑥ National Palaces Painting Museum
Milli Saraylar Resim Müzesi

Hayrettin Paşa İskelesi Sok, Beşiktaş.
Map 8 B4. **Tel** (0212) 261 42 98.
🚌 25E, 28, 40, 56. **Open** 9am–
5pm Tue, Wed, Fri–Sun.
🌐 millisaraylar.gov.tr

This building adjacent to
Dolmabahçe Palace *(see pp130–
31)* houses a fine collection of
19th- and 20th-century paintings
and sculpture. In the 1800s, the
westernization of the Ottoman
Empire *(see pp32–3)* led
artists such as Osman Hamdi
Bey (1842–1910, *see p64*) to
experiment with Western-style
painting. While their styles rely
heavily on European art forms,
the subject matter of their work
gives a glimpse into the Oriental
history of the city. Look out
for *Woman with Mimosas,
Portrait of a Young Girl* and
Man with a Yellow Robe, all

Woman with Mimosas by Osman Hamdi
Bey, National Palaces Painting Museum

by Osman Hamdi Bey, *Sultan
Ahmet Mosque* by Ahmet Ziya
Akbulut (1869–1938), and
Âşık, a statue of a poet by
İsa Behzat (1867–1944).

⑦ Dolmabahçe Palace

See pp130–31.

⑧ Palace Collections Museum
Saray Koleksiyonları Müzesi

Barbaros Hayrettin Paşa İskelesi Sok,
Beşiktaş. **Map** 8 B4. **Tel** (0212) 236 90
00. 🚌 25E, 40. 🚋 Kabataş. **Open** 9am–
5pm Tue–Sun. 🌐 millisaraylar.gov.tr

Located in the impressive former
kitchens of the Dolmabahçe
Palace, this museum offers an
insight into the domestic life
of the palace. There are over
43,000 objects on display,
including toys once played with
by future sultans, calligraphy
tools, Singer sewing machines
and Limoges porcelain wares.

⑨ Dolmabahçe Mosque
Dolmabahçe Camii

Meclis-i Mebusan Cad, Kabataş.
Map 8 A5. 🚋 Kabataş. 🚌 25E, 40.
Open daily.

Completed at the same time
as Dolmabahçe Palace, in 1853,
the mosque standing beside it
was also built by the wealthy
Balyan family. Its slim minarets
were constructed in the form of
Corinthian columns, while great
arching windows lighten the
interior. Inside, the decoration
includes fake marbling
and *trompe l'oeil*.

⑩ Military Museum
Harbiye Askeri Müzesi

Vali Konağı Cad, Harbiye. **Map** 7 F1.
Tel (0212) 233 27 20. 🚌 46H.
🚇 Osmanbey. **Open** 9am–5pm
Wed–Sun. Mehter Band performances:
3–4pm Wed–Sun. 📷 🅿

This impressive museum traces
the history of Turkey's conflicts
from the conquest of Constantinople in 1453 *(see p28)*
through to modern warfare. The
building used to be the military
academy where Atatürk studied
from 1899 to 1905. His classroom
has been preserved as it was.
  The museum is also the main
venue for performances by the
Mehter Band, which was formed
in the 14th-century during the
reign of Osman I *(see p27)*. Until
the 19th century, the band's
members were Janissaries, who
would accompany the sultan
into battle and perform songs

Dolmabahçe Mosque, a landmark on the Bosphorus shoreline

about Ottoman hero-ancestors and battle victories.

Some of the most striking weapons on display on the ground floor are the curved daggers *(cembiyes)* carried by foot soldiers in the 15th century. These are decorated with plant and geometric motifs in relief and silver filigree. Other exhibits are 17th-century copper head armour for horses, and Ottoman shields made from cane and willow covered in silk thread. A moving portrayal of trench warfare, commissioned in 1995, is included in the section concerned with the ANZAC landings of 1915 at Chunuk Bair on the Gallipoli peninsula *(see p32)*.

Upstairs, the most spectacular of all the exhibits are the tents used by sultans on their campaigns. They are made of silk and wool with embroidered decoration.

⓫ Santralistanbul Museum of Energy

Kazim Karabekir Cad 1, Eyüp. **Tel** (0212) 311 78 78. 🚌 47; also free shuttle every 30 minutes from Kabataş ferry port. **Open** 10am–6pm Tue–Fri, 10am–8pm Sat & Sun. 🆆 santralistanbul.org

Housed in the first power station built in the city, the museum has preserved the plant's working parts and control centre. It also has a few interactive features for inquisitive children.

⓬ Aynalı Kavak Palace
Aynalı Kavak Kasrı

Kasımpaşa Cad, Hasköy. **Map** 6 A3. **Tel** (0212) 250 40 94. 🚌 47, 54. **Open** 9:30am–4pm. **Closed** Mon & Thu. 🖼

This is the last vestige of a large Ottoman palace complex on the once lovely Golden Horn *(see p91)*. Originally it stood in extensive gardens covering an area of 7,000 sq m (75,300 sq ft). Inscriptions dated 1791 can be found all over the palace, but it is thought to have been built earlier by Ahmet III during the Tulip Period *(see p29)*, because of traces around the building of an older style of architecture.

The palace is built on a hill and as a result has two storeys on the southwest side and a single storey to the northeast. It retains some beautiful Ottoman features. These include the upper windows on the southwest façade, which are decorated with stained glass set in curvilinear stucco tracery. Particularly striking is the composition room, which Sultan Selim III (1789–1807) is thought to have used for writing music.

The audience chamber is adorned with an inscription in gold on blue which describes the activities of Selim III while he stayed at the palace.

There is also an exhibition of archaic Turkish musical instruments, in honour of Selim III,

who contributed a great deal to Turkish classical music. In summer, concerts of classical Turkish music are held here.

⓭ Miniatürk

İmrahor Caddesi, Sütlüce. **Tel** (0212) 222 28 82. 🚌 47, 47C, 47E, 54HT. 🆆 miniaturk.com.tr

This well-planned attraction on the banks of the Golden Horn is home to more than a hundred 1:25 scale models of major sights in Turkey. These include 45 places from Istanbul, ranging from the Haghia Sophia to the Atatürk International Airport.

Audience chamber of Aynalı Kavak Palace on the Golden Horn

⓮ Rahmi M Koç Museum
Rahmi M Koç Müzesi

Hasköy Cad 27, Eyüp. **Tel** (0212) 369 66 00. 🚌 47. **Open** Apr–Sep: 10am–7pm Tue–Fri (till 8pm Sat & Sun); Oct–Mar: 10am–5pm Tue–Fri (till 6pm Sat & Sun). 🖼

This old 19th-century factory, which once produced anchors and chains, now houses an eclectic collection named after its industrialist founder, Rahmi M Koç. The building itself, with its four small domes, vaulted passageways and original wooden fittings, is a highlight.

The theme of the industrial age loosely connects exhibitions on aviation, transport, steam engines and scientific instruments. Exhibits range from mechanical toys and scale models of machinery to an entire recreated ship's bridge. Two fine restaurants are located on the premises.

Janissaries

The Janissary (New Army) corps was formed in the 14th century to serve as the sultan's elite fighting force. Its ranks were filled by *devşirme*, the levy of Christian youths brought to Istanbul to serve the sultan. A highly professional and strong army, it was instrumental in the early expansion of the Ottoman Empire and, as well as a fighting force, it acted as the sultan's personal guard. However, discipline eventually began to weaken, and by 1800 the Janissaries had become a destabilizing element in society. They mutinied and overthrew many sultans until their final demise under Mahmut II in 1826 *(see p32)*.

Janissaries depicted in a 16th-century miniature

Dolmabahçe Palace
Dolmabahçe Sarayı

Sultan Abdül Mecit *(see p35)* built Dolmabahçe Palace in 1856. As its designers he employed Karabet Balyan and his son Nikoğos, members of the great family of Armenian architects who lined the Bosphorus *(see pp138–51)* with many of their creations in the 19th century. The extravagant opulence of the Dolmabahçe belies the fact that it was built when the Ottoman Empire was in decline. The sultan financed his great palace with loans from foreign banks. The palace can only be visited on a guided tour, of which two are on offer. The best tour takes you through the Selamlık (or Mabeyn-i Hümayun), the part of the palace that was reserved for men and which contains the state rooms and the enormous Ceremonial Hall. The other tour goes through the Harem, the living quarters of the sultan and his entourage. If you only want to go on one tour, visit the Selamlık.

★ **Crystal Staircase**
The apparent fragility of this glass staircase stunned observers when it was built. It is constructed in the shape of a double horseshoe, and made from Baccarat crystal and brass with a polished mahogany rail.

Imperial Gate
Once used only by the sultan and his ministers, this gate is now the main entrance to the palace. The Mehter, or Janissary, Band *(see p129)* performs in front of the gate every Tuesday afternoon throughout the summer.

Entrance

Swan Fountain
This fountain stands in the Imperial Garden. The original 16th-century garden here was created from recovered land, hence the palace's name, Dolmabahçe, meaning "Filled-in Garden".

★ **Ceremonial Hall**
This magnificent domed hall was designed to hold 2,500 people. Its chandelier, reputedly the heaviest in the world, was bought in England.

VISITORS' CHECKLIST

Practical Information
Dolmabahçe Cad, Beşiktaş.
Map 8 B4. **Tel** (0212) 236 90 00.
Open 9am–4pm (last adm) Tue,
Wed & Fri–Sun (Oct–Feb: last adm
3pm). **Closed** the first day of
religious festivals. 🎫 🅿 🖵 📷

Transport
🚌 25E, 40.

Blue Salon
On religious feast days the sultan's mother would receive his wives and favourites in the Harem's principal room.

KEY

① **The Red Room** was used by the sultan to receive ambassadors.

② **The Süfera Salon**, where ambassadors waited for an audience with the sultan, is one of the most luxurious rooms in the palace.

③ **Selamlık**

④ **The Zülveçheyn, or Panorama Room**

⑤ **Main shore gate**

⑥ **Reception room of the sultan's mother**

⑦ **Sultan Abdül Aziz's bedroom** had to accommodate a huge bed built especially for the 150-kg (23-stone) amateur wrestler.

⑧ **Atatürk's Bedroom** is part of the palace tour. Atatürk *(see pp32–3)* died in this room at 9:05am on 10 November 1938. All the clocks in the palace, such as this one near the crystal staircase, are stopped at this time.

⑨ **The Rose-coloured salon** was the assembly room of the Harem.

⑩ **Harem**

★ **Main Bathroom**
The walls of this bathroom are revetted in finest Egyptian alabaster, while the taps are solid silver. The brass-framed bathroom windows afford stunning views across the Bosphorus.

The Asian Side

The Asian side of Istanbul comprises the two major suburbs of Üsküdar and Kadıköy, which date from the 7th century BC *(see p21)*. Üsküdar (once known as Scutari after the 12th-century Scutarion Palace which was located opposite Leander's Tower) was the starting point of Byzantine trade routes through Asia. It retained its importance in the Ottoman period and today is renowned for its many classical mosques. Üsküdar can be reached from the European side of the city by either ferry or the Marmaray Metro line.

Regular ferries also link Kadıköy to the European side of the city. It lacks Üsküdar's beautiful Ottoman sights but has a lively market area, some excellent restaurants and a vibrant nightlife.

The distinctive Leander's Tower, on its own small island

❷ Şemsi Paşa Mosque
Şemsi Paşa Camii

Sahil Yolu, Üsküdar. **Map** 10 A2.
🚇 Üsküdar. 🚢 Üsküdar. **Open** daily.

This is one of the smallest mosques to be commissioned by a grand vizier *(see p31)*. Its miniature dimensions combined with its picturesque waterfront location make it one of the most attractive mosques in the city.

Şemsi Ahmet Paşa succeeded Sokollu Mehmet Paşa *(see p84)* as grand vizier, and may have been involved in his murder. Sinan *(see p93)* built this mosque for him in 1580.

The garden, which overlooks the Bosphorus, is surrounded on two sides by the *medrese* *(see p40)*, with the mosque on the third side and the sea wall on the fourth. The mosque itself is unusual in that the tomb of Şemsi Ahmet is joined to the main building, divided from the interior by a grille.

Sights at a Glance

① Leander's Tower
② Şemsi Paşa Mosque
③ Mihrimah Sultan Mosque
④ Yeni Valide Mosque
⑤ Atik Valide Mosque
⑥ Tiled Mosque
⑦ Karacaahmet Cemetery
⑧ Selimiye Barracks
⑨ Haydarpaşa Station
⑩ Big Pine Hill

Key
━━━ Main road
═══ Other road

0 kilometres   1
0 miles   1

---

❶ Leander's Tower
Kız Kulesi

Üsküdar. **Map** 10 A3. **Tel** (0216) 342 47 47. 🚢 Üsküdar.
🌐 kizkulesi.com.tr

Located offshore from Üsküdar, the tiny, white Leander's Tower is a well-known Bosphorus landmark. The islet on which this 18th-century tower stands was the site of a 12th-century Byzantine fortress built by Manuel I Comnenus.

The tower has served as a quarantine centre during a cholera outbreak, a lighthouse, a customs control point and a maritime toll gate. It is now a restaurant and nightclub.

The tower is known in Turkish as the "Maiden's Tower" after a legendary princess, said to have been confined here after a prophet foretold that she would die from a snakebite. The snake duly appeared from a basket of figs and struck the fatal blow. The English name of the tower derives from the Greek myth of Leander, who swam the Hellespont (the modern-day Dardanelles, *see p172*) to see his lover Hero.

Şemsi Paşa Mosque, built by Sinan for Grand Vizier Şemsi Ahmet Paşa

❸ Mihrimah Sultan Mosque
Mihrimah Sultan Camii

Hakimiyeti Milliye Cad, Üsküdar.
Map 10 B2. 🚇 Üsküdar. ⛴ Üsküdar.
Open daily.

One of Üsküdar's most prominent landmarks, the Mihrimah Sultan Mosque (also known as İskele Mosque), is named after the daughter of Süleyman the Magnificent and wife of Grand Vizier Rüstem Paşa (see p90). A massive structure on a raised platform, it was built by Sinan between 1547 and 1548.

Without space to build a courtyard, Sinan constructed a large protruding roof which extends to cover the şadırvan (ablutions fountain) in front of the mosque. The porch and interior are rather gloomy as a result. This raised portico is an excellent place from which to look down on the main square below, in which stands the Baroque Fountain of Ahmet III, built in 1726.

Fountain set into the platform below the Mihrimah Sultan Mosque

❹ Yeni Valide Mosque
Yeni Valide Camii

Hakimiyeti Milliye Cad, Üsküdar.
Map 10 B2. 🚇 Üsküdar. ⛴ Üsküdar.
Open daily.

Across the main square from Mihrimah Sultan Mosque, the Yeni Valide Mosque, or New Mosque of the Sultan's Mother, was built by Ahmet III between

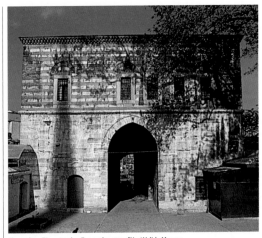

The *mektep* (Koranic school) over the gate of Yeni Valide Mosque

1708 and 1710 to honour his mother, Gülnuş Emetullah. The complex is entered through a large gateway, with the *mektep* (Koranic school) built above it. This leads into a spacious courtyard. The buildings in the complex date from an important turning point in Ottoman architecture. The mosque is in the classical style, yet there are Baroque embellishments on the tomb of the Valide Sultan, the neighbouring *sebil* (kiosk from which drinks were served), and the *şadırvan*.

❺ Atik Valide Mosque
Atik Valide Camii

Çinili Camii Sok, Üsküdar. **Map** 10 C3.
🚌 12C (from Üsküdar). **Open** prayer times only.

The Atik Valide Mosque, set on the hill above Üsküdar, was among Istanbul's most extensive mosque complexes. Translated as the Old Mosque of the Sultan's Mother, the mosque was built for Nur Banu, the Venetian-born wife of Selim II ("the Sot") and the mother of Murat III. She was the first of the sultans' mothers to rule the Ottoman Empire from the harem (see p29).

Dome in the entrance to Atik Valide Mosque

Sinan completed the mosque, which was his last major work, in 1583. It has a wide shallow dome which rests on five semidomes, with a flat arch over the entrance portal.

The interior is surrounded on three sides by galleries, the undersides of which retain the rich black, red and gold stencilling typical of the period. The mihrab apse is almost completely covered with panels of fine İznik tiles (see p163), while the mihrab itself and the *minbar* are both made of beautifully carved marble. Side aisles were added to the north and south in the 17th century, while the grilles and architectural *trompe l'oeil* paintings on the royal loge in the western gallery date from the 18th century.

Outside, a door in the north wall of the courtyard leads down a flight of stairs to the *medrese*, where the *dershane* (classroom) projects out over the street below, supported by an arch. Of the other buildings in the complex, the *şifahane* (hospital) is the only one which has been restored and is open to the public. Located just to the east of the mosque, it consists of 40 cells around a courtyard and was in use well into the 20th century.

Women attending an Islamic class in the Tiled Mosque

❻ Tiled Mosque
Çinili Camii

Çinili Camii Sok, Üsküdar. **Map** 10 C3. 🚌 Üsküdar, then 20 mins walk.
Open prayer times only.

This pretty little mosque is best known for the fine tiles from which it takes its name. It dates from 1640 and is noticeably smaller than other royal foundations of the 17th century. This is partly because by the middle of the century much of Istanbul's prime land had already been built on, and the size of the plot did not allow for a larger building. There was also a trend away from endowing yet more enormous mosque complexes in the city.

The mosque was founded by Mahpeyker Kösem Sultan. As the wife of Sultan Ahmet I (see p35), and mother of sultans Murat IV and İbrahim the Mad, she wielded great influence. Indeed, she was one of the last of the powerful harem women (see p29).

In the courtyard is a massive, roofed ablutions fountain. The adjacent medrese (see p40), however, is tiny. The façade and interior of the mosque are covered with İznik tiles (see p163) in turquoise, white, grey and a range of blues. There are none of the red and green pigments associated with the heyday of İznik tile production, but the designs are still exquisite. Even the conical cap of the marble minbar is tiled, and the carving on the minbar itself is picked out in green, red and gold paint.

The mosque's Turkish bath is on Çinili Hamam Sokağı. It has been renovated and is used by local residents.

❼ Karacaahmet Cemetery
Karacaahmet Mezarlığı

Nuh Kuyusu Cad, Selimiye.
Map 10 C4. 🚌 12. **Open** daily.
Tomb: **Open** daily.

Sprawling over a large area, this cemetery is a pleasant place in which to stroll among old cypress trees and look at ancient tombstones. The earliest dated stone is from 1521, although the cemetery itself, one of the largest in Turkey, is thought to date from 1338.

The carvings on each tombstone tell a story (see p123). A man's tomb is indicated by a fez or a turban. The style of the turban denotes the status of the deceased. Women's stones are adorned with carved flowers, hats and shawls.

Standing on the corner of Gündoğumu Caddesi and Nuh Kuyusu Caddesi is the tomb of Karaca Ahmet himself. This warrior died fighting in the Turkish conquest of the Byzantine towns of Chrysopolis and Chalcedon (Üsküdar and Kadıköy) in the mid-14th century. The tomb and monument to his favourite horse date from the 19th century.

Crimean War memorial in the British War Cemetery

❽ Selimiye Barracks
Selimiye Kışlası

Çeşme-i Kebir Cad, Selimiye. **Map** 10 B5. **Tel** (0216) 343 73 10. 🚌 Harem. 🚌 12. **Open** 9am–5pm Sat.

The Selimiye Barracks were originally built by Selim III in 1799 to house his New Army, with which he hoped to replace the Janissaries (see p129). He failed in his attempt, and was deposed and killed in a Janissary insurrection in 1807–8 (see p32). The barracks burnt down shortly afterwards. The present building, which dominates the skyline of the Asian shore, was started by Mahmut II in 1828, after he had finally disbanded the Janissary corps. Abdül Mecit I added three more wings between 1842 and 1853.

The barracks were used as a military hospital during the Crimean War (1853–6). They became famously associated with Florence Nightingale, who lived and worked in the northeast tower from 1854. The rooms she occupied are now a museum, and are the only part of the barracks open to the public. They contain their original furniture and the lamp from which she gained the epitaph "Lady of the Lamp". Visits must be arranged well in advance by faxing 0216 333 10 09.

Two other sites near the barracks – the Selimiye Mosque

Visitor praying at the tomb of the warrior Karaca Ahmet

Haydarpaşa Station, terminus for trains arriving from Anatolia

built. Haydarpaşa, the grandest of these, was completed in 1908. Trains run from Haydarpaşa into the rest of Asia.

⓾ Big Pine Hill
Büyük Çamlıca

Çamlıca. 🚌 11F, KÇ1; then 30 mins walk. Park: **Open** 9am–11pm daily.

On a clear day the view from the top of this hill takes in the Princes' Islands, the Sea of Marmara, the Golden Horn and Beyoğlu, and the Bosphorus as far as the Black Sea. It is even possible to see snow-capped Mount Uludağ near Bursa *(see p171)* to the south. Big Pine Hill, 4 km (2.5 miles) east of Üsküdar, is the highest point in Istanbul, at 261 m (856 ft) above sea level. Even the forest of radio and TV masts further down the slopes of the hill does not obscure the view.

The park at the summit, which was created by the Turkish Touring and Automobile Club *(see p245)* in 1980, is laid out with gardens, marble kiosks and two 18th-century-style cafés.

The park might lose some of its character if plans to build a gigantic, mock Ottoman mosque atop it reach fruition.

and the British War Cemetery – are both worth seeing. Built in 1804, the mosque is in a peaceful, if somewhat neglected, garden courtyard. The interior is filled with light from tiers of windows set in high arches. It is simply decorated with a classically painted dome and grey marble *minbar*. The royal pavilion in the northwest corner of the compound is flanked by graceful arches.

The British War Cemetery is a short walk south, on Burhan Felek Caddesi. It contains the graves of men who died in the Crimean War, in World War I at Gallipoli *(see p172)* and in World War II in the Middle East. There is no sign outside and opening hours vary, but the caretaker will usually be there to let you in.

⓽ Haydarpaşa Station
Haydarpaşa Garı

Haydarpaşa İstasyon Cad, Haydarpaşa. 🚢 Haydarpaşa or Kadıköy. **Open** daily.

The waterfront location and grandeur of Haydarpaşa Station, together with the neighbouring tiled jetty, made it an impressive point of arrival or departure in Istanbul. Its importance has, however, diminished with the introduction of the Marmaray Metro line and it is likely to become a luxury hotel or shopping mall in the near future. The first Anatolian railway line, which was built in 1873, ran

from here to İznik *(see p162)*. The extension of this railway was a major part of Abdül Hamit II's drive to modernize the Ottoman Empire. Lacking sufficient funds to continue the project, he applied for help to his German ally, Kaiser Wilhelm II. The Deutsche Bank agreed to invest in the construction and operation of the railway. In 1898 German engineers were contracted to build the new railway lines running across Anatolia and beyond into the far reaches of the Ottoman Empire. At the same time a number of stations were

Florence Nightingale

A 19th-century painting of Florence Nightingale in Selimiye Barracks

The British nurse Florence Nightingale (1820–1910) was a tireless campaigner for hospital, military and social reform. During the Crimean War, in which Britain and France fought on the Ottoman side against the Russian Empire, she organized a party of 38 British nurses. They took charge of medical services at the Selimiye Barracks in Scutari (Üsküdar) in 1854. By the time she returned to Britain in 1856, at the end of the war, the mortality rate in the barracks had decreased from 20 to 2 percent, and the fundamental principles of modern nursing had been established. On her return home, Florence Nightingale opened a training school for nurses.

BEYOND ISTANBUL

THE BOSPHORUS

If the noise and bustle of the city get too much, nothing can beat a trip up the Bosphorus *(see pp146–51)*, the straits separating Europe and Asia, which join the Black Sea and the Sea of Marmara. The easiest way to travel is by boat. An alternative is to explore the sights along the shores at your own pace. For much of their length the shores are lined with handsome buildings: wooden waterside villas known as yalıs, graceful mosques and opulent 19th-century palaces. The grander residences along the Bosphorus have

waterfront entrances. These date from the days when wooden caïques, boats powered by a strong team of oarsmen, were a popular form of transport along the straits among the city's wealthier inhabitants. Interspersed between the monumental architecture are former fishing villages, where you will find some of Istanbul's finest clubs and restaurants. The Bosphorus is especially popular in summer, when the cool breezes off the water provide welcome relief from the heat of the city.

Sights at a Glance

Museums, Galleries and Palaces

- ❷ Beylerbeyi Palace
- ❹ Küçüksu Palace
- ❺ Aşiyan Museum
- ❼ Borusan Contemporary
- ❿ Sakıp Sabancı Museum
- ⓫ Maslak Pavilions
- ⓬ Khedive's Palace
- ⓮ Sadberk Hanım Museum

Towns and Villages

- ❸ Bebek
- ❽ Kanlıca
- ⓭ Beykoz
- ⓯ Rumeli Kavağı

Historic Buildings

- ❶ Bosphorus Bridge
- ❻ Fortress of Europe

Parks

- ❾ Emirgan Park

Key

- ▓ Central Istanbul
- ░ Greater Istanbul
- ▬ Motorway
- ▭ Main road

The Bosphorus Trip

This vital navigational channel is 30 km (19 miles) long and varies between 700 m (2,300 ft) and 3.6 km (2 miles) wide. The trip has been divided into three stages, indicated by the boxes on this map.

Black Sea

Kilyos

Rumeli Feneri

Bosphorus Bridge

See pp150–1

See pp148–9

See pp146–7

Sea of Marmara

◀ The imposing Bosphorus Bridge, also known as the Atatürk Bridge

For map symbols *see back flap*

The Bosphorus suspension bridge between Ortaköy and Beylerbeyi

❶ Bosphorus Bridge

Boğaziçi Köprüsü

Ortaköy and Beylerbeyi. **Map** 9 F2.
🚌 40, 200, 202 (double-deckers from Taksim).

Spanning the Bosphorus between the districts of Ortaköy and Beylerbeyi, this was the first bridge to be built across the straits that divide Istanbul. Construction began in February 1970 and finished on 29 October 1973, the 50th anniversary of the inauguration of the Turkish Republic (see p33). It is the world's ninth-longest suspension bridge, at a length of 1,074 m (3,524 ft), and it reaches 64 m (210 ft) above water level.

❷ Beylerbeyi Palace

Beylerbeyi Sarayı

Beylerbeyi Cad, Asian side. **Tel** (0216) 321 93 20. 🚌 15 (from Üsküdar).
🚇 from Üsküdar. **Open** 8:30am–5pm Tue, Wed & Fri–Sun (Oct–Apr until 4pm). 🐾 📷

Designed in the Baroque style by Sarkis Balyan, Beylerbeyi Palace seems fairly restrained compared to the excesses of the earlier Dolmabahçe (see pp130–31) or Küçüksu (see p142) palaces. It was built for Sultan Abdül Aziz (see p32) in 1861 as a summer residence and a place to entertain visiting heads of state. Empress Eugénie of France visited Beylerbeyi on her way to the opening of the Suez Canal in 1869 and had her face slapped by the sultan's

mother for daring to enter the palace on the arm of Abdül Aziz. Other regal visitors to the palace included the Duke and Duchess of Windsor.

The palace looks its most attractive from the Bosphorus, from where its two bathing pavilions – one for the harem and the other for the selamlık (the men's quarters) – can best be seen.

The most attractive room is the reception hall, which has a pool and fountain. Running water was popular in Ottoman houses for its pleasant sound and cooling effect in the heat.

Egyptian straw matting is used on the floor as a form of insulation. The pretty crystal chandeliers are mostly Bohemian and the carpets (see pp218–19)

Detail of the gate of the Egyptian Consulate, Bebek

Landing at the top of the stairs in Beylerbeyi Palace

are from Hereke. Despite her initial reception, Empress Eugénie of France was so delighted by the elegance of the palace that she had a copy of the window in the guest room made for her bedroom in Tuileries Palace, in Paris.

❸ Bebek

European side. 🚌 25E, 40.

Bebek is one of the most fashionable villages along the Bosphorus. It is famous for its marzipan (badem ezmesi, see p213), and for the cafés which line its waterfront. It was once a favourite location for summer residences and palaces of Ottoman aristocrats, and at the end of the 19th century, caïques (see p128) of merry-makers would sail off on moonlit cruises from the bay, accompanied by a boat of musicians. The women in the party would trail pieces of velvet or satin edged with silver fishes in the water behind them while the musicians played to the revellers.

One of the hosts of these parties was the mother of the last Khedive of Egypt (see p31), Abbas Hilmi II. Built in the late 19th century, the only remaining monumental architecture in Bebek is the Egyptian Consulate, which, like the Khedive's Palace (see p144), was commissioned by Abbas Hilmi II. The steep, mansard roof of this yalı is reminiscent of 19th-century northern French architecture. There are lighter Art Nouveau touches including the railings draped in wrought-iron vines and a rising sun between the two turrets, symbolizing the beginning of the new century.

The khedive used the yalı as a summer palace until he was deposed by the British in 1914. From then on to the present day it has been used as the Egyptian Consulate.

Yalıs on the Bosphorus

Old yalı at Kandilli, Asian side

At the end of the 17th century, *paşas*, grand viziers and other distinguished citizens of Ottoman Istanbul began to build themselves elegant villas – yalıs – along the shores of the Bosphorus. These served as summer residences, and the styles employed reflected their owners' prestige. Since then, the yalıs that have been built have become larger and more elaborate, adopting Baroque, Art Nouveau and modern styles of architecture. Most of them still conform to a traditional plan, making maximum use of the waterfront and, inside, having a large sitting room surrounded by bedrooms.

Köprülü Amcazade Hüseyin Paşa Yalı *(see p149)*, near Anadolu Hisarı, was built in 1699 and is the oldest building on the shores of the Bosphorus. Early yalıs, like this one, were built at the water's edge, but in later years they were constructed a little way inland.

A *cumba*, or bay window, projects over the water.

Traditional wooden yalıs were normally painted rust red, a colour known as "Ottoman rose".

Later yalıs, built from the 18th century, were painted in pastel shades.

A bracket supports the projecting upstairs rooms.

Fethi Ahmet Paşa Yalı *(see p147)*, or Mocan Yalı, at Kuzguncuk, was built in the late 18th century. Among visitors were the composer Franz Liszt and the architect Le Corbusier. Famous as the "Pink Yalı", after its boldly decorated exterior, the house is almost invisible from the land.

Baroque influence is clearly visible in the ornately carved balcony.

Ethem Pertev Yalı *(see p149)*, at Kanlıca, is a prime example of the so-called "cosmopolitan period" of yalı building, between 1867 and 1908. It has a boat house below and combines intricate woodcarving, a later development, with the more traditional features of a yalı.

Boat house under the yalı

The Egyptian Consulate *(see p148)* at Bebek clearly shows the influence of Art Nouveau, with its wrought-iron railings worked into a leaf design. It was commissioned by the Khedive of Egypt *(see p140)* in around 1900.

A narrow quay often separates 19th-century yalıs from the shore.

French-style mansard roof

Ornamental details were inspired by Austrian Art Nouveau designs.

❹ Küçüksu Palace
Küçüksu Kasrı

Küçüksu Sahili–Anadoluhisarı Beykoz,
Asian side. **Tel** (0216) 332 02 37. 🚌 15
(from Üsküdar) or 101 (from Beşiktaş).
Open 9:30am–5pm Tue, Wed, Fri–Sun
(Oct–Apr until 4pm).

Marble-fronted Küçüksu Palace
has one of the prettiest façades
on the shores of the Bosphorus.
Sultan Abdül Mecit I *(see p32)*
employed court architect
Nikoğos Balyan *(see p130)* to
build this palace to accommodate his entourage on their
visits to the Sweet Waters of
Asia. This was the romantic name
European visitors gave to the
Küçüksu and Göksu rivers. For
centuries the Ottoman nobility
liked to indulge in picnics in the
meadows between the streams.
On the completion of Küçüksu
Palace in 1856, the sultan
complained that it was too plain
and demanded more ornamentation, including his monogram
engraved on the façade. Later,
in the reign of Abdül Aziz *(see
p32)*, the façade was further
embellished, with the result
that it is hard to follow the lines
of the original architecture.
The room arrangement is
typically Ottoman, with a large
central salon opening on to
four corner rooms on each floor.
The interior decor was carried
out by Séchan, the decorator
of the Paris Opera, soon after
the palace was finished. The
carpets are fine examples from
Hereke *(see pp218–19)* and the
chandeliers Bohemian crystal.
On the shore near Küçüksu
Palace is the picturesque,
turreted Fountain of the Valide
Sultan Mihrişah. Dating from
1796, it is in the Baroque style.

Küçüksu Palace, an ornate Bosphorus residence built in 1856

Kıbrıslı Yalı, just south of the
palace, was built in 1760. At over
60 m (200 ft), its brilliant white
façade is the longest of any yalı
(see p141) along the Bosphorus.
A little further south again is
Kırmızı Yalı, the Red Yalı, which
is so called for its distinctive
crimson colour and was built
for one of Sultan Mahmut II's
gardens in the 1830s.

❺ Aşiyan Museum
Aşiyan Müzesi

Aşiyan Yolu, Bebek, European side.
Tel (0212) 263 69 86. 🚌 25E, 40.
Open 9am–4pm Tue–Sat.

Aşiyan, or bird's nest, is the
former home of Tevfik Fikret
(1867–1915), a teacher,
utopian visionary and one
of Turkey's leading poets.
The wooden mansion, built
by Fikret himself in 1906, is an
attractive example of Turkish
vernacular architecture. The
views from its upper-storey
balcony are stunning.
On show are the poet's
possessions and *Sis* (Fog), a
painting by Caliph Abdül
Mecit (1922–24), inspired by
Fikret's poem of that name.

❻ Fortress of Europe
Rumeli Hisarı

Yahya Kemal Cad, European side.
Tel (0212) 263 53 05. 🚌 25E, 40.
Open 9:30am–4:30pm Thu–Tue. 📷

This fortress was built by
Mehmet the Conqueror in 1452
as his first step in the conquest
of Constantinople *(see p28)*.
Situated at the narrowest point
of the Bosphorus, the fortress
controlled a major Byzantine
supply route. Across the straits
is Anadolu Hisarı, or the Fortress
of Asia, which was built in the
14th century by Beyazıt I.
The Fortress of Europe's layout
was planned by Mehmet himself.
While his grand vizier *(see p31)*
and two other viziers were each
responsible for the building of
one of the three great towers,
the sultan took charge of the
walls. In the spirit of competition
which evolved, the fortress was
completed in four months.
The new fortress was soon
nicknamed Boğazkesen –
meaning "Throat-cutter" or
"Strait-cutter". It was garrisoned
by a force of Janissaries *(see
p129)*. These troops trained
their cannons on the straits to
prevent the passage of foreign

The Fortress of Europe, built by Mehmet the Conqueror to enable him to capture Constantinople ships. After they had sunk a Venetian vessel, this approach to Constantinople was cut off. Following the conquest of the city, the fortress lost its importance as a military base and was used as a prison, particularly for out-of-favour foreign envoys and prisoners of war.

The structure was restored in 1953. Open-air theatre performances are now staged here during the Istanbul Music Festival (see p47).

❼ Borusan Contemporary

Perili Köşk, Hisar Cad 5.
Tel (0212) 393 52 00. 🚌 22, 25E, 40.
Open 10am–8pm Sat & Sun.
🌐 borusancontemporary.com

This early 20th-century mansion block faces the Bosphorus and serves as the headquarters for Borusan Holdings on weekdays. During the weekend, it transforms into one of the city's best contemporary art spaces. The sculpture-studded rooftop provides spectacular views of the Second Bosphorus Bridge and Fortress of Europe.

❽ Kanlıca

Asian side. 🚌 15, 101.

A delicious, creamy type of yogurt is Kanlıca's best-known asset. The İskender Paşa Mosque, overlooking the village square, is a minor work by Sinan (see p93), built for Sultan Süleyman's vizier İskender Paşa in 1559–60. There have been changes to the original building: the wooden dome has been replaced by a flat roof, and the porch was added later.

There are a number of yalıs in and around Kanlıca, including the Köprülü Amcazade Hüseyin Paşa Yalı (see p141), the oldest surviving Bosphorus yalı, just south of the village. This was built in 1698 by Mustafa II's grand vizier Hüseyin Paşa, the fourth grand vizier from the Köprülü family. The Treaty of Karlowitz, in which the Ottomans acknowledged the loss of territory to

Austria, Venice, Poland and Russia, was signed here in 1699 (see p29). All that remains of the yalı, which is not open to visitors, is a T-shaped salon, its dome only saved by wooden props.

❾ Emirgan Park
Emirgan Parkı

Emirgan Sahil Yolu, European side.
Tel (0212) 277 57 82. 🚌 25E, 40.
Open 7am–10:30pm daily.
🚗 for vehicles.

Emirgan Park is the location of some famous tulip gardens, which are at their finest for the annual Tulip Festival in April (see p46). Tulips originally grew wild on the Asian steppes and were first propagated in large quantities in Holland. They were later reintroduced to Turkey by Mehmet IV (1648–87). The reign of his son Ahmet III is known as the Tulip Period (see p29) due to his fascination with the flowers.

In the late 19th century Sultan Abdül Aziz gave the park to the Egyptian Khedive (see p31), İsmail Paşa, and its three pavilions date from that era. They are known by their colours. The Sarı Köşk (Yellow Pavilion), built in the style of a Swiss chalet, suffered fire damage in 1954 and was re-built in concrete with a façade resembling the original. The Beyaz Köşk (White Pavilion) is a Neo-Classical style mansion, while the Pembe Köşk (Pink Pavilion) is in the style of a traditional Ottoman house. All three are now cafés.

Pretty tulips at Pembe Köşk in Emirgan Park

❿ Sakıp Sabancı Museum
Sakıp Sabancı Müzesi

İstinye Cad 22, Emirgan 34467.
Tel (0212) 229 55 18. 🚌 40, 41 from Taksim Sq; any bus to İstinye or Sarıyer.
Open 10am–5pm Tue, Thu, Fri; 10am–7pm Wed & Sat; noon–5pm Sun. **Closed** 1 Jan, 1st day of religious hols. 🎫 🔲 🔲 🔲 🔲
🌐 muze.sabanciuniv.edu

With a superb view over the Bosphorus, the Sakıp Sabancı Museum is also known as the Horse Mansion (Atlı Köşk). Exhibitions comprise over 400 years of Ottoman calligraphy and other Koranic and secular art treasures. The collection of paintings is exquisite, with works by Ottoman court painters and European artists enthralled with Turkey. It hosts some of the city's most prestigious art and culture exhibitions. The works of Picasso and Dali have been showcased here. The museum also houses the Muze de Changa restaurant.

Birds of the Bosphorus

In September and October, thousands of white storks and birds of prey fly over the Bosphorus on their way from their breeding grounds in eastern Europe to wintering regions in Africa. Large birds usually prefer to cross narrow straits like the Bosphorus rather than fly over an expanse of open water such as the Mediterranean. Among birds of prey on this route you can see the lesser spotted eagle and the honey buzzard. The birds also cross the straits in spring on their way to Europe but, before the breeding season, they are fewer in number.

The white stork, which migrates over the straits

Hot-house plants in the conservatory at Maslak Pavilions

⓫ Maslak Pavilions

Maslak Kasırları

Büyükdere Cad, Maslak. **Tel** (0212) 346 19 07. 📻 40S (from Taksim). **Open** 9:30am–5pm Tue, Wed & Fri–Sun (Nov–Feb until 4pm).

This small group of buildings was a royal hunting lodge and country residence, much prized for its glorious views. The pavilions were built in the early and mid-19th century, when the focus of Istanbul court life moved away from Topkapı Palace *(see pp56–61)*, in the centre of the city, to the sultans' lavish estates along the shore of the Bosphorus.

The buildings are thought to date mainly from the reign of Abdül Aziz (1861–76). He gave Maslak to his nephew Abdül Hamit in the hope that he would then stop sailing at Tarabya *(see p150)*, which his uncle regarded as unsafe.

The four main buildings are less ornate than other 19th-century pavilions in Istanbul. This is possibly due to the austere character of Abdül Hamit. He personally crafted the balustrades of the beautiful central staircase in the Kasr-ı Hümayun (the Pavilion of the Sultan) during his stay here. His initials in Western script – AH – can also be seen in the

headpieces over the mirrors. The pavilion's lounge retains an Oriental feel, with a low sofa and a central coal-burning brazier.

Behind the small but elegant Mabeyn-i Hümayun (the Private Apartments) is a large conservatory full of camellias, ferns and banana plants. Nearby, at the edge of the forest stands a tiny octagonal folly with an ornate balcony called the Çadır Köşkü, or Tent Pavilion, which now serves as a bookshop.

⓬ Khedive's Palace

Hidiv Kasrı

Hidiv Kasrı Yolu 32, Çubuklu. **Tel** (0216) 413 96 64. 📻 15, 15A, 15P (from Üsküdar) or 221 (from Taksim), then 5 mins' walk from Kanlıca. **Open** 9am–11pm daily (May–Oct: to 10:30pm). 💻 🔲 hidivkasri.com

Built in 1907 by the last khedive (hereditary viceroy of Egypt, *see p31*), Abbas Hilmi II, this summer palace is one of the city's most striking buildings of its era. Its tower is an imposing landmark for those travelling up the Bosphorus.

The Italian architect Delfo Seminati based the design of the palace on an Italianate villa, throwing in Art Nouveau and Ottoman elements. Most impressive of all is the round entrance hall. This is entered through Art Nouveau glass doors and features a stained-glass skylight above a central fountain surrounded by eight pairs of elegant columns.

Renovated by the Turkish Touring Club (TTOK, *see p245*), the palace is now a luxury restaurant.

⓭ Beykoz

Asian shore. 📻 15 (from Üsküdar) or 221 (from Taksim).

Beykoz is famous for its walnuts (*beykoz* means "prince's walnut") and for the glass produced here in the 1800s. The distinctive, mainly opaque,

Jason and the Symplegades

The upper Bosphorus features in the Greek myth of Jason's search for the Golden Fleece. The Argonauts, Jason's crew, helped a local king, Phineus, by ridding him of the harpies (female demons) sent by Zeus to torment him. In return, the king advised them on how to tackle the Symplegades, two rocks at the mouth of the Bosphorus which were reputed to clash together, making passage impossible. His advice was to send a dove in advance of the ship; if it went through safely, so would the ship. This the Argonauts duly did, and the rocks clipped the dove's tail feathers. The Argo then went through with only some damage to its stern.

Jason and the Argonauts making their way through the Symplegades

Fountain in the village square at Beykoz

Beykoz glass *(see p213)*, with its rich colours and graceful designs, can be seen in museums all over Turkey. Nowadays, the village's main attraction is its fish restaurants, which serve excellent turbot.

A fine fountain stands in the central square. Built on the orders of Sultan Mahmut I *(see p35)*, it is called the İshak Ağa Çeşmesi, after the customs inspector who commissioned it in 1746. It has a large domed and colonnaded loggia, and 10 conduits spouting a constant stream of water.

Industrialization, mainly bottling and leather factories, has taken its toll, and only a remaining few buildings hint at the village's former splendour.

⓮ Sadberk Hanım Museum
Sadberk Hanım Müzesi

Piyasa Cad 27–29, Büyükdere.
Tel (0212) 242 38 13. 🚌 25E.
Open 10am–6pm Thu–Tue. 🅿 🖂
🌐 sadberkhanimmuzesi.org.tr

Occupying two archetypal wooden Bosphorus yalıs *(see p141)*, the Sadberk Hanım Museum was the first private museum to open in Turkey, in 1981. The larger of these yalıs,

the Azaryan Yalı, is the former summer house of the wealthy Koç family. A four-storey mansion, it was built in 1911 and, like many buildings of the time, was inspired by European architecture. The distinctive criss-crossed wooden slats on its façade distinguish it from the neighbouring buildings. It contains some fine ethnographic artifacts collected by Sadberk Hanım, wife of the industrialist Vehbi Koç, to whom the museum is dedicated. She found many of them in the Grand Bazaar *(see pp100–101)* and in Istanbul's other markets. A number of exhibits are laid out in tableaux depicting 19th-century Ottoman society. These include a henna party, at which the groom's female relatives would apply henna to the hands of his bride; and a circumcision bed, with a young boy dressed in traditional costume. Also worth seeking out in this section is a display of infinitely delicate *oya*, Turkish embroideries. These remarkably life-like pieces imitate garlands of flowers, such as carnations, roses, hyacinths and lilies and were used to fringe scarves and petticoats. Some of the examples on show were made in palace harems in the 18th century.

Attic vase, Sadberk Hanım Museum

The neighbouring building is called the Sevgi Gönül Wing. Also dating from the early 20th century, it was bought to house the archaeological collection of Hüseyin Kocabaş, a friend of the Koç family. Displays are ordered chronologically, ranging from the late Neolithic period (5400 BC) to the Ottoman era.

Exhibits are changed from time to time, but typically include Assyrian cuneiform tablets dating from the second millennium BC, Phrygian metalwork and Greek pottery from the late Geometric Period (750–680 BC). Among other items are Byzantine reliquary and pendent crosses, and a selection of Roman gold jewellery.

⓯ Rumeli Kavağı

European shore. 🚌 25A (from Beşiktaş). ⛴ Rumeli Kavağı.

This pretty village has a broad selection of restaurants specializing in fish and fried mussels. They are clustered around the harbour from where there are views of the wild, rocky shores on the approach to the Black Sea. On the hill above Rumeli Kavağı are the scant remains of a castle, İmros Kalesi, built by Manuel I Comnenus *(see p23)* in the 12th century to guard his customs point.

Further up the Bosphorus, the shore road leads from Rumeli Kavağı to Altın Kum beach. This small strip of sand backed by restaurants is popular with local people.

The fishing village of Rumeli Kavağı, on the upper Bosphorus

The Bosphorus Trip

One of the great pleasures of a visit to Istanbul is a cruise up the Bosphorus. You can go on a pre-arranged guided tour or take one of the small boats that tout for passengers at Eminönü. But there is no better way to travel than on the official trip run by Istanbul Sea Bus Company (İDO, *see pp242–3*), which is described on the following pages. The İDO Bosphorus Cruise makes a round trip to the upper Bosphorus two or three times daily, stopping at six piers along the way. You can return to Eminönü on the same boat or make your way back by bus, dolmuş or taxi. A 2-hour cruise also departs daily from Eminönü and Üsküdar.

Locator Map

Naval Museum
(see p128)

Dolmabahçe Palace
This opulent 19th-century palace *(see pp130–31)* has a series of ornate gates along the waterfront. These were used by the sultan to enter the palace from his imperial barge.

Barbaros
Hayrettin
Paşa

Beşiktaş FC
Stadium

Kabataş

National Palaces Painting Museum *(see p128)*

View of the City
As the ferry departs, you have a view of many of the old monuments of Istanbul, including Süleymaniye Mosque, seen in this picture.

Dolmabahçe Mosque was completed in 1855, a year before the palace *(see p128)*.

Galata
Bridge

Karaköy

Eminönü

Eminönü Port
The official Bosphorus ferry departs from Istanbul's busiest ferry terminal.

Leander's Tower
One the landmarks of the city, this white tower stands prominently in mid-channel, a short way off the Asian shore *(see p132)*.

See pages 148–9

Key

- ▬ Motorway
- ▬ Main road
- ▬ Other road
- Built-up area
- ▬ ▬ Route of Bosphorus trip

Kuleli Military School has a pretty wooden mosque beside it

Arnavutköy

Mecidiye Mosque
Sultan Abdül Mecit I ordered the construction of this Baroque mosque on a promontory near the ferry pier at Ortaköy (see p124).

Galatasaray Island is a public pool and bar/ restaurant.

Çengelköy

Sadullah Paşa Yalı, built in 1783, is painted red-brown, as are many old yalıs (see p141).

Ortaköy (see p124)

Beylerbeyi

Yıldız Park (see pp126–7)

Bosphorus Bridge (see p140)

Kuzguncuk

Çırağan Palace dates from 1874, but had to be rebuilt after a devastating fire in 1910. It is now a luxury hotel (see p125).

Fethi Ahmet Paşa Yalı (see p141)

Beylerbeyi Palace
The palace grounds contain two shore-side bathing pavilions: one for men and the other for the women of the harem (see p140).

Mihrimah Sultan Mosque (see p133)

Üsküdar

Şemsi Paşa Mosque
The circular windows of this 16th-century mosque by Sinan (see p132) are an allusion to Şemsi Paşa, whose name derives from the word "shams", meaning "sun" in Arabic.

VISITORS' CHECKLIST

Practical Information
Eminönü Pier 3 (Boğaz Hattı).
Map 3 D2. **Tel** (0212) 444 18 51.
Tickets should be purchased at the departure pier.
W sehirhatlari.com.tr

Transport
Eminönü. May–Sep: 10:30am & 1:30pm daily; Oct–Apr: 10:30am daily. Round trip takes 6 hours.

For map symbols see back flap

The Middle Bosphorus

North of Arnavutköy, the outskirts of Istanbul give way to attractive towns and villages, such as Bebek with its bars and cafés. The Bosphorus flows fast and deep as the channel reaches its narrowest point – 700 m (2,300 ft) across – on the approach to the Fatih Sultan Mehmet bridge. It was at this point that the Persian emperor Darius and his army crossed the Bosphorus on a pontoon bridge in 512 BC, on their way to fight the Greeks. Two famous old fortresses face each other across the water near here. Several elegant yalıs are also found in this part of the strait, particularly in the region known to Europeans as the Sweet Waters of Asia.

Locator Map

İstinye Bay
This huge natural bay, the largest inlet on the Bosphorus, has been used as a dock for centuries. There is a fish market along the quay every morning.

Emirgan Park
Situated above the pretty village of Emirgan, this park is famous for its tulips in spring (see p46). The grounds contain pleasant cafés and pavilions (see p143).

The Bosphorus University, one of the most prestigious in Turkey, enjoys spectacular views. Almost all teaching here is in English.

Bebek (see p140)
Egyptian Consulate (see p140)
Kandi

Fortress of Europe
Situated at the narrowest point on the Bosphorus, this fortress (see p142) was built by Mehmet II in 1452, as a prelude to his invasion of Constantinople (see p28).

See pages 146–7

Arnavutköy

See pages 150–51

Yeniköy
Handsome 19th-century villas define the waterfront of this village dating from Byzantine times.

Paşabahçe

Sait Halim Paşa Yalı

Kanlıca is a pretty village (see p143) with a mosque built by Sinan (see p93). It is also known for its delicious yogurt.

İstinye

Çubuklu

Khedive's Palace
Above çubuklu stands the palace built by the last viceroy of Egypt (see p31), Abbas Hilmi Paşa, in around 1900. It is now a hotel and restaurant (see p144).

Kanlıca

Ethem Pertev Yalı (see p141)

Fortress of Asia
Fifty years older than the Fortress of Europe, this fortress was built by Beyazıt I just before the failed Ottoman siege of Constantinople in 1396–7.

tih Sultan ehmet idge

rülü azade eyin Yalı (see 3)

Anadolu Hisarı

üksu ace (see 2)

ı Yalı 142)

Göksu River
This pretty little river and the Küçüksu River south of it are together known as the Sweet Waters of Asia (see p142).

Key

▬ Motorway

▬ Main road

▬ Other road

▦ Built-up area

– – Route of Bosphorus trip

0 metres   750
0 yards   750

For map symbols see back flap

The Upper Bosphorus

In the 19th-century ambassadors to Turkey built their summer retreats between Tarabya and Büyükdere, on the European side of the Bosphorus. As the hills fall more steeply towards the shore along the upper reaches of the straits, the built-up area peters out. There is time to explore and take lunch at Anadolu Kavaği on the Asian side before the boat returns to Eminönü. You can also catch a bus or dolmuş back to the city. The Bosphorus itself continues for 8 km (5 miles) or so to meet the Black Sea, but the land on both sides of this stretch is now under military control.

Locator Map

Sadberk Hanım Museum
This museum, housed in two wooden yalıs, has a variety of interesting exhibits. These include antiquities from Greece and Rome, and Ottoman craftwork (see p145).

Sarıyer

Büyükdere

Tarabya Bay
The small village set within a lovely bay first attracted wealthy Greeks in the 18th century. The bay still thrives as an exclusive resort with upmarket fish restaurants.

Huber Köşkı
a 19th-centu
yalı owned b
the governmer

Fishing on the Bosphorus

A multitude of fishing vessels ply the waters of the Bosphorus, ranging from large trawlers returning from the Black Sea to tiny rowing boats from which a line is cast into the water. On a trip up the Bosphorus you often see seine nets spread out in circles, suspended from floats on the surface. The main types of fish caught are mackerel, mullet, hamsi (similar to anchovy, see p192) and sardine. Much of the fish caught is sold at Istanbul's principal fish market in Kumkapı.

Fishing boats at Sarıyer, the main fishing port on the Bosphorus

Rumeli Kavağı

This village is the most northerly ferry stop on the European side *(see p145)*. From here the Bosphorus widens out to meet the Black Sea.

🚢 Rumeli
    Kavağı

🚢
Anadolu
Kavağı

Anadolu Kavağı

A short climb from this village – the last stop on the trip – brings you to a ruined 14th-century Byzantine fortress, the Genoese Castle, from which there are great views over the straits.

Beykoz

Beykoz is the largest fishing village along the Asian shore. Close to its village square, which has this fountain dating from 1746, are several fish restaurants which are very popular in summer *(see p144)*.

🚢
Beykoz

🕌
Halil
Ethem Yalı
(see p145)

Key

▮▮▮	Main road
▮▮▮	Other road
▦	Built-up area
– –	Route of Bosphorus trip

| 0 metres | 750 |
| 0 yards | 750 |

See pages 148–9

For map symbols *see back flap*

EXCURSIONS FROM ISTANBUL

Standing at a natural crossroads, Istanbul makes a good base for excursions into the neighbouring areas of Thrace and Anatolia – European and Asian Turkey respectively. Whether you want to see great Islamic architecture, immerse yourself in a busy bazaar, relax on an island or in a lakeside town, you will find a choice of destinations within easy reach of the city.

On public holidays and weekends, nearby resorts become crowded with Istanbul residents taking a break from the noisy city. For longer breaks, they head for the Mediterranean or Aegean, so summer is a good time to explore the Marmara and western Black Sea regions while they are quiet.

The country around Istanbul varies immensely from lush forests to open plains and, beyond them, impressive mountains. The Belgrade Forest is one of the closest green areas to the city if you want a short break. The Princes' Islands, where the pine forests and monasteries can be toured by a pleasant ride in a horse and carriage, are also just a short boat trip away from the city. Further away, through rolling fields of bright yellow sunflowers, is Edirne, the former Ottoman capital, famed for its fine mosques, especially the Selimiye.

South of the Sea of Marmara is the pretty spa town of Bursa, originally a Greek city which was founded in 183 BC. The first Ottoman capital, it has some fine architecture. The pretty lakeside town of İznik, a major producer of ceramics in Ottoman times, lies across the Sea of Marmara.

Near the mouth of the straits of the Dardanelles (which link the Sea of Marmara to the Aegean) lie the ruins of the legendary city of Troy, dating from as early as 3600 BC. North of the Dardanelles are cemeteries commemorating the battles which were fought over the Gallipoli peninsula during World War I.

Boats in Burgaz Harbour on the Princes' Islands, a short ferry ride from Istanbul

◀ Yeşil Türbe, also known as the Green Tomb, Bursa

Exploring Beyond Istanbul

Within a radius of 250 km (150 miles) of Istanbul there are many destinations worth visiting. To the northwest is Edirne, an attractive riverside town and the location of several fine mosques. South of Istanbul is Bursa, which lies at the foot of Uludağ, a mountain famed for its skiing. Closer to Istanbul are the Black Sea resorts of Şile, Polonezköy and Kilyos, and the Princes' Islands, which are easily reached by ferry. The war cemeteries of the Dardanelles and the site of ancient Troy require a longer trip.

The 15th-century Beyazıt II Mosque in Edirne

Key

— Motorway

— Main road

⋯ Minor road

— Scenic route

— Main railway

— Minor railway

▬ International border

For map symbols see back flap

Sights at a Glance
1. Edirne pp156–9
2. Kilyos
3. Belgrade Forest
4. Şile
5. Princes' Islands
6. Termal
7. İznik
8. Bursa pp164–70
9. Uludağ National Park
10. Bird Paradise National Park
11. Marmara Islands
12. The Dardanelles
13. Troy

View over the picturesque city of Bursa

Getting Around

The road network around Istanbul is steadily improving, and modern, cheap and efficient coaches (see p244) will get you to most places. Ferries and sea buses (see p244) cross the Sea of Marmara to ports on its southern shore and reach both the Princes' and Marmara Islands.

One of the main ski runs in Uludağ National Park

❶ Edirne

Standing on the river Tunca near the border with Greece, Edirne is a provincial university town which is home to one of Turkey's star attractions, the Selimiye Mosque (see pp158–9). As this huge monument attests, Edirne was historically of great importance. It dates back to AD 125, when the Roman Emperor Hadrian joined two small towns to form Hadrianopolis, or Adrianople. For nearly a century, from when Murat I (see p27) took the city in 1361 until Constantinople was conquered in 1453 (see p28), Edirne was the Ottoman capital. The town has one other claim to fame – the annual grease wrestling championships in June.

Entrance arch, Mosque of the Three Balconies

Entrance to Beyazıt II Mosque viewed from its inner courtyard

◧ Beyazıt II Mosque

Beyazıt II KülliyesiYeniimaret Mah Beyazıt Cad. **Open** daily. Health Museum: **Tel** (0284) 212 09 22. **Open** 9am–5:30pm daily. 🏛 ♿

Beyazıt II Mosque stands in a peaceful location on the northern bank of the Tunca River, 1.5 km (1 mile) from the town centre. It was built in 1484–8, soon after Beyazıt II (see p34) succeeded Mehmet the Conqueror (see p28) as sultan.

The mosque and its courtyards are open to the public. Of the surrounding buildings in the complex, the old hospital, which incorporated an asylum, has been converted into the Health Museum. Disturbed patients were treated in the asylum – a model of its time – with water, colour and flower therapies.

The Turkish writer Evliya Çelebi (1611–84) reported that singers and instrumentalists would play soothing music here three times a week. Overuse of hashish was one of the commonest afflictions. The colonnaded inner mosque courtyard, unlike most later examples, covers three times the area of the mosque itself. Inside, the weight of the impressive dome is supported on sweeping pendentives.

◧ Mosque of the Three Balconies

Üç Şerefeli Camii Hükümet Cad. **Open** daily. 🖂

Until the fall of Constantinople, this was the grandest building in the early Ottoman state. It was finished in 1447 and takes its name from the three balconies adorning its southeast minaret, at the time the tallest in existence. In an unusual touch, the other three minarets of the mosque are each of a different design and height. Unlike its predecessors in Bursa (see pp164–70), the mosque has an open courtyard, setting a precedent for the great imperial mosques of Istanbul. The plan of its interior was also innovative. With minimal obstructions, the mihrab and minbar can both be seen from almost every corner of the prayer hall. Like the minarets, the dome, too, was the largest of its time.

◧ Old Mosque

Eski Cami Talat Paşa Asfaltı. **Open** daily. 🖂

The oldest of Edirne's major mosques, this is a smaller version of the Great Mosque in Bursa (see p166). The eldest son of Beyazıt I (see p34), Süleyman, began the mosque in 1403, but it was his youngest son, Mehmet I, who completed it in 1414.

A perfect square, the mosque is divided by four massive piers into nine domed sections. On either side of the prayer hall entrance there are massive Arabic inscriptions proclaiming "Allah" and "Mohammed".

Grease Wrestling

The Kırkpınar Grease Wrestling Championships take place at the end of June, in Sarayiçi Er Meydanı, a field near Edirne. Established in 1346, the event is famed throughout Turkey. Before competing,

Grease wrestlers parading before they fight

the wrestlers dress in knee-length leather shorts (kispet) and grease themselves from head to foot in diluted olive oil. The master of ceremonies, the cazgır, then invites the competitors to take part in a high-stepping, arm-flinging parade across the field, accompanied by music played on a deep-toned drum (davul) and a single-reed oboe (zurna). Wrestling bouts can last up to 2 hours and involve long periods of frozen, silent concentration interspersed by attempts to throw down the opponent.

🏠 Rüstem Paşa Caravanserai

Rüstem Paşa Kervansarayı
İki Kapılı Han Cad 57.
Tel (0284) 212 61 19.

Sinan *(see p93)* designed this caravanserai for Süleyman's most powerful grand vizier, Rüstem Paşa *(see p90)*, in 1560–61. It was constructed in two distinct parts. The larger courtyard, or han *(see p98)*, which is now the Rüstempaşa Kervansaray Hotel *(see p188)*, was built for the merchants of Edirne, while the smaller court-yard, now a student hostel, was an inn for other travellers.

A short walk away, on the other side of Saraçlar Caddesi, is the Semiz Ali Paşa Bazaar, where Edirne's merchants still sell their wares. This is another work of Sinan, dating from 1589. It consists of a long, narrow street of vaulted shops.

🏛 Museum of Turkish and Islamic Arts

Türk ve İslam Eserleri Müzesi
Kadir Paşa Mektep Sok.
Tel (0284) 225 16 25.
Open 8am–6pm Tue–Sun.

Edirne's small collection of Turkish and Islamic works of art is attractively located in

the *medrese* of the Selimiye Mosque *(see pp158–9)*.
The museum's first room is devoted to the local sport of grease wrestling. It includes enlarged reproductions of miniatures depicting 600 years of the sport. These show the wrestling stars resplendent in their leather shorts, their skin glistening with olive oil.

Other objects on display include the original doors of the Beyazıt II Mosque. There are also military exhibits. Among them are some beautiful 18th-century Ottoman shields, with woven silk exteriors, and paintings of military subjects.

The tranquil 15th-century Muradiye Mosque

🕌 Muradiye Mosque

Muradiye Camii
Küçükpazar Cad.
Open prayer times only.

This mosque was built as a *zaviye* (dervish hospice) in 1421 by Murat II *(see p34)*, who dreamt that the great dervish leader Celaleddin Rumi *(see p107)* asked him to build one in Edirne. Only later was it converted into a mosque. Its interior is notable for its massive inscriptions, similar to those in the Old Mosque, and for some fine early 15th-century İznik tiles *(see p163)*.

Edirne City Centre

① Beyazıt II Mosque
② Mosque of the Three Balconies
③ Old Mosque
④ Rüstem Paşa Caravanserai
⑤ Selimiye Mosque *see pp158–9*
⑥ Museum of Turkish and Islamic Arts
⑦ Muradiye Mosque

Key to symbols *see back flap*

Edirne: Selimiye Mosque

Selimiye Camii

The Selimiye is the greatest of all the Ottoman mosque complexes, the apogee of an art form and the culmination of a lifetime's ambition for its architect, Sinan (see p93). Built on a slight hill, the mosque is a prominent landmark. Its complex includes a medrese (see p40), now housing the Museum of Turkish and Islamic Arts (see p157), a school and the Kavaflar Arasta, a covered bazaar.

Selim II (see p29) commissioned the mosque. It was begun in 1569 and completed in 1575, a year after his death. The dome was Sinan's proudest achievement. In his memoirs, he wrote: "With the help of Allah and the favour of Sultan Selim Khan, I have succeeded in building a cupola six cubits wider and four cubits deeper than that of Haghia Sophia". In fact, the dome is of a diameter comparable to and slightly shallower than that of the building (see pp74–7) Sinan had so longed to surpass.

★ Minarets
The mosque's four slender minarets tower to a height of 84 m (275 ft). Each one has three balconies. The two northern minarets contain three intertwining staircases, each one leading to a different balcony.

KEY

① **The columns** supporting the arches of the courtyard are made of old marble, plundered from Byzantine architecture.

② **The müezzin mahfili** (see p40) still retains original, intricate 16th-century paintwork on its underside. Beneath it is a small fountain.

③ **Mihrab**, cut from Marmara marble

④ **Entrance from Kavaflar Arasta**

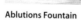

Ablutions Fountain
Intricate, pierced carving decorates the top of the 16-sided open şadırvan (ablutions fountain), which stands in the centre of the courtyard. The absence of a canopy helps to retain the uncluttered aspect of the courtyard.

Courtyard Portals
Alternating red and honey-coloured slabs of stone were used to build the striking arches above the courtyard portals. This echoes the decoration of the magnificent arches running around the mosque courtyard itself.

★ Dome
The dome masterfully dominates the entire interior of the mosque. Not even the florid paintwork – the original 16th-century decoration underwent restoration in the 19th century – detracts from its effect.

★ Minbar
Many experts claim that the Selimiye's *minbar*, with its conical tiled cap, is the finest in Turkey. Its lace-like side panels are exquisitely carved.

The Interior
The mosque is the supreme achievement of Islamic architecture. Its octagonal plan allows for a reduction in the size of the buttresses supporting the dome. This permitted extra windows to be incorporated, making the mosque exceptionally light inside.

Sultan's Loge
The imperial loge is supported on green marble columns. They are connected by pointed arches, whose surrounds are adorned with floral İznik tiles *(see p163)*. Unusually, its ornately decorated mihrab contains a shuttered window, which opened on to countryside when the mosque was first built.

Main entrance

❷ Kilyos

27 km (17 miles) N of Istanbul.
🏯 1,665. **D** from Sarıyer.

Kilyos, on the shore of the Black Sea, is the closest seaside resort to Istanbul and very popular. It has a long, sandy beach and temptingly clear water, but visitors should not swim here in the absence of a lifeguard because there are dangerous currents.

A 14th-century Genoese castle perches on a clifftop overlooking the town but it is not open to visitors. There are a couple of private beach clubs here, such as Dalia (www.clubdalia.com) and Solar Beach (www.solarbeach.com.tr). Both offer loungers, sunshades and water sports. Solar Beach hosts a popular Electronic Music festival every June.

❸ Belgrade Forest

Belgrad Ormanı

20 km (12 miles) N of Istanbul. 🚌 42, 40S from Taksim to Çayırbaşı, then 42 to Bahçeköy. Park: **Tel** (0212) 226 13 14. **Open** May–Sep: 6am–9pm daily; Oct–Apr: 7am–7:30pm. 🅿 ♿

One of the most popular escapes from the city, the Belgrade Forest is the only sizeable piece of woodland in the immediate vicinity of Istanbul. The forest is made up of pines, oaks, beeches, chestnuts and poplars, beneath which a profusion of wild flowers grow in spring. Within it is a huge woodland park, best visited during the week, since it attracts hordes of picnickers at weekends. The main entrance to the park is near the village of Bahçeköy and the popular Neşetsuyu picnic area is a half-hour stroll from this gate.

The park's other attractions are the relics of the dams, reservoirs and aqueducts used for over 1,000 years to transport spring water in to Istanbul.

Büyük Bent, a Byzantine dam and reservoir in the Belgrade Forest

The oldest structure, Büyük Bent (Great Reservoir), dates back to the early Byzantine era. It is a pleasant half-hour walk from Neşetsuyu picnic area. Meanwhile, the Sultan Mahmut Dam, outside the park's gate, is a fine curve of marble which dates from 1839.

Eğri Kemer (Crooked Aqueduct) and Uzun Kemer (Long Aqueduct) are on the D010 road between Levent and Kısırmandıra and are best reached by taxi. Both have impressive rows of arches. The former probably dates from the 12th century, while Sinan (see p93) built the latter for Süleyman the Magnificent (see p28).

❹ Şile

72 km (45 miles) NE of Istanbul.
🏯 25,372. 🚌 from Üsküdar.

The quintessential Black Sea holiday village of Şile has a number of fine, sandy beaches and a black-and-white striped

Şile, a holiday resort and centre for cotton production

clifftop lighthouse. In antiquity, the village, then known as Kalpe, was a port used by ships sailing east from the Bosphorus.

Şile's lighthouse, the largest in Turkey, was built by the French for Sultan Abdül Mecit (see p32) in 1858–9; it can be visited after dusk. Apart from tourism, the main industry is now the production of a coarse cotton which is made into clothing and sold in shops along Üsküdar Caddesi.

❺ Princes' Islands

Adalar

12 km (7 miles) SE of Istanbul.
🏯 16,171. ⛴ 8–10 crossings daily from Kabataş to Büyükada (in winter, 15 in summer). ℹ (0216) 382 70 71.

The pine-forested Princes' Islands are a welcome break from the bustle of the city and are just a short ferry or sea bus ride southeast from Istanbul so are ideal for day trips. The most frequently used ferries depart from Kabataş. Most ferries stop at the four largest islands, namely Kınalıada, Burgazada, Heybeliada and Büyükada. The journey time to the nearest island, Kınalıada, is less than one hour and to the largest and furthest island, Büyükada, 1.5 hours. Less frequent high-speed catamarans or sea buses cover the journey to Büyükada in a little over half an hour, but are more expensive.

The islands take their name from a royal palace built by

Justin II on Büyükada, then known as Prinkipo (Island of the Prince) in 569. During the Byzantine era the islands became infamous as a place of exile. Members of the royal family and public figures were often banished to the monasteries here.

In the latter half of the 19th century, with the launch of a steamboat service from Istanbul, several wealthy expatriates settled on the islands, including Leon Trotsky. From 1929–33 he lived at 55 Çankaya Caddesi, one of the finest mansions on Büyükada.

Büyükada, the largest island, attracts the most visitors with its sandy beaches and *fin-de-siècle* elegance. Its 19th-century atmosphere is enhanced by the omni-presence of horse-drawn phaetons. These quaint carriages are the only form of public transport on the islands since motorized transport is banned. Another popular alternative is the bicycle. There are rental outlets in the main town on each of the four main islands.

At the top of Büyükada's wooded southern hill, in a clearing, stands the Monastery of St George. It is a 20th-century structure, built on Byzantine foundations. On the eastern side of the island, the small but interesting Adalar Müzesi or Museum of the Princes' Islands (open 9am–5pm Tue–Sun) has

Door to the Monastery of St George

material on the flora and fauna, geology and history of the islands.

To the left of the ferry pier on Heybeliada, the second-largest island, is the imposing former Naval High School (Deniz Harp Okulu), built in 1942. The island's northern hill is the stunning location of the Greek Orthodox School of Theology (built in 1841). The school is now closed but its library, famous among Orthodox scholars, is still open and can be visited by appointment. The island also has a pleasant beach on its south coast at Çam Limanı Köyü.

Kınalıada is favoured by Istanbul's dwindling Armenian community as a summer retreat. The slightly larger Burgazada is crowned by a ruined Byzantine monastery and the 19th-century Orthodox Greek church of John the Baptist.

Another major attraction is the opportunity to swim in one of the pay beaches and sunbathe along the shores.

❻ Termal

38 km (24 miles) SE of Istanbul.
🚏 5,018. 🚢 from Kabataş to Yalova.
ℹ️ Termal-Yalova, (0226) 675 74 00.

This small spa buried deep in a wooded valley has been patronized by ruling elites since the Roman era. Termal is 12 km

Ornamental fountain at Atatürk's former house at Termal

(7 miles) from the port of Yalova. Its popularity was revived by Sultan Abdül Hamit II *(see p35)* in the early 20th century, when he refurbished the **Yalova Termal Baths**, now part of the Ministry of Health complex of five baths and four hotels. Facilities include Turkish baths *(see p69)*, a sauna and a swimming pool.

Atatürk enjoyed taking the waters here. The small chalet-style house he built at the bottom of the valley, now the **Atatürk Museum**, preserves some of his possessions.

🛁 Yalova Termal Baths
Termal. **Tel** (0226) 675 74 00.
Open 8am–10pm daily.

🏛 Atatürk Museum
Atatürk Köşkü, Termal. **Tel** (0226) 675 70 28. **Open** May–Oct: 9am–5pm Tue, Wed, Fri–Sun; Nov–Apr: 9:30am–4pm.

The harbour of Burgazada, one of the relaxed and picturesque Princes' Islands near Istanbul

❼ İznik

87 km (54 miles) SE of Istanbul.
🏔 42,000. 🚌 Yeni Mahalle, Yakup
Sok, (0224) 757 25 83. 🚌 to Yalova.
🚇 to İznik. 🛈 Belediye Hizmet Binasi,
Kılıçaslan Cad 97, (0224) 757 10 10.
🛒 Wed. 🎪 İznik Fair (5–10 Oct);
Liberation Day (28 Nov).

A charming lakeside town, İznik gives little clue now of its former glory as, at one point, the capital of the Byzantine Empire. Its most important legacy dates, however, from the 16th century, when its kilns produced the finest ceramics ever to be made in the Ottoman world.

The town first reached prominence in AD 325, when it was known as Nicaea. In that year Constantine (see p22) chose it as the location of the first Ecumenical Council of the Christian Church. At this meeting, the Nicene Creed, a statement of doctrine on the nature of Christ in relation to God, was formulated.

The Seljuks (see p23) took Nicaea in 1081 and renamed it İznik. It was wrested back from them in 1097 by the First Crusade on behalf of Emperor Alexius I Comnenus. After the capture of Constantinople in 1204 (see p28), the city was capital of the 'Empire of Nicaea', a remaining fragment of the Byzantine Empire, for half a century. In 1331,

Grand domed portico fronting the Archaeological Museum

Orhan Gazi (see p34) captured İznik and incorporated it into the Ottoman Empire. İznik still retains its original layout. Surrounded by the city walls, its two main streets are in the form of a cross, with minor streets running out from them on a grid plan. The walls still more or less delineate the town's boundaries. They were built by the Greek Lysimachus, then ruler of the town, in 300 BC, but they were frequently repaired by both the Byzantines and later the Ottomans. They cover a total of 3 km (2 miles)

Istanbul Gate from within the city walls

in circumference and are punctuated by huge gateways. The main one of these, Istanbul Gate (İstanbul Kapısı), is at the city's northern limit. It is decorated with a carved relief of fighting horsemen and is flanked by Byzantine towers.

The **Haghia Sophia Mosque**, stands at the intersection of the main streets, Atatürk

Caddesi and Kılıçaslan Caddesi. The current building was erected after an earthquake in 1065. The remains of a fine mosaic floor, and also of a Deësis, a fresco that depicts Christ, the Virgin and John the Baptist, are protected from damage behind glass screens. Just off the eastern end of Kılıçaslan Caddesi, the 14th-century **Green Mosque** (Yeşil Cami) is named after the tiles covering its minaret. Unfortunately, the originals have been replaced by modern copies of an inferior quality.

Opposite the mosque, the Kitchen of Lady Nilüfer (Nilüfer Hatun İmareti), one of İznik's loveliest buildings, now houses the town's **Archaeological Museum**. This imaret was set up in 1388 by Nilüfer Hatun, wife of Orhan Gazi, and also served as a hospice for wandering dervishes. Entered through a spacious five-domed portico, the central domed area is flanked by two further domed rooms. The museum has displays of Roman antiquities and glass as well as some examples of Seljuk and Ottoman tiles.

🕌 **Haghia Sophia Mosque**
Müze Cad. **Tel** (0224) 757 12 06.
Open daily (after prayer).

🕌 **Green Mosque**
Müze Sok. **Open** daily (after prayer).

🏛 **Archaeological Museum**
Müze Sok. **Tel** (0224) 757 10 27.
Open by appointment.

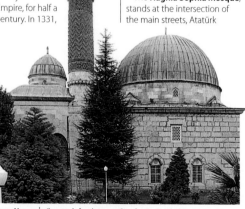

Green Mosque, İznik, named after the green tiles adorning its minaret

İznik Ceramics

Towards the end of the 15th century, the town of İznik began to produce large quantities of ceramic bowls, jars and, later, tiles for the many palaces and mosques of Istanbul. Drawing on local deposits of fine clay and inspired by imported Chinese ceramics, the work of the craftsmen of İznik soon excelled, both technically and aesthetically. İznik pottery is made from hard, white "fritware", which is akin to porcelain. This style of pottery was invented in Egypt in around the 12th century. It is covered by a bright, white slip (a creamy mixture of clay and water) and a transparent glaze. Early İznik pottery is brilliant blue and white. Later, other colours, especially a vivid red, were added. The potteries of İznik reached their height in the late 16th and early 17th centuries but shortly after fell into decline.

Chinese porcelain, which was imported into Turkey from the 14th century and of which there is a large collection in Topkapı Palace *(see pp56–61)*, often inspired the designs used for İznik pottery. During the 16th century, İznik potters produced imitations of pieces of Chinese porcelain such as this copy of a Ming dish.

Rock and wave border pattern

Cobalt blue and white was the striking combination of colours used in early İznik pottery (produced between c.1470–1520). The designs used were a mixture of Chinese and Arabesque, as seen on this tiled panel on the wall of the Circumcision Chamber in Topkapı Palace. Floral patterns and animal motifs were both popular at this time.

Damascus ware was the name erroneously given to ceramics produced at İznik during the first half of the 16th century. They had fantastic floral designs in the new colours of turquoise, sage green and manganese. When such tiles were discovered at Damascus, the similar İznik pots were wrongly assumed to have been made there.

Armenian bole, an iron-rich red colour, began to be used in around 1550, as seen in this 16th-century tankard. New, realistic tulip and other floral designs were also introduced, and İznik ware enjoyed its heyday, which lasted until around 1630.

Miniature depicting potters

Wall tiles were not made in any quantity until the reign of Süleyman the Magnificent (1520–66). Süleyman used İznik tiles to refurbish the Dome of the Rock in Jerusalem. Some of the best examples are seen in Istanbul's mosques, notably in the Süleymaniye *(see pp92–3)*, Rüstem Paşa Mosque *(pp90–91)* and, here, in this example from the Blue Mosque *(pp80–81)*.

ⓐ Bursa

Bursa extends in a swathe along the northern foothills of Mount Uludağ *(see p171)*. A settlement known as Prusa was reputedly established here in the 3rd century BC by Prusias I of Bithynia. However, it was the Romans who first spotted the potential of Bursa's mineral springs: today there are an estimated 3,000 baths in the city. In 1326 Bursa became the first capital of the Ottoman Empire, following its capture by Orhan Gazi *(see p27)*.

View over the rooftops of the city of Bursa

Today Bursa is a provincial capital whose status as one of Turkey's foremost centres of commerce and industry is evident in its broad boulevards and busy shops and bazaars. Apart from the central market area *(see pp166–7)*, the most frequented sightseeing area is Yeşil, on the eastern side of the Gök River, where the Green Mosque and Green Tomb are the main attractions.

📷 Yıldırım Beyazıt Mosque

Yıldırım Beyazıt Camii, Yıldırım Cad. **Open** daily.

This mosque is named after Beyazıt I *(see p34)*, whose nickname was "Yıldırım", meaning "thunderbolt". This referred to the speed with which he reacted to his enemies. Built in 1389, just after Beyazıt became sultan, the mosque at first doubled as a lodge for Sufi dervishes *(see p106)*. It has a lovely portico with five domed bays.

Inside, the interior court (a covered "courtyard" in Bursa mosques, which prefigures the open courtyards preferred by later Ottoman architects) and prayer hall are divided by an impressive arch. This rises from two mihrab-like niches. The walls of the prayer hall itself are adorned with several bold and attractive pieces of calligraphic design *(see p97)*.

🕌 Green Tomb
Yeşil Türbe, Yeşil Cad. **Open** daily. 📷 donation.

The tomb of Mehmet I *(see p32)*, which stands elevated above the mosque among tall cypress trees, is one of the city's most prominent landmarks. It was built between 1414 and 1421. The tomb is much closer to the Seljuk *(see p23)* style of architecture than Classical Ottoman. Its exterior is covered in green tiles, although these are mainly 19th-century replacements for the original faïence. However, a few older tiles survive around the entrance portal.

The interior, entered through a pair of superbly carved wooden doors, is simply dazzling. The space is small and the ornamentation, covering a relatively large surface area, is breathtaking in its depth of colour and detail. The mihrab has especially intricate tile panels, including a representation of a mosque lamp hanging from a gold chain between two candles.

The sultan's magnificent sarcophagus is covered in exquisite tiles and adorned by a long Koranic inscription. Nearby sarcophagi contain the remains of his sons, daughters and nursemaid.

📷 Green Mosque
Yeşil Cami, Yeşil Cad. **Open** daily.

Bursa's most famous monument was commissioned by Mehmet I in 1412, but it remained unfinished at his death in 1421 and still lacks a portico. Nevertheless, it is the finest Ottoman mosque built before the conquest of Constantinople *(see p28)*.

The main portal is tall and elegant, with an intricately carved canopy. It opens into the entrance hall. Beyond this is an interior court, with a carved fountain at its centre. A flight of three steps leads up from here into the prayer hall. On either side of the steps are niches where worshippers once left their shoes *(see p41)*. Above the entrance to the court is the sultan's loge, resplendent in richly patterned tiles created using the *cuerda seca* technique. They are in beautiful greens, blues and yellows, with threads of gold which were added after firing. The tiling of the prayer hall was carried out by Ali İbn İlyas Ali, who learnt his art in Samarkand. It was the first

The Green Tomb and Green Mosque, Bursa's most distinctive monuments

time that tiles were used extensively in an Ottoman mosque and set a precedent for the later widespread use of İznik tiles (see p163). The tiles covering the walls of the prayer hall, which is well lit by floor-level windows, are simple, green and hexagonal. Against this plain backdrop, the effect of the mihrab is especially glorious. Predominantly turquoise, deep blue and white, with touches of gold, the mihrab's tiles depict flowers, leaves, arabesques and geometric patterns. The mosque's exterior was also

once clad in tiles, but they have since disappeared.

🏛 Museum of Turkish and Islamic Arts

Türk ve İslam Eserleri Müzesi, Yeşil Cad. **Tel** (0224) 327 76 79. **Open** 10am–5pm Tue–Sun. 🎟

This museum is housed in a fine Ottoman building, the former *medrese* (see p40) of the Green Mosque. A colonnade surrounds its courtyard on three sides and the cells leading off from it, formerly used by the students, are now exhibition galleries. At the far end of the

VISITORS' CHECKLIST

Practical Information
90 km (60 miles) S of Istanbul.
🚊 2,740,000. 🅿 Atatürk Cad;
Osman Gazi Cad. 🛈 Ulucami
Parkı, Orhangazi Altgeçidi, No. 1
(0224) 220 18 48. 🎭 Textiles Fair
(mid-Apr); Bursa Festival
(12 Jun–12 Jul).

Transport
✈ 20 km (12 miles) NW.
🚌 Kıbrıs Şehitler Cad, (0224)
261 54 00. ⛴ to Yalova.

courtyard is the large, domed hall which was originally the main classroom.

Exhibits dating from the 12th–20th centuries include Seljuk and Ottoman ceramics, elaborately decorated Korans and costumes ranging from linen dervish robes to ornate wedding gowns. A display on Turkish baths (see p69) features embroidered towels and exotic high-heeled silver bath clogs. There is also a recreated setting of a traditional circumcision room, complete with a four-poster bed.

Façade of the Museum of Turkish and Islamic Arts

Bursa City Centre

① Yıldırım Beyazıt Mosque
② Green Tomb
③ Green Mosque
④ Museum of Turkish and Islamic Arts
⑤ Tophane Citadel
⑥ Osman Gazi Tomb
⑦ Alaeddin Mosque
⑧ Muradiye Mosque
⑨ Hüsnü Züber House
⑩ Archaeological Museum

Key

⬛ Street-by-Street area
see pp166–7

0 metres 750
0 yards 750

For map symbols see back flap

Bursa: The Market Area

Bursa's central market area is a warren of streets and ancient Ottoman courtyards (hans). The area is still central to Bursa's commercial activity and is a good place to experience the life of the city. Here too you can buy the local fabrics for which the town is famous, particularly handmade lace, towelling and silk. The silkworm was introduced to the Byzantine Empire in the 6th century and there is still a brisk trade in silk cocoons carried out in Koza Han all year round. Among the many other items on sale today are the lovely hand-painted, camel-skin Karagöz puppets *(see p170)*.

★ Covered Bazaar
The great bazaar, built by Mehmet I in the 15th century, consists of a long hall with domed bays, adjoined by a high, vaulted hall. The Bedesten is home to jewellers' shops.

★ The Great Mosque
A three-tiered ablutions fountain stands beneath the central dome of this monumental mosque, which was erected in 1396–9.

Şengül Hamamı Turkish baths

FEVZI ÇAKMAK CAD

Bey Han (also called Emir Han) was built as part of the Orhan Gazi Mosque complex, to provide revenue for the mosque's upkeep.

Cafés

KOZA PARKI

ATATÜRK CAD

The Bey Hamamı
(1339) is the oldest Turkish baths building in the world. It now houses workshops.

Koza Park
The gardens in front of Koza Han, with their fountains, benches and shaded café tables, are a popular meeting place for locals and visitors throughout the day.

★ Koza Han
This is the most attractive and fascinating building in the market area. Since it was built in 1491 by Beyazıt II, it has been central to the silk trade.

Flower Market
The numerous bunches of flowers for sale in the streets around the town hall make a picturesque sight in the midst of Bursa's bustling market area.

Geyve Han is also known as Ivaz Paşa Han.

Fidan Han dates from around 1470, when it was built by a grand vizier of Mehmet the Conqueror.

İçkoza Han

BORSA SOK

UZUN ÇARŞI CAD

CÖMLEK SOK

0 metres 40
0 yards 40

The Belediye, Bursa's town hall, is a Swiss chalet-style, half-timbered building that forms a surprising landmark in the centre of the town.

BELEDİYE CAD

Orhan Gazi Mosque
Built in 1339, just 13 years after the Ottoman conquest of Bursa, this mosque is the oldest of the city's imperial mosques.

Key
— Suggested route

Bursa: Tophane and Muradiye

Tophane, the most ancient part of Bursa, is distinguished by its clock tower which stands on top of a hill. This area was formerly the site of the citadel and is bounded by what remains of the original Byzantine walls. It is also known as Hisar, which means "fortress" in Turkish. If you continue westwards for 2 km (1mile), crossing the Cilimboz River, you come to the historic district of Muradiye. The 15th-century Muradiye Mosque, from which this suburb takes its name, is one of the most impressive royal mosque and tomb complexes in the city.

brought his father's body to be buried in the baptistry of a converted church and he himself was later buried in the nave. The tombs that can be seen today date from 1868. They were rebuilt after the destruction of the church and the original tombs in an earthquake in 1855. Fragments of the church's mosaic floor survive inside the tomb of Orhan Gazi.

Exploring Tophane

Tophane's northern limit is marked by the best preserved section of the citadel walls, built on to an outcrop of rock. At the top is a pleasant park filled with cafés, which also contains the imposing clock tower and the tombs of the founders of the Ottoman dynasty. From here you can look down on the lower part of Tophane, where archetypal Ottoman houses still line many of the twisting streets. Pınarbaşı Kapısı, at Tophane's southern point, is the gate through which Orhan Gazi entered Bursa in 1326 (see p27).

🚇 Tophane Citadel

Hisar Osman Gazi Cad. **Open** daily. 🚻
The citadel walls can be viewed from a set of steps which lead uphill from the intersection of Cemal Nadir Caddesi and Atatürk Caddesi. These steps end at the tea gardens above. The citadel fell into Turkish hands when Orhan Gazi's troops broke through its walls. Later, he built a wooden palace inside the citadel and had the old Byzantine ramparts refortified. The walls had until this era delimited the entire circumference of the ancient

city. However, Orhan began to encourage Bursa's expansion and developed the present-day commercial heart of the city further to the east.

South of Hastalaryurdu Caddesi is an area notable for its old Ottoman houses (see p63). Most of these have over-hanging upper storeys. They consist of a timber frame filled in with adobe and plastered over, then painted in bright colours. Kaleiçi Sokağı, which can be reached down Karadut Sokağı from Hastalaryurdu Caddesi, is one of the best streets of such houses.

🕌 Tombs of Osman and Orhan Gazi

Osman & Orhan Gazi Türbeleri. Ulu Cami Cad. **Open** daily. 🚻 donation.
Osman Gazi began the process of Ottoman expansion in the 13th century (see p27) and attempted to capture Bursa. But it was his son, Orhan, who took the city just before his father died. Orhan

Tomb of Osman Gazi, the first great Ottoman leader

🕌 Alaeddin Mosque

Alaeddin Camii
Alaeddin Mahallesi.
Open prayer times only. 🚻

Further exploration in the Tophane area reveals the Alaeddin Mosque, the oldest in Bursa, built within 10 years of the city's conquest. It is in the form of a simple domed square, fronted by a portico of four Byzantine columns with capitals. The mosque was commissioned by Alaeddin Bey, brother of and vizier (see p41) to Orhan Gazi.

Exploring Muradiye

Muradiye is a leafy, largely residential district. Close to the Muradiye Mosque are the Hüsnü Züber House and the Ottoman House, two fine examples of traditional Turkish homes. To the north is a park, among the attractions of which are a boating lake and the Archaeological Museum.

🕌 Muradiye Mosque

Muradiye Külliyesi Murat II Cad.
Open daily. 🚻 donation.
This mosque complex was built by Murat II, father of Mehmet the Conqueror (see p28), in the early 15th century. The mosque itself is preceded by a graceful domed portico. Its wooden door is finely carved and the interior decorated with early İznik tiles (see p163). The medrese, beside the mosque, now serves as a dispensary.

Popular café in the park above the ancient citadel walls in Tophane

Octagonal tomb of Mustafa in the grounds of Muradiye Mosque

It is a perfectly square building, with cells surrounding a central garden courtyard. Its *dershane*, or main classroom, is richly tiled and adorned with an ornate brickwork façade.

The mosque garden, with its cypresses, well-tended flower beds and fountains, is one of Bursa's most tranquil retreats. Murat II was the last Ottoman sultan to be buried in Bursa and his mausoleum, standing in the garden beside the mosque and *medrese*, was completed in 1437. His earth-filled sarcophagus lies beneath an opening in the roof. The eaves above the tomb's 16th-century porch still retain their original painted decoration. There are 11 other tombs in the garden, several of which were built for murdered princes. One such is the tomb of Mustafa, a son of Süleyman the

Magnificent, who was disposed of to clear the way for his younger brother, Selim II, "the Sot" (see p78). According to an inscription, Selim had the octagonal mausoleum built for his brother. The interior is decorated with some particularly beautiful İznik tile panels depicting carnations, tulips and hyacinths. The tiles date from the best İznik period, the late 16th century.

🏛 Hüsnü Züber House

Hüsnü Züber Evi, Yaşayan Müze Uzunyol Sok 3, Muradiye. **Tel** (0224) 221 35 42. **Open** 10am–midday, 1–5pm Tue–Sun. 🅿 🚻 Ottoman House: **Tel** (0224) 285 48 13. **Open** 10am–5pm Tue–Sun.

Among the numerous well-preserved houses in the Muradiye district is the Hüsnü Züber House. This 150-year-old mansion has been opened as a museum by its present owner, the artist Hüsnü Züber. It was originally a guest house for visiting dignitaries, later becoming the Russian Consulate and, most recently, a private residence. The house is an interesting example of vernacular architecture. The upper storey projects over the street in the traditional manner of Ottoman houses (see p63). Overlooking the interior courtyard, which has rooms arranged around it

on three sides, there is a loggia. Originally this would have been open, but it is now glazed. Meanwhile, inside the house, the decorative wooden ceilings (some with hand-painted borders) are particularly attractive.

Hüsnü Züber's private collection of interesting carved wooden objects is now displayed here. These include spoons, musical instruments and even farming utensils. They are all decorated with Anatolian motifs by a unique technique of engraving by burning known as pyrogravure.

The 18th-century **Ottoman House** (Osmanlı Evi) stands on the square in front of the Muradiye Mosque. The upper storey of this fine house is adorned with elaborately patterned brickwork. Shutters and grilles hide the windows.

Hüsnü Züber House, dating from the mid-19th century

🏛 Archaeological Museum

Arkeoloji Müzesi, Kültür Parkı. **Tel** (0224) 234 49 18. **Open** 10am–5pm Tue–Sun. 🅿

Finds dating from the third millennium BC up to the Ottoman conquest of Bursa are collected in this museum. In the first hall there are clasps, vessels and an inscription from the Phrygian period. Other exhibits include Roman and Hellenistic jewellery and ceramics, a number of Roman statues of Cybele, goddess of nature, and a Roman bronze of the god Apollo with strange, lifelike eyes. There are also displays of Byzantine religious objects and coins.

Muradiye Mosque, constructed by Murat II

Bursa: Çekirge

With a name which translates literally as "Realm of the Crickets", Çekirge still earns Bursa the tag of yeşil, or "green", by which it is known in Turkey. This leafy western spa suburb of the city has attracted visitors to its mineral springs since Roman times. In the 6th century the Emperor Justinian (see p22) built a bathhouse here and his wife Theodora later arrived with a retinue of 4,000. Çekirge is also the location of most of the city's finest hotels and the area's hillside setting affords some spectacular views.

Çekirge's Old Spa, dating back to the 14th-century reign of Murat I

🔥 New Spa

Yeni Kaplıca Mudanya Yolu 6.
Tel (0224) 236 69 68.
Open 7am–11pm daily.

Despite their name, the New Spa baths have a substantial pedigree. They were rebuilt in 1552 by Rüstem Paşa, grand vizier (see p31) to Süleyman the Magnificent (see p28). The sultan is said to have ordered their rebuilding in gratitude after his recovery from gout when bathing in the Byzantine baths that stood on this site.

The central pool is surrounded with bays adorned with beautiful but damaged İznik tiles (see p163). They are not open to women. Within the same complex, however, there are two other baths: the modern Kaynarca baths which is for women and the Karamustafa baths for couples.

🏨 Çelik Palas Hotel

Çelik Palas Otel Çekirge Cad 79.
Tel (0224) 233 38 00.
🌐 celikpalas.com

This five-star hotel stands on one of Bursa's main thorough-fares. Built in 1933, it is the city's oldest, most prestigious spa hotel. Atatürk (see pp32–3) frequented its baths. Open to both sexes, their centrepiece is an attractive circular pool in a domed marble room.

🔥 Old Spa

Eski Kaplıca Hotel Kervansaray,
Çekirge Meydanı, Kervansaray.
Tel (0224) 233 93 00.
Open 7am–10:30pm daily.

The Old Spa baths were established by Murat I in the late 14th century and renovated in 1512, during the reign of Beyazıt II. Remnants of an earlier building, said to date from the reign of Emperor Justinian (see p22), are also visible. These include some Byzantine columns and capitals in the hararet (steam room) of the men's section (see p69). You enter the baths through the Kervansaray Termal Hotel. Spring water, said to cure skin diseases and rheumatism, bubbles into the central pool of both the men's and women's sections at 45 °C (113 °F). The women's baths are not as old or grand, but are still the most attractive women-only ones in Bursa.

🕌 Murat I Hüdavendigar Mosque

Murat I Hüdavendigar Camii
I. Murat Cad, Çekirge. **Open** daily.

Bursa's most unusual mosque was built for Murat I, self-styled Hüdavendigar, meaning "Creator of the Universe", in 1385. It is unlike any other mosque in the Ottoman world: its prayer hall is on the ground floor, with the medrese built around a second storey.

The façade looks more like that of a palace than a mosque, with a five-arched portico surmounted by a colonnade. This colonnade in turn has five sets of double-arched windows divided by Byzantine columns. Inside, the domed court and prayer hall rise through both storeys. The upper storey colonnade leads to the cells of the medrese.

On this level, passageways lead around both sides of the mosque to a mysterious room, located over the mihrab, whose original purpose is unknown.

Karagöz Shadow Puppets

Suspended above Çekirge Caddesi is an imposing monument to the town's two famous scapegoats, Karagöz and Hacıvat. According to legend, these local clowns were executed in the 14th century for distracting their fellow workers while building the Orhan Gazi Mosque (see p167). It is said that Sultan Orhan (see p34) created a shadow play about them in remorse.

In fact, shadow puppet theatre arrived in Turkey later and is thought to have originated in Southeast Asia. Selim I is reported to have brought it back to Istanbul after his Egyptian campaign in 1517. The camel-skin puppets are 35–40 cm (14–16 in) high, brightly dyed and oiled to aid translucency. They are still made today and can be purchased in an antique shop in the Bedesten run by Şinasi Çelikkol, who also occasionally puts on shows.

Cadı, a witch in the Karagöz puppet shows

Uludağ National Park, a popular ski resort in winter

❾ Uludağ National Park

Uludağ Milli Parkı

100 km (60 miles) S of Istanbul. **Tel** (0224) 283 21 97. 🚠 *Teleferik* to Sarıalan, then dolmuş. **Open** daily. 🚗 only for vehicles.

One of a number of Turkish mountains to claim the title of Mount Olympus, Uludağ was believed by the Bithynians (of northwest Asia Minor) to be the home of the gods. In the Byzantine era, it was home to several monastic orders. After the Ottoman conquest of Bursa, Muslim dervishes *(see p106)* moved into their abandoned monasteries. Nowadays, how-ever, no traces of Uludağ's former religious communities remain.

A visit to Uludağ National Park is especially enjoyable in spring or summer, when its alpine heights are relatively cool and it becomes a popular picnic area. The park includes 109.26 sq km (258.6 sq miles) of woodland. As you ascend, the deciduous beech, oak and hazel gradually give way to juniper and aspen, and finally to dwarf junipers. In spring, hyacinths and crocuses blanket the wooded slopes.

In winter, Uludağ is transformed into Turkey's most fashionable ski resort. The industry centres on the Oteller region, which has good alpine-style hotels.

Osman Gazi *(see p27)* is supposed to have founded seven villages for his seven sons and their brides in the Bursa region. **Cumalıkızık**,

on the lower slopes of Uludağ, is the most perfectly preserved of the five surviving villages and is now registered as a national monument. It is also a UNESCO World Heritage Site. Among its houses are many 13th-century semi-timbered buildings. The village can be reached by minibus from Bursa.

❿ Bird Paradise National Park

Kuşcenneti Milli Parkı

115 km (70 miles) SW of Istanbul. **Tel** (0266) 735 54 22. 🇩 from Bandırma. **Open** 8am–8pm daily. ♿

An estimated 255 species of birds visit Bird Paradise National Park at the edge of Kuş Gölü, the lake formerly known as Manyas Gölü. Located on the great migratory paths between Europe and Asia, the park is a happy combination of plant cover and reed beds, and it includes a lake, which supports at least 20 species of fish.

At the entrance to the park, there is a small museum with displays about various birds.

Spoonbill wading in the lake at Bird Paradise National Park

Binoculars are provided at the desk and visitors make their way to an observation tower.

Two main groups of birds visit the lake: those that come here to breed (March–July), and those which pass by during migration, either heading south (November) or north (April–May). Among the numerous different birds that breed around the lake are the endangered Dalmatian pelican, the great crested grebe, cormorants, herons, bitterns and spoonbills. The migratory birds, which can be seen in spring and autumn, include storks, cranes, pelicans and birds of prey such as sparrowhawks and spotted eagles.

Sandy beach on Avşa, the most popular of the Marmara Islands

⓫ Marmara Islands

Marmara Adaları

120 km (75 miles) SW of Istanbul. 🚢 from Yenikapı. 🛈 Neyire Sıtkı Cad 31/3, Erdek, (0266) 835 11 69.

This beautiful archipelago in the Sea of Marmara is a popular destination with Turkish holiday-makers, particularly with residents of Istanbul.

The loveliest of the islands is Avşa, whose sandy beaches and regular summer ferry service make it popular with Turks and, increasingly, foreign tourists. The ferry arrives at Türkeli on the west coast. Transport to the most popular beach, at Mavi Koy, is by a tractor-pulled train.

Marmara, the largest island, has one beach, north of Marmara village at Çınarlı. It is famous for producing the prized Proconnesian marble.

⑫ The Dardanelles

Çanakkale Boğazı

200 km (125 miles) SW of Istanbul. 🚌 Çanakkale–Eceabat car ferry. 🚌 Çanakkale. ℹ️ Çanakkale İskele Meydanı 27, (0286) 217 11 87.

Named after Dardanus, an ancient king of Çanakkale, the Dardanelles are the straits that link the Aegean Sea to the Sea of Marmara, and which separate European Turkey from Asia. Some 40 km (25 miles) long and narrowing to little more than a kilometre (half a mile) wide, they are steeped in legend and have been of strategic importance for thousands of years. In modern times they are probably best known as the setting for a disastrous Allied campaign during World War I.

The classical name for this channel of water was the Hellespont. According to legend, the Greek goddess Helle fell into the straits from the back of a golden winged ram. In another tale, the lovelorn Leander swam nightly across the Hellespont to meet his lover, Hero, until one night he drowned. The English Romantic poet Byron swam across the straits in 1810, in emulation of Leander, and remarked on the hazardous nature of the currents.

Çanakkale, the old town at the mouth of the Dardanelles, has two museums. The **Military and Naval Museum** is a short walk from the ferry docks. Its collection includes a pocket

Locator Map

① Suvla Bay
② Chunuk Bair
③ Anzac Cove
④ Kabatepe Museum and Simulation Centre
⑤ National Park Information Centre
⑥ Çanakkale
⑦ Cape Helles

Key

☐ Area of war memorials
▬ Road
--- Ferry route

The Çanakkale Şehitleri Memorial, honouring the Turkish dead

watch that saved the life of Atatürk (see pp32–3) when he was hit by shrapnel. The **Archaeological Museum**, south of the town centre, has exhibits from ancient Troy.

To the west is the beautiful **Gallipoli** (Gelibolu) **Peninsula**. Part of this land is a national park, with an information centre near Eceabat. The peninsula, which is now quite tranquil, was the scene of horrific battles that took place in 1915. The objectives of the Allied forces' invasion of Gallipoli were to capture Istanbul, force Turkey into submission and open a strategic supply route to Russia. The campaign began on 25 April 1915 with the landings of British and French troops at **Cape Helles**, and the Anzacs (Australian and New Zealand forces) at what they thought was the beach at Kabatepe. But currents had swept the Anzac force about 1.5 km (1 mile) to the north, to a place now known as **Anzac Cove**, near Arı Burnu. Here the soldiers were faced with unknown and tough terrain, including a cliff.

The Turks managed to retain the high ground of **Chunuk Bair**. The battle here lasted three days, during which 28,000 men were

Mehmetcik Memorial near Anzac Cove

killed. When the Allied forces failed to make headway, more British troops landed at **Suvla Bay** on 6 August. This new offensive might have been successful, but Allied intelligence continually underestimated the Turks and the difficult ground. The terrible slaughter of deadlocked trench warfare continued until the Allies were finally evacuated on 19 December. More than 500,000 Allied and Turkish troops lost their lives and the whole peninsula is scattered with battlefield sites and war memorials. The best place to begin a tour of the war memorials and cemeteries is at the **Kabatepe Museum and Simulation Centre**, which opened in 2013, replacing the Kabatepe Visitors' Centre. It has 11 rooms with exhibits of uniforms, weapons and other memorabilia, as well as realistic video simulations of the Gallipoli campaign. North of here, near Anzac Cove, are several cemeteries and monuments. Chunuk Bair, now a peaceful pine grove above the beaches, has a memorial to the New Zealanders who died and some reconstructed Turkish trenches. The British Memorial is at Cape

Helles, on the peninsula's tip. Further east along the coast stand both the French Memorial and the vast Çanakkale Şehitleri Memorial to the Turks who died defending Gallipoli.

🏛 Military Museum

Çimenlik Kalesi, Çanakkale. **Tel** (0286) 213 17 30. **Open** 9am–noon, 1:30–5:30pm Tue, Wed & Fri–Sun. 🗺

🏛 Archaeological Museum

Atatürk Cad, Çanakkale.
Tel (0286) 217 67 40. **Open** 8am–5pm. **Closed** Mon. 🗺

ℹ National Park Information Centre

Near Eceabat. **Tel** (0286) 814 11 28.
Open 9am–6pm Mon–Fri.
Park: **Open** daily. 🗺

ℹ Kabatepe Museum and Simulation Centre

Near Kabatepe. **Tel** (0286) 814 12 97.
Open 9am–6pm daily. 🗺

⑱ Troy

Truva

350 km (220 miles) SW of Istanbul.
🚌 from Çanakkale. ℹ Çanakkale
İskele Meydanı 27, (0286) 217 11 87.
Open 8am–7pm daily (Nov–Apr: until 5pm). 🗺

In Homer's epic poem, the *Iliad*, the city of Troy is besieged by the Greeks for ten years. For centuries Troy was assumed by many to be as mythical as

Model of the legendary wooden horse at Troy

Achilles, Hector and the other heroes in the tale. But a handful of 19th-century archaeologists were convinced that Homer had based his story on the events that happened to a real city and that traces of it could be found by searching near the Dardanelles. In 1865 British Consul Frank Calvert began investigating some ruins in Hisarlık. This interested the German archaeologist Heinrich Schliemann who soon found evidence of an ancient city resembling the layout of Homer's Troy. Over the last hundred years most historians have come to accept that this city must at least have inspired Homer, and was possibly even called Troy and besieged at the time specified in the story.

The settlement mound in fact has nine distinct levels (labelled Troy I–IX) representing 3,000 years of habitation. Although the remains are sparse compared to major sites such as Ephesus, what is left of Troy has been superbly presented for visitors. There are explanatory boards which allow you to self-guide, describing major features and locating everything from Athena's temple to the ramp where cavalier Schliemann supposedly found the Treasure of Priam.

The city Homer refers to is probably Troy VI (1800–1250 BC), while the Greek and Roman levels, when the city was known as Ilion, are Troy VIII (700–300 BC) and Troy IX (300 BC–AD 1) respectively.

At the entrance is a kitsch wooden horse made in the 1970s, which can be entered by visitors, much like the Trojan horse, which was entered by the Greeks. There is also a small visitors' centre on site.

Schliemann's Search for Ancient Troy

Heinrich Schliemann used a fortune amassed in business to realize his life-long dream of discovering ancient Troy. He began

Schliemann's wife wearing some of the excavated treasure

excavating some likely sites in the 1860s and started on the ruins at Hisarlık in 1870. An amateur, Schliemann drove a great trench through the mound, destroying some walls in his haste. He soon claimed to have found Troy, though he knew not all his findings pointed to this. His greatest find – a hoard of gold and silver jewellery that he smuggled to Germany, calling it "Priam's Treasure" *(see p67)* – predates Homer's Troy by 1,000 years. Some of the treasure disappeared after World War II only to reappear spectacularly in Moscow in August 1994.

THREE GUIDED WALKS

With its frenetic atmosphere, traditional cafés at almost every corner and historic sights from centuries of different rulers, Istanbul is a wonderful city for walkers.

On the following five pages are routes for three walks that take you through three different areas of Istanbul. They will take you past many of the most interesting sights. The areas covered range from the old Greek and Jewish neighbourhoods of Balat and Fener, where historic synagogues can still be seen amid traditional tripe shops, to the wonderful aromas of coffee, spices and fresh fish permeating the air in the Galata region of the city. For a little more elegance, take a stroll along İstiklâl Caddesi in order to confirm why this area of Istanbul has the reputation for celebrating its European rather than its Asian side, taking in the Istanbul Modern *(see p109)*, the finest venue in the city for contemporary art, as you do so. All the walks are intended to be done at a leisurely pace, and there are plenty of suggestions for refreshment stops along each route. In addition to these walks, each of the four areas of Istanbul described in the *Area by Area* section of this book has a walk on its *Street-by-Street* map.

CHOOSING A WALK

Spices from the Spice Bazaar in Eminönü *(see p90)*

The Three Walks
This map shows the location of the three guided walks in relation to the main sightseeing areas of Istanbul.

The Beyoğlu district seen from the Golden Horn *(see pp102–9)*

Balat and Fener *(p175)*

Taksim to the Istanbul Modern *(pp176–7)*

Beyazıt to Galata *(pp178–9)*

Golden Horn

Beyoğlu

Bosphorus

The Bazaar Quarter

Seraglio Point

Sultanahmet

0 kilometres   1

0 miles   1

Key

· · · Walk route

A 75-Minute Walk in Balat, Fener and Ayvansaray

The Balat and Fener neighbourhoods epitomize the cultural diversity and tolerance that was the hallmark of the Ottomans. Fener was predominantly a Greek area, while Balat was Jewish, and this walk guides you around the ancient churches, synagogues, Turkish baths and mosques in the atmospheric backstreets. Although the area may have seen better days, a rejuvenation scheme is putting life back into this picturesque locality.

Tips for Walkers

Starting point: Ahrida Synagogue.
Length: 1.5 km (1 mile).
Getting there: From Eminönü bus terminus, take No. 99 or any bus displaying Eyüp or Ayvansaray. Ask the driver to let you off at Balat. There are also ferry points at Fener and Balat.
Stopping-off points: Hotel Daphnis ⑬ is a good spot to stop for a meal.

⑫ Fener Greek Boys High School

Key

• • • Walk route

This walk starts in the heart of Balat at the Ahrida Synagogue ① (see p112), which was founded before the Ottoman conquest in 1453. It has been restored many times, most recently in 1992. The 19th-century Yanbol synagogue ②, however, is now boarded up but its position indicates its former significance. The Church of Holy Angels ③ dates from Byzantine times. Below it flows a sacred spring and every 14 September supplicants of all religions gather here to pray for cures from their ailments.

Walk to Leblebiciler Sokak and nearby is Afilli Cezve ④, a small café popular for its Turkish coffee. Further along is Agora ⑤, one of Istanbul's nicest taverns (meyhane). Turn left on Hızır Çavuş Köprü Sokak and continue down this road until you reach Köfteci Arnavut ⑥. This traditional meatball restaurant has been serving its loyal customers since 1947.

0 metres 250
0 yards 250

Turn right and then left on to Vodina Caddesi and on your right is Tahtalı Minare Hamam ⑦, one of the oldest Turkish baths in the city, dating from the 1500s. Note the boiler room chimney on the roof. A short distance further on your right is Tahtalı Minare Mosque ⑧, built by Fatih Sultan Mehmet II in 1458. Next door is the Tomb of Hazreti Hüseyin Sadık ⑨, who was buried as a gazi (warrior of the faith) in the 1450s. Continue down the road and you will be able to see the cross of Aya Yorgi Metokhi Church ⑩ (no public access) above its high wall.

At the end of the road turn left and on the right is the Greek Orthodox Patriarchate ⑪ (see p113), seat of the Greek church since 1601. Look at the red-brick building on the ramparts above. This is the Fener Greek Boys High School ⑫, established in Byzantine times. Turn left onto Abdülezel Paşa Caddesi ⑬ and the stone building on your right is the Women's Library ⑭, the city's sole female-only information centre. Further up is the Church of St Stephen of the Bulgars ⑮ (see p112). From here, walk to the Golden Horn waterfront, past the old Galata Bridge, to the Ayvansaray pier for a ferry back to the city centre.

The narrow, winding backstreets of the Balat district

For map symbols see back flap

A 90-Minute Walk from Taksim Square to the Istanbul Modern

It was in the Pera district, where the embassies and palatial residences mirrored the lifestyle of Topkapı Palace, on the opposite side of the Golden Horn, that Constantinople's cosmopolitan population lived and worked in the 19th century. Once known as the "Paris of the East", life centred on the Grand Rue de Pera, today's İstiklâl Caddesi. Even today the Avrupa Pasajı and Balık Pazar markets seem wistfully unchanged, especially when contrasted with the remarkable Pera Museum and the sophisticated Istanbul Modern.

④ A Çiçek Pasajı restaurant

⑥ Avrupa Pasajı bazaar

Along İstiklâl Caddesi

Begin the walk in Taksim Square ① at the Independence Monument. Completed by Pietro Canonica in 1928, it depicts Atatürk with his political contemporaries. Before following the vintage tram line down İstiklâl Caddesi, have a look at the octagonal stone tower, known as the Maksem ②, on the corner of Taksim Caddesi. Dating from 1832, it was once used as a reservoir – you can still see carved bird houses and remains of a fountain. It now houses an art gallery. On your right is the French Cultural Centre, while on the left, further down at No. 83 is a traditional sweet shop, Hacı Bekir, dating from 1777. Saray Muhallebicisi ③ is perfect for a coffee and one of its renowned pastries.

Market Shopping

Pass Yeşilcam Sokak, once the home of Turkish cinema, and at Şarabi Wine House, turn into the former flower market, Çiçek

Pasajı ④, built by Italian architect Michel Capello in 1856, and now filled with restaurants. At Stop Restaurant, veer left then right on Sahne Sokak, which forms the backbone of the Fish Market, or Balık Pazar ⑤.

Return along Sahne Sokak and stroll down the arcaded Hall of Mirrors, or Avrupa Pasajı ⑥ on the right. The Neo-Renaissance interior, with marble floors and classical statues, was once lit by gas lamps, and mirrors amplified the light.

Turn right and then left onto Meşrutiyet Caddesi and follow the road around to the left, keeping the British Consulate General ⑦ on your right. Follow this street down, past TRT (Turkish Radio and Television) and the celebrated but now faded Grand Hotel de Londres, until you reach the exquisite Pera Museum ⑧ (once the Bristol Hotel), where the philanthropic Suna and İnan Kiraç Foundation exhibits its art collection and Turkish tiles.

⑯ Dome of the Kılıç Ali Paşa Mosque

Historic Buildings

Walk through the Odakule Arkade and turn left on to İstiklâl Caddesi. On the east side of a tiny square, Galatasaray Meydanı, is the prominent Galatasaray High School ⑨, lost in greenery behind wrought-iron railings. In 1905, a group of students got together here to form Galatasaray, one of Turkey's leading football clubs.

From here, go onto Turnacıbaşı Sokak, which takes you

⑳ Istanbul Modern

past the Greek Orthodox school, Zografyon ⑩ on the left. In front of you is Galatasaray Hamamı ⑪, Turkish baths built in 1481 and in use ever since.

Take the steep cobbled street that descends beside the Turkish baths, Çapanoğlu Sokak, which becomes a staircase at the bottom. Turn right onto Harbiye Sokak and you will reach French Street, or Fransız Sokağı ⑫ on the left, where an elegant French ambience meets classy Beyoğlu. Enjoy lunch or a glass of wine at one of the French-style cafés.

Refreshed, continue along French Street and at the end turn right onto Boğazkesen Caddesi and continue left down the hill until you reach Tomtom Kaptan Mosque ⑬. The pretty 17th-century fountain here, which was once a grand landmark, is now sadly neglected.

⑮ Interior of the Tophane cannon foundry

Tips for Walkers

Starting point: Taksim Square.
Length: 2.5 km (1.5 miles).
Getting there: From Sultanahmet, take the tramway to Karaköy, from where you can ride the Tünel funicular train to Tünel Square at the southern end of İstiklâl Caddesi in Beyoğlu. Travel up İstiklâl Caddesi by nostalgic tram to Taksim Square.
Stopping-off points: The fish market on Sahne Sokak has lots of cheerful eateries. Cezayir Street is ideal for an elegant drink.

Shopping and Museums

Çukurcuma Caddesi (see p109) and Tomtom Kaptan Sokak intersect here and both have curio shops such as Tüterler ⑭ at No. 186. At the bottom of this street on the corner of Defterdar Yokuşu is the Tophane ⑮, once an Ottoman cannon foundry.

Cross Necatibey Caddesi over the tram line to the 16th-century Kılıç Ali Paşa Mosque ⑯ (see p108), one of the last masterpieces of architect Mimar Sinan. Attached to it is a beautifully restored Turkish bathhouse, the Kılıç Ali Paşa Hamamı. Opposite is the Tophane Fountain ⑰ (see p108) built in 1732, which now bestows locally bottled drinking water. From here you can also see the Baroque Clock Tower ⑱.

Continue left along Salı Pazarı ⑲ with its shops, restaurants and narghile (bubble pipe) smokers. A sign directs you to the Istanbul Modern ⑳ (see p109), with its collection of contemporary Turkish art.

To get back to the city centre, catch the west-bound tram which takes you back to Sultanahmet over the Galata Bridge.

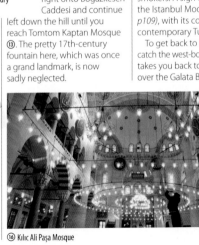

⑯ Kılıç Ali Paşa Mosque

0 metres 500
0 yards 500

Key

••• Walk route

For map symbols see back flap

A 90-Minute Walk from Beyazıt to Galata

Istanbul is a seductive mix of ancient and modern, religious and secular, and this walk will give you a flavour of both. Starting at Beyazıt Tower in the city's historic quarter, the route takes you through narrow shopping streets brimming with energy, over the Galata Bridge with its stunning views of the Bosphorus, to the Beyoğlu district, where the shops, bars and cafés lend Istanbul its chic reputation.

Magnificent façade of Süleymaniye Mosque

Mimar Sinan Architecture

Start from the Kalenderhane Mosque ① *(see pp94)*, once an important Byzantine church and today a mosque. Walk north under one of the arches of the Valens Aqueduct ② *(see pp91)*, a masterpiece of late Roman engineering. Continue up 16 Mart Şehitelri Caddesi to join Prof Sıddık Sami Onar Caddesi in the shadow of the Süleymaniye

Tips for Walkers

Starting point: Kalenderhane Mosque.
Length: 4 km (2.5 miles).
Getting there: From the Old City, take the T1 tram going west to Laleli/Üniversite and walk up Büyük Reşit Paşa Caddesi to Kalenderhane Mosque. From Taksim/Beyoğlu, catch the M2 Metro to Vezneciler station, just south of Kalenderhane Mosque.
Stopping-off points: You are never far from a café or bar in Istanbul, but the obvious halfway stopping-off point is at one of the numerous cafés or bars on Galata Bridge. The streets around Galata Tower and the southern end of İstiklal Caddesi also have plenty of elegant taverns (meyhanes) and restaurants.

Mosque ③ *(see pp92–3)*. This breathtaking structure was completed in 1557 by architect Mimar Sinan *(see p93)*. Keep going until you reach Şifahane Sokak. Turn right into the street and, if you are feeling peckish or thirsty, you can make a pit stop at historic Dârüzziyafe restaurant ④, with its 16th-century detailing, housed in the former soup kitchens of the Süleymaniye Mosque *(see p199)*. Turn right on to Mimar Sinan Caddesi and at the bottom of the street, on the corner in front of you, is the tomb of the architect Mimar Sinan ⑤ – a poignant tribute to the great man even if its design is humble compared to his own creations.

Coffee and Spices

Turn left onto Ismetiye Caddesi and then left again on to Uzunçarsi Caddesi. Walk to the end of the street until you reach bustling Tahtakale Caddesi, where you can jostle with the locals who come here to shop for bargains on everything from electronic goods to clothing. On the right is the Tahtakale Hamamı Çarşısı ⑥, a 16th-century Turkish bathhouse that has been renovated and turned into a shopping centre. There is also a lovely café under the domed roof where you can stop to refuel. Turn down any of the side streets to the left and you will come to Hasırcılar Caddesi ⑦, famed for its spice shops, coffee stalls and delis. Walk towards the end of the street, turn left on to Tahmis

Caddesi and you will reach Kurukahreci Mehmet Efendi ⑧, a traditional coffee shop, opened in 1871, famous for its range of blends.

Galata Bridge

Walk to Galata Bridge ⑨ for fantastic views of the city. You can either stroll across the top and watch the many amateur fishermen suspending their

Fishermen hoping for a catch on Galata Bridge

Judaism to Islam

Walk up Harraççi Ali Sokak until you reach the Jewish Museum ⑪ on Perçemli Sokak, close to Karaköy Tünel station. This 17th-century museum, once a synagogue, now contains a fascinating collection of old photographs, documents and religious objects relating to the city's Jewish population.

From here, walk up Camekan Sokak to the Gothic-looking Beyoğlu Hospital ⑫, built in 1904 as a British naval hospital. Continue until you come to the Galata Tower ⑬ (see p107) in Galata Square, the focal point of the district. The 360° viewing deck at the top of the tower gives the perfect vantage point from which to see almost the entire city laid out before you.

Now turn right and left on to Yüksek Kaldırım Caddesi ⑭, a steep cobblestone street lined with music shops selling just about every conceivable musical instrument you can think of, both traditional and

hi-tech. Tucked away off to the right on Galip Dede Caddesi is the Mevlevi Lodge ⑮ (see p106), once home to the Whirling Dervishes.

Chic Tünel

At the top of the street, at Tünel Square on the southern terminus of İstiklal Caddesi , you have the option of catching the underground funicular ⑯ back down to Karaköy. The one-stop subway was opened in 1876 and is the third-oldest underground system in the world after that of London and New York. However, do not miss the opportunity to experience this fashionable neighbourhood. Just opposite the funicular is Tünel Geçidi, an open-air passage lined with late 19th-century European-style buildings, most of which have now been turned into apartments with shops and cafés at ground level. For a refreshing iced coffee in sumptuous Viennese-style surroundings, pop into the KV restaurant ⑰, before making your way to ARtrium ⑱ to pick up some high-class antiques.

To return to Sultanahmet/Old City, catch the Tünel funicular back to Karaköy and walk through the underground shopping centre to the Karaköy T1 tram station.

⑧ Coffee machine, Kurukahveci Mehmet Efendi

Key

••• Walk route

0 metres 250
0 yards 250

rods into the water below in hope of a catch, or go down the steps and walk along the lower deck, where there are a number of cafés, bars and restaurants. After a leisurely moment spent taking in the breathtaking views of the Bosphorus below, continue to the bustling and aromatic Karaköy fish market ⑩, home to cafés serving delicious fish meals and sandwiches at bargain prices.

Fresh fish at the Karaköy fish market

TRAVELLERS' NEEDS

WHERE TO STAY

Whether you feel like staying in an Ottoman palace, taking a room in a restored mansion or a traditional wooden house, or even spending a night in a converted prison, you will find the hotel of your choice in Istanbul. As tourism continues to boom, the city's hotels and guesthouses now cater to every kind of taste and budget. Accommodation in Istanbul tends to be clustered around the main sightseeing areas. Sultanahmet has many of the city's historic hotels, guesthouses and boutique hotels. Beyoğlu, across the Golden Horn, is a good place to look for three- and four-star hotels, including the

grand old hotels of the 19th century. Design hotels are also proliferating in all areas.

The hotels listed on pages 186–9 have been chosen from the best the city can offer across all price ranges. Each hotel is given a brief description and details are provided about the facilities available. For a broad range, check the website www.istanbulhotels.com. *Cornucopia*, a glossy magazine about Turkey, offers a hand-picked selection available for booking at www.cornucopiahotels.com. Information on other types of accommodation can be found on page 185.

Choosing a Hotel

Many hotels in Istanbul are rated by the Ministry of Culture and Tourism according to a star system. They range from comfortable but basic one-star hotels to five-star luxury hotels. Other types of accommodation licensed by the Ministry are the converted buildings known as Special Licence hotels. A further category is the accommodation licensed by the Greater Istanbul Municipality. These hotels offer perfectly reasonable facilities, but with less stringent standards.

Accommodation is available in most central areas of the city. The Sultanahmet district is conveniently situated within walking distance of most of the city's major sights. Many of the Special Licence hotels in this area are tucked away on formerly residential side streets. There are guesthouses along Divanyolu Caddesi, the main road, and along the slopes leading down

Elegant furnishing at Baylo Suites

to the Sea of Marmara. Along with these, there are also middle-range hotels in central Sultanahmet.

Beyoğlu, the old European centre of Istanbul, is within easy reach of the best sights in the city. This area has innumerable impressive hotels that are comfortable and dependable, international chain hotels and some stylish recent additions.

The Asian side of Istanbul is mainly residential, but has some hotels, though they are generally used more by Turks than foreigners and tourists.

Luxury Hotels

There has been rapid growth in the number of luxury hotels in the city, and most international chains are now represented in Istanbul. Almost all five-star

hotels here boast spectacular views of Marmara or the Bosphorus, and between them they have some of the best international restaurants in the city. All the major hotels have swimming pools and health clubs. Many of them also have Turkish baths. Conference facilities are provided, and many hotels have extensive entertainment facilities. Most of them can also arrange tours of Istanbul and nearby places through local companies. They also provide facilities for disabled visitors, arrange special activities for children *(see p184)* and have wireless Internet in all their rooms.

Special Licence Hotels

A number of the city's old buildings have been renovated

The luxurious Four Seasons Hotel *(see p187)*, formerly a prison

◄ An array of Turkish lanterns for sale

and transformed into historic hotels. However, due to the nature of the buildings in which they are housed, some of these hotels cannot provide facilities such as lifts. They belong to a separate category, the Special Licence hotels, and are under independent private management.

These hotels constitute some of Istanbul's most interesting and attractive hotels. They are often located in the residential streets of historic areas, and range from small, modestly priced traditional wooden houses to luxury Ottoman mansions and town houses. Special Licence hotels, whether large or small, are generally of a high standard.

The authentic period decor of many of them gives even the larger ones a warm atmosphere.

The listings on the following pages provide plenty of examples, especially of boutique Special Licence hotels in Sultanahmet. Increasingly, many of the city's boutique-style hotels are opting not to apply for official ratings or stars.

This does not, however, imply any lack of standards or amenities. In fact, these establishments are contributing to the continually rising

Lovely view from the rooftop terrace of the historic Adahan Istanbul *(see p 187)*

standards of accommodation in the city. All have their own websites on which you can take a virtual tour, compare prices and facilities, and make a booking.

Cheaper Hotels

Istanbul has plenty of cheap, comfortable accommodation, which meets the standards of the Turkish Ministry of Culture and Tourism.

However, if you are choosing one of the cheaper hotels, do not base your decision on the façade or lobby, which may look brand new.

One-star hotels provide the most basic facilities, but often have rooms with a private shower and toilet. Two- and three-star hotels have more comfortable rooms and usually a café or bar. Many three-star hotels offer rooms with a TV and mini-bar.

Guesthouses vary in terms of facilities. Most provide bedlinen and towels, and the better ones will have rooms with en-suite bathrooms. All should have communal cooking facilities. While cheaper hotels usually have central heating, they are unlikely to have air conditioning, but an electric fan may be provided. Some small hotels

Pretty façade of Yeşil Ev *(see p 186)*, a Special Licence hotel

may not provide hot water 24 hours a day.

What to Expect

All hotels listed in this book are comfortable and welcoming. Front desk staff usually speak English, and will be able to offer information on sights and travel.

At some budget and mid-range hotels you may need to specify if you want a double bed rather than two singles when booking or checking in.

Most hotels with three or more storeys will have a lift. However, there may not be a lift in a Special Licence hotel because of the problems of installing one in an older building. Facilities for wheelchair users are increasingly found in hotels these days.

Noise can be a problem even in some smart hotels, so in busy areas choose a room that does not face a main street. If you are not satisfied with your room, you can always ask for another.

Breakfast is included in the price of the room and typically consists of a generous open buffet, including cold meats, fruits, cereals and yogurt. Many larger hotels have restaurants that serve à la carte meals. Upmarket hotels have at least one dining room serving evening meals, but some of the smaller, cheaper hotels do not. It is a good idea to check while booking and confirm by email or fax before you visit.

Grand entrance to Pera Palace Hotel Jumeirah (see p188)

Prices and Discounts

Hotel prices are quoted in US dollars, Euros and Turkish lira (₺). Prices are per room, not per person. All prices usually include breakfast and tax. Apart from top-class hotels, which have standard prices that do not change through the year, tariffs differ according to the season. The busy season, when hotel prices tend to be at their highest, is from April to the end of October. During the brief Christmas and New Year period, the higher summer tariffs are applied. There are few single rooms, but all hotels offer a single room rate of slightly more than half the price of a double room.

Lounge area of the Empress Zoe (see p186)

It is always worth attempting to bargain with hotels, but do not expect to get a discount. For longer stays of a week or more, you may be able to get a reduction. Some hotels also offer discounts for Internet bookings, cash payments, or out-of-season stays. However, do not expect a room with any kind of a view if you have got it at a discount.

While you will always be able to find a room of a reasonable standard, it is advisable to book in advance for the best hotels or those of your choice during the busy season. You can book any hotel listed in this guide directly, by telephone, fax and email. Nearly all hotels also have their own website registration forms and are included in the major booking websites. You may be asked to give your credit card details, which will guarantee your reservation. If you cannot find a place in any of the hotels that fall in your preferred price range, try one of the established travel companies based in Istanbul, such as **Gazella Travel Designer**, **Meptur**, **Plan Tours** (see p245) or **VIP Tourism**. If you arrive without a reservation, the tourist information offices (see p229) in the airport, Sirkeci Station, Sultanahmet Square or Karaköy International Maritime Terminal will help you find a hotel, but they will not make a reservation for you.

Checking Out and Paying

Guests are expected to check out by midday, but hotels will usually keep luggage for collec-

tion later. All hotels accept the major credit cards, as well as Turkish lira and other currencies. VAT is always included in the room price. It is usual to leave a few dollars, or its equivalent, in the room for the cleaner, and to give a tip to the receptionist to be divided among the staff. Phone calls and mini-bar drinks can add to the size of your bill.

Children

Children up to six years of age are often not charged for rooms, and pay 50 per cent until 12 years old. It is possible to negotiate a discount for older children who share a room with their parents. Most hotels also have cots.

Some hotels arrange special entertainment for children. The Swissôtel (see p189) offers a weekend package.

Hostels

For those on a tight budget, Istanbul has a number of inexpensive hostels, mostly in the Sultanahmet area. The **Sultan Hostel** is located right in the heart of the Sultanahmet district, close to Haghia Sophia, Topkapı Palace and the Grand Bazaar. The Sultan is a member of the International Youth Hostel Federation (IYHF) and offers a discount for members. There are many other hostels in the city; those on the north side of the Golden Horn in Galata and Beyoğlu, such as **#Bunk**, are popular among youngsters due to the area's vibrant nightlife. On the same street is the **Orient**

Indoor pool at The Edition (see p189)

Classy interiors at the excellent design hostel, #Bunk *(see p188)*

Hostel, a youth hostel with excellent facilities, including a rooftop café, a bar and a safe. The tour operator Gençtur is also affiliated to the IYHF and can provide information on other hostels.

Camping

Camping and caravanning in Turkey have steadily gained popularity in recent years. There is an ever-increasing variety of excellent camp sites with self-catering facilities open in the summer season, which lasts from May until October. **Londra Kamping** is open through the year. It has facilities for washing and cooking, a fast-food restaurant, bar, pool table and football pitch. As well as providing facilities for camping, it also has two-room bungalows for rent.

For further details, contact the **Turkish Camping and Caravanning Association**, which is helpful and informative. The association also has a website with comprehensive listings of sites throughout the country.

Self-catering

Istanbul has a growing number of apartment hotels providing fully furnished apartments for those who prefer more homely surroundings. In the listings, we have included a number of stand out apartments, which are handy for tourists. The **Akmerkez Residence**, which is mostly used by businessmen, is in the upmarket Akmerkez shopping mall in Etiler *(see p211)*. Its luxuriously decorated flats have air conditioning and all the domestic appliances.

The **Entes Apart Hotel** has compact modern apartments. Global real estate franchises, such as **Century 21** and **Remax**, can assist in finding long- or short-term rental accommodation.

The Dolmabahçe Mosque as viewed from the Swissôtel *(see p189)*

Recommended Hotels

The accommodation options featured in this guide have been selected from across a wide price range for their excellent facilities, good location and value. These include stylish, modern hotels as well as hotels steeped in history. Visitors can also consider staying in one of the well-furnished apartment hotels. For a more intimate experience, there are several acclaimed guesthouses and boutique options, along with hostels for those on a budget. The places highlighted as DK Choice are the very best of the pack, chosen for being outstanding in some way. They may stand in beautiful surroundings, be located within a historically important building or simply offer a particularly special and memorable experience.

DIRECTORY

Travel Agents

Gazella Travel Designer
Ulus Mah Öztopuz Cad 16, Beşiktaş.
Tel (0212) 233 15 98.
W gazella.com

Meptur
Büyükdere Cad 26, Mecidiyeköy.
Tel (0212) 275 02 50.
W meptur.com.tr

VIP Tourism
Cumhuriyet Cad 167A, Harbiye.
Tel (0212) 368 48 00.
W viptourism.com.tr

Youth Hostels

#Bunk
Balık Sok 7, Beyoğlu.
Map 7 D4. **Tel** (0212) 244 88 08.
W bunkhostels.com

Orient Hostel
Akbıyık Cad 9, Sultanahmet.
Map 3 E5 (5 E5). **Tel** (0212) 517 94 93. W orienthostel.com

Sultan Hostel
Akbıyık Cad 17, Sultanahmet.
Map 3 E5 (5 E5). **Tel** (0212) 516 92 60. W sultanhostel.com

Camping

Londra Kamping
Londra Asfaltı, Bakırköy.
Tel (0212) 560 42 00.
Fax (0212) 559 34 38.

Turkish Camping and Caravanning Association
Bestekar sok, No. 62/12 Kavaklıdere, Ankara.
Tel (0312) 466 19 97.
W kampkaravan.org.tr

Self-catering

Akmerkez Residence
Akmerkez Shopping & Business Centre, Etiler.
Tel (0212) 282 01 20.
W akmerkez.com.tr

Century 21
Topçular Kışla Cad 5, Rami-Eyüp.
Tel (0212) 493 26 00.
W century21.com.tr

Entes Apart Hotel
İpek Sok 19, Taksim.
Map 7 E4.
Tel (0212) 293 22 08.
W entesapart.com

Remax
Tel (0212) 232 48 20.
W remax.com.tr

Where to Stay

Apartments
Seraglio Point

Romantic Mansion Istanbul ₺₺
*Nöbethane Cad, Tayahatun
Sok 28, Sirkeci*
Tel *(0212) 638 96 35*   **Map** 5 E1
Ⓦ romanticmansion.com
Three lovely flats in a self-sufficient
pink and white building. Views of
Gulhane Park from the terrace.

Beyoğlu

DK Choice

Baylo Suites ₺₺
Galata Kulesi Sok 24, 34420
Tel *(0212) 245 98 60*   **Map** 3 D1
Ⓦ baylosuites.com
Four self-contained apartments
in a historic Galata building,
lovingly restored by a mother-
daughter team. It is Istanbul's
first historic restoration project
to meet American ecological
standards. Many original features
have been preserved, and a
gallery downstairs sells historic
prints, postcards and maps.

Galata Flats ₺₺
Tünel Meydanı 84, 34430
Tel *(0212) 244 26 76*   **Map** 7 D5
Ⓦ galataflats.com
Ideal for longer stays, with homely
comforts and plenty of space.
Flats are serviced daily.

Istanbul Place Apartments ₺₺₺
Serdar-ı Ekrem Cad, Galata
Tel *(0772) 925 16 76*
Ⓦ istanbulplace.com
Friendly Anglo-Turkish couple
offer a range of beautifully
restored period apartments.

Simple and classy bedroom interiors
at Baylo Suites, Beyoğlu

Boutique Hotels
Seraglio Point

DK Choice

The Kybele Hotel ₺₺
*Yerebatan Cad 35,
Sultanahmet, 34410*
Tel *(0212) 511 77 66*   **Map** 5 E3
Ⓦ kybelehotel.com
Four thousand coloured glass
lamps decorate this wooden
Sultanahmet town house, while
antique gramophones vie for
attention with heavy fabrics and
equally fat rich wallpaper. Yet, the
Kybele never feels overdone,
only welcoming and relaxed.

Sirkeci Mansion ₺₺₺
Taya Hatun Sok 5, 34120, Sirkeci
Tel *(0212) 528 43 44*   **Map** 5 E2
Ⓦ sirkecimansion.com
Extremely well-run hotel set in a
period building abutting the outer
walls of the Topkapı Palace complex. A gym, sauna and great
rooftop terrace make it special.

Sultanahmet

Aruna ₺
*Cankurtaran Mah, Ahırkapı
Sok 74, 34122*
Tel *(0212) 458 54 88*   **Map** 5 F5
Ⓦ arunahotel.com
Homely, with Jacuzzis or *hamam*-
style bathrooms in suites. Some
rooms have separate living areas.

Hotel Nena ₺
Klodfarer Cad 8–10, 34122
Tel *(0212) 516 52 64*   **Map** 5 D4
Ⓦ istanbulhotelnena.com
Stylish and charming hotel
with a leafy courtyard café and
terrace restaurant.

Dersaadet ₺₺
*Küçük Ayasofya Cad, Kapıağası
Sok 5, 34400*
Tel *(0212) 458 07 60*   **Map** 5 D5
Ⓦ dersaadethotel.com
A striking, red, wooden building
close to the Blue Mosque. Antique
decor; friendly, professional staff.

Hotel Empress Zoe ₺₺
Akbıyık Cad 10, 34122
Tel *(0212) 518 43 60*   **Map** 5 F4
Ⓦ emzoe.com
Lovely garden courtyard, Byzantine substructures and a roof
terrace with great Haghia Sophia
and Blue Mosque views. Individually designed rooms and
professional management.

Hotel Ibrahim Pasha ₺₺
Terzihane Sok 5, 34110
Tel *(0212) 518 03 94*   **Map** 5 D4
Ⓦ ibrahimpasha.com
Stylish, well-run hotel housed in a
pair of atmospheric town houses
away from traffic. Elegant rooms
where old meets new.

Hotel Nomade ₺₺
Ticarethane Sok 15, 34410
Tel *(0212) 513 81 72*   **Map** 5 D3
Ⓦ hotelnomade.com
This designer hotel makes a
refreshing change from the faux-
Ottoman hotels around it. Stylish
roof terrace with commanding
views of the Haghia Sophia.

Hotel Turkoman ₺₺
Asmalı Çeşme Sok 2, Adliye Yanı, 34490
Tel *(0212) 516 29 56*   **Map** 5 D4
Ⓦ turkomanhotel.com
Down-to-earth, with 18 simple
and comfortable rooms, helpful
staff and incredible views.

**Hotel Valide
Sultan Konağı** ₺₺
*Ishakpasa Cad Kutlugün Sok 1,
34122*
Tel *(0212) 517 65 58*   **Map** 5 F4
Ⓦ hotelvalidesultan.com
Family-run, with an emphasis on
service. Quaint, antique furnishings,
but all modern conveniences.

White House Hotel ₺₺
Çatalçeşme Sok 21, 34122
Tel *(0212) 526 00 19*   **Map** 3 D4
Ⓦ istanbulwhitehouse.com
Plush Neo-Ottoman style hotel
with ultra-high standards of service.
Well-located and has major sights
at easy walking distance.

Yeşil Ev ₺₺
Kabasakal Cad 5, 34122
Tel *(0212) 517 67 85*   **Map** 5 E4
Ⓦ yesilev.com.tr
This hotel ushered in a new era of
boutique tourism in Sultanahmet.
It is one of the best options here.

Beyoğlu

Sub Hotel ₺₺
Necatibey Cad 91, Karaköy, 34435
Tel *(0212) 243 00 05*   **Map** 3 E1
Ⓦ subistanbul.com
Hip hotel with a trendy bar on
the roof terrace. Rooms are in

bold colours with rivetted iron bathroom stalls. The organic breakfast here is a treat.

The House Hotel Galatasaray ₺₺
Firuzağa Mah, Bostanbaşı Cad 19, 34425
Tel *(0212) 252 04 22*   **Map** 7 E4
Ⓦ thehousehotel.com
Homeliest of the House Hotels in a stylishly restored 19th-century town house located on a quiet street below bustling İstiklal Caddesi. Lovely views from the roof terrace.

Georges Hotel Galata ₺₺₺
Serdar-ı Ekrem Cad 24, 34425
Tel *(0212) 244 24 23*   **Map** 7 D5
Ⓦ georges.com
First-class luxury and great views in a grand town house. Contemporary features include iPad docking stations and flatscreen TVs.

Vault Karaköy ₺₺₺
Bankalar Cad 5, Karaköy, 34421
Tel *(0212) 244 34 00*   **Map** 3 D1
Ⓦ thehousehotel.com
A grandiose 19th-century bank converted into a superb boutique hotel run by the House group. Stocked with fine wines.

Witt Istanbul Suites ₺₺₺
Defterdar Yokuşu 26, Cihangir, 34433
Tel *(0212) 293 15 00*   **Map** 7 E5
Ⓦ wittistanbul.com
Well-run designer hotel with a stunning roof terrace. Great location adds to its charm.

Greater Istanbul
Kariye Hotel ₺
Kariye Camii Sok 6, Edirnekapi
Tel *(0212) 534 84 14*   **Map** 1 B1
Ⓦ kariyeotel.com
Next door to the Church of St Saviour in Chora, this period building makes for an unusual stay in Istanbul. The excellent Asitane restaurant *(see p204)* is attached.

The House Hotel Nişantaşı ₺₺
Abdi İpekçi Cad 34, Nişantaşı, 34367
Tel *(0212) 224 59 99*   **Map** 7 F1
Ⓦ thehousehotel.com
The House chain's most fashionable address; set above the Prada store. Features include a well-stocked library and lavish buffet breakfast.

Bosphorus
The House Hotel Bosphorus ₺₺₺
Salhane Sok 1, Ortaköy, 34347
Tel *(0212) 327 77 87*   **Map** 8 A3
Ⓦ thehousehotel.com
Celebrity favourite; by a scenic waterside square and close to the city's exclusive night spots.

Picturesque setting of The House Hotel Bosphorus

Beyond Istanbul
Acqua Verde ₺₺
Kurfallı Yakuplu Cad 34980, Şile
Tel *(0216) 721 71 43*
Ⓦ acquaverde.com.tr
Set on the reed-lined banks of a river, this hotel offers a mix of stylish standard rooms and bungalows with a rustic feel.

A'jia ₺₺
Çubuklu Cad 27, Kanlıca, 34810
Tel *(0216) 413 93 00*
Ⓦ ajiahotel.com
Converted traditional wooden waterfront *yalı* (mansion), at a Bosphorus-front location, with contemporary décor.

Aya Nikola Butik Pansiyon ₺₺
Aya Nikola Mevki 104, Büyükada, 34970
Tel *(0126) 382 41 43*
On the waterfront in Büyükada, this 11-room hotel is a real getaway and the perfect antidote to teeming Istanbul.

Hotel des Etrangers ₺₺
Yalı Cad 25, Çanakkale
Tel *(0286) 214 24 24*
Charming eight-room boutique hotel, close to the waterfront in the seaside town of Çanakkale.

Mehtap 45 ₺₺
Burgazada
Tel *(0126) 381 26 60*
Set on the most peaceful of the four main Princes' Islands, Burgazada, with sea views across to metropolitan Istanbul.

Historic Hotels
Seraglio Point
Ayasofya Konakları ₺₺
Soğuk Çeşme Sok, Sultanahmet, 34400
Tel *(0212) 513 36 00*   **Map** 5 F3
Ⓦ ayasofyakonaklari.com
19th-century wooden Ottoman mansions along a leafy cobbled street. Pretty courtyard café.

Ottoman Hotel Imperial ₺₺
Caferiye Sok 6/1, 34400, Sultanahmet
Tel *(0212) 513 61 51*   **Map** 5 E3
Ⓦ ottomanhotelimperial.com
A converted Ottoman hospital that offers sheer opulence. Traditional Ottoman-style rooms.

Sultanahmet
Deluxe Golden Horn Hotel ₺₺
Binbirdirek Meydanı Sok 1, 34400
Tel *(0212) 518 17 17*   **Map** 5 D4
Ⓦ goldenhornhotel.com
One of the few hotels to maintain an atmosphere of the Orient Express era. Pleasingly traditional.

Four Seasons Sultanahmet ₺₺₺
Tevkifhane Sok 1, 34110
Tel *(0212) 402 30 00*   **Map** 5 F4
Ⓦ fourseasons.com
Originally an Ottoman prison, this luxurious hotel now offers ample pampering, plus a herb-scented garden.

Bazaar Quarter
Legacy Ottoman ₺₺
Hamidiye Cad 16, Eminönü, 34112
Tel *(0212) 527 67 67*   **Map** 5 D1
Ⓦ legacyottomanhotel.com
Impressive early 20th-century complex that dominates the bustling market. Simple rooms.

Beyoğlu
Büyük Londra Oteli (Grand Hotel de Londres) ₺
Meşrutiyet Cad 53, 34430, Tepebaşı
Tel *(0212) 245 06 70*   **Map** 7 D4
Ⓦ londrahotel.net
This period hotel is one of the most famous in Istanbul and great value.

Adahan Istanbul ₺₺
General Yazgan Sokağı 14, 34430
Tel *(0212) 243 85 81*   **Map** 7 D5
Ⓦ adahanistanbul.com
Sensitively restored historic apartment building. Large rooms, high ceilings and simple design.

For more information on types of hotels *see page 182*

Impressive entrance to the Pera Palace Hotel Jumeirah, Beyoğlu

Palazzo Donizetti ₺₺₺
Asmali Mescit Sok 55, 34400
Tel *(0212) 249 51 51*   Map 7 D5
ⓦ palazzodonizetti.com
A grand old building reminiscent of a European château, with a continental approach to luxury.

Pera Palace
Hotel Jumeirah ₺₺₺
Meşrutiyet Cad 52, 34430, Tepebaşı
Tel *(0212) 377 40 00*   Map 7 D5
ⓦ jumeirah.com
Quintessential Istanbul hotel with suites named after famous guests.

Bosphorus

Çırağan Palace Kempinski ₺₺₺
Çırağan Cad 32, Beşiktaş
Tel *(0212) 326 46 46*   Map 9 E3
ⓦ kempinski.com
The only Istanbul hotel to occupy a royal Ottoman palace. Waterside terrace with heated infinity pool.

DK Choice

Sumahan on the Water ₺₺₺
Kuleli Cad 43, 34684
Tel *(0216) 422 80 00*
ⓦ sumahan.com
A multi-award-winning converted distillery. Every room has a sea view, and some open onto a lawn terrace. The hotel offers a boat shuttle service, in case guests ever feel like leaving the spa and excellent restaurant.

Beyond Istanbul

Splendid Palas Hotel ₺₺
23 Nisan Cad 53, Büyükada
Tel *(0216) 382 69 50*
ⓦ splendidhotel.net
The most venerable hotel on the Princes' Islands. Undeniable charm, and a historic heritage.

Les Ottomans ₺₺₺
Muallim Nacı Cad 68
Tel *(0212) 359 15 00*
ⓦ lesottomans.com
Housed in an old waterfront mansion, Les Ottomans offers superlative Bosphorus views. Relax in the sumptuous Caudalie spa or dine at the Şamadan restaurant.

Hostels and Guesthouses
Sultanahmet

Agora Guest
House and Hostel ₺
Amiral Tafdil Sok 6
Tel *(0212) 458 55 47*   Map 5 F5
ⓦ agoraguesthouse.com
Well-renovated accommodation with a communal lounge and TV, computer terminals, and a great terrace. Choose between mixed-sex dorms or private doubles.

Akdeniz Hotel
Guest House ₺
Haci Tahsin Bey Sok 7, 34410
Tel *(0212) 520 20 99*
ⓦ istanbulakdenizhotel.com
Modest guesthouse with clean, comfortable rooms, and a *hamam* nearby. Ask for a discount.

Sultan Hostel ₺
Akbıyık Cad 17, 34122
Tel *(0212) 516 92 60*   Map 5 F4
ⓦ sultanhostel.com
Ideal for backpackers; choose between private and dorm rooms. Safe, close to main sights, and a pub downstairs.

Beyoğlu

DK Choice

#Bunk ₺
Balik Sok 7, 34435
Tel *(0212) 244 88 08*   Map 7 D4
ⓦ bunkhostels.com
A great and original idea – low-price accommodation with a cool design philosophy – makes #Bunk the perfect base for a social city break. The group hopes to expand to more properties soon.

Rapunzel Guest House ₺
Kardibey Çıkmaz 4, Galata, 34420
Tel *(0212) 292 50 34*   Map 6 D5
ⓦ rapunzelistanbul.com
A mix of trendy dorms and doubles in a well-restored and artistically decorated period house close to the landmark Galata Tower. Friendly, well-run and serves huge breakfasts.

Beyond Istanbul

Geçim Pansiyon ₺
Avşaadası, 10940, Avşaadası
Tel *(0535) 926 10 20*
ⓦ gecimpansiyon.net
On an island in the Sea of Marmara reached by ferry from Istanbul and Tekirdağ.

Rustempaşa Kervansaray ₺
Iki Kapılıhan Cad 57, Edirne, 22100
Tel *(0284) 212 61 19*
ⓦ edirnekervansarayhotel.com
Converted 16th-century caravanserai. Small, but comfortable rooms.

Modern Hotels
Seraglio Point

Gulhane Park Hotel ₺
Nöbethane Cad 1, 34112, Sirkeci
Tel *(0212) 519 68 68*   Map 5 E1
ⓦ gulhaneparkhotel.com.tr
Overlooking the Topkapı Palace gardens, with fairly priced rooms, a gym and *hamam*.

Arden City Hotel ₺₺
Kazım Ismail Gürkan Cad 2, Sultanahmet
Tel *(0212) 528 93 93*   Map 5 E3
ⓦ hotelarden.com
Recently renovated, with some rooms overlooking the Sea of Marmara. Quick service, good value for money.

Hagia Sophia Hotel
Istanbul Old City ₺₺₺
Yerebatan Cad 13, 34110, Sultanahmet
Tel *(0212) 444 93 32*   Map 5 E3
ⓦ hsoldcity.com
Smart and modern option in the heart of the Old City, with an

Elegant room interior at #Bunk, a design hostel in Beyoğlu

English-style pub. Good for business clients and sightseers. It also has a spacious and lovely garden restaurant.

Sultanahmet

Armada ₺
Ahır Kapı Sok 24, 34122
Tel *(0212) 455 44 55* **Map** 5 F5
Ⓦ armadahotel.com.tr
Popular with tour groups serious about seeing the sights. The terrace restaurant has one of the best views in the city.

Blue House/Mavi Ev ₺₺
Dalbasti Sok 14
Tel *(0212) 638 90 10* **Map** 5 E5
Ⓦ bluehouse.com.tr
Family-run, with first-class service. Tasteful rooms, three restaurants and all the necessary amenities.

Pierre Loti Hotel ₺₺
Piyer Loti Cad 1, 34400
Tel *(0212) 518 57 00* **Map** 4 C4
Ⓦ pierrelotihotel.com
Everything needed for a comfortable and hassle-free stay, including spa and *hamam* treatments.

Sura Hotel ₺₺
Ticarethane Sok 45
Tel *(0212) 513 66 66* **Map** 5 D3
Ⓦ surahotels.com
This hotel has many striking features: rooms are colour-coded by floor and suites come with rain showers or free-standing baths.

Bazaar Quarter

Antik Cisterna ₺₺
Sekbanbaşı Sok 10, Beyazıt, 34130
Tel *(0212) 638 58 58* **Map** 4 A3
Ⓦ antikhotel.com
Four-star hotel with a 1,500-year-old cistern in the basement now used as an entertainment venue. Floors are themed by historical events.

Grand Beyazid Hotel ₺₺
Mithat Paşa Cad, Abuhayat Sok 5 34490, Beyazıt
Tel *(0212) 638 46 41* **Map** 4 A4
Ⓦ hotelbeyazid.com
Just outside the main tourist area, and of a similar standard to more expensive hotels.

Niles Hotel ₺₺
Dibekli Cami Sok 13, Beyazıt, 34130
Tel *(0212) 517 32 39* **Map** 2 C4
Ⓦ hotelniles.com
Good value, extremely well-run and located on a quiet (for Istanbul) side street running down to the Sea of Marmara. Nicely-furnished, faux-Ottoman rooms.

Sophisticated and luxurious lobby of The Edition in Levent, Greater Istanbul

Beyoğlu

Martı ₺₺
Abdülhak Hamit Cad 25/B, Taksim, 34435
Tel *(0212) 987 40 00* **Map** 7 E3
Ⓦ martiistanbulhotel.com
Elegant five-star hotel, one of the latest projects by interior designer Zeynep Fadillioglu. Top-floor spa and gym have wonderful views.

Ceylan Intercontinental ₺₺₺
Asker Ocağı Cad 1, Taksim, 34435
Tel *(0212) 368 44 44* **Map** 7 F3
Ⓦ istanbul.intercontinental.com.tr
High-quality hospitality from this world-renowned group of hotels. Centrally located.

Taksim Marmara ₺₺₺
Taksim Meydanı
Tel *(0212) 334 83 00* **Map** 7 E4
Ⓦ taksim.themarmara hotels.com
Landmark hotel, which towers over much of the city. Even the relatively low gym and pool areas offer superb bird's-eye views.

Greater Istanbul

DK Choice

The Edition ₺₺₺
Büyükdere Cad 136, 34330
Tel *(0212) 317 77 00*
Ⓦ editionhotels.com
The Edition is in the heart of Istanbul's business district, but once inside, you enter a private world of luxury. Should visitors want to venture out, there is a convenient metro connection to the sightseeing and shopping areas. The bar and restaurant is managed by Cipriani's.

Hilton Istanbul ₺₺₺
Cumhuriyet Cad, Harbiye, 34367
Tel *(0212) 315 60 00* **Map** 7 F2
Ⓦ placeshilton.com
Surrounded by a park; the brand's first foray beyond the USA has built up quite a reputation.

Swissôtel The Bosphorus ₺₺₺
Bayildim Cad 2, 34330, Beşiktaş
Tel *(0212) 326 11 00* **Map** 8 A4
Ⓦ swissotel.com
Huge windows give jaw-dropping vistas across the Bosphorus. One of Istanbul's top five luxury hotels, Swissôtel features the award-winning Purovel Spa and Sport.

W Hotel ₺₺₺
Suleyman Seba Cad 22, Akaretler Beşiktaş, 34357
Tel *(0212) 381 21 21* **Map** 8 B4
Ⓦ wistanbul.com.tr
Set among shops, galleries and restaurants, this hotel is aimed squarely at a young, cool crowd. Rooms and suites have either gardens, terraces or cabanas.

Beyond Istanbul

Anzac ₺
Saat Kulesi Meydanı 8, 17100 Canakkale
Tel *(0286) 217 77 77*
Ⓦ anzachotel.com
A good base from which to explore the beaches and vineyards of the Dardanelles. The Gallipoli campaign is commemorated here on 25 April.

Kervansaray ₺
Fatvahane Sok 13, Çanakkale
Tel *(0286) 217 81 92*
Ⓦ canakkalekervansarayhotel.com
Along with Hotel des Etrangers, this is the most characterful hotel in Çanakkale. Converted red-brick early 20th-century mansion with a leafy courtyard out back.

Almira, Bursa ₺₺
Ulubatlı Hasan Bulvarı 5, 16200, Bursa
Tel *(0224) 250 20 20*
Ⓦ almira.com.tr
A large, luxurious hotel with a music venue, restaurants, bars, shopping and swimming pools on site. There is also a terrace overlooking the city.

Hotel Çelik Palace Thermal Spa ₺₺
Çekirge Cad 79, 16000, Bursa
Tel *(0224) 233 38 00*
Ⓦ celikpalasotel.com
The star attraction is the biggest thermal pool in the city. Best to relax after skiing on Uludağ or exploring Bursa's Ottoman sights.

For more information on types of hotels *see page 182*

WHERE TO EAT AND DRINK

Istanbul's restaurants range from the informal *lokanta* and kebab house, which are found on almost every street corner, to the gourmet restaurants *(restoran)* of large hotels. There are a variety of international restaurants in the city that offer fare from France to Japan at middle to high prices. Pages 192–4 illustrate the most typical Turkish dishes, and the phrase book on pages 279–80 will help you tackle the menu. On page 195, you will find a guide to drinks available. The restaurants listed on pages 196–207 have been chosen from the best that Istanbul has to offer across all price ranges, from casual eateries to award-winning restaurants. They have been recommended for their quality of food, service and value for money. A detailed description is provided with examples of signature dishes. Light meals and snacks sold by street vendors and served in cafés and bars are described on pages 208–9.

Where to Look

Istanbul's smartest and most expensive restaurants are concentrated in the European parts of the city: along the Bosphorus in Ortaköy; in and around Taksim; in the chic shopping districts of Nişantaşı, Maçka, Bebek and Teşvikiye; and in the modern residential suburbs of Levent and Etiler, west of the Bosphorus. The best gourmet restaurants for both Western and Turkish food are often in five-star hotels.

Beyoğlu district has the liveliest restaurants, cafés and fast-food eateries, particularly around İstiklal Caddesi *(see pp104–105)*, which cater to a young crowd. Many Sultanahmet restaurants cater primarily to tourists, while those in the neighbouring districts of Sirkeci, Eminönü and Beyazıt are full of inexpensive restaurants serving the local population. There are also some stylish restaurants with modern decor in these areas. Further afield, in areas such as Fatih, Fener, Balat and Eyüp, there are plenty of cheap restaurants, cafés and bakeries.

Types of Restaurant

The most common type of restaurant is the traditional *lokanta* – an ordinary restaurant offering a variety of dishes, often listed by the entrance. Homemade dishes comprise hot meat and vegetable dishes displayed in steel containers. Other options may be *sulu yemek* (a stew) and *et* (grilled meat and kebabs).

Equally ubiquitous is the Turkish kebab house *(kebapçı* or *ocakbaşı)*. Along with grilled meats, most kebab houses serve *lahmacun*, a very thin dough base with minced meat, onions and tomato sauce on top. Cheaper restaurants also serve *pide*, a flattened bread base, served with toppings like eggs, cheese or lamb. There are also a few specialist *pide* restaurants.

If you have had too much to drink you may welcome tripe soup *(işkembe)*, a Turkish cure for hangovers, before going to bed. *İşkembe* restaurants stay open until early morning. The atmosphere is always informal and lively in Istanbul's innumerable fish restaurants

Spectacular views of the Old City from 360 East *(see p204)*

(balık lokantası). The best ones are located on the shores of the Bosphorus *(see pp204–206)* and in Kumkapı, on the Sea of Marmara, which is like one large open-air restaurant in summer. A typical fish restaurant will offer a large variety of *mezes (see p194)* before you order your main course from the day's catch. Skipjack tuna *(palamut)*, fresh sardines *(sardalya)* and sea bass *(levrek)* are the most popular fish. Also popular are Black Sea *hamsi* (a kind of anchovy), *istavrit* (bluefin) and *mezgit* (whiting). As fish become scarcer and more expensive, farmed fish has become more widely accepted, particularly *çipura* (sea bream). Fish is served fried or grilled and often accompanied by a large salad and a bottle of rakı *(see p195)*. Most fish restaurants in busy areas will not accept reservations, but if you cannot find a table at one restaurant,

Beautiful hanging garden at Nar Lokanta *(see p199)*, Bazaar Quarter

Elegant dining area at Park Şamdan *(see p203)*

you will probably find one at another nearby.

International culinary experiences are encouraging local chefs to be more adventurous; the best are crafting superb, original food in a beautiful ambience. Wealthier Turks frequent the foreign restaurants found in a number of neighbourhoods, while global icons such as Starbucks and Gloria Jean's are becoming part of everyday life.

A *meyhane* is a tavern, serving alcohol and a variety of *mezes*. These are more casual and attract a younger crowd. The accent is mostly on drinking; there is usually *fasıl* music and musicians who play atmospheric tunes on a zither or drum.

Opening Hours

Turks eat lunch between 12:30 and 2pm, and dinner around 8pm. Ordinary restaurants and kebab houses are open from about 11am to 11pm, while fish restaurants serve all day and stay open later. International restaurants have strict opening hours, usually from noon to 3:30pm and 7:30pm to midnight. *Meyhanes* will be open from 7pm until well after midnight. Most restaurants are open daily, but some are closed only on Sunday. During Ramazan *(see p49)*, when Muslims fast from sunrise to sunset, many restaurants are closed. Some only shut during daylight hours and then serve special Ramazan meals, while others, especially in religious areas such as Fatih and Eyüp, close for the whole month. In sightseeing areas, however, there is always one open somewhere.

What to Expect

Since July 2009, smoking has been banned in all indoor establishments, although illegal lighting up is not unheard of.

Cheaper restaurants and kebab houses often do not serve alcohol. Others cannot because they are near a mosque or religious site. When alcohol is served, it can be expensive.

Accessibility for wheelchairs is somewhat hit or miss. Restaurants are often multilevel with family rooms on the upper floors, and ground-floor restaurants often have a step leading up to the entrance. Lifts are not common outside of large hotels and offices. Many restaurants offer options for vegetarians.

In local Turkish restaurants in conservative parts of the city and outside Istanbul, women should look for the *aile salonu* sign. This denotes an area set aside for women and children; single women will be unwelcome in the main restaurant.

Turks are proud of their hospitality and service. Upmarket restaurants offer good service, but the same standards may not always apply in cheaper places.

Service and Paying

The major credit cards are widely accepted, except in the cheaper restaurants, kebab houses, local *bufés* (snack kiosks) and some *lokantas*. Restaurants usually display the credit card sign if they accept this form of payment. Value-added tax (*KDV* in Turkish) is always included. Some places add 10 per cent for service while others leave it to the discretion of the customer.

A selection of pastries

Recommended Restaurants

All the restaurants on the pages that follow have been carefully selected to offer a cross-section of the best options from across the city – from the smartest and most upmarket establishments to the best budget food eateries. Restaurants and cafés in Istanbul offer a wide range of cuisines, including Ottoman, fusion, and international dishes, but you should not miss the traditional Turkish restaurants (*lokanta*, *meyhane*) either. The DK Choice restaurants are extra special. These are the truly exceptional establishments – those that boast superb cuisine, presentation, service and location, or just offer a unique and unmissable experience.

Delicious fried and grilled mackerel sold on the Eminönü quayside *(see p208)*

The Flavours of Istanbul

The wide range of climatic zones across Turkey make it one of the few countries that can grow all its own food. Tea is cultivated in the mountains by the Black Sea and bananas in the sultry south. The Anatolian plain in between is criss-crossed by wheat fields and rich grasslands on which cattle graze, providing top-quality meat and dairy produce. Fruit and vegetables flourish everywhere and fish abound in the salty seas that lap the nation's shores. Freshness is the hallmark of this varied cuisine, drawn from the many cultures that were subject to nearly five centuries of Ottoman rule.

Nar (pomegranates)

A stall in the Spice Bazaar, one of Istanbul's oldest markets

The Anatolian Steppe

The steppe stretching from Central Asia to Anatolia is one of the oldest inhabited regions of the world. Dishes from this vast area are as varied as the different ethnic groups that live here, but are mainly traditional and simple. To fit in with a mainly nomadic way of life, food generally needed to be quick and easy to prepare. Turkey's most famous culinary staples, yogurt, flatbread and the kebab, originate in this region.

The common use of fruits, such as pomegranates, figs and apricots, in Turkish savoury dishes stems from Persian influences, filtering down with the tribes that came from the north of the steppe. From the Middle East, further south, nomads introduced the occasional fiery blash of chilli. Its use was once an essential aid to preserving meat in the searing desert heat.

Ottoman Cuisine

It was in the vast, steamy kitchens of the Topkapı Palace that a repertoire of mouthwatering dishes to rival the celebrated cuisines

A selection of typical Turkish kebabs

Lamb şiş kebab / Chicken şiş kebab / Stuffed aubergine (eggplant) / Spicy tomato sauce / Prawn (shrimp) kebab / Lamb cutlet / Döner kebab

Local Dishes and Specialities

Turkish Delight

Because of Istanbul's proximity to the sea, fresh fish is readily available and is a key ingredient on the city's menus. Since ancient times the Bosphorus has been known for its excellent fishing. In the winter months especially, there is a bounty of oil-rich fish, such as bluefish, bream, bonito tuna, sea bass, mullet and mackerel, waiting to be reeled in. From the Black Sea, Istanbul is also provided with a steady supply of juicy mussels and *hamsi*, a type of anchovy. Sweets are also popular and eaten throughout the day, not just after a meal. They are sold in shops, on stalls and by street vendors. Istanbul is renowned for its baklava (sweet pastries coated with syrup and often filled with nuts).

Midye dolması Mussels are stuffed with a spiced rice mixture, steamed and served with a squirt of lemon juice.

A splendid array of fruit, vegetables and dried goods in the Spice Bazaar

Bazaar Culture

A visit to the market that spills out around Istanbul's Spice Bazaar *(see p90)* is an absolute must. A cornucopia of fine ingredients is brought here daily from farms that surround the city. Apricots, watermelons, cherries and figs sit alongside staple vegetables, such as peppers, onions, aubergines and tomatoes. Fine cuts of lamb and beef, cheeses, pickles, herbs, spices and honey-drenched pastries and puddings are also on offer.

KNOW YOUR FISH

The profusion of different species in the waters around Istanbul makes the city a paradise for fish-lovers:

Barbunya Red mullet

Çipura Sea bream

Dilbalığı Sole

Hamsi Anchovy

Kalamar Squid

Kalkan Turbot

Kefal Grey mullet

Kılıç Swordfish

Levrek Sea bass

Lüfer Bluefish

Midye Mussels

Palamut Bonito tuna

Uskumru Mackerel

of France and China grew up. At the height of the Ottoman Empire, in the 16th and 17th centuries, legions of kitchen staff slaved away on the sultan's behalf. Court cooks usually specialized in particular dishes. Some prepared soups, while others just grilled meats or fish, or dreamed up combinations of vegetables, or baked breads, or made puddings and sherberts. As Ottoman rule expanded to North Africa, the Balkans and parts of southern Russia, influences from these far-flung places crept into the Turkish imperial kitchens. Complex dishes of finely seasoned stuffed meats and vegetables, often with such fanciful names as "lady's lips", "Vizier's fingers" and the "fainting Imam", appeared. This imperial tradition lives on

in many of Istanbul's restaurants, where dishes such as *karnıyarık* (halved aubergines (eggplant) stuffed with minced lamb, pine nuts and dried fruit) and *hünkar beğendili köfte* (meatballs served with a smooth purée of smoked aubergine and cheese) grace the menu.

Fresh catch from the Bosphorus on a fish stall in Karaköy

İmam bayıldı Aubergines, stuffed with tomatoes, garlic and onions, are baked in the oven until meltingly soft.

Levrek pilakisi This stew is made by simmering sea bass fillets with potatoes, carrots, tomatoes, onions and garlic.

Kadayıf Rounds of shredded filo pastry are stuffed with nuts and doused with honey to make a sumptuous dessert.

Mezes

As in many southern European countries, a Turkish meal begins with a selection of appetizing starters known as *mezes*, which are placed in the middle of the table for sharing. In a basic *meyhane* restaurant, you may be offered olives, cheese and slices of melon, but in a grander establishment the choice will be enormous. Mainly consisting of cold vegetables and salads of various kinds, *mezes* can also include a number of hot dishes, such as *börek* (cheese pastries), fried mussels and squid. *Mezes* are eaten with bread and traditionally washed down with *rakı* (a clear, anise-flavoured spirit).

Haydarı (strained yogurt and garlic dip) with bread

Zeytinyağlı enginar (artichokes)

Çoban salatası (tomato, red onion and cucumber salad)

Ayşe fasulye (green beans with tomato sauce)

Kavun with beyaz peynir (melon with a creamy, feta-like cheese)

Yaprak dolması (stuffed vine leaves)

Tarama (a dip made with cod's roe, garlic and olive oil)

Turkish Breads

Bread is the cornerstone of every meal in Turkey and comes in a wide range of shapes and styles. Besides *ekmek* (crusty white loaves) the other most common types of Turkish bread are *yufka*, *lavaş* and *pide*. *Yufka*, the typical bread of nomadic communities, is made from thinly rolled sheets of dough cooked on a griddle. *Lavaş* is the urban equivalent of *yufka* and is usually served as a starter in kebab restaurants. *Pide* is a semi-leavened flatbread, often served with *mezes* and kebabs in restaurants. It consists of a flattened circle or oval of dough, sometimes brushed with beaten egg and sprinkled with sesame seeds or black cumin, and then baked in an oven. It is a staple during many religious festivals. In the month of Ramazan, no meal is considered complete without *pide*. Another popular bread is *simit*, a crisp, ring-shaped savoury loaf that comes covered in sesame seeds.

A delivery of freshly baked *simit* loaves

What to Drink in Istanbul

The most common drink in Istanbul is tea *(çay)*, which is normally served black in small, tulip-shaped glasses. It is offered to you wherever you go: in shops and bazaars, and even in banks and offices. Breakfast is usually accompanied by tea, whereas small cups of strong Turkish coffee *(kahve)* are drunk mid-morning and also at the end of meals. Cold drinks include a variety of fresh fruit juices, such as orange and cherry, and refreshing syrup-based sherbets. Although Turkey does produce its own wine and beer, the most popular alcoholic drink in Istanbul is rakı, which is usually served to accompany *mezes*.

Fruit juice seller

Soft Drinks

Bottled mineral water *(su)* is sold in corner shops and served in restaurants everywhere. If you are feeling adventurous, you may like to try a glass of *ayran*, salty liquid yogurt. *Boza*, made from bulgur wheat, is another local drink to sample *(see p94)*. There is always a variety of refreshing fruit and vegetable juices available. They include cherry juice *(vişne suyu)*, turnip juice *(şalgam suyu)* and *şıra*, a juice made from fermented grapes.

Vişne suyu   Ayran

Alcoholic Drinks

The national alcoholic drink in Turkey is rakı – "lion's milk" – a clear, anise-flavoured spirit, which turns cloudy when water is added. It is drunk with fish and *mezes*. The Turkish wine industry produces some good reds and whites, served in many restaurants. Doluca and Kavaklıdere are two of the leading brands. Foreign and imported wines are widely available at high prices. Turkey's own Efes Pilsen beer is widely sold. Note that alcohol is not served in most of the cheaper restaurants and kebab houses.

White wine
Rakı   Beer   Red wine

Coffee and Tea

Turkish coffee *(kahve)* is dark and strong and is ordered according to the amount of sugar required: *az* (little), *orta* (medium), or *çok* (a lot). You may have to ask for it especially, as some restaurants may give you instant coffee. The ubiquitous drink is tea *(çay)*. It is served with sugar but without milk, and in a small, tulip-shaped glass. Apple tea *(elma çay)*, is the popular alternative to traditional Turkish tea, but there are also linden *(ıhlamur)*, rosehip *(kuşburnu)* and mint *(nane)* teas.

Traditional samovar for tea

Turkish coffee is a very strong drink and an acquired taste for most people.

Apple tea   Linden tea

Sahlep is a hot, winter drink made from powdered orchid root.

Where to Eat and Drink

Seraglio Point

Hocapaşa Pidecisi ₺
Turkish Pizza   **Map** 5 D2
Hocapaşa Sok 19, Sirkeci
Tel *(0212) 512 09 90*
Pide, best described as a long, chewy Turkish pizza, is the speciality. The one with mince is deliciously spicy, and can come with or without an egg in it.

Paşazade ₺
Ottoman   **Map** 5 D2
Ibn-i Kemal Sok 5A, Sirkeci
Tel *(0212) 513 37 57*
Many restaurants purport to serve Ottoman cuisine, but Paşazade doesn't take this duty lightly. The menu boasts hard-to-find dishes such as *mahmudiye*, a fruity chicken dish. Good value for money; attentive service.

Şehzade Erzurum Cağ Kebabı ₺
Kebab   **Map** 5 D1
Hocapaşa Sok 3A, Sirkeci
Tel *(0212) 520 33 61*
This unassuming place serves up a delicious alternative to the döner kebab, which hails from the eastern city of Erzurum. The meat is laterally skewered before being served. Try the tasty marinated lamb.

Café Mese ₺₺
Café   **Map** 5 E2
Hudavendigar Cad 27, Sirkeci
Tel *(0212) 519 18 00*
Pastas, desserts, coffees and pints of beer (hard to find in the Old City) are popular choices at this friendly café. Close to the train station and tram lines.

Can Oba ₺₺
Turkish Fusion   **Map** 5 D1
Hocapaşa Sok 10, Sirkeci
Tel *(0212) 522 12 15*
A relative newcomer to the Sirkeci restaurant scene, chef Can Oba trained abroad before returning to set up his own place. While there are few tables at his restaurant, the imaginatively prepared dishes make sure there's always a crowd here.

DK Choice

Imbat ₺₺
Aegean   **Map** 5 D2
Hudavendigar Cad 34, Sirkeci
Tel *(0212) 520 71 91*
Popular Aegean restaurant located at the top of the Orient Express Hotel. Reserving ahead is almost essential, and is the best way to secure a coveted Bosphorus-facing spot on the terrace. The succulent lamb is highly rated, but the menu also caters to vegetarians without compromising on originality. Attentive staff.

Neyzade ₺₺
Meyhane   **Map** 5 E2
Taya Hatun Sokak 5, Sirkeci
Tel *(0212) 528 43 44*
Nestled outside the wall of the Topkapı Palace, Neyzade's carefully chosen menu showcases different regional Turkish cuisines. Instead of trying to specialize in all of them, the restaurant picks a few dishes – *mezes*, soups and kebabs – and does them well.

Orient Express Restaurant ₺₺
Traditional   **Map** 5 E1
Inside Sirkeci Train Station
Tel *(0212) 522 22 80*
Housed in the terminus building of the Orient Express, the station and restaurant are a fading monument to a gentler age. Not the best value place, but with tables spilling out onto the station platform, its atmospheric setting can't be beaten.

Karakol ₺₺₺
Turkish Fusion   **Map** 5 F3
Inside Topkapı Palace grounds, next to Haghia Eirene
Tel *(0212) 514 94 94*
Most of the seating here is outside, but in winter, patrons can sit in the recently restored sentry post building.

Konyalı ₺₺₺
Kebab
Inside Topkapı Palace   **Map** 3 F3
Tel *(0212) 513 96 96*
This upmarket restaurant has many branches through the city. The Topkapı Palace branch offers breathtaking views of the Bosphorus, although guests have to pay the Topkapı Palace entry fee to eat here.

Olive Restaurant ₺₺₺
Ottoman   **Map** 5 E2
Hotel Yaşmak Sultan (top floor), 18 Ebusuud Cad
Tel *(0212) 528 13 47*
Elegant Ottoman-inspired cuisine, along with sweeping views of the Haghia Sofia, Topkapı Palace and the Bosphorus from the terrace.

Sarnıç ₺₺₺
Meyhane   **Map** 5 F3
Soğukçeşme Sok 38, Sultanahmet
Tel *(0212) 512 42 91*
Dramatically set in a millennium-old Byzantine cistern from which it takes its name. Enjoy an evening meal in its brick and wrought-iron, candlelit interior.

Gently lit interiors at Café Mese, Seraglio Point

Sultanahtem

Doy Doy
Traditional   ₺
Map 5 D5
Sifa Hamami Sok 13
Tel *(0212) 517 15 88*
Doy Doy is a predictable and reasonable place for the uninitiated to try Turkish cuisine. It's worth hiking up four flights of stairs for the view from the terrace.

Köfteci Ramiz
Kebab   ₺
Map 5 D3
Bab-ı Ali Cad, Himaye-i Ekfal Sok 17, Fatih
Tel *(0212) 527 13 40*
Part of a chain specializing in meatballs. Clean and predictable with no alcohol – try the *ayran*.

DK Choice

Tarihi Sultanahtem Köftecisi
Traditional   ₺
Map 5 E4
Divanyolu Cad 12
Tel *(0212) 520 05 66*
Along a strip of imitators, this is the most original. The *köfte*, (grilled meatballs) have many famous admirers, whose comments are framed upon the walls. Eat your *köfte* with *piyaz*, or white bean salad, and follow up with the semolina halva dessert. The menu may not be diverse, but whatever they do, they do well.

Ahırkapı Balıkçısı
Meyhane   ₺₺
Map 5 F5
Keresteci Hakkı Sok 46
Tel *(0212) 518 49 88*
A tiny neighbourhood fish restaurant, which caters to locals and tourists alike. Be sure to save room for the delicious baked halva dessert.

Albura Kathisma
Kebab   ₺₺
Map 5 F5
Akbıyık Cad 26
Tel *(0212) 517 90 31*
Waiters here seem less pushy than in other restaurants which makes for a relaxing meal. A good range of meat and vegetarian dishes caters to all palates and preferences.

Aloran Café & Restaurant
Traditional   ₺₺
Map 5 F4
Adliye Sok 11, Cankurtaran
Tel *(0212) 458 85 28*
Try an array of Turkish *mezes* and meats at this warm and welcoming restaurant. Interesting flavours, generous portions and reasonable prices. Ask the staff for their recommendations

DK Choice

Amedros
Turkish Fusion   ₺₺
Map 5 D3
Hoca Rüstem Sok 7
Tel *(0212) 522 83 56*
Reliable restaurant located up an atmospheric alley, Amedros is known for its tasteful interiors, reasonable prices and attentive service. Try the *Testi* kebab, an Anatolian stew cooked in a sealed clay pot.

Dubb
Indian   ₺₺
Map 5 E3
Incili Çavuş Sok 10
Tel *(0212) 513 73 08*
Popular Indian restaurant. The atmosphere here is jolly – dancing lessons are given on Saturdays.

Fuego Restaurant
Kebab   ₺₺
Map 5 E3
Incili Cavus Sok 15A
Tel *(0212) 531 36 97*
A deceptively named restaurant serving not Spanish cuisine, but Turkish and Kurdish specials, backed by a well-stocked bar.

Port Shield
Pub   ₺₺
Map 5 E4
Yerebatan Cad 13
Tel *(0212) 527 09 31*
It would be hard to claim that people come here for the standard international cuisine on offer – most come for the cold beer, and the many screenings of football.

Balıkçı Sabahattin
Seafood   ₺₺₺
Map 5 F4
Seyit Hasan Kuyu Sok 1, Cankurtaran, Eminönü
Tel *(0212) 458 18 24*
Housed in a restored wooden mansion near the Armada hotel, this old Istanbul favourite specializes in seafood. In summer, diners spill out onto the pretty garden.

Faros Hotel Restaurant
International   ₺₺₺
Map 5 D3
Divanyolu Cad 76, Sultanahtem
Tel *(0212) 518 83 88*
Located on the top floor of the Faros hotel, this restaurant has a variety of international cuisine with some Turkish-influenced dishes.

Giritli Restaurant
Meyhane   ₺₺₺
Map 5 F5
Keresteci Hakkı Sok, Cankurtaran
Tel *(0212) 458 22 70*
Cretan restaurant tucked away in a charming courtyard down an alley. The only option here is a good value all-you-can-eat menu, which includes limitless alcoholic drinks and about 20 kinds of *meze*. Book ahead.

Intimate dining at the well-reviewed Amedros

Karışma Sen Meyhane
Meyhane   ₺₺₺
Map 2 A5
Kennedy Cad 28–30 , Sahil Yolu, Cankurtaran
Tel *(0212) 458 00 81*
A proper historical Istanbul *meyhane*, which started life as a nightclub in the 1930s. Serves a variety of *mezes* and fish as well as desserts.

Khorasani
Kebab   ₺₺₺
Map 5 D3
Ticarethane Sok 39/41
Tel *(0212) 519 59 59*
Visitors won't find bargain prices at Khorasani, but they are serious about their kebabs. Flavours of southeast Turkey and an array of spicy starters; try the slow-cooked pistachio encrusted kebab.

Mozaik Restaurant
Turkish   ₺₺₺
Map 5 E3
Incili Cavus Sok 1
Tel *(0212) 512 41 77*
Plenty of intimate corners in this converted old house. Try the *meze* platter for starters, or the oven-baked seafood.

Patara Restaurant
Meyhane   ₺₺₺
Map 4 A5
Samsa Sok 13, Kumkapı
Tel *(0212) 517 99 19*
A number of set menu options save guests from the hassle of choosing dishes. Book ahead and they will also arrange a free pick-up from your hotel.

Seasons Restaurant
International   ₺₺₺
Map 5 F4
Four Seasons Hotel, 1 Tevkifhane Sok, Cankurtaran
Tel *(0212) 402 30 00*
The restaurant at this converted late Ottoman prison is a popular destination for high-end dining. Enjoy the all-you-can-eat spread, to more traditional Turkish choices.

For more information on types of restaurants *see page 190*

Sultanahmet Fish House ₺₺₺
Meyhane **Map** 3 E4
Prof K Ismail Gürkan Cad 14
Tel *(0212) 527 44 45*
Good choice for seafood, with
helpful and knowledgeable staff.
Seasonal specials like salt-baked
sea bass follow a range of *mezes*.
There are some kebabs too.

Tria Elegance ₺₺₺
Kebab **Map** 5 F4
Akbıyık Cad 11
Tel *(0212) 518 45 18*
Pleasant restaurant where dishes
like sea-bass stew or lamb shank
with saffron are served against a
breathtaking rooftop view.

Vonalı Celal ₺₺₺
Meyhane **Map** 5 F5
*Kennedy Cad 40, Sahil Yolu,
Cankurtaran*
Tel *(0212) 516 18 93*
The Vonalı Celal stands out among
a string of restaurants looking out
over the Marmara. It serves special
Black Sea dishes along with more
ubiquitous fish grills, but the real
passion here is for pickles, which
form the centrepiece of the menu.

Bazaar Quarter

Aslan Restaurant ₺
Lokanta **Map** 4 C3
Vezirhan Cad 66, Çemberlitaş
Tel *(0212) 513 76 10*
A reliable *esnaf* or tradesman's
restaurant, serving the best in
Turkish comfort food. Vegetable
dishes and soups form the core
of the menu, but there are meat
options on offer as well.

Aynen Dürüm ₺
Kebab **Map** 4 C3
*Muhafazacılar Sok 29, near gate 20
of the Grand Bazaar*
Tel *(0212) 527 47 28*
Useful bolt-hole for tasty kebabs

when on the go. Keeps bazaar
hours, so closes by early evening.

Bizim Mutfak ₺
Lokanta **Map** 5 D1
*Şeyhülislam Hayri Efendi
Cad 2 , Eminönü*
Tel *(0212) 522 78 46*
A modern dining room tucked
away behind the New Mosque.
Local workers flock here at
lunchtime for the variety of
soups, desserts, meat and
vegetable choices. Fantastic
value, lots of seating available.
Self service.

Borsa ₺
Traditional **Map** 5 D1
*Yalı Köşkü Han 60–62, Yalı Köşkü
Cad, Eminönü*
Tel *(0212) 511 80 79*
A clean, efficient family eatery
that serves breakfast, lunch and
dinner, and is never without a
throng of people. Convenient
pit-stop for sightseers along the
Eminönü shoreline.

Can Restaurant ₺
Lokanta **Map** 4 B3
*Sorguclu Han No 19–24,
Kapalıçarşı*
Tel *(0212) 511 91 53*
An out-of-the-way lunch
spot where both bazaar workers
and shoppers come to get
their fill of hearty home-style
cooking. The meat broth
thickened with egg is worth
the trip.

Çiğ Köfteci Ali Usta ₺
Café **Map** 5 D1
*Mimar Vedat Sok, in the alley behind
Kral Kokoreç*
Join the queue for a portion
of *cig kofte* (balls of a spicy
mixture of raw meat and tomato
paste). Get yours wrapped in
crispy lettuce or in a tub to
take away.

Doyuran Lokantası ₺
Lokanta **Map** 4 A5
*Ördekli Bakkal Sok 10,
Kumkapı*
Tel *(0212) 458 26 37*
Eat like the locals and skip
tourist fare in favour of the daily
specials at Doyuran. Far from
fancy, the home-made meals
are filling and won't set you
back by very much.

Fes Café ₺
Café **Map** 4 C3
Ali Baba Türbe Sok 25, Nuruosmaniye
Tel *(0212) 526 30 70*
Glamorous café located in a
peaceful sidestreet just off the
bazaar. Fruit sherbets, coffees,
baklava and modest lunch
options are served in cool,
retro surroundings. Relaxed
and ambient atmosphere.

Gaziantep Burç Ocakbaşı ₺
Kebab **Map** 4 B3
Parçacilar Sok 12, Kapalıçarşı
Tel *(0212) 527 15 16*
This narrow bazaar restaurant
serves meat dishes from the
southeastern region of Turkey,
which is famed for its flavourful
kebabs. Stuffed and dried vegetables are a delicious alternative
for vegetarian guests.

Imren Lokantasi ₺
Lokanta **Map** 4 B5
*Kadırga Liman Cad 81 Kumkapı,
Fatih*
Tel *(0212) 638 11 96*
Utilitarian, inexpensive and very
popular for its tasty and plentiful
meals. Pick from a series of daily
specials, but come early in the
day for the widest selection.
Don't be deterred by its
busy atmosphere, the service
is fast.

Kahve Dünyası ₺
Café **Map** 4 C3
Kızılhan Sok 18, Eminönü
Tel *(0212) 520 02 04*
Turkey's answer to Starbucks is
a good place to grab a coffee –
whether Turkish or the more
familiar latte. It always comes
with a sweet of some kind,
showing off the other speciality
of this chain: chocolate.

Kardeşler Pilav Evi ₺
Café **Map** 4 C1
Tahtakale Cad 48
Tel *(0212) 514 63 62*
A classic tradesman's lunch spot
with a humble menu consisting
of chicken, rice and chickpeas.
Wash everything down with
ayran (a salty yogurt drink).
Don't come after dark though –
things pack up at 5:30pm.

Glass and tile decor of Fes Café in the Bazaar Quarter

Kral Kokoreç ⏻
Kebab   **Map** 5 D1
Büyük Postane Cad 54, Sirkeci
Tel *(0212) 526 71 69*
Serving only sandwiches of spicy but delicious grilled lamb innards, this place is not for the faint-hearted. However, those who try it will find themselves wooed by Istanbul's favourite hangover cure.

Nuruosmaniye Köftecisi ⏻
Kebab   **Map** 4 C3
Vezirhan Cad 73, Çemberlitaş
Tel *(0212) 526 71 69*
Meatballs and beans are the staples here. Cheap, delicious and fulfilling – a great place to refuel on the way to the bazaar.

Ocakbası Dürüm Ve Kebap Salonu
Kebab   **Map** 5 D1
Hasırcılar Cad 62, Eminönü
Tel *(0212) 526 32 29*
Chicken or lamb grills are almost all there is at this pitstop near the Spice Bazaar. Reasonable and delicious lunch options served on a platter or in a wrap.

Şark Kahvesi ⏻
Café   **Map** 4 B2
Yağlıkçılar Cad 134, Kapalıçarşı, Beyazıt
Tel *(0212) 512 11 44*
All roads in the bazaar lead to Şark Kahvesi, or so it seems. Enjoy coffee and a game of backgammon.

Siirt Şeref Büryan ⏻
Traditional   **Map** 2 A2
Itfaiye Cad 4, Husambey Mah, Fatih
Tel *(0212) 635 80 85*
A good choice among a strip of restaurants purveying delicious tandoori lamb from the Kurdish southeastern region. *Perde pilavı*, a chicken and almond rice dish, and *mumbar*, a kind of stuffed sausage, are some other options.

Darüzziyafe ⏻⏻
Kebab   **Map** 2 B3
Şifahane Sok 6 , Süleymaniye
Tel *(0212) 511 84 14*
Located in the grounds of the recently restored Süleymaniye Mosque, this spacious, airy restaurant caters mostly to tour groups, but is a pretty setting.

Havuzlu ⏻⏻
Lokanta   **Map** 4 B3
Gani Çelebi Sok 3 , inside the Grand Bazaar
Tel *(0212) 527 33 46*
Because of its size, Havuzlu is a rare dining option in the Grand Bazaar. It does not offer the best value but is nevertheless a pleasant sit-down restaurant in the centre of the bazaar.

Buffet spread at Nar Lokanta, Bazaar Quarter

Hamdi ⏻⏻⏻
Kebab   **Map** 4 C1
Kalçin Sok 17, Rüstem Paşa, Fatih
Tel *(0212) 528 03 90*
A multi-storey kebab emporium serving up meats from the spiced to the pistachioed to the aubergined. Book ahead for a seat that looks out across the confluence of the Golden Horn and the Bosphorus.

DK Choice

Nar Lokanta ⏻⏻⏻
Lokanta   **Map** 4 C3
Top floor of Armaggan store, 65 Nuruosmaniye Cad, 5th Floor
Tel *(0212) 522 28 00*
A special choice in the hit-and-miss culinary fringes of the bazaar. Nar makes a point of only using seasonal ingredients, and from these they manage to fashion 50 daily dishes. One option inside this glamorous tiled dining room is an open buffet of vegetable specials, made using their own brand of pressed olive oil. Has an extensive list of Turkish wines too.

Surplus ⏻⏻⏻
Ottoman   **Map** 3 D2
Zindan Han, Ragıp Gümüş Pala Cad 54
Tel *(0212) 520 10 02*
Overlooking the Golden Horn and Galata Bridge, this top-floor restaurant offers gorgeous views, excellent food and superior service. If you're feeling particularly hungry (or if you fancy a challenge) order the enormous mixed grill.

Beyoğlu

Café Grand Boulevard ⏻
Café   **Map** 7 D4
Hazzo Pulo Pasajı, 116 Hengecidi Sok, Istiklal Cad
Tel *(0212) 293 34 46*
Take a rest from sightseeing in this relaxing cafe in the pleasant courtyard of Hazzo Pulo Pasaj. It is the perfect spot to drink tea and play backgammon.

Café Privato ⏻
Breakfast   **Map** 6 5C
Tımarcı Sok 3B, Galata
Tel *(0212) 293 20 55*
A full-spread breakfast served till noon and home-cooked food thereafter. Delicious Georgian pancakes are paired with organic jams and cheeses.

Datlı Maya ⏻
Lokanta   **Map** 7 E5
Türkgücü Cad 59/A, Cihangir
Tel *(0212) 292 90 56*
The latest project from eccentric and exuberant chef, Dilara Erbay. Housed in an old *simit* factory, it has a menu of creatively reimagined Turkish street-food staples – *dürüm* wraps, which diners may encounter elsewhere, but not the vegan version.

Durumzade ⏻
Kebab
Kamer Hatun Cad 26/A
Tel *(0212) 249 01 47*
Considered to be among the best in Beyoğlu, the kebabs here are cooked over charcoal and served with tasty flatbreads rubbed with a mix of spices. Expect long queues.

For more information on types of restaurants *see page 190*

Modern dining area at the Culinary Institute in Beyoğlu

Fasuli 𝓉
Lokanta Map 7 E5
Kılıçalipaşa Cad 6, Tophane
Tel *(0212) 243 65 80*
This Black Sea restaurant is famous for the beans after which it is named. Corn bread, a cheesy fondue called *mihlama* and healthy salads are executed with aplomb.

Güllüoğlu Baklavacısı 𝓉
Café Map 3 E1
Katlı Otopark Altı, Karaköy
Tel *(0212) 293 09 10*
Come to the baklava kings of Turkey for the best example of this delectable filo dessert.

İsmail Kebab 𝓉
Café Map 7 E4
Hocazade Sok 7, Siraselviler Cad
Tel *(0212) 252 34 87*
Great place for cheap, crisp and tasty Turkish *lahmacun* pizzas. Roll them up with lemon and salad.

Mandabatmaz 𝓉
Café Map 7 E4
Olivia Gecidi, off Istiklal Cad
Sit inside or in the narrow alley outside to enjoy rich and aromatic Turkish coffee, at a bargain price.

Saray Muhallebicisi 𝓉
Patisserie Map 7 D4
Istiklal Cad 173
Tel *(0212) 292 34 34*
Less a restaurant than a five-storey temple to dessert – 10 kinds of baklava, milky puddings and cakes are served here till 3 in the morning. Don't miss the *tavuk gogusu* – a sweet milky pudding made with boiled chicken.

Solera 𝓉
Wine Bar Map 7 D5
Yeni Çarşı Cad 44, Galatasaray
Sample an array of Turkish *meze*, and wash them down with a well-priced selection of domestic wines. Intimate atmosphere.

Van Kahvaltı Evi 𝓉
Breakfast Map 7 E5
Defterdar Yokuşu 52A, Cihangir
Tel *(0212) 293 64 37*
Welcome to a cornucopia of regional specialities at this hip Kurdish breakfast joint. It is so popular that there can be a long wait to get in, but the management usually ply guests with tea till they can be seated.

Yirmibir Kebab 𝓉
Kebab Map 7 D4
Hazzo Pulo Pasajı, off Istiklal Cad
Tel *(0212) 244 38 73*
A tranquil historic arcade, perfect to gorge on tender kebabs grilled over charcoal. Vegetarians can start with the delicious *meze* platter.

Ada Café & Bookstore 𝓉𝓉
International Map 7 D5
Istiklal Cad 158
Tel *(0212) 251 55 44*
A bookshop-cum-café on Beyoglu's main pedestrian thoroughfare. Previously housing nothing but books, some of the floor was cleared to accommodate diners, who can be spotted perusing their purchases along with Italian-influenced pastas and salads.

Ara Kafe 𝓉𝓉
Café Map 7 D4
Tosbağa Sok 2, Tomtom Mah, Galatasaray
Tel *(0212) 245 41 05*
Housed in the building where photographer Ara Guler has his studio, the decor as much as the photographs on the wall at Ara Kafe are a slice of old-world Istanbul. No alcohol is served, but Indian teas and home-made lemonades keep things rolling along.

Canım Ciğerim 𝓉𝓉
Kebab Map 7 D5
Istiklal Cad 162
Tel *(0212) 243 10 05*
Famous for its skewers of liver, this inexpensive restaurant is popular with locals and tourists alike. Get your food on the skewer or wrapped up with onions and greens. There is also chicken and meat and sweet cheesy *kunefe* for dessert.

Culinary Institute 𝓉𝓉
Turkish Fusion Map 7 D4
Meşrutiyet Cad 59, Asmalı Mescit
Tel *(0212) 251 22 14*
The dining room of a cookery school, the Culinary Institute serves a full monthly menu. Some of the interesting twists on Turkish favourites to be found here are persimmon martini and dried aubergine stuffed kebab, as well as a few international meals.

Date 𝓉𝓉
Turkish Fusion Map 7 D5
Asmalı Mescit Mah, Ensiz Sok 1/B, Asmalı Mescit
Tel *(0212) 243 81 27*
Some of the large shared tables may make it hard to indulge in the romantic tête-à-tête it promises, but Date boasts a number of cosy corners too. Try the samphire and scallops, or the steak tartare.

Fıccın 𝓉𝓉
Traditional Map 7 D4
Kallavı Sok 7/1–13/1
Tel *(0212) 293 37 86*
Circassian-influenced *meze* place that comprises a series of venues lining the same street. A worthy dinner stop for small groups, away from the chaos of Nevizade. Don't miss the *cerkez tavuk*, a garlicky chicken walnut dish. The restaurant's eponymous meat pie is also hard to match. Serves alcohol.

Fürreyya 𝓉𝓉
Seafood Map 7 D5
Serdari Ekrem Sok 2b
Tel *(0212) 252 48 53*
Miniature restaurant that serves excellent fish, a stone's throw away from the Galata Tower. Fish soups, wraps, and sandwiches brimming with caramelized onions are great value. There are also more elaborate plates of whitebait and shrimp to choose from.

Hacıbaba 𝓉𝓉
Traditional Map 7 E4
İstiklal Cad 49
Tel *(0212) 244 18 86*
Conveniently situated restaurant serving traditional Turkish food, if visitors don't mind competing with tour groups. Open buffet with a big vegetarian selection, and kebab choices for the main courses.

Key to Price Guide *see page 196*

Helvetia 租租
Lokanta **Map** 7 D5
Gen Yazgan Sok 12, Asmalı Mescit Mah
Tel *(0212) 245 87 80*
A vegetarian restaurant without being strictly vegetarian. A few choices for carnivores nestle alongside the day's specials. Pick from home-style vegetable gratins, followed by aromatic herbal teas.

Jash 租租
Meyhane **Map** 7 F4
Cihangir Cad 9, Pürletaş Mah
Tel *(0212) 244 30 42*
This intimate *meyhane* serves Armenian *mezes*. But when the musicians move in with their accordions, things can get a bit raucous!

DK Choice
Kahve6 租租
Breakfast **Map** 7 E5
Anahtar Sok 13, Cihangir
Tel *(0212) 293 08 49*
Kahve6's name is a pun on the word "breakfast", but the riffs on the best meal of the day don't end there. From poached eggs with a garlic sauce to the life-saver *simit* (a seeded bread ring served with all the essential Turkish breakfast jams, cheeses and olives), this Cihangir hang-out serves creative versions of old favourites.

Karaköy Lokantası 租租
Lokanta **Map** 3 E1
Kemankeş Cad 37 , Karaköy
Tel *(0212) 292 44 55*
A buzzing, stylish take on the *lokanta,* spread across two storeys with a beautifully tiled interior. A popular lunch choice for

businesspeople in the area. Booking is essential.

Kitchenette 租租
International **Map** 7 E3
Tak-ı Zafer Cad 3, Gümüşsuyu Mah, Taksim
Tel *(0212) 292 68 62*
A reliable chain of brasseries. Among their menus is one called "fit-for-you" which counts the calories in your salmon and vegetables *en papillote*. There is also a kids' menu as well as burgers, breakfasts and *quesadillas* – the objective is to cater to all kinds of tastes.

Sensus 租租
Wine Bar **Map** 6 C5
Büyükhendek Cad 5, Galata
Tel *(0212) 245 56 57*
Packed with people on weekend nights, this trendy basement wine bar stocks a variety of Turkish wines and a range of cheeses to complement them.

Zencefil 租租
Lokanta **Map** 7 E4
Kurabiye Sok 8, Şht Muhtar Mah
Tel *(0212) 243 82 34*
Pretty café in a glasshouse of a building. Mainly vegetarian dishes on offer, with some non-vegetarian options. A calm oasis away from the noise and traffic of Taksim's busier end.

5 Kat 租租租
International **Map** 7 E4
Soğancı Sok 7, Cihangir
Tel *(0212) 293 37 74*
Popular Cihangir restaurant and bar. The upbeat atmosphere and lovely views are more enticing than the food, although the *prix fixe* menu is useful for large parties.

Ca'd'oro Salt Restaurant and Café 租租租
International **Map** 3 D1
SALT Galata, Bankalar Cad
Tel *(0212) 243 82 92*
Housed in the newly restored Ottoman Bank building/SALT gallery and research library. A purpose-built glass cube at the back has a small café menu, while an upstairs restaurant offers cuisine with Italian and Turkish influences. Views of the Golden Horn.

Cezayir 租租租
Turkish Fusion **Map** 7 E4
Hayriye Cad 12, Galatasary
Tel *(0212) 245 99 80*
Housed in the restored Italian Workers' Association. This elegant building has a dining room on the ground floor and a large garden downstairs.

Çok Çok Thai 租租租
International **Map** 7 D4
Mesrutiyet Cad 51
Tel *(0212) 292 64 96*
Upmarket Thai restaurant with a hip ambience and friendly staff. The honey-grilled salmon with mung bean salad is a winner.

Klemuri 租租租
Meyhane **Map** 7 E4
Büyükparmakkapı, Tel Sok 2
Tel *(0212) 292 32 72*
A friendly Laz *meyhane*. Besides serving dishes from Turkey's lush Black Sea region, the proprietors also curate cultural shows from the east, and sometimes host guest cooks. The menu indicates vegan or vegetarian suitability, but there plenty to satisfy a meat-eate

Meze by Lemon Tree
Meyhane
Meşrutiyet Cad 83/B, Beyo
Tel *(0212) 252 83 02*
This stylish restaurant contemporary take o traditional Turkish m The main course is and the *meze* are e Sophisticated and book in advance for weekend ni

Mikla 租租租
Turkish Fusio *tel, Meşrutiyet* **Map** 7 D4
The Marmar Cad 15
Tel *(0212) 2* erial views of Enjoy an sprawling, chic the city e fixed menu is restaura priced and showcases reason of Turkish classics.
updat

Vibrant and colourful tables at Çok Çok Thai, Beyoğlu

For more information on types of restaurants *see page 190*

Convivial atmosphere at the popular Pierre Loti Coffee House, Eyüp

Münferit ₺₺₺
Turkish Fusion **Map** 7 D4
Yeni Çarşı Cad 19, Galatasaray
Tel *(0212) 252 50 67*
With an interior by local design
team Autoban, this is a cool
place to go to for both dinner
and after-dinner dancing. Indoor
and outdoor seating.

Ninja ₺₺₺
Japanese **Map** 7 F4
İnönü Cad 43, Gümüşsuyu
Tel *(0212) 245 35 95*
One of the first Japanese
restaurants in Turkey, Ninja serves
these grills as well as noodles
sushi. There are small booths
private parties.

⟩nesi ₺₺₺
Map 7 D4
51 60
esi doesn't feel
y up the nostalgic
food, like
ass and grilled
yhane fare, but
Ser and younger.
Me
Sofyo
Tel *(0*
Proper
meyhan
changed Istanbul
list, which ing that's
wide selec the rakı
boutique bl ontains a
ewer

Yakup 2
Meyhane
Asmalı Mescit Sok 3 **Map** 7 D5
Mescit Mah
Tel *(0212) 249 29 25*
A well-established mey
plenty of character, serv with
the old favourites: rakı is ll
consumed liberally here.
Popular among locals.

Key to Price Guide *see page 196*

Yeni Lokanta ₺₺₺
Meyhane **Map** 7 D5
Kumbaracı Yokuşu 66
Tel *(0212) 292 25 50*
An upmarket restaurant giving
a modern twist to strong Turkish
flavours. Book well in advance,
especially on weekends.

Greater Istanbul

Ali Haydar ₺
Kebab **Map** 5 D5
Gümüşyüzük Sok 6, Samatya
Tel *(0212) 584 21 62*
This popular eatery features
in its own popular Turkish soap
series, *The Second Spring*. Set in
an old Armenian neighbourhood,
it has a hearty and well-priced
menu of kebab dishes. On
summer nights, find yourselves
being serenaded by Samatya
street musicians.

Egg & Burger ₺
International
*Nispetiye Cad, Yıldızçiçeği
Sok 2/E, Etiler*
Tel *(0212) 265 09 99*
A pastiche American burger
joint near Etiler's Akmerkez
shopping centre. Be sure to try
their house burger, which comes
with caramelized onions as well
as the eponymous egg.

Fenerbahçe Büfe ₺
Café
*Rahmi M Koç Museum,
5 Hasköy Cad*
Tel *(0212) 369 66 00*
There's not much on the menu
here besides tea with bread rings
and white cheese – but that's not
the point. Part of industrialist
Rahmi Koc's eccentric collection,
this café is housed in a retired
Bosphorus ferry, and serves the
kind of fare diners may have
tasted on their way across.

Pastel ₺
Café
Cevdetpasa Cad 123, Bebek
Tel *(0212) 265 01 45*
Recently opened by a returning
Turkish expat, Pastel is the answer
to the prayers of a generation of
sophisticated Turks brought up
on *patisserie* outside their shores,
and for whom only a genuine
opera cake or *millefeuille* will do.
Light lunches are also offered.

DK Choice

Pierre Loti Coffee House ₺
Café
*Gümüşsuyu Balmumcu
Sok 1, Eyüp*
Tel *(0212) 581 26 96*
Named after the French
novelist and naval officer, this
modest tea spot is famous for
its spectacular views of the
Golden Horn. Walk up the green
slope from Eyüp Mosque, or
take the funicular to the top,
crossing over the cemetery
en route to the hill. Either way,
on sunny days, the views are
worth the trip, even if the
rickety chairs and simple menu
wouldn't be worth the detour
on their own.

Yanyalı Fehmi Lokantası ₺
Traditional
Yağlıkçı İsmail Sok 1, Kadıköy
Tel *(0216) 336 33 33*
The encyclopedic menu belies
this restaurant's unconventional
appearance – but it showcases
quality as well as breadth. The
meatballs are delicious, and the
saffron rice makes an intriguing
change from plain old *pilav*.
Save room for dessert.

Akasya ₺₺
International
*Nisan Cad 23, 49 Nizam Mah,
Büyükada*
Tel *(0216) 382 10 50*
Charming new restaurant
on the island of Buyukada; offers
an Italian-influenced
menu featuring meat, pastas
and gourmet dishes from around
the world.

Akdeniz Hatay Sofrası ₺₺
Traditional **Map** 1 B4
Ahmediye Cad 44, Fatih
Tel *(0212) 444 72 47*
A wonderful showcase of
the Antakya region's flavourful
cuisine. Try the sour minced
meat, chickpea and pomegranate
soup. Call ahead to sample the
special chicken, which is stuffed
with rice and spices and then
salt-baked.

Aziyade Restaurant ₺₺
Ottoman
Pierre Loti Tepesi, Eyüp
Tel *(0212) 497 13 13*
Magnificent views of the Golden Horn, an open buffet breakfast, followed by lunch and dinner. It also hosts events such as meetings and Ramazan dinners.

Baccim ₺₺
Ottoman
Aytar Cad 14 Levent, Beşiktaş
Tel *(0212) 283 87 44*
An intriguing restaurant near the financial district, specializing in a kind of traditional Turkish stew. Garish, gold-leaf interior and occasional live *fasil* music.

Beymen Brasserie ₺₺
International   **Map** 7 F1
Abdi İpekçi Cad 23/1, Nişantaşı
Tel *(0212) 343 04 43*
This elegant restaurant has a predominantly French menu. On warm summer evenings, diners occupy the lovely outdoor tables.

Brasserie La Brise ₺₺
French   **Map** 7 F1
Mim Kemal Öke Cad 11A, Nişantaşı
Tel *(0212) 244 48 46*
Authentically French menu with wines to match. The price tags on the alcohol are very much Turkish, however, and are liable to make your eyes water more than the onions.

bread & butter ₺₺
Café   **Map** 7 F1
Mim Kemal Öke Cad 1/C,Nişantaşı
Tel *(0212) 248 40 00*
The smell of freshly baked breads and pastries tempts Nişantaşı's shoppers off the streets and into bread & butter. Salads and sandwiches are also on offer.

Çiya Kebap ₺₺
Lokanta
48/B Güneşli Bahçe Sokak, Caferağa, Kadıköy
Tel *(0216) 336 30 13*
Çiya is a humble trio of restaurants along this Kadıköy street. They serve no alcohol, but a recent spate of press activity means that the chef's encyclopedic menu is no longer the secret it once was. Guests here can sample dishes that don't exist anywhere else.

Develi ₺₺
Kebab
Gümüş Yüzük Sok 7, Samatya
Tel *(0212) 529 08 33*
Renowned as one of Istanbul's best kebab restaurants, Develi also serves a mouthwatering baklava dessert. Alcohol is served.

Fener Köşkü ₺₺
Meyhane   **Map** 1 C1
Abdülezelpaşa Cad 311, Fener
Tel *(0212) 621 90 25*
Located next to the city walls, the decor reflects historical events. Drink rakı while enjoying a wide range of seafood dishes.

Mabeyin ₺₺
Kebab
Eski Kısıklı Cad 7 , Burhaniye, Kısıklı
Tel *(0216) 422 55 80*
Delicious kebab restaurant in the hills above the Bosphorus Bridge. Try the *içli köfte*, a stuffed bulgur and meat dumpling, which comes laced with pistachios.

Mahal ₺₺
Ottoman
Kanyon AVM, Büyükdere Cad 185, Kat 1 B/169, Levent
Tel *(0212) 353 51 53*
Ottoman fast food is the unlikely staple of Mahal. The two branches are both good places to take a break from your shopping schedule. Be sure to try the *börek*, or traditional Turkish cheese pastry.

Malta Köşkü ₺₺
Kebab   **Map** 9 D2
Yıldız Park, Beşiktaş
Tel *(0212) 258 94 53*
Hidden away in the gardens of Yıldız Palace, this late Ottoman mansion houses a restaurant that serves brunches, lunches, dinners and everything in between.

Mezzaluna ₺₺
Italian   **Map** 7 F1
Mim Kemal Oke Cad 21, Nişantaşı
Tel *(0212) 231 31 42*
Istanbul's original Italian restaurant now has branches through the city – this one is where the shoppers of Nişantaşı go for pizzas.

Nusr-Et ₺₺
Kebab
Bebek Mah, Manolya Sok 244–1, Bebek
Tel *(0212) 265 45 02*
Try the mouthwatering steaks and burgers or rarer cuts at this popular steakhouse. Great for meat-lovers. Completing the menu are American-style desserts.

Paper Moon ₺₺
Italian
Adnan Saygun Cad, Akmerkez, Residence Entrance No 224, Akmerkez AVM-Etiler
Tel *(0212) 282 16 16*
Perhaps more high-end than it has the right to be, this long-established restaurant continues to draw in a jet-setting crowd.

Park Şamdan ₺₺
International   **Map** 7 F1
Mim Kemal Öke Cad 18 , Nişantaşı
Tel *(0212) 225 07 10*
Continental as well as Turkish food in an upmarket bistro environment. Set amid luxury hotels and art galleries, this has long been a fashionable spot for the glitterati of Nişantaşı.

Zanzibar ₺₺
Turkish Fusion
Cemil Topuzlu Cad 102–A, Caddebostan
Tel *(0216) 385 64 30*
This is not a traditional Turkish restaurant, because the plates here are not for sharing. But when your chocolate cheesecake or grilled sea-bass is this delicious, why would diners want to share?

Outdoor tables at bread & butter, Greater Istanbul

For more information on types of restaurants *see page 190*

Zinnet   ₺₺
Traditional
Türk Dünyasi Kültür Evleri 6, Topkapı Kültür Parkı
Tel *(0212) 567 10 77*
A fascinating place to try a mix of cuisines from Uzbekistan, Kyrgyzstan, Kazakhstan and surrounding regions. Located outside the Theodisian Walls but easy to reach by the T1 tram.

360 East   ₺₺₺
Turkish Fusion
Albay Faik, Sozdener Cad 31, Kadikoy
Tel *(0216) 542 43 50*
The upmarket 360 chain has now opened this expansive diner and nightclub in Istanbul's Moda neighbourhood. The boat ride over is part of the fun, as are the views of the Old City. The programme of events includes international DJs and musicians.

Asitane   ₺₺₺
Ottoman   **Map** 1 B1
Kariye Camii Sok 6 , Edirnekapl
Tel *(0212) 635 79 97*
This smart outfit offers a well-researched menu of Ottoman palace cuisine. Each dish comes with expansive notes. Combine a meal here with a trip to the beautiful, mosaic-filled Kariye Museum.

Beyti   ₺₺₺
Kebab
Orman Sok 8, Florya
Tel *(0212) 663 29 90*
A pilgrimage site for meat-lovers, as might be expected if the patron is the only living Turk to have a kebab named after him. The portions are enormous, so a mixed grill might give a better chance of trying a range of tastes.

Delicatessen   ₺₺₺
International   **Map** 7 F1
Mim Kemal Oke Cad19/1, Nişantaşı, Harbiye
Tel *(0212) 225 06 04*
One of the Nişantaşı restaurant scene's swankier venues: not content with flogging fish salads and burgers, it has even expanded into a range of homeware. Good wine list.

Divan Lokanta   ₺₺₺
Turkish Fusion   **Map** 7 F3
Asker Ocağı Cad, 34367, No 1 Şişli
Tel *(0212) 315 55 00*
An Istanbul landmark for more than 50 years. Having undergone renovation, it now boasts a range of new restaurants, including this venue for high-end Turkish cuisine. Sensitively executed glass sculptures by Robert du Grenier feature throughout, while service is diligent and attentive.

The ultra modern and stylish 360 East, Greater Istanbul

Hünkar   ₺₺₺
Lokanta   **Map** 7 F1
Mim Kemal Oke Cad 21, Nişantaşı
Tel *(0212) 225 46 65*
Meat dishes like *hunkar begendi* (meat chunks on aubergine mash) are popular, but there are also a great number of vegetarian options to try at this upmarket tradesman's restaurant.

Müzede Changa   ₺₺₺
Turkish Fusion
Sakıp Sabancı Cad 42, Emirgan
Tel *(0212) 323 09 01*
Inventive fusion cuisine in the leafy surroundings of the Sabanci Museum. Try grilled octopus with black-olive paste and caper-berry sauce, or clove-flavoured Turkish meatballs. There is a shuttle from the museum to the restaurant.

Sıçanlı Meyhane   ₺₺₺
Meyhane
Hurşit Efendi Sok 6, Çinaralti, Emirgan
Tel *(0212) 277 63 03*
A notorious *fasil* venue: a restaurant offering not just *mezes*, but also singing and dancing – and lots of it. This traditional music form, often associated with belly dancing, is a boisterous affair, so don't come expecting to sit quietly in a corner.

Tahtasaray   ₺₺₺
Meyhane
4 Levent Meşeli Sok 25, Dördüncü, Levent
Tel *(0212) 283 85 85*
In the business district of Levent, packed with devoted patrons who come here for the *mezes* and meats on offer. Hot starters, like a thin hazelnut and mince pizza, are part of Tahtasaray's appeal.

Ulus 29   ₺₺₺
Turkish Fusion
Yol Sok 1, Kuruçeşme
Tel *(0212) 358 29 29*
Set in the hills overlooking the Bosphorus Bridge, Ulus 29 was the closest Istanbul dining got to haute and even molecular cuisine for many years. The excellent sommelier has put together a list that champions new Turkish grapes to match the wonderful fine-dining experience.

The Bosphorus
Aşşk Kahve   ₺
Café
Muallim Naci Cad 64/B, Kurucesme, Besiktas
Tel *(0212) 265 47 34*
Assk's encyclopedic menu manages to cover everything from breakfast to bellinis, and all its dishes are infused with a sense of fun. On the Bosphorus coast by Kurucesme, it has a great location as well.

Asude   ₺
Lokanta
Perihan Abla Sok 4 , Kuzguncuk, Üsküdar
Tel *(0216) 334 44 14*
Crowded, family-run lunch spot with a few revolving specials. On Monday, the speciality is homemade Turkish ravioli with a garlic yogurt sauce.

Çengelköy Börekçisi   ₺
Café
Çengelköy Cad 26 , Çengelköy
Tel *(0216) 318 34 68*
This store serves tasty and filling *böreks*, or savoury pastries, of all varieties. While it has expanded into other parts of the city, this one is the original.

Çengelköy Kokoreççisi Mehmet Erözcan   ₺
Café
Halk Cad 15 , Çengelköy
Tel *(0216) 318 76 56*
Delicious spot to sample *kokoreç*, or grilled and spiced lamb's

intestines. Get your portion stuffed into a sandwich in this kitsch family-run café.

Kanaat ₺
Lokanta
Selmanipak Cad 9, Üsküdar
Tel *(0216) 341 54 44*
A good choice in Üsküdar for its wide range of olive oil dishes and meat lunch specials. Cold yogurt and cucumber soup for starters and milky pudding for dessert are tasty options.

Ortaköy Mantı Evi ₺
Lokanta   **Map** 9 F2
Değirmenci Sok 3, Ortaköy
Tel *(0212) 261 45 50*
Purveyors of delicious *mantı*, or Turkish ravioli served in a garlicky yogurt sauce.

Pide Ban ₺
Lokanta
Dereboyu Cad 23, Sariyer
Tel *(0212) 242 42 39*
Traditional cuisine from the Black Sea region. Huge range of *pide* on offer, and an extensive menu of vegetable dishes and meats from the grill.

Adem Baba Balık ₺₺
Meyhane
Satışmeydanı Sok 2, Arnavutköy
Tel *(0212) 263 29 33*
Fun fish restaurant filled with fishing memorabilia. Expect all the usual *meyhane* repast, except without alcohol.

House Café ₺₺
International   **Map** 9 F3
Salhane Sok 1, Ortaköy
Tel *(0212) 227 26 99*
This chic restaurant is such an Istanbul institution that it even has its own radio station. Enjoy tasty pastas, pizzas and fresh lemonade alongside live beats.

İncir Altı ₺₺
Meyhane
Arabacılar Sok 4, Beylerbeyi
Tel *(0216) 557 66 86*
Particularly charming, secret-walled garden offering old-fashioned Istanbul *mezes*.

Kıyı Fish Restaurant ₺₺
Meyhane
Kefelikoy Cad 126, Tarabya
Tel *(0212) 262 00 02*
Although there is no outdoor seating at this long-established fish restaurant, in the summer, large glass panels open out into the fresh air.

Kosinitza ₺₺
Meyhane
Bereketli Sok 2, Kuzguncuk, Üsküdar
Tel *(0216) 334 04 00*
While most Istanbul restaurants serve their fish plain and grilled, here, they think a bit more about combinations of flavours – so patrons are just as likely to find an elegantly spiced fish stew as a plain grilled offering.

Ortaköy Sefarad ₺₺
Meyhane   **Map** 9 F2
Muvakkit Sok 21, Ortaköy
Tel *(0212) 261 29 83*
Jolly, traditional *meyhane* just far enough away from this waterside neighbourhood's worst tourist traps.

Suna'nın Yeri ₺₺
Meyhane
Kandilli İskele Cad 4, Kandilli
Tel *(0216) 332 32 41*
Unpretentious fish restaurant on the waterside. Located in the shadow of a mosque, it has no wine list as such, but ask around and you might be surprised by what can be brought to your table.

Tike ₺₺
Kebab   **Map** 8 C4
Beylerbeyi iskele Cad 19, Beylerbeyi
Tel *(0216) 422 69 37*
Tike is justly famous for its kebabs. Multiple branches exist in the city; this one is a good excuse to visit the quiet Bosphorus neighbourhood of Beylerbeyi.

Angel Salacak ₺₺₺
Meyhane
Salacak Sahil Yolu 46, Üsküdar
Tel *(0216) 553 04 26*
A smart *meyhane*, which looks out towards Seraglio Point. Creative fish *mezes* are a big draw here, as is salt-baked John Dory, which is wheeled to your table girded by blue flames.

Balıkçı Kahraman ₺₺₺
Meyhane
Iskele Cad 15, Rumeli Kavağı
Tel *(0212) 242 64 47*
Although this restaurant doesn't have a seafront, it is still packed to the rafters on evenings and weekends. Crowds from the city are drawn to Kahraman's famous turbot, cooked in a clay-lined oven.

Boğaziçi Borsa ₺₺₺
Turkish Fusion   **Map** 7 F1
Lütfi Kırdar complex, Harbiye
Tel *(0212) 232 42 01*
A grand restaurant set in the rolling hills of Lütfi Kırdar. Ideal for business lunches or fancy dinners. Everything tastes exquisite, and meat dishes feel less greasy than in Anatolian cuisine elsewhere.

Fish Var Balıkçı ₺₺₺
Meyhane
İstinye Cad 26, İstinye
Tel *(0212) 277 25 82*
A popular fish restaurant near the water on the İstinye inlet, serving a wide range of fresh fish dishes, but no alcohol.

Hanedan ₺₺₺
Meyhane
Çiğdem Sok 27, Beşiktaş
Tel *(0212) 259 40 17*
Next to the Besiktas boat terminal, this popular place is really several restaurants in one. One floor focuses on meat, the other on fish, while there is a bar on the ground floor. Rakı is popular throughout.

Istanbul Modern ₺₺₺
Turkish Fusion   **Map** 3 F1
Antrepo No 4, Liman İşletmeleri Sahası, Meclis-i Mebusan Cad, Karaköy
Tel *(0212) 334 73 00*
The dining room of the museum is a great place to sip a cocktail and sample a varied menu, while enjoying stunning views of the Bosphorus and the Old City.

Spectacular sea view from the House Café in Ortakoy, The Bosphorus

For more information on types of restaurants *see page 190*

Kızkulesi †††
International **Map** 10 A3
Kızkulesi, the Maiden's Tower
Tel *(0216) 342 47 47*
Situated right in the middle of the Bosphorus on a landmark site, this restaurant boasts a unique view – though there is a surcharge. Boats leave from Kadıköy or Kabataş.

Lacivert †††
Meyhane
Körfez Cad 57, Anadolu Hisarı
Tel *(0216) 413 37 53*
Set practically under the second Bosphorus bridge, this *meyhane's* waterside location served as a set for Turkish films of the 1970s. Seafood is the focus.

Lucca †††
International
Cevdetpaşa Cad 51 B, Bebek
Tel *(0212) 257 12 55*
Trendy and informal celebrity hangout that serves a range of modern fusion cuisine.

Sur Balık †††
Seafood
Arnavutköy Cad 52, Bebek
Tel *(0212) 257 27 43*
Fine-dining option with excellent views of the Bosphorus. A great place for lovers of seafood. Set in Körükçü Yalısı, the beautiful 150-year-old summer house, which is said to be among the best examples of Ottoman civilian architecture.

Takanik Balik †††
Meyhane
Birinci Cad 87, Arnavutköy
Tel *(0212) 263 83 46*
Pickles and fresh fish form the main dishes at this dependable, delicious fish restaurant. No alcohol is served.

DK Choice

Tapasuma †††
Turkish Fusion
Kuleli Cad 43, Çengelköy
Tel *(0216) 401 13 33*
Tapasuma plays with great originality on the links between tapas and *meze*. The result is an ingenious tableau of flavours. The restored distillery that houses the restaurant is owned by a pair of architects, whose eye for detail is evident in the elegant decor. Guests can make their own way over to Çengelköy, or can go in the restaurant's boat.

Villa Bosphorus Beylerbeyi †††
Meyhane
İskele Cad 18, Beylerbeyi
Tel *(0216) 318 68 10*
Lovely waterside fish restaurant in the former fishing village neighbourhood of Beylerbeyi.

Beyond Istanbul

Ciğerci Kazım ve Ilhan Usta †
Kebab
Balıkpazarı, Osmaniye Cad 43, Edirne
Tel *(0284) 212 12 80*
With a menu of liver, vegetable side dishes and not much else, this is a quick, cheap and tasty dining option. Their method of cooking crispy liver is outstanding. Twelve kinds of breakfast are also on offer.

Doyum Pide ve Kebab Restaurant †
Café
Demircioğlu Cad, Cumhuriyet Meydanı, Çanakkale
Tel *(0286) 217 48 10*
Functional café that serves not

---

just *pide*, but a range of kebabs as well. It is worth saving room for *kadayıf*, the shredded pastry dessert.

Karadeniz Pide Salonu †
Turkish Pizza
Kılıcaslan Cad, İznik
Tel *(0224) 757 01 43*
Located in agricultural İznik, this busy little place has a wood-fired oven that churns out steady supplies of tasty *pide* (flatbread topped with cheese or meat).

Kebabçı İskender †
Kebab
Tayyare Kültür Merkezi Yanı, Atatürk Cad 60, Bursa
Tel *(0224) 221 10 76*
This place has a worthy claim to being the home of *iskender kebap*, a delicious take on the döner kebab whose peculiarity is the soft bread layer below the meat and the lashings of tomato, yogurt and melted butter above.

Tahmis Köftecisi †
Kebab
Sabuni Mah, Tahmis Çarşısı No 6, Edirne
Tel *(0284) 213 30 92*
The menu here is sparse – expect meatballs, beans and soup. That's basically it, but the meatball speciality of this small Edirne eatery is cooked to such perfection that it's hard to complain.

Burç Beach ††
Café
Boğaziçi Üniversitesi Gümüşdere Mevki, Sarıtepe Campus, Kumköy (Kilyos) Köyü, Sarıyer
Tel *(0212) 203 02 36*
The café at Burç Beach offers plenty of snacks to keep patrons fuelled all day, with occasional concerts adding to the carnival atmosphere.

Cafeka ††
Turkish Fusion
Cumhuriyet Meydan 28, Çanakkale
Tel *(0286) 217 49 00*
Sit back in the modern, tasteful interiors of Cafeka to enjoy healthy bowls of salad, tasty pasta dishes and international variations of classic Turkish dishes.

Çamlık Motel ††
Meyhane
Göl Sahil Yolu, İznik
Tel *(0224) 757 13 62*
Set amid pine trees near the lake, this pleasant restaurant serves an extensive range of *mezes*. Locally caught catfish is a speciality.

View of Maiden's Tower, surrounded by the stunning Bosphorus

Splendid views from the outdoor seating area at Lacivert

DK Choice

Çiçek Izgara   ₺₺
Traditional
Belediye Cad, Heykel
Tel *(0216) 532 33 00*
Well-located behind the town hall, this homely restaurant with an old-fashioned charm is set in a period house. Do not miss the rich, tender *köfte* stuffed with cheese. The service is efficient. There is no alcohol on the menu.

Dalia Beach Club   ₺₺
Meyhane
Kilyos Yolu, Üzeri Dalyan Mevkii, Demircıköy
Tel *(0212) 204 03 68*
Quieter than Burç Beach, Dalia is a resort with more of a family feel to it, as well as a fish restaurant.

Hünkar Köşkü Sosyal Tesisi   ₺₺
Ottoman
Sabiha Gökçen Sok 2, Mollaarap Mah, Bursa
Tel *(0224) 800 20 70*
An Ottoman-inspired menu is offered at this restaurant, housed in premises built over 160 years ago by Sultan Abdulmecid. The view has been altered by the addition of skyscrapers, but the terrace is still a good vantage point.

Ilhan Restaurant   ₺₺
Meyhane
Liman İçi Balıkhane Sok 2, Gelibolu
Tel *(0286) 566 11 24*
Fish restaurant right on the Gallipoli Pier, notable not just for its reliable seasonal fish dishes and its great view but also for the friendliness of its staff.

İskele Balık   ₺₺
Meyhane
İskele Meydanı No 2/1, Rumeli Kavağı
Tel *(0212) 242 22 73*
Located conveniently near the ferry terminal at the mouth of the Black Sea, this is a pleasant, casual fish restaurant for a leisurely summer lunch before exploring the castle up on the hill.

Kitap Evi   ₺₺
International
Burç Üstü 21, Tophane, Bursa
Tel *(0224) 225 41 60*
An elegantly restored Ottoman mansion, which used to be a bookshop with an adjoining café. The place is now a hotel, but it retains its charm with a pleasant garden seating area. The menu features salads, pastas and sandwiches.

Lalezar   ₺₺
Kebab
Lozan Cad 6, Karaağaç Mahallesi, Edirne
Tel *(0284) 223 06 00*
With a children's playground and a ballroom, Lalezar has it set when it comes to catering for grand events – but there is much in their excellent kebab selection and riverside location that will also appeal to the more casual Edirne diner.

Saki Rum Meyhanesi   ₺₺
Meyhane
Eski Mudanya Yolu 25, Bademli Girisi, Bursa
Tel *(0224) 549 02 89*
The leafy and spacious setting sets this place apart. Whether the grilled octopus and beef steaks are actually Greek is open to question, but the menu does not disappoint. A fish or meat set menu for groups of six or above is an economical choice that ensures countless dishes and unlimited local booze.

Yalova Liman Restaurant   ₺₺
Meyhane
Entrance at Gümrük Sok 7, Çanakkale
Tel *(0286) 217 10 45*
Overlooking Canakkale harbour, and brimming with character.

Popular with locals who come for the stews and soups at lunch, and then fill the place again for more formal fish, steaks and grills in the evening.

Yoros Café Restaurant   ₺₺
Meyhane
Feneryolu Cad, Yoros Kalesi Yanı, Anadolu Kavağı, Beykoz
Tel *(0216) 320 20 56*
Fish and *meze* form a menu that guests can enjoy seated atop the castle hill, while taking in sweeping views of the Bosphorus. However, the trek up the hill is not for the faint-hearted.

Yusuf Restaurant   ₺₺
Kebab
Kültür Park, Bursa
Tel *(0224) 234 49 54*
Yusuf serves some of the city's tastiest food. Locals flock here for the lamb *tandir* (lamb baked in a clay oven). There is a huge choice of *mezes*, grills, vegetarian dishes – and football screens, which keep the place packed.

Balıkçı Yaşar Restaurant   ₺₺₺
Meyhane
Opposite the Piri Reis fountain, Atatürk Cad 333, Çanakkale
Tel *(0286) 218 04 41*
Near the university campus, this is one of the best local fish venues. *Meze* and salad choices are vast, but leave room for the traditional quince and pumpkin desserts. Wide selection of rakı.

Gizli Bahçe Restaurant   ₺₺₺
Meyhane
Sazgeyin Mevkii Kopru Yanı No 1, Ağva, Şile
Tel *(0216) 721 72 23*
A secluded lunch spot in the village of Ağva. Worth the detour, not just for the menu, which has specialities like *hodan* or *ebegumeci* (a kind of boiled marrow), but also because between the boats, the hammock area and children's amusements, there are enough activities to fill the day.

Leonardo Restaurant   ₺₺₺
International
Köyiçi Sok 32, Polonezköy
Tel *(0216) 432 30 82*
With a menu of French, Polish and Austrian cuisine, Leonardo seems to be becoming more popular with time. Set in lush garden surroundings, it gets very crowded on weekends, when the buffet brunch is served and guests flock here to use the pool.

For more information on types of restaurants *see page 190*

Light Meals and Snacks

Eating on the streets is a part of life in Istanbul. You cannot go far without coming across a café, street stall or pedlar selling snacks to appease the hunger of busy passers-by. Savoury snacks like kebabs, *lahmacun*, *pide* and *börek* (see pp190–95) are eaten at any time of day, as are sweets and puddings. On every street corner you will find a *büfe* or *simit sarayı* (sandwich kiosk). If you want to sit down, try a traditional *kahve*, or one of the increasing number of European-style cafés in the more affluent and cosmopolitan parts of Istanbul. There are also dozens of American-style restaurants in the city, selling hamburgers, pizzas and other types of fast food.

Street Food

A common sight on the streets of Istanbul is the seller of *simits* – chewy bread rings coated with sesame. The traditional *simit*-seller (*simitçi*) carries his fare on his head on a wooden tray; better-off ones push a glass-fronted cart from which they also sell *poğaça* (flaky pastry filled with cheese or mince), *su böreği* (filled layered pastry), *açma* (a fluffy *simit* shaped like a doughnut) and *çatal* (sweeter, eye-shaped *simits* without sesame seeds). They are all best eaten fresh.

During the summer, street vendors sell grilled or boiled corn on the cob (*mısır*), generously sprinkled with salt. In winter they sell roast chestnuts (*kestane*).

Kağıt helvası, a sweet, is another summer snack. *Kağıt* means "paper", and the thin, crumbly layers of pastry filled with sugar melt in your mouth.

Street food in Ortaköy is dominated by *Kumpir*, baked potatoes smothered with every imaginable topping.

Sandwich and Pastry Shops

Delicious sandwiches are on sale from small kiosks or *büfes*, usually near bus stops. They include inexpensive thin, toasted sandwiches (*tost*) and hot dogs (*sosisli sandviç*).

The snack bars of Ortaköy (see p124) specialize in pastries from southern Turkey like *gözleme* and *dürüm*. Both consist of thin layers of bread, grilled on a hot sheet of iron and stuffed with meat, cheese and vegetables. *Dürüm* bread is cooked first,

then stuffed and rolled, while *gözleme* is cooked with the ingredients inside, then folded over in a triangle.

Fish

Fish sandwich sellers offer delicious grilled or fried fresh fish inside a large piece of bread. *Midye tava* (fried mussels), dressed with ground hazelnuts, garlic and oil, are also served inside bread or on a stick.

Fish and mussel sandwiches are sold at the Galatasaray Fish Market in Beyoğlu (see p214). Here you can also buy *midye dolma*, mussels stuffed with pine nuts, rice and currants (see p192). However, be vigilant when purchasing food that may have had a long street life, particularly in the summer months.

Kahvehanes

The typical Turkish café, *kahvehane* (or *kahve*), is a male-dominated local coffee shop. The original Ottoman name, *kıraathane*, means "a place to read", but such cafés are more a place where men play backgammon and cards, puff on a nargile (bubble pipe) and drink endless cups of coffee and tea. No alcoholic drinks or food are served.

In tourist areas like Beyazıt and Sultanahmet, however, female foreigners will be welcome in *kahves* and, although they may be stared at, they will not be disturbed. **Çorlulu Ali Paşa Medresesi** (see p98) is a *kahve* popular with artists and students. The **Basilica Cistern Café** offers a cooling retreat in

an unusual setting although you have to pay to get into the cistern (see p78). **Café Kafka** is frequented by academics and intellectuals. They serve delicious coffee, cake and snacks in a convivial atmosphere. In Eyüp (see p122) the **Pierre Loti Café** is another traditional *kahve*. Decorated with memorabilia and antique wall tiles, it serves good apple tea and claims to have been the haunt of Pierre Loti. **İsmail Ağa Café**, by the waterside in Kanlıca (see p143), is famous for delicious yogurt.

Next to the Bebek ferry jetty (see p140) is **Bebek Kahvesi**. This café is a favourite with students and middle-class families who read their Sunday newspapers on the terrace while enjoying the breeze of the Bosphorus.

Patisseries and Pudding Shops

The best patisseries are in two Beyoğlu hotels: the Divan and Pera Palace (see p106). **Divan** is known for its chocolates. **Patisserie de Pera** retains its charm with period decor, classical music and tasty biscuits. It has a good selection of English teas. **İnci Patisserie**, founded in 1944, is famous for its excellent profiteroles and baklava.

Conveniently located next to the tram stop in Sultanahmet, **Edebiyat Kıraathanesi** is a patisserie popular among local intellectuals.

Pudding shops (*muhallebici*) sell traditional sweet milk puddings. **Sütiş Muhallebicisi** is a long-established chain.

Ice-Cream Shops

Itinerant ice-cream vendors are a common sight in residential districts in the summer. Turkish ice cream (*dondurma*) is thick and very sweet. It comes in milk chocolate and fruit varieties and is served in cones. One of the best places to eat ice cream is **Mado**, which has several outlets. Also try **Mini Dondurma** in Bebek.

European-style Cafés

European-style cafés serving light meals such as salads, croque-monsieur, omelettes and crêpes are now common in Istanbul. Sweets usually include cheesecake, chocolate brownies, tiramisu and ice cream in summer.

The best are around Taksim and İstiklal Caddesi in Beyoğlu *(see pp104–105)*. The elegant, late 19th-century **Lebon** serves savoury dishes such as vol-au-vents, as well as sumptuous Viennese cakes. **House Café** is much favoured by Istanbul's westernized middle classes, and has branches on Asmalı Mescit, İstiklal Caddesi and in Ortaköy.

Sultanahmet has a few chic, designer cafés. The **Lale Restaurant**, a hippie spot in the 1970s, now serves inexpensive casseroles and grilled chicken, as well as Turkish milk puddings.

Zanzibar, in the smart shopping district of Nişantaşı, is popular with a stylish young clientele. It serves dishes such

as vegetable grill, Waldorf salad and toast provençale. Also in Nişantaşı is the **Next Café**, which offers European-style cakes and pies as well as savoury dishes such as *börek*.

The area around Ortaköy *(see p124)*, with its market, many craft shops and a good nightlife scene, is a haven of street food and light snacks.

Further up along the shores of the Bosphorus, in Rumeli Hisarı *(see p142)*, there is an exclusive English café called **Tea Room**. Decorated in a colonial style, it serves scones and, of course, a variety of English teas.

Among a new generation of Internet cafés *(see p234)* springing up in the city, one of the best is **Antique**.

Cafés are now beginning to open on the Asian side, too. One of the most interesting is **Kadife Chalet** near Moda. Housed in a 19th-century wooden building, it offers home-made cakes and dishes made

with home-grown ingredients, as well as a range of herbal teas.

Bars

Despite the Islamic edict against alcohol, there are plenty of bars in Istanbul. The majority of the city's fashionable cafés turn into bars in the evening, signalled by a change of music from soft tunes to loud pop. It is possible just to sit with a drink, but for those who wish to have food, many serve pasta, steaks, grills and salads at the bar. Even bars that are not cafés during the day will serve snacks.

Sensus is a basement wine and cheese bar, specializing in Turkish wines. **Leb-ı Derya** is a sophisticated restaurant and bar, offering splendid views of the Bosphorus. Down in Karaköy, **Unter** is a fashionable waterfront bar with excellent decor. Many bars feature live bands playing rock or jazz music. For further details see page 221.

DIRECTORY

Kahvehanes

Bebek Kahvesi
Cevdetpaşa Cad 137, Bebek.
Tel (0212) 257 54 02.

Café Kafka
Yeni Çarşi Cad 26/1, Galatasaray.
Map 7 D4.
Tel (0212) 245 19 58.

Çorlulu Ali Paşa Medresesi
Yeniçeriler Cad 36, Çemberlitaş.
Map 2 C4 (4 B3).
Tel (0212) 528 37 85.

İsmail Ağa Café
Simavi Meydanı, Kanlıca.

Pierre Loti Café
Gümüşsuyu Karyağdı Sok 5 (inside Eyüp cemetary), Eyüp. **Tel** (0212) 581 26 96.

Patisseries and Pudding Shops

Divan
Cumhuriyet Cad 2, Elmadağ. **Map** 7 F3.
Tel (0212) 231 41 08.

Edebiyat Kıraathanesi
Divanyolu Cad 14, Sultanahmet. **Map** 5 D4.
Tel (0212) 526 16 15.

İnci Patisserie
İstiklal Cad, Mis Sok 18, Beyoğlu. **Map** 7 E4.
Tel (0212) 293 92 24.

Patisserie de Pera
Pera Palace Hotel, Meşrutiyet Cad 98–100, Tepebaşı. **Map** 7 D5.
Tel (0212) 251 45 60.

Sütiş Muhallebicisi
Sıraselviler Cad 9/A, Taksim. **Map** 7 E4.
Tel (0212) 252 82 68.

Ice Cream Shops

Mado
Osmanzade Sok 26, Ortaköy. **Map** 9 F3.
Tel (0212) 227 38 76.

Mini Dondurma
Cevdetpaşa Cad 107, Bebek.
Tel (0212) 257 10 70.

European-style Cafés

Antique
Kutlugün Sokak 51, Sultanahmet. **Map** 3 E4.
Tel (0212) 517 67 89.

House Café
Asmalı Mescit Sok 9/1–2, Beyoğlu. **Map** 7 D5.
Tel (0212) 245 95 15.
Mısır Apt, İstiklal Cad 163, Beyoğlu. **Map** 7 D4.
Tel (0212) 251 79 91.
Salhane Sok 1, Ortaköy.
Map 9 F3.
Tel (0212) 227 26 99.

Kadife Chalet
Kadife Sok 29, Kadıköy.
Tel (0216) 347 85 96.

Lale Restaurant
Divanyolu Cad 6, Sultanahmet.
Map 3 E4 (5 E4).
Tel (0212) 522 29 70.

Lebon
Richmond Hotel, İstiklal Cad 445, Beyoğlu.
Map 7 D5.
Tel (0212) 252 54 60.

Next Café
Ihlamur Yolu 3–1, Nişantaşı. **Map** 7 D5.
Tel (0212) 247 80 43.

Tea Room
Yahya Kemal Cad 36A, Rumeli Hisarı.
Tel (0212) 257 25 80.

Zanzibar
Teşvikiye Cad 43–57, Reassürans Çarşısı No. 60, Teşvikiye. **Map** 8 A2.
Tel (0212) 233 80 46.

Bars

Leb-ı Derya
Kumbaracı Yokuşu 57, Beyoğlu. **Map** 7 D5.
Tel (0212) 293 49 89.

Sensus
Büyükhendek Cad 5, Galata. **Map** 6 C5.
Tel (0212) 245 94 43.

Unter
Kara Ali Kaptan Sok, Karaköy. **Map** 3 E1.
Tel (0212) 244 51 51.

SHOPPING IN ISTANBUL

Istanbul's shops and markets, crowded and noisy at most times of the day and year, sell a colourful mixture of goods from all over the world. The city's most famous shopping centre is the Grand Bazaar and there are many other bazaars and markets to browse around *(see pp214–15)*. Turkey is a centre of textile production, and Istanbul has a wealth of carpet and fashion shops. If you prefer to do all your shopping under one roof, head for one of the city's modern shopping malls which offer a variety of international and Turkish brand goods. Wherever you shop, be wary of imitations of famous brand products – even if they appear to be of a high standard and the salesman maintains that they are authentic. Be prepared to bargain where required: it is an important part of a shopping trip.

Brightly decorated candle lanterns in the Grand Bazaar

Opening Hours

Shops are open, in general, from 9am to 8pm Monday to Saturday; open-air markets from 8am onwards. Large shops and department stores open slightly later in the morning. The Grand Bazaar and Spice Bazaar open their gates at 8:30am and close at 7pm. Big shopping malls open from 10am to 10pm seven days a week. Shops do not close for lunch, although a few small shops may close briefly at prayer times, especially for the midday prayers on Fridays. Most shops close for the religious holidays of Şeker Bayramı and Kurban Bayramı, but remain open on national holidays *(see pp46–9)*.

How to Pay

Most shops that cater to tourists will be happy to accept foreign currency. If you can pay in cash, you can usually get a discount. Exchange rates are often displayed in shops and also appear in daily newspapers.

Credit cards are widely accepted (except in markets and smaller shops) and most vendors do not charge a commission. Resist any attempts to make you pay a small compensatory commission. It is not unusual to be asked to draw the money out from a bank on your card. Very few shops now accept traveller's cheques. Cash and haggling are expected in the markets and bazaars. Start by offering half the asking price. In rural markets merchants may accept foreign currency.

VAT Exemption

If you spend at least 118 TL in one shop, you can claim back VAT (known as KDV in Turkey), which is 18 per cent. More than 2,200 retail outlets display the Tax Free Shopping logo. The retailer will give you a Global Refund Cheque, which you should then present to the customs officials with your invoices and purchases for a cash refund when leaving Turkey.

Fezes for sale on a street stall

Sizes and Measures

Turkey uses continental European sizes for clothes and shoes. Food and drink are sold in metric measures. This book has a conversion chart on page 229.

Buying Antiques

Before purchasing antique items, it is important to know what can and cannot be taken out of Turkey. The rule is that objects which are over 100 years old may be exported only when a certificate stating their age and granting permission to remove them from the country has been issued by the relevant authority. Museums issue these certificates, as does

Turkish delight and boiled sweets, sold by weight at market stalls

Antiques shop in Çukurcuma

the Ministry of Culture in Ankara, who will also undertake to authenticate the correct age and value of an object, if necessary. The shopkeeper from whom you bought your goods will often know which museum will be authorizing your purchases for export. In theory, a seller should already have registered with a museum all goods for sale that are over 100 years old. In practice, sellers usually only seek permission after a particular item has been sold. In the past, antiques could be removed from Turkey without a certificate. Although this has changed, the export of antiques is not forbidden, as some believe. If the proper authorities permit your purchase to be exported, you can either take it with you or send it home, whether or not it is over 100 years old. Do take note, however, that taking antiques out of Turkey without proper permission is regarded as smuggling, and is a punishable offence.

Van cats and Kangal dogs have recently been included in this category.

Shopping Malls and Department Stores

Istanbul's modern shopping malls are popular for their entertainment as well as their shopping facilities. They have multiscreen cinemas, food courts selling fast food, chic cafés, and hundreds of shops.

Istanbul has almost 100 shopping malls, at central and convenient locations for visitors. **Demirören** on İstiklal Caddesi, is designed to complement the historic surroundings. **City's Mall**, with its upmarket shops and cinema, caters to Nişantaşı's prosperous inhabitants. The award-winning **Zorlu Centre**, with its state-of-the-art performance centre and designer shops, is extremely stylish. **Kanyon**, in Levent, boasts 160 stores, a cinema, gourmet restaurants and a fitness centre. The mall is anchored by a Harvey Nichols.

Swanky interiors of the Kanyon shopping mall in Levent

Seasonal Sales

Clothes shops are the main places for seasonal sales *(indirim)*, although department stores and a number of speciality shops also have them. They begin in June or July and continue to the end of September. The winter sales start as soon as New Year shopping is over in early January and continue until mid-April. There are no sales in bazaars – every day of the year offers bargains depending on your haggling skills.

How to Bargain

In upmarket shops in Istanbul, bargaining is rarely practised. However, you will probably do most of your shopping in the Grand Bazaar and the shops located in or around the Old City (Sultanahmet and Beyazıt). In these places haggling is a necessity, otherwise you may be cheated. Elsewhere you can try making an offer but it may be refused.

Bazaar shopkeepers, characterized by their abrasive insistence, expect you to bargain. Always take your time and decide where to buy after visiting a few shops selling similar goods. The procedure is as follows:
• You will often be invited inside and offered a cup of tea. Feel free to accept, as this is the customary introduction to any kind of exchange and will not oblige you to buy.
• Do not feel pressurized if the shopkeeper turns the shop upside down to show you his stock – this is normal practice and most salesmen are proud of their goods.
• If you are seriously interested in any item, be brave enough to offer half the price you are asked.

Haggling over the price of a rug

• Take no notice if the shopkeeper looks offended and refuses, but raise the price slightly, aiming to pay a little more than half the original offer. If that price is really unacceptable to the owner he will stop bargaining over the item and turn your attention to other goods in the shop.

Where to Shop in Istanbul

Istanbul is home to a vast range of shops and bazaars. Often shops selling particular items are clustered together, competing for custom. In the Old City, the Grand Bazaar (see pp100–101) is a centre for carpets and kilims, gold jewellery and leather jackets, as well as every type of handicraft and souvenir. Nişantaşı and İstiklal Caddesi over the Golden Horn, and Bağdat Caddesi on the Asian side, have a good range of clothes and shoe shops. The best choices for food are the Spice Bazaar (see p90) and the Galatasaray Fish Market (see p214).

Carpets and Kilims

One of the best places to buy carpets and kilims in Istanbul is in the Grand Bazaar (see pp100–101), where **Şişko Osman** has a good range of carpets. **Nakkas** offers a range of quality carpets and kilims in a huge variety of sizes, colours and patterns. The **Arasta Bazaar** (see p73) has many kilim shops, and **Hazal Halı**, in Ortaköy, is run by a wonderfully professional lady who knows the history of almost all of the carpets.

Fabrics

As well as rugs, colourful fabrics in traditional designs from all over Turkey and Central Asia are widely sold. **Sivaslı Yazmacısı** sells village textiles, crocheted headscarves and embroidered cloths. Centrally located behind the Blue Mosque, **Khaftan** offers a wide selection of

Brightly coloured Central Asian *suzani* wall hangings

traditional Ottoman textiles. The antiques dealer **Aslı Günşiray** sells both original Ottoman and reproduction embroidered cloths. Jennifer's Hamam in Arasta Bazaar sells a wide range of quality textiles, including *peştemals* (Turkish bath wraps).

Jewellery

Istanbul's substantial gold market centres on Kalpakçılar Caddesi in the Grand Bazaar. Here gold jewellery is sold by weight, with a modest sum added for craftsmanship, which is generally of good quality. The daily price of gold is displayed in the shop windows. Other shops in the Grand Bazaar sell silver jewellery, and pieces inlaid with precious stones.

Icons for sale in the Grand Bazaar

Urart stocks collections of unique gold and silver jewellery inspired by the designs of ancient civilizations. **Antikart** specializes in restored antique silver jewellery made by Kurds and nomads in eastern Turkey.

Leather

Turkish leatherwear, while not always of the best quality hides, is durable, of good craftsmanship and reasonably priced. The Grand Bazaar is full of shops selling leather goods. **B B Store**, for example, offers a good range of ready-to-wear and made-to-order garments.

Meb Deri sells designer handbags and small leather goods, and **Desa** has classic and fashionable designs.

Antiques and Books

The best area for antiques is Çukurcuma (see p109), in the backstreets of Beyoğlu. Shops worth a visit are **Aslı Günşiray**, **Antikhane** and **Antikarnas** for their Turkish, Islamic and Western stock. A vast array of Ottoman antique brassware, furniture and pottery, including Turkish coffee cups and vases, are sold in the Grand Bazaar.

The best bookshop in the Old City is **Galeri Kayseri**, which sells a wide selection of English-language titles. **Homer**, in Beyoğlu, stocks every possible book on Istanbul and Turkey.

Handicrafts and Souvenirs

All types of Turkish arts and crafts can be found in the Grand Bazaar. Ideal gifts and souvenirs include embroidered hats, waistcoats and slippers, mother-of-pearl inlaid jewellery boxes, meerschaum pipes in the shape of heads, prayer beads made from semi-precious stones, alabaster ornaments, blue-eye charms to guard against the evil eye, nargiles (bubble pipes) and reproductions of icons. At the **Istanbul Handicrafts Centre** (see p78), watch the traditional art of calligraphy being practised. **Rölyef** in Beyoğlu, the **Book Bazaar** (see p96), **Artrium** and **Sofa** also sell antique and reproduction calligraphy, as well as *ebru* (marbled paintings) and reproductions of Ottoman miniature paintings.

Pottery, Metal and Glassware

Hundreds of shops in the Grand Bazaar are stocked with traditional ceramics, including many pieces decorated with exquisite blue-and-white İznik designs (see p163). Other types of pottery come from Kütahya – distinguished by its free style of decoration – and Çanakkale (see p172) – which uses more modern designs, often in yellows and greens. **İznik Classics** has three branches in the city selling beautiful handcrafted pottery, the most convenient outlet being in Arasta Bazaar. Most museum shops also have a good range of pottery for sale, including reproduction pieces.

The Grand Bazaar and the Arasta Bazaar *(see p215)* are centres of the copper and brass trade and offer a huge selection to the browsing visitor. For glassware, **Paşabahçe**, the largest glass manufacturer in Turkey, creates delicate *çeşmibülbül* vases (decorated with blue and gold stripes) and Beykoz-style ware (with gilded decoration).

Food, Drink, Herbs and Spices

The Spice Bazaar *(see p90)* is the place to buy nuts (especially pistachios) and dried fruits, herbs and spices, jams and the many types of herbal tea produced in Turkey. These include sage *(adaçayı)*, linden *(ıhlamur)* and camomile *(papatya)*. However, other foods can be bought here as well, including such luxuries as caviar. Another place with a wide variety of good quality herbs, jams, teas and spices is the Galatasaray Fish Market.

Several shops specialize in particular foods. **Şekerci Hacı Bekir** is renowned for its delectable Turkish delight and baklava. Also popular is **Bebek Badem Ezmesi**, on the Bosphorus, widely acclaimed for its pistachio and almond fondants. Over the course of more than a century in business, **Kurukahveci Mehmet Efendi** *(see p88)* has become the best-known producer of Turkish coffee. The quintessential Turkish spirit, rakı *(see p195)*, can be bought in any grocery or duty-free store.

Pickled fruits and vegetables, sold in markets and on street stalls

DIRECTORY

VAT Exemption

Global Refund
Teşvikiye, Ferah Sokak 19/A-2.
Tel (0212) 232 11 21.
🅦 globalrefund.com

Shopping Malls

City's Mall
Tesvikiye Cad 162, Nişantaşı.
Tel (0212) 373 33 33.

Demirören
İstiklal Cad, Beyoğlu.
Map 7 E4.
Tel (0212) 249 99 99.

Kanyon
Büyükdere Cad 185, Levent.
Tel (0212) 353 53 00.

Zorlu Centre
Zincirlikuyu. **Map** 7 E4.
Tel (0212) 336 91 60.

Carpets and Kilims

Hazal Halı
Mecidiye Köprüsü Sok 27–9, Ortaköy. **Map** 9 F3.
Tel (0212) 261 72 33.

Nakkas
Nakilbent Sok 33, Sultanahmet. **Map** 3 D5 (5 D5).**Tel** (0212) 516 52 23.

Şişko Osman
Halıcılar Cad 49, Grand Bazaar. **Map** 2 C4 (4 B3).
Tel (0212) 528 35 48.

Fabrics

Khaftan
Nakilbent Sok 32, Sultanahmet. **Map** 3 D5 (5 D5). **Tel** (0212) 458 54 25.

Sivaslı Yazmacısı
Yağlıkçılar Sok 57, Grand Bazaar. **Map** 2 C4 (4 B3).
Tel (0212) 526 77 48.

Jewellery

Antikart
İstiklal Cad 207, Beyoğlu.
Map 7 D4.
Tel (0212) 252 44 82.

Urart
Abdi İpekçi Cad 18/1, Nişantaşı. **Map** 7 F1.
Tel (0212) 246 71 94.

Leather

B B Store
Gani Çelebi Sok 4–6, Grand Bazaar.
Map 2 C4 (4 B3).
Tel (0212) 527 53 38.

Desa
İstiklal Cad 140, Beyoğlu.
Map 7 D4.
Tel (0212) 243 37 86.

Meb Deri
Abdi İpekçi Cad 14/2, Nişantaşı. **Map** 1 C1.
Tel (0212) 225 56 80.

Antiques

Antikarnas
Faik Paşa Yok 15, Çukurcuma. **Map** 7 E4.
Tel (0212) 251 59 28.

Antikhane
Faik Paşa Yok Restohan 41, Çukurcuma. **Map** 7 E4.
Tel (0212) 251 95 87.

Aslı Günşiray
Çukurcuma Cad 72–74, Çukurcuma. **Map** 7 E4.
Tel (0212) 252 59 86.

Books

Galeri Kayseri
Divanyolou Caddesi 11, Sultanahmet. **Map** 3 D4.
Tel (0212) 516 33 66.

Homer
Yeni Çarşı Cad 28, Beyoğlu. **Map** 7 D4.
Tel (0212) 249 59 02.

Handicrafts

Atrium
9th floor, Swissôtel, Maçka. **Map** 8 A4.
Tel (0212) 2559 02 28.

Rölyef
Emir Nevruz Sok 16, Beyoğlu. **Map** 7 D4 (4 C3).
Tel (0212) 244 04 94.

Sofa
Nuruosmaniye Cad 42, Cağaloğlu. **Map** 3 D4 (4 C3). **Tel** (0212) 527 41 42.

Pottery, Metal and Glassware

İznik Classics
Arasta Çarşısı 119, Sultanahmet. **Map** 5 E5.
Tel (0212) 517 17 05.

Paşabahçe
İstiklal Cad 314, Beyoğlu.
Map 7 D5.
Tel (0212) 244 05 44.

Food

Bebek Badem Ezmesi
Cevdetpaşa Cad 238/1, Bebek.
Tel (0212) 263 59 84.

Kurukahveci Mehmet Efendi
Tahmis Cad 66, Eminönü.
Map 3 D2.
Tel (0212) 511 42 62.

Şekerci Hacı Bekir
Hamidiye Cad 83, Eminönü. **Map** 3 D3.
Tel (0212) 522 06 66.

Istanbul's Markets

Whether you want to lose yourself in the aromas of exotic spices, rummage for old prints and miniatures among secondhand books, hunt for souvenirs or just shop for food, you will find a market or bazaar catering to your tastes somewhere in Istanbul. An obvious first stop is the Grand Bazaar, but several others are well worth visiting for their more specialized produce and their atmospheric settings. Every neighbourhood in Istanbul has its own open-air market on a specific day of the week. At these markets, crowded with budget-conscious housewives, you will find a huge variety of merchandise at the cheapest possible prices.

Şişli Feriköy
Organic Market

Galatasaray Fish Market
The best fish market in Istanbul runs along a historic alleyway. Constantly sprinkled with water to keep them cool, fresh fish from the Sea of Marmara and elsewhere lie waiting to be sold *(see p105).*

Wednesday Street Market
One of Istanbul's colourful neighbourhood markets, the Wednesday market, is next to the Fatih Mosque *(see p115)* and sells everything from fresh produce and household goods to bulbs and seeds.

Spice Bazaar   Arasta Bazaar

Book Bazaar
Next to the Grand Bazaar, the Book Bazaar (Sahaflar Çarşısı) offers a wealth of printed matter in various languages, from tourist guides to academic tomes and old magazines *(see p96).*

Grand Bazaar
The largest market in the world, the Grand Bazaar contains about 4,000 shops. In this roofed labyrinth of passages you can find every commodity associated with Turkey, from costly jewellery to basic foodstuffs. It has operated for hundreds of years *(see pp100–101).*

Şişli Feriköy Organic Market
Istanbul's first organic fruit and vegetables market is open every Saturday in Feriköy.

Ortaköy Flea Market
Every Sunday the main square of Ortaköy is filled with stalls selling souvenirs to suit every budget, from junk to fine jewellery and original Turkish handicrafts *(see p124)*.

BARBAROS BULVARI

ÇIRAĞAN CADDESİ

B o s p h o r u s

PAŞA LIMANI CADDESİ

ÜSKÜDAR HAREM SAHIL YOLU

GÜNDOĞUMU CAD

TIBBİYE CADDESİ

0 metres	500
0 yards	500

S e a   o f
M a r m a r a

Kadıköy Street Market
The main market for food on the Asian side of the city can be found in Kadıköy Square, behind the post office.

Spice Bazaar
The Spice Bazaar is an exotic trading house for dried herbs, spices and other foodstuffs *(see p90)*.

Arasta Bazaar
Converted Ottoman stables are the setting for this bazaar below the Blue Mosque *(see pp80–81)*. Carpets *(see pp218–19)* are the main items touted, but handicrafts and jewellery are also on sale *(see p73)*.

What to Buy in Istanbul

With its endless bazaars, markets, shops and stalls, Istanbul is a souvenir hunter's paradise. If you are seeking a bargain, jewellery and leather can be worth investing in. For something typically Turkish, there is a wide selection of ceramics and copperware based on the designs of traditional Ottoman handicrafts and arts. The city's antique shops *(see p212)* are also worth a visit. Istanbul is possibly most famous for its carpets and kilims *(see pp218–19)*, but check the quality before you buy.

Copperware

Antique copperware can be very expensive. Newer items, however, are also available, at more affordable prices.

Copper goblets

Pipes
Classic nargiles (bubble pipes) are still used by older Turkish men. They make attractive ornaments even if you do not smoke.

Jewellery
Jewellery includes pendants made from gold, silver, semi-precious stones and other materials. A simple blue glass eye is said to ward off evil.

Antique copper water ewer

Blue glass-eye pendants

Ceramics

Ceramics form a major part of Turkey's artistic tradition. The style varies according to the area of origin. Blue-and-white pottery is in the İznik style *(see p163)*; other areas of production include Kütahya and Çanakkale *(see p172)*.

Colourful Kütahya ware

Green jugs from Çanakkale

Blue and white decorated plate

İznik-style tile

Miniatures

Istanbul has a history of miniature painting, examples of which can be seen in the city's museums, especially Topkapı Palace *(see p59)*. These tiny works of art, often depicting the sultan at court, were once bound in books. Those for sale are copies of originals.

Miniature from the Grand Bazaar

Box inlaid with mother-of-pearl

Box with painted scenes on bone inlay

Handicrafts

Jewellery boxes crafted from wood or bone, alabaster figurines and other handmade ornaments make unusual souvenirs.

Textiles

Hand-woven cloths, including ikat work (where the cotton is dyed as it is woven), fine embroidery and knits are just some of the range of textiles that can be bought.

Embroidered scarves, known as *oyalı*

Cotton ikat work

Glassware

This elegant jug is an example of the blue-and-white striped glassware, *çeşmibülbül*, made in the Paşabahçe works *(see p149)*.

Çeşmibülbül jug

Local Delicacies

Delicious sweets such as halva, Turkish delight and baklava are very popular. A huge range of fragrant spices, dried fruit and nuts are sold loose by weight in the city's bazaars.

Halva

Nuts in honey

Turkish delight

Dried red peppers and aubergines

Mulberries

Sunflower and pumpkin seeds

Chickpeas

Apricots

Almonds

Pistachio nuts

Turkish Carpets and Kilims

The ancient skill of weaving rugs has been handed down from generation to generation in Turkey. Rugs were originally made for warmth and decoration in the home, as dowry items for brides, or as donations to mosques. There are two main kinds of rug: carpets *(halı)*, which are knotted, and kilims, which are flat-woven with vertical (warp) and horizontal (weft) threads. Many foreign rugs are sold in Istanbul but those of Turkish origin come in a particularly wide range of attractive colours. Most of the carpets and kilims offered for sale will be new or almost new; antique rugs are rarer and far more expensive.

A carpet may be machine-made or handmade. Fold the face of the rug back on itself: if you can see the base of the knots and the pile cannot be pulled out, it means that it is handmade.

Weaving a Carpet
Wool for rugs is washed, carded, spun and dyed before it is woven. Weaving is a cottage industry in Turkey; the women weave in winter leaving the summer months for farming duties.

Carpets are made using three different combinations of material: wool on wool, silk on silk, or wool on cotton.

Rug-making Areas of Western Turkey

The weaving industry in Turkey is concentrated into several areas of production, listed below. Rug designs are traditional to their tribal origins, resulting in a wide range of designs and enabling the skilled buyer to identify the area of origin.

Carpets
① Hereke
② Çanakkale
③ Ayvacık
④ Bergama
⑤ Yuntdağ
⑥ Balıkesir
⑦ Sındırgı
⑧ Milas
⑨ Antalya
⑩ Isparta

Kilims
⑪ Denizli
⑫ Uşak

Carpets and Kilims
⑬ Konya

Carpet
This reproduction of a 16th-century Uşak carpet is known as a Bellini double entrance prayer rug.

Indigo

Madder

Camomile

Dyes

Before chemical dyes were introduced in 1863, plant extracts were used: madder roots for red; indigo for blue; and camomile and other plants for yellow.

The **"prayer design"** is inspired by a mihrab, the niche in a mosque that indicates the direction of Mecca *(see p40)*.

The **tree of life** motif at the centre of the kilim is symbolic of immortality.

Buying a Rug

Before you buy a rug, look at it by itself on the floor, to see that it lies straight – without waves or lumps. Check that the pattern is balanced, the borders are of the same dimensions, and the ends are roughly the same width. The colours should be clear and not bleeding into one another. Bargaining is essential *(see p211)*, as the first price given is likely to be at least 50 per cent higher than the seller really expects.

Buying a good quality old rug at a reasonable price, however, is a job for an expert. The age of a rug is ascertained from its colour, the quality of the weaving and the design. Check the pile to make sure that the surface has not been painted and look for any repairs – they can easily be seen on the back of the rug. Restoration of an old carpet is acceptable but the repair should not be too visible. Make sure the rug has a small lead seal attached to it, to prove its authenticity and that it may be exported, and ask the shop for a receipt.

Kilim
Kilims are usually made using the slit weave technique by which a vertical slit marks a colour change.

The **width** of a rug is limited by the size of the loom. Most rugs are small because a large loom will not fit into a village house.

Kilim pieces are used to make a variety of smaller craft objects, also for sale in carpet shops.

Burdock motif

Chest motif

Motifs

The recurring motifs in rugs – some of them seemingly abstract, others more figurative – often have a surprising origin. For instance, many are derived from marks that nomads and villagers used for branding animals.

Motif from wolf track, crab or scorpion

Modern motif of a human figure

ENTERTAINMENT IN ISTANBUL

Istanbul offers a great variety of leisure pursuits, ranging from arts festivals, folk music and belly dancing to sports centres and nightclubs. The main event in the cultural calendar is the series of festivals organized by the Istanbul Foundation for Culture and the Arts *(see pp46–9)*. The festivals take place between March and November, and always draw international performers and large audiences. Throughout the year, traditional Turkish music, opera, ballet, Western classical music and plays are performed at the Lütfi Kırdar Kongre Merkezi (Istanbul Convention &

Exhibition Centre, ICEC), the Cemal Reşit Rey Concert Hall (CRR) and other venues around the city. Beyoğlu is the main centre for entertainment of all kinds. This area has the highest concentration of cinemas in the city as well as several cultural centres, both Turkish and foreign. In the evening the bars and cafés here play live music. Ortaköy, on the European shore of the Bosphorus, is another popular venue where, on summer nights, dining, music and dancing continue into the small hours of the morning.

Copies of *The Guide*, a good source for information on entertainment in Istanbul

Entertainment Guides

Istanbul has a bi-monthly entertainment and listings magazine in English called *The Guide*. This publishes the programmes of the ICEC and CRR, and information on other cultural events, as well as bars and nightclubs around the city. *The Guide* is sold at the larger, central newsagents and bookshops. *Time Out Istanbul* is published monthly in both English and Turkish.

Lists of events taking place at individual theatres and cultural centres (including those attached to foreign consulates) can be obtained from tourist information offices *(see p229)*.

The Turkish Airlines in-flight magazine, *Skylife*, has details of major events, and the daily English-language Turkish newspaper *Hürriyet Daily News* has listings in Turkish.

Booking Tickets

Tickets for performances at the Lütfi Kırdar Congress and Exhibition Centre and Cemal Reşit Rey Concert Hall can be purchased one week in advance from their box offices. The fastest and most convenient ways to book and pay for tickets to any event is online through **Biletix** (www.biletix.com). **Vakkorama** department store and **Galleria, Akmerkez** and **Capitol** shopping centres sell tickets for large pop and jazz concerts, and also for performances at the Cemal Reşit Rey Concert Hall.

Late-night Transport

The metro and tram systems close around midnight. The last late-night buses and dolmuşes leave at midnight from Taksim, which is close to many entertainment venues. Taxis run throughout the night. During music festivals in June and July there is a special bus service which runs between venues and central parts of Istanbul.

Festivals

Five arts festivals, four annual and one biennial, are organized by the **Istanbul Foundation for Culture and the Arts**. The Film Festival runs from March to April every year, the Theatre Festival is in May and June, the Music and Dance Festival – the original and biggest festival – is

in June and July, and the Jazz Festival is in July. The biennial Fine Arts Festival takes place in the autumn. Tickets for all these festivals can be bought over the phone from the Istanbul Festival Committee, which also has programme details, and from the venues.

The Yapı Kredi Arts Festival, Akbank Jazz Festival and Efes Pilsen Blues Festival are also in the autumn *(see p48)*.

Western Classical Music and Dance

Every season the Istanbul State Opera and Ballet companies, State Symphony Orchestra and State Theatre perform a wide repertoire of classical and modern works. The companies share the same venue: the **Lütfi Kırdar Congress and Exhibition Centre**. Early booking is essential for shows here.

Classical concert in the church of Haghia Eirene *(see p62)*

Folk dancing at Kervansaray, a long-established venue

The **Cemal Reşit Rey Concert Hall** stages concerts of Western classical music as well as hosting a wide variety of music and dance groups from all over the world. Concerts, operettas and ballets are also performed at smaller venues throughout the city.

Laser-disc screenings of opera, ballet and classical music performances are held most days at 2pm and 6pm at the **Aksanat Cultural Centre**. It also sometimes stages live plays and music recitals.

Rock Music and Jazz

Istanbul has an increasing number of bars and clubs playing good live music. **Hayal Kahvesi** is a bar dedicated to jazz, rock and blues by groups from Turkey and abroad. It also has an outdoor summer branch next to the Bosphorus in Çubuklu. **Babylon** is Istanbul's leading club venue and hosts performances on rock, electronic and world music. **Nardis**, located beneath Galata Tower, is the city's best jazz club.

Peyote features a mix of live alternative rock and electronica. **Roxy** and **Mojo** present local bands that fuse Turkish and foreign musical styles. The unique and low-key **Salon IKSV**, backed by the Istanbul Foundation for Culture and Arts, hosts jazz, folk, rock and electronic acts from around the world. Kadıköy, with places like **Shaft**, has a thriving rock culture.

Clubs

The luxurious, summer-only **Ulus 29** is probably the most glamorous nightclub in Istanbul. It has a restaurant, swimming pool and torchlit garden with glorious views of the Bosphorus. Every half-hour a boat ferries guests to and from İstinye on the European side. The bar becomes a disco after midnight. **Reina**, also open in summer only, is the city's biggest nightspot, with a large dance floor right beside the Bosphorus, as well as several bars and restaurants.

Blackk is a high-end club replete with lavish decoration and jaw-dropping lighting and sound systems. Uniquely for Ortaköy, it offers a fantastic view of the Bosphorous. There is also a restaurant/lounge on the upper floor. **Supperclub** hosts a talented line-up of local and international DJs and shows atmospheric movies. **Minimüzikhol** and **Indigo** in Beyoğlu are popular among fans of electronic music.

Avoid the seedier-looking clubs in Beyoğlu, as these have been known to coerce clients into paying extortionate bills.

Traditional Turkish Music and Dance

Traditional Turkish music is regularly performed at the Cemal Reşit Rey Concert Hall. This includes Ottoman classical music, performed by an ensemble of singers and musicians, mystical Sufi music and folk music from various regions of Turkey. Another good venue to see a mix of traditional Turkish folk music and dance is the stunning Hodja Pasha Culture Centre in Sirkeci, located in a beautifully restored Ottoman bathhouse.

Fasıl is a popular form of traditional music best enjoyed live in *meyhanes* such as **Ece** and **Istanbulin Dinner Show**. It is usually performed by gypsies on instruments which include the violin, *kanun* (zither), *tambur* and *ut* (both similar to the lute).

Belly dancing is performed mainly in nightclubs. Shows are aimed at the tourist market, invariably including a belly dance performance and Turkish folk music, along with dinner. Venues featuring top performers include **Kervansaray, Orient House** and **Manzara**.

Whirling Dervishes perform their traditional religious dances at the Mevlevi Lodge (see p106) in Galata on most Sundays.

The traditional *ut*, a lute-like instrument played in *fasıl* music

Musicians at the
Jazz Festival

Cinemas

The latest foreign films are on general release in Istanbul at the same time as other European countries. They are screened in their original languages with Turkish subtitles.

Most of the city's cinemas are on İstiklal Caddesi. **AFM Fitas** and **Atlas** tend to show a mix of mainstream and art-house films, while **Yeşilçam** only screens art-house movies. There are also numerous cinemas in Kadıköy, on the Asian side, while all the main shopping centres have multi-screen cinemas, the best being City Life in Nişantaşı's City Mall.

The first screening of the day is half-price, and many cinemas offer tickets at half-price all day on Wednesdays. Students with a valid card are entitled to a discount for all showings. There is usually an interval.

Theatre

Plays by Turkish and international playwrights are staged in Istanbul's theatres, but only in Turkish. A popular company is the Istanbul State Theatre. They perform at theatres across the city, such as at the Cevahir stage in the Cevahir Shopping and Entertainment Centre in Şişli, the Küçük Sahne in Beyoğlu and the Üsküdar stage in Paşa Limanı.

Health Clubs and Sports Centres

All the main five-star hotels have good swimming pools and welcome non-residents for a daily fee. Health clubs such as the **Vakkorama Gym**, the **Alkent Hillside Club** and the **Cihangir Sports Center** can also be used by non-members for a daily fee.

At the edge of the Belgrade Forest, the **Kemer Country Riding and Golf Club** has stables and a 9-hole golf course. It also offers riding and golf lessons. For ice-skaters, the rink in the **Galleria** shopping centre (see p211) is open to the public after 7pm. Skates are available for hire. Yoga and detox centres, such as

Cihangir Yoga, are cheaper than in the rest of Europe and are very popular.

Spectator Sports

Football has a large following in Turkey. The three major Istanbul teams, **Beşiktaş JK**, **Fenerbahçe SK** and **Galatasaray AS** usually qualify for European Cup competitions every year.

Horse racing takes place at **Veli Efendi Hipodromu** racecourse between 14 April and 31 October, on Wednesdays, Fridays and at weekends. In summer there are yacht regattas in the Sea of Marmara (see p47). For an unusual spectator sport, head to Edirne at festival time, to see the grease wrestling (see p156).

Galatasaray team logo

Beaches

The best place to swim, water-ski and windsurf in Istanbul is the Princes' Islands (see p160). Yörükali Plajı, on Büyükada, is a public beach, but it is safe to swim anywhere around the islands.

There are large beaches at Kilyos (see p160) and Gümüşdere on the Black Sea, about 30 minutes' drive from central Istanbul, and Şile (see p160). The Black Sea can be rough at times, however, with big waves and dangerous undercurrents, so always exercise caution on these beaches. The Marmara Islands (see p171), are also popular for their beaches.

Children

Little in Istanbul has been designed with children in mind. Nevertheless, there are many things to interest children and increasingly activities and sights that will attract them.

However, children are welcome and will be made a fuss of almost everywhere they go. With a little thought you can find plenty of things for children to do.

The **Turkuazoo Aquarium** at Forum Istanbul shopping centre is open daily and boasts an 80 metre (262 ft) underwater tunnel.

There are parks at Yıldız (see pp126–7) and Emirgan (see p143), though the smaller Gülhane Park in Sultanahmet is more suitable for a visit with the family. Another park near Emirgan, the **Park Orman**, is a family complex situated in woods, with picnic areas, a swimming pool and a theatre. **Miniatürk** in Sütlüce, on the edge of the Golden Horn, boasts an extensive model village of miniature replicas of Turkey's cultural landmarks, as well as restaurants, shops and a pool. The Rahmi M Koç Industrial Museum (see p129) and Santralistanbul Museum of Energy (see p129) will appeal to children. On the Princes' Islands, where there are no cars, children can cycle safely, or take a tour in a horse-drawn carriage. The **Toy Museum** in Göztepe is the first of its kind in Turkey. In Darica, 28 miles (45 km) from Istanbul, the **Faruk Yalçın Zoo** has exotic animals in natural habitats.

A theme park near Istanbul

DIRECTORY

Booking Tickets

Akmerkez
Nispetiye Cad, Etiler.
Tel (0212) 282 01 70.

Biletix
Tel (0216) 556 98 00.
W biletix.com

Capitol
Mahir İz Cad, Altunizade.
Tel (0216) 554 77 77.

Galleria
Sahil Yolu, Ataköy.
Tel (0212) 559 95 60.

Vakkorama
Abdi İpekçi Cad 29,
Nişantaşı. **Map** 7 E4.
Tel (0212) 224 31 72.

Festivals

**Istanbul Foundation
for Culture and Arts**
Tel (0212) 334 07 00.
W iksv.org

Western Classical Music and Dance

**Aksanat Cultural
Centre**
İstiklal Cad 16, Taksim.
Map 7 D4.
Tel (0212) 252 35 00.

**Cemal Reşit Rey
Concert Hall (CRR)**
Darülbedayi Cad,
Harbiye. **Map** 7 F1.
Tel (0212) 231 54 97.
W ccrkonsersalonu.org

**Lütfi Kırdar Congress
and Exhibition
Centre (ICEC)**
Gümüş Cad 4,
Harbiye. **Map** 7 F1.
Tel (0212) 373 11 00.
W icec.org

Rock Music and Jazz

Babylon
Şehbender Sok 3, Asmalı
Mescit, Beyoğlu.
Tel (0212) 292 73 68.
W babylon.com.tr

**Hayal Kahvesi
(Beyoğlu)**
Büyükparmakkapı
Sok 19, Beyoğlu.
Map 7 E4.
Tel (0212) 244 25 58.

**Hayal Kahvesi
(Çubuklu)**
Burunbahçe Mevkii,
Çubuklu. **Open** May–Oct.
Tel (0216) 413 68 80.

Mojo
Büyük Parmakkapı Sok,
Beyoğlu. **Map** 7 E4.
Tel (0212) 243 29 27.
W mojobeyoglu.net

Nardis Jazz Club
Kulebdibi Sok 14, Galata.
Map 3 D1. **Tel** (0212) 244
63 27. W nardisjazz.com

Peyote
Kamariye Sok 4, Balık
Pazarı. **Map** 7 D4.
Tel (0212) 251 43 98.
W peyote.com.tr

Salon IKSV
Sadi Konuralp Cad 5,
Beyoğlu. **Map** 6 C5.
Tel (0212) 334 07 52.
W saloniksv.com

Shaft
Osmancık Sok 13, Kadıköy.
Tel (0216) 349 99 56.
W shaftclub.com

Clubs

Blackk
Muallim Naci Cad 71,
Ortaköy. **Map** 9 F2.
Tel (0212) 236 72 56.
W blackk.net

Indigo
Akarasu Sok 1/2, Beyoğlu.
Map 7 D4.
Tel (0212) 244 85 67.

Minimüzikhol
Soğancı Sok 7,
Beyoğlu. **Map** 7 E4.
Tel (0212) 245 19 96.
W minimuzikhol.com

Reina
Muallim Naci Cad 44,
Kuruçeşme. **Map** 9 F2.
Tel (0212) 259 59 19.
W reina.com.tr

Roxy
Siraselviler Cad,
Aslanyatagi Sok 1–3,
Taksim **Map** 7 E4
Tel (0212) 249 1283.

Supperclub
Muallim Naci Cad 65,
Ortaköy. **Map** 9 F2.
Tel (0212) 261 19 88.
W supperclub.com

Ulus 29
A Adnan Saygun Cad,
Ulus Parki içi, Ulus.
Tel (0212) 358 29 29.
W club29.com

Traditional Turkish Music and Dance

Ece
Tramvay Cad 104,
Kuruçeşme.
Tel (0212) 265 96 00.

**Istanbulin Dinner
Show**
Cumhuriyet Cad, Cebel
Topu Sokak 2, Harbiye.
Tel (0212) 291 84 40.
W istanbulin.org

Kervansaray
Cumhuriyet Cad 52/A,
Harbiye. **Map** 7 F2.
Tel (0212) 247 16 30.

Manzara
Conrad Hotel, Yıldız Cad,
Beşiktaş. **Map** 8 C3.
Tel (0212) 227 30 00.

Orient House
Tiyatro Cad 27, next to
President Hotel, Beyazıt.
Map 2 C4 (4 A4). **Tel** (0212)
517 61 63. W orienthouse
istanbul.com

Cinemas

AFM Fitas
İstiklal Cad 24, Beyoğlu.
Map 7 E4.
Tel (0212) 251 20 20.

Atlas
İstiklal Cad 209, Beyoğlu.
Map 7 D4.
Tel (0212) 252 85 76.

Nişantaşı Citylife
Nişantaşı Shopping Mall,
Teşvikiye Cad 162. **Map** 8
A2. **Tel** (0212) 373 35 35.

Yeşilçam
İman Adna Sok 10.
Tel (0212) 249 68 00.
W yesilcamsinemasi.
com

Health Clubs and Sports Centres

Alkent Hillside Club
Alkent Residential
Complex, Tepecik Yolu,
Etiler. **Tel** (0212) 257 78 22.

Cihangir Sports Center
Sıraselviler Cad 118, Mavi
Plaza, Cihangir. **Tel** (0212)
245 12 55.

Cihangir Yoga
Meclisi Mebusan Yokuşu
51, Cihangir.
Tel (0539) 572 84 37.
W cihangiryoga.com

**Kemer Country Riding
and Golf Club**
Göktürk Beldesi,Uzun
Kemer Mevkii, Eyüp.
Tel (0212) 239 70 10.

Vakkorama Gym
Osmanlı Sok 13, Taksim.
Map 7 E4.
Tel (0212) 251 15 71.

Spectator Sports

Beşiktaş JK
Vodafone Arena, Beşiktaş.
Map 8 A4.
Tel (0212) 227 87 80.

Fenerbahçe SK
Fenerbahçe Spor Kulübü,
Kızıltoprak, Kadıköy.
Tel (0216) 345 09 40.

Galatasaray AŞ
Türk Telekom Arena.
Map 7 E4.
Tel (0212) 259 59 19.

**Veli Efendi
Hipodromu**
Türkiye Jokey Kulübü,
Osmaniye, Bakırköy.
Tel (0212) 543 70 96.

Children

Faruk Yalçın Zoo
Tuzla Cad, Darica.
Tel (0212) 265 99 65.

Miniatürk
İmrahor Cad, Sütlüce.
Tel (0212) 222 28 82.
W miniaturk.com.tr

Park Orman
Fatih Çocuk Ormanı,
Maslak Cad, Maslak.
Tel (0212) 285 95 47.

Toy Museum
Dr. Zeki Zeren Sokak 17,
Göztepe.
Tel (0216) 359 45 50.

Turkuazoo Aquarium
Bayrampaşa.
Tel (0216) 640 27 40.
W turkuazoo.com

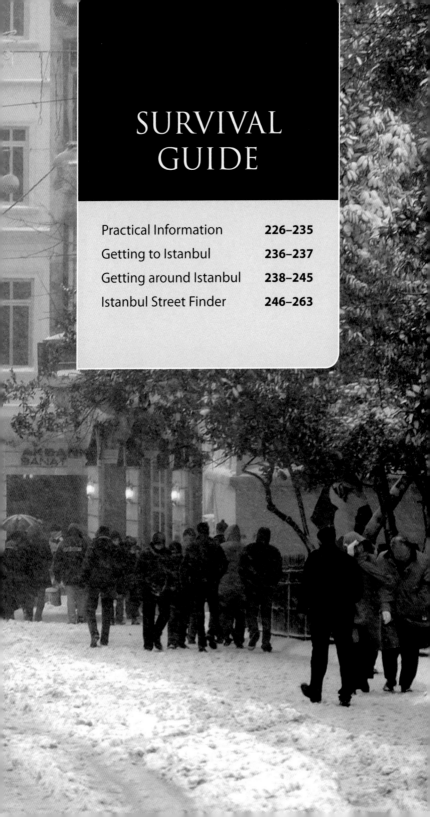

SURVIVAL GUIDE

PRACTICAL INFORMATION

Rapidly expanding Istanbul has the transport, banking and medical facilities of any large modern city. However, in remoter suburbs of the city, and less-visited parts of the Bazaar Quarter, banks and ATM machines may be thin on the ground, so it is worth carrying a day's supply of Turkish lira. It also makes sense to carry the Istanbul Card travel pass *(see p241)*, a mobile phone and/or phonecard. Certain aspects of Turkish culture may seem strange to the foreign visitor, especially if you have never travelled in a Muslim country. It is not considered rude to stare and foreigners are objects of attention in quarters less visited by tourists. *Istanbullu* (Istanbul residents) are subject to the same pressures as any modern urban dweller, but in general are friendly and hospitable, and appreciate any effort to show respect for their traditions.

When to Go

With its hot, humid summers and cold, wet winters, Istanbul is best visited in May and June or September and October, when the weather is usually warm and sunny enough to enjoy open-air cafés but not too hot to explore on foot. This said, mid-summer temperatures seldom exceed 30°C (86°F) and sightseeing is manageable if you avoid walking around in the midday heat. Bear in mind that you will need to be suitably dressed (shoulders and knees must be covered) when visiting mosques *(see p227)*. The city is at its least busy (and best value) in winter, and the sights are all the better for the lack of crowds. However, you may encounter fog and rain so take a coat and umbrella.

Tourists on the steps of Dolmabahçe Palace on a sunny day

◀ Trams cutting through a snowy street in Beyoğlu

Customs Information

Only airports and main road entry points offer a full customs service. At major ports or marinas, customs hours are 8:30am–5:30pm on weekdays. Outside these hours a fee must be paid to consult a customs official. You can buy duty-free items at the airport on entering the country. Visitors over 18 years old can bring in reasonable amounts of coffee (1.5 kg/3 lb), perfume (5 bottles), spirits (1 litre/34 fl oz) and cigarettes (200). There is no limit on the amount of foreign currency or Turkish lira you can bring in. The maximum when leaving is US$5,000 (or Turkish lira equivalent). In practice, this is rarely enforced.

Turkey is very strict with regard to illegal drugs. Sniffer dogs are used at Atatürk and Sabiha Gökçen airports. You need to have a permit to export antiquities *(see p210)*.

Visas and Passports

Visitors to Turkey should have a full passport with at least six months validity. Overstaying your visa incurs a fine, which escalates rapidly. Citizens of many countries require a visa, which must be purchased in advance from www.evisa.gov.tr. Visas are multi-entry and issued for 180 days, out of which they are valid for 90 days.

Requirements can and do change, so for up-to-date information contact the Turkish consulate in your country or visit www.mfa.gov.tr.

Tourist Information

The sign for a tourist information office is a white "i" on a green background in a white box. The

Travellers outside the tourist information office in Sirkeci

offices themselves are named in English and Turkish. They hand out city maps and pamphlets with useful information. The main office in Sultanahmet Square, in particular, will be able to answer questions on all aspects of your stay in Istanbul. Edirne, Bursa, İznik and Çanakkale have offices near the town centre. Most information offices are open 9am–5pm, Mon–Sat. Some stay open later in summer, while the one in the arrivals terminal of Atatürk airport is open 24 hours daily.

Admission Fees and Opening Hours

Entry fees to Istanbul's major monuments and museums are comparable to elsewhere in Europe, although smaller, less well known establishments are considerably cheaper. In some monuments there is an additional charge for a special section, for example the Harem in Topkapı Palace *(see pp56–61)*.

Most sights are closed one day a week, usually Monday or

Tuesday. Exhibits in the most-visited museums are generally labelled in Turkish and English. Museum opening times are usually 8:30 or 9am to 5 or 6pm, with a break for lunch in smaller establishments. The larger museums are often open between 9am and 5pm from November to March and 9am to 7pm from April to October. Remember that it is best to avoid mosques at prayer times *(see below)*.

Shops generally open from 8:30 or 9am to 7 or 8pm *(see p210)*. Shopping malls are open from 10am to 10pm. For information on opening times of banks and exchange offices *(döviz)* see page 232.

Public offices are closed on Saturdays and Sundays, and some shops on Sundays, although shopping malls, supermarkets and small grocers are invariably open seven days a week.

Etiquette

In Istanbul around 10 per cent of women cover their arms, legs and heads in public. Residents of devout areas such as Fatih *(see pp112–15)* may be offended at exposed limbs in the street. In many areas such as Beyoğlu *(see pp103–109)* most Turkish women dress as they choose and visitors can do the same, except when visiting a mosque *(see below)*.

Although areas like Beyoğlu are lined with bars and restaurants, most Turks drink alcohol in moderation, and overt drunkenness is frowned upon. Visitors who transgress the law while

Wearing the veil, a matter of personal choice for Turkish women

The venerable Blue Mosque *(see pp80–81)*

drunk will get little sympathy. Traditional rules of etiquette and hospitality are still an important aspect of Turkish society. Always show respect for Atatürk *(see p33)*, whose picture you will see often.

Discreet gay and lesbian visitors are unlikely to experience problems and Istanbul has a lively gay scene, though overt displays of affection are best kept to a minimum.

Since 2009 smoking has been prohibited in all enclosed spaces, including government offices, public transport, restaurants, bars and even nargile cafés, establishments devoted to smoking the traditional water pipe.

Visiting Mosques

Most large mosques are open all day, closing after last prayers in the evening. Smaller mosques open only for the five daily prayer times *(namaz)*. At these mosques it may be difficult to gain entrance outside prayer times unless there is a caretaker around to open up for you. Non-Muslims should refrain from entering any mosque during prayers.

The times of prayer change throughout the year according to sunrise and sunset. They are displayed on a board either outside or inside the mosque, but are always signalled by the call to prayer *(ezan)* from a loudspeaker that is fixed to

the minaret of the mosque. When visiting a mosque, women and men should dress appropriately. Most mosques in Istanbul have a prominent notice outside, in English, noting the entry requirements: cover your head (women) and bare shoulders (both sexes); no skirts above the knee or shorts; remove shoes. Some mosques provide shawls to cover head, arms and shoulders. Shoes are usually left on racks in the entryway, but you may prefer to carry them with you as theft is not unknown. Some mosques provide elasticated plastic bags to slip over your shoes instead of removing them. Make as little noise as possible inside and show consideration for anyone who is praying there.

Taxes and Tipping

The rate of VAT (KDV in Turkish) varies between 1 and 23 per cent, though the most common rate is 18 per cent. It is included in hotel prices as well as in the purchase price of most goods and services.

A service charge of 10 to 15 per cent is usually charged in upmarket and licensed restaurants and cafés, and it is customary to tip the waiters here a further 5 per cent. Waiters working in more basic establishments will also appreciate a gratuity.

Language

As a rule, Turks will make every effort to communicate with foreigners. In areas frequented by tourists it is easy to find English-speakers, but it is worth making an effort to learn a few words and phrases in Turkish. The Phrase Book on pages 279–80 is a useful place to start.

Public Conveniences

Public toilets are thin on the ground in Istanbul, usually located in prominent underpasses and at transport terminals. Entrances are marked *Bay* for men and *Bayan* for women. The attendant sitting outside, whom you pay on exit (a sign generally shows the charge), may supply toilet paper, but it is a good idea to carry tissues with you. Fortunately, virtually every mosque (of which there are many) has facilities attached for both men and women. Like public toilets, there is usually an attendant and a small fee is charged.

Sign for a public toilet

If you are reluctant to use the squat toilets generally found in public and mosque facilities, you can ask to use the modern flush-style toilets in most restaurants, hotels or cafés. Museums and major sights all have toilets and, outside the city, motorway service areas have excellent, free washroom facilities.

Travellers with Special Needs

Istanbul has few facilities for disabled people and the poor state of the streets can make it difficult to get around. Few mosques allow wheelchairs, but an increasing number of museums are making provisions for those with a disability. Toilets with special facilities are also very rare. Conversely, museum staff and the public will go to great lengths to assist with entry to buildings, and there are some low-level public telephones and special access buses *(see p239)*. Trams are

accessible to wheelchair users, although accessing some of the underground stations will be difficult. Other stations have platforms with gentle ramps from street level *(see p240)*.

The **Turkish Tourist Office** in London publishes a guide to facilities for the disabled in Turkey. This contains specific details of hotels as well as general information.

The **Turkish Association for the Disabled** (Türkiye Sakatlar Derneği) helps disabled people living in Istanbul, and can arrange bus tours around the city for small groups of disabled tourists.

Women Travellers

Women travelling in Turkey may receive unwelcome attention from men, but are rarely in danger of physical attack. To avoid harassment, dress respectably and look purposeful when walking around. Avoid being out alone at night. Traditional cafés *(see pp208–209)* tend to be male preserves, while restaurants often have a section reserved for women and families *(see p191)*.

The Beyoğlu area of Istanbul, along with many of the more prosperous suburbs, is a different proposition, and women can and do go out and about without male company, even at night.

Students outside the Moorish-style gateway of Istanbul University

Students

Apart from a small discount on intercity trains, an ISIC card is of little use in Turkey. Budget accommodation is easy to find. In July and August you can get a bed in a student dormitory through the Sultanahmet tourist information office. There are quite a few youth hostels *(see p185)*, and some cheap hotels and guesthouses in the city centre *(see pp186–9)*.

Photography

Museums do not usually charge visitors for using cameras, but there is often a charge for the use of a video camera. Flash is forbidden in most museums, as are tripods. Some mosques do

Groups of friends socializing at a café in Beyoğlu

not permit the use of a flash, but discreet photography is usually allowed. It is polite to ask permission before taking photographs of people.

Time

Turkey is 2 hours ahead of GMT and BST.

Electricity

As in Europe, the electric current is 220V AC. Plugs have two round pins and adaptors are readily available in Turkey.

Conversion Chart

Imperial to Metric
1 inch = 2.54 centimetres
1 foot = 30 centimetres
1 mile = 1.6 kilometres
1 ounce = 28 grams
1 pound = 454 grams
1 pint = 0.6 litres
1 gallon = 4.6 litres

Metric to Imperial
1 centimetre = 0.4 inches
1 metre = 3 feet, 3 inches
1 kilometre = 0.6 miles
1 gram = 0.04 ounces
1 kilogram = 2.2 pounds
1 litre = 1.8 pints

Colourful display of fruit and vegetables at a market stall

Responsible Tourism

Traditionally, recycling is carried out by members of the Roma community who, pulling hand-carts fitted with giant sacks, scavenge through the large waste bins left out on the street for collection. Plastics, paper, metal and glass are sold to private operators for recycling. Some Turks help by leaving recyclable materials next to bins rather than putting them in – visitors could do the same.

Environmental awareness in Turkey is improving, with municipality-controlled recycling bins beginning to appear on the streets of Istanbul and other cities. Visitors should make use of these when available.

Electricity is expensive, so many Turks use solar-energy systems for their hot-water needs. If you are serious about energy conservation, check that your proposed accommodation has a system installed. For the same reason low-energy light bulbs have caught on in a big way here.

Street markets are abundant in Istanbul (see pp214–15) and buying from them reduces the amount of packaging – try the Wednesday market (Çarşamba Pazarı) in Fatih.

DIRECTORY

Consulates

Australia
Asker Ocağı Cad 15, Elmadağ-Taksim. **Map** 7 F3. **Tel** (0212) 243 13 33.

Canada
İstiklâl Cad 189/5, Beyoğlu. **Map** 7 D4. **Tel** (0212) 251 98 38.

New Zealand
İnönü Cad 48/3, Taksim. **Map** 7 F4. **Tel** (0212) 244 02 72.

United Kingdom
Meşrutiyet Cad 34, Tepebaşı. **Map** 7 D4. **Tel** (0212) 334 64 00.

United States
Kaplıcalar Mevkii 2, İstinye. **Tel** (0212) 335 90 00.

Tourist Information

Atatürk Airport
International Arrivals Hall. **Tel** (0212) 465 31 51.

Hilton Hotel Arcade
Cumhuriyet Cad, Elmadağ. **Map** 7 F2. **Tel** (0212) 233 05 92.

Karaköy International
Maritime Passenger Terminal (Terminal 2). **Map** 3 E1. **Tel** (0212) 249 57 76.

Sirkeci Station
Sirkeci İstasyon Cad, Sirkeci. **Map** 3 E3 (5 E1). **Tel** (0212) 511 58 88.

Sultanahmet Square
Divanyolu Cad 3, Sultanahmet. **Map** 3 E4 (5 E4). **Tel** (0212) 518 18 02.

Religious Services

Anglican Christ Church (Crimean Memorial Church)
Serdar-ı Ekrem Sok 82, Tünel. **Map** 7 D5. **Tel** (0212) 251 56 16.

Greek Orthodox St George's Cathedral
Sadrazam Ali Paşa Cad 35, Fener. **Tel** (0212) 525 21 17.

Jewish Neve Shalom Synagogue
Büyük Hendek Cad 61, Şişhane. **Map** 6 C5. **Tel** (0212) 293 75 66.

Presbyterian All Saints Church
Yusuf Kamil Sok Paşa 10, Moda. **Map** 3 D5 (4 C5). **Tel** (0216) 449 39 74.

Roman Catholic St Anthony of Padua
İstiklâl Cad 325, Galatasaray. **Map** 7 D4. **Tel** (0212) 244 09 35.

Travellers with Special Needs

Turkish Association for the Disabled
Tel (0212) 521 49 12.
W tsd.org.tr

Turkish Tourist Office
170–73 Piccadilly, London W1V 9DD, UK. **Tel** (020) 7839 7778.

Personal Security and Health

Istanbul is safer than many other European cities, and visitors rarely encounter violence. It is, however, a fast-growing city with huge disparities between rich and poor, and burglary, pickpocketing and petty theft are all on the rise. Keep an eye on your valuables in crowded areas and do not wander the streets late at night on your own. The standard of health care in the city is very good, with excellent private hospitals. For minor complaints, pharmacists will be able to provide advice.

Police

There are several police forces in Turkey. The Security Police (*Emniyet Polisi*), the city's main force, wear dark-blue uniforms and caps, and pale-blue shirts. The Tourist Police (*Turizm Polisi*) is a branch of the *Emniyet Polisi*. Most officers have some knowledge of one or two European languages. The Tourist Police station in Sultanahmet, opposite the Basilica Cistern (*see p78*), is open 24 hours daily, and has an English–Turkish translator available 8:30am to 5pm Monday to Friday.

The Dolphin Police (*Yunus Polisi*) is a rapid-reaction branch of the *Emniyet Polisi*. Dolphin officers ride motorbikes and wear black biking leathers with a red stripe.

The Traffic Police (*Trafik Polisi*) wear the same blue uniform as the *Emniyet Polisi* but with a white belt, hat and gloves. Officers patrol the streets in black and white cars equipped with loudspeakers.

The navy-blue-uniformed Market Police (*Zabıta*) is a municipal police force, which patrols bazaars and other areas of commerce.

The Military Police (*Askeri İnzibat*) controls Turkey's many conscripts and officers wear an army uniform and white helmet bearing the abbreviation "As İz". The Gendarme (*Jandarma*) polices rural areas.

Dolphin Motorbike Police badge

What to be Aware of

When looking after your personal safety use common sense as you would in any large city. Be alert for pickpockets, particularly at markets, as well as on public transport and at termini. Keep your cash in a money belt and other valuables well out of sight. Carry bags on your front with the strap worn across your shoulder. In the event of any

trouble, shout *"imdat"* (help) to alert fellow passengers or officials. If necessary contact the Tourist Police. Women travelling alone or in groups without a male escort may need to take extra care. After dusk, avoid the areas bordering the Old City walls as muggings have taken place here. The Tarlabaşı neighbourhood of Beyoğlu is notorious for petty theft, drug-dealing and prostitution, and Taksim Square, especially around the Tarlabaşı Bulvarı exit, can be unsavoury at night.

Meetings are forbidden in Taksim Square but the upper section of İstiklal Caddesi, between Galatasaray Meydanı and Taksim Square, often witnesses protests, which can lead to heavy-handed policing. Do not leave valuables in your hotel room (use the hotel safe), and remember that Turkish law requires that you carry ID, preferably your passport (or at least a photocopy of it), at all times. Official tourist guides all carry photo ID around their necks – avoid any who do not. Finally, make sure your taxi driver turns on his meter before setting off.

In an Emergency

For emergency telephone numbers see the directory opposite. If your condition is serious or life-threatening you should be treated automatically, but carry your insurance details with you to prove your ability to pay. The state-run **Taksim Ilkyardım Hastanesi** (Taksim Emergency Hospital) has a decent reputation. The American and German hospitals listed in the directory have emergency dental practitioners.

Lost and Stolen Property

Turks are generally very honest and will go to great lengths to return lost property. It is worth

Security policeman

Traffic policeman

Dolphin policeman

Fire engine

Turkish Security Police *(Emniyet Polisi)* car

State ambulance

returning to the last place the item was seen, or going to the Tourist Police. Property left on public transport can be reclaimed from **IETT Buses**. If you have anything stolen, contact the Tourist Police. In order to make an insurance claim, you will need to give (and sign) a statement, preferably at the Tourist Police station in Sultanahmet.

Hospitals and Pharmacies

The Turkish health system has public and private hospitals. Both are usually well equipped but state-owned hospitals can be over-crowded and bureaucratic. Private establishments tend to be more efficient and more comfortable, have a higher proportion of English-speaking doctors, and some run their own ambulance services.

There are also a number of public clinics *(poliklinik)*

all over the city offering treatment for minor ailments, as well as private general practitioners *(tibbi doktorlar)* offering the same services.

The first port of call with a minor complaint, however, should be a pharmacy *(eczane)*. Pharmacists are well-trained, many speak some English, and antibiotics can be purchased at pharmacies without a prescription. Outside opening hours, the address of the nearest *nöbetçi eczane* (duty pharmacist) is usually posted in the pharmacy window.

Minor Hazards

Before leaving, make sure that your basic inoculations (diphtheria, polio, typhoid and tetanus) are all up to date. Check with your doctor about hepatitis A and hepatitis B vaccinations.

Do not drink tap water (bottled water is readily available everywhere), and exercise care when choosing restaurants and meals. Avoid anything that has been standing around, especially seafood, and only eat salads in more upmarket restaurants.

Some travellers to Turkey experience stomach upsets, often as a result of the amount of oil used in cooking or from drinking tap water. Take the usual precautions and medicines in case you get ill. If you are still unwell after 24 hours it is almost certainly some kind of food poisoning and antibiotics will be required.

Mosquitoes can be a minor irritant, so bring some repellent from your home country or buy a plug-in locally.

Sign for a state hospital in Şişli

Typical sign for a pharmacy in Istanbul

Travel and Health Insurance

The state health system in Turkey has few reciprocal agreements with other countries and private hospital costs are high, so be sure to take out travel and medical insurance before you leave.

DIRECTORY

Emergency Numbers

Ambulance
Tel 112.

Fire Service
Tel 110.

Hospital Call Line
Tel (0212) 444 09 11.

Police
Tel 155.

Tourist Police
Yerebatan Cad 6, Sultanahmet.
Map 3 E4.
Tel (0212) 527 45 03 or 528 53 69.

Lost Property

IETT Buses
Tünel, Beyoğlu. **Map** 7 D5.
Tel (0212) 245 07 20 ext 3205.

Hospitals and Pharmacies

American Admiral Bristol Hospital
Güzelbahçe Sok 20, Nişantaşı.
Map 8 A2. Tel (0212) 444 37 77.
w amerikanhastanesi.org

Ayasofya Eczanesi
Divanyolu Cad 28, Sultanahmet
Map 3 D4. Tel (0212) 513 72 15.

Cerrahpaşa Hospital
Koca Mustafa Paşa Cad, Fatih.
Map 1 C5. Tel (0212) 414 30 00.
w ctf.edu.tr

German Hospital
Sıraselviler Cad 119, Taksim.
Map 7 E4. Tel (0212) 2448 26 18
w almanhastanesi.com.tr

İstiklâl Eczanesi
İstiklâl Cad 423, Beyoğlu
Map 7 D4. Tel (0212) 2448 26 18.

Taksim Ilkyardım Hastanesi
Sıraselviler Cad 1, Taksim.
Map 7 E4. Tel (0212) 252 4300.

Banking and Currency

There is no limit to the amount of currency (foreign or Turkish) you can bring into Turkey. Following decades of inflation, the Turkish lira (*Türk Lirası*) has stabilized, with inflation running at around 9 per cent in 2015. An indicator of this stability was first seen in 2012 with the introduction of the ₺ symbol to denote the currency. However, it should be noted that although the prices of many goods are indicated using the ₺ symbol or TRY, the old abbreviation for the Turkish lira, TL, is still used in many places. For those visiting Istanbul and its surrounding areas, it is easy to withdraw money from ATMs and to pay for everything using credit or debit cards.

Cash dispenser with instructions in a range of languages

Banks and Bureaux de Change

Most private banks, such as Garanti and Yapıkredi, are open 9am–5pm Mon–Fri and some bigger branches also offer limited Saturday opening. State banks, such as Ziraat, close 12:30–1:30pm. Banks can be found in all main areas, on Divanyolu Caddesi in Sultanahmet and on İstiklâl Caddesi in Beyoğlu. The İş Bankası at Atatürk airport is open 24 hours daily. Apart from Turkish banks, there are many foreign banks like Citibank and HSBC, with familiar logos and services.

Most banks have an automated queuing system. Take a numbered ticket from the dispenser (for currency exchange there is usually a button marked *döviz*) and wait for your number to flash up on screen.

Several Turkish banks have outlets at airports, offering a full range of banking services.

With relatively modest inflation, there is no need to worry about exchanging foreign currency at the most beneficial time. Exchange offices (*döviz*) still exist, but not in the numbers they once did. Well-established offices include **Bamka Döviz** in Taksim and **Çetin Döviz** on İstiklâl Caddesi. *Döviz* are open for longer hours than banks, and also on Saturdays, but the exchange rate is often better in banks.

ATMs

ATMs are found outside all banks and near major tourist, business and shopping areas. They accept most debit cards, allowing you to withdraw the equivalent of about £250 daily. There is an English-language option on every machine. You can also use some credit cards such as MasterCard and Visa. It is

worth remembering that using a debit or credit card at an ATM involves a fee.

Traveller's Cheques and Credit Cards

Credit and debit cards, along with ATMs, have made traveller's cheques almost obsolete. Travellers are advised not to bring them into Turkey because they are difficult to cash. If you need to have large sums of money to hand, consider using a money-order (*havale*) service such as Western Union. They have an association with the Turkish Post Office (PTT – *see p235*) and some banks. This is a safe and

DIRECTORY

Banks and Bureaux de Change

Bamka Döviz
Cumhuriyet Cad 23, Taksim.
Map 7 E3. **Tel** (0212) 253 70 00.

Çetin Döviz
İstiklal Cad 39, Beyoğlu.
Map 7 E4. **Tel** (0212) 225 64 28.

Ziraat Bankası
Yeniçeriler Cad 55, Beyazıt
Map 2 C4 (4 B3).
Tel (0212) 517 06 00.

Credit Cards

American Express
Tel (0212) 444 25 25.

Diners Club, VISA, MasterCard and Eurocard
Tel (0212) 225 00 80.

A branch of HSBC in Istanbul

speedy, although expensive, way to transfer money.

Credit cards, such as VISA and MasterCard, and, to a lesser extent, American Express and Diners Club are universally accepted in hotels, shops and restaurants. Smaller restaurants and grocery stores, however, may not accept card payment. A number of debit cards issued by international banks, such as HSBC and Citibank, are also accepted, but check before leaving that your card is valid internationally. Ensure you know your PIN because swipe readers use chip and PIN protocol. It is also a good idea to inform your bank of your travels so that they expect your card to be used in Turkey.

There is no commission on paying with credit cards, though many hotels offer discounts for paying with cash (see p184). If you buy an airline ticket from a travel agent however, they will charge about 3 per cent commission.

Currency

The Turkish currency is known as the Turkish lira (TL) or, more officially (as your credit card statement will show), TRY. A ₺ symbol for the currency was introduced in 2012. The sub-division of the lira is the kuruş, with 100 kuruş equalling 1 lira. The lowest denomination note is ₺5, the highest ₺200. Beware that some Turks, out of habit, still talk in old, hyper-inflated lira terms, asking *bir milyon* (one million) for a glass of tea (1 lira). You are allowed to take up to US$5,000 out of Turkey in cash.

Banknotes

Turkish banknotes come in six denominations: 200 TL, 100 TL, 50 TL, 20 TL, 10 TL and 5 TL, and each denomination has its own distinctive colour. All the notes display the head of Atatürk on the front, with other Turkish notables on the reverse. Those shown here are 50 TL, 20 TL, 10 TL and 5 TL.

50 lira

20 lira

10 lira

5 lira

Coins

Coins are in denominations of 1 kuruş, 5 kuruş, 10 kuruş, 25 kuruş and 50 kuruş, and 1 lira (100 kuruş). All coins feature Atatürk on one side.

1 lira

50 kuruş

25 kuruş

10 kuruş

5 kuruş

Communications and Media

All major cities in Turkey enjoy easy access to efficient high-speed Internet and broadband connections. Internet cafés abound, though they are now being challenged by an ever-increasing number of places offering wireless connection. The formerly state-owned company, Türk Telekom, has a monopoly on all fixed-line telecommunications.

Post offices are clearly identified by the letters PTT and, although slow, the postal service is fairly reliable. Making phone calls from counter-top metered phones within a PTT building is economical, and many change foreign currency and offer the Western Union service for sending and receiving money.

Dozens of Turkish papers vye for readers' attention, ranging from the pro-Islamic to the staunchly secular, and all persuasions in between. Satellite TV has revolutionized the country's once staid, parochial broadcasting, and many foreign-language channels are widely available.

International and Local Telephone Calls

Istanbul has two area codes, 0212 (European side) and 0216 (Asian side). When calling a number within the same area, it is not necessary to use the code.

When calling the European side from the Asian, you must prefix the number with 0212; use the prefix 0216 when calling the Asian side from the European.

To call another city in Turkey, use the appropriate area code, for example 0224 for Bursa. To make an international call from Turkey, dial 00 followed by the code for the country, eg: Australia: 61; US and Canada: 1; New Zealand: 64; Republic of Ireland: 353 and UK: 44.

Mobile Phones

Mobile (cell) phones are essential items in modern Turkey. The market is dominated by three players – **Turkcell**, **Vodafone** and **Avea**. Most visitors with a roaming facility can use their existing mobile phone as they would at home because Turkey uses the standard 900 or 1800 MHz frequencies. Most North American phones are not compatible with the Turkish system and will not work here.

It costs less to make calls from a Turkish SIM than to pay roaming charges. For short stays in the country, consider buying a SIM card from a local mobile operator. All the three main phone companies have sales outlets at Atatürk and Sabiha Gökçen airports, as well as across the city. The SIM card costs around ₺50 but is usually sold as part of a package, with calling credit.

A phone brought in from outside Turkey will be blocked for use here within a week to 10 days. This is part of a government regulation to prevent Turkish phones from being undermined by cheaper ones, smuggled in from other countries.

Public Telephones

Telephone calls in Istanbul can be made from public phone boxes, post offices (PTT) and Türk Telekom (TT) centres using phonecards. The Alokart, with its scratch-off code, allows you to make

Chipped Türk Telekom Kontörlü prepaid phonecard

calls from any landline in Turkey. Chipped Türk Telekom Kontörlü cards are available in units of 50, 100, 200 and 350. Both can be purchased at PTT and TT centres and, for an additional charge, from street sellers and kiosks.

Internet Access

Istanbul has plenty of Internet cafés, although they are in short supply in the major tourist hub of Sultanahmet. Hourly rates are very modest. The Turkish keyboard can be frustrating to use so ask for help. Look out for the dotless Turkish "ı", for example, which will render web and email addresses invalid if used inadvertently. The "@" sign is usually made by pressing the "alt" and "q" keys at the same time.

Wireless Internet (Wi-Fi) connection is now found in many hotels and guesthouses and, although some business-oriented hotels charge, it is

Public telephone boxes in Istanbul

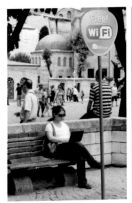

Woman using free Wi-Fi point in a street in Istanbul

usually free. Most hotels also have fixed terminals where you can check your mail. Many cafés in the city now offer wireless connection free of charge.

Postal Services

Post offices are found throughout Istanbul. There are large branches, with a full range of postal services, in **Sirkeci**, **Taksim** and **Karaköy**. Other locations are marked on the Street Finder (see pp246–63). Opening hours are usually 8:30am–5:30pm Monday to Friday and 8:30am–noon on Saturday. Stamps are only available from post offices.

Letters and postcards can be handed over the counter at post offices or posted in letter boxes, which are yellow and labelled **PTT**. Common signs indicating which box or slot to put your letter in are: Şehiriçi (local), Yurtiçi (domestic) and Yurtdışı (international).

Use air mail (uçak ile) when posting items abroad as surface post is slow. If you want to send a parcel by surface mail, use registered (kayıtlı) post. The contents of a package must be inspected at the post office, so take tape with you to seal your parcel at the counter. Letters and postcards to the rest of Europe take around a week, but may take twice as long to reach other continents. A recorded delivery service (called APS) is available from post offices, with

delivery in three days within Turkey. Local courier companies such as **Aras Kargo** and **Yurtiçi Kargo** will deliver letters and parcels in Turkey in a day or so at a comparable price.

Newspapers and Magazines

Turkey has three English-language daily papers, the liberal, pro-Islamic Today's Zaman, the nationalist, secular Hürriyet Daily News and the pro-AKP government Daily Sabah. All of them give round-ups of Turkish and foreign news. Foreign newspapers and magazines can be obtained from newsstands wherever there are substantial numbers of tourists or foreign residents. For current events listings try The Guide (see p220), which also has good features on Istanbul and Turkish culture, or Time Out Istanbul. Both are available from larger newsagents and bookshops.

Television and Radio

Satellite TV has blossomed in Turkey, with dozens of channels vying for viewers. Widely available foreign news channels include BBC World, CNN and Al Jazeera, with English-language entertainment provided by CNBCE, E2, BBC Entertainment and MTV. For foreign sports, look out for Eurosport and Spormax. Most hotels receive global

Newspaper stand outside the Topkapı Palace

satellite TV but check before booking if you particularly want foreign channels.

The state-owned TRT (Türk Radyo ve Televizyon) has 16 television channels and 14 radio stations. TRT3 radio (FM 88.2) broadcasts news bulletins in English, French and German.

GETTING TO ISTANBUL

The easiest way to reach Istanbul is to fly to one of the city's two international airports, Atatürk Airport, on the European side of the city, or Sabiha Gökçen on the Asian side. Turkish Airlines (THY) offers regular, direct flights from more than 100 destinations worldwide. Several major European carriers, such as Lufthansa and KLM, also fly direct to Istanbul. Most carriers fly into Atatürk Airport, but many budget and charter firms use Sabiha Gökçen. There are well-established coach services between Istanbul and several European cities, and a more rudimentary rail service. There are no direct ferry sailings from Europe, although cruises of the Aegean and Mediterranean usually include a one-day stopover in Istanbul.

Planes parked at Atatürk Airport

Arriving by Air

Turkey's main international airline, **Turkish Airlines** (THY), has direct flights to Istanbul from all major cities in Europe and some in Asia. **KLM** and **British Airways** both have at least one flight daily to Istanbul.

A number of budget airlines also serve Istanbul's airports. These include **EasyJet**, which connects the UK with Sabiha Gökçen airport, the Turkish carrier **Pegasus**, which flies into both Istanbul airports from the UK and several European cities, and **Atlas Global**, with flights from Luton. German/ Turkish carrier **Sunexpress** serves Sabiha Gökçen airport from many northern European countries.

Turkish Airlines flies direct to Istanbul from Chicago and New York, and **Delta Airlines**, among others, also has regular direct flights from New York. **American Airlines**, **Qatar Airways** and several other international carriers serve the city, but not always directly.

Atatürk Airport

Istanbul's **Atatürk Airport** (Atatürk Hava Limanı) lies 25 km (16 miles) west of the city centre in Yeşilköy. Its huge international (Dış Hatları) terminal and separate domestic (İç Hatları) terminal are internally connected by a series of moving walkways; the walk between them takes about 5 minutes.

The international terminal has all the facilities you would expect, including 24-hour banking, car hire outlets, tourist information and a hotel reservation desk. Allow at least 2 hours to check in for departures from busy Atatürk Airport.

Taxis (see p238) wait outside the arrivals hall of the international terminal. The fare to Taksim or Sultanahmet will be about ₺50.

The airport bus is a cheaper way of getting to the city centre. Buses depart every half-hour between 4am and 1am, take 30–40 minutes and cost ₺11. The bus stop, marked "Havaş", is situated outside the main doors of the arrivals hall. Stops include Aksaray, (from where tram/taxis run to Sultanahmet), and it terminates in Taksim Square (see p109).

The most economical way to the city centre is by metro and tramway. Buy two tokens (jeton) at the airport terminus of the metro or take a combination of metro and tram. For Old City/ Sultanahmet, take the M1 Metro to Zeytinburnu, and then take the T1 tram. For Galata, Beyoğlu or Taksim, take the M1 Metro to Yenikapı, and then the M2 Metro to either Şişhane or Taksim. To use the system, buy an Istanbul Card (see p241) from a vending machine and top it up with credit, or buy a couple of jeton.

Sabiha Gökçen Airport

Many domestic carriers and budget international airlines use **Sabiha Gökçen Airport**. Set in the suburbs of Asian Istanbul, 32 km (20 miles) southeast of the city centre, it has car hire outlets, banks, duty-free shops and cafés.

A taxi ride to Taksim takes 1 hour and costs about ₺95. Havaş buses travel to Taksim half-hourly between 4am and 1am. The 1-hour journey costs ₺14.

The cheapest option is to take the IETT (see p239) E3 bus to IV Levent, then the metro to Taksim. Alternatively, take the E10 bus to Kadıköy and the ferry across the Bosphorus to Eminönü (for Sultanahmet). The E3 operates every 15 minutes between 6am and 11:10pm;

A modern tram on the ancient streets of Istanbul

the E10 runs very frequently between 5am and 3:30am.

Arriving by Rail

The Orient Express *(see p68)* no longer runs as far as Istanbul. The overland route, which takes two days, is from Munich via Vienna, Budapest and Bucharest. Information can be obtained on **The Man in Seat 61** website, but bookings are best done via **European Rail Ltd**.

Major transport infrastructure projects are underway in Istanbul. Trains from Europe will terminate at Halkalı, 16 km (10 miles) west of the city centre, with onward travel on the new metro system.

Arriving by Coach

The Turkish coach companies **Ulusoy** and **Varan** operate direct services from several European cities to Istanbul, with tickets available online. Ulusoy coaches depart from Munich and Thessalonica, among other European cities, while Varan coaches depart from Berlin, Prague and Vienna. For services from the UK, contact **Eurolines**.

Coaches arrive at Esenler coach station *(otogar)*, 10 km (6 miles) northwest of Istanbul city centre. Esenler is also the main terminal for domestic connections *(see p244)*. Coach companies usually operate a courtesy minibus to the city centre. If not, take the metro, *(see pp240–41)* from the *otogar* to Aksaray, or the IETT 91 bus to Eminönü, or 830 bus to Taksim.

Arriving by Car

Drivers bringing cars into Turkey must show registration documents and a valid driving licence at the port of entry. Your passport will be stamped to show you have brought in a vehicle, and you cannot leave the country without it. You will also be issued a certificate by the Turkish customs authorities and this should be carried at all times, with your driving licence and passport. You must have a Green Card (available from your insurance company) if arriving from Europe, and appropriate insurance. A fire extinguisher, a first-aid kit and two hazard warning triangles are mandatory. Driving in Istanbul is taxing and public car parks *(otopark or katlıotopark)* are scarce and often full.

Motorway sign showing Turkish and European road numbers

DIRECTORY

Arriving by Air

American Airlines
Tel (1 800) 433 7300 (US).
W aa.com

Atlas Global
W atlasglb.com

British Airways
Tel (0870) 850 9850 (UK).
W britishairways.com

Delta Airlines
Tel (0800) 414 767 (UK).
Tel (404) 765 5000 (US).
W delta.com

EasyJet
Tel (0871) 244 2366 (UK).
W easyjet.com

KLM
Tel (0871) 222 740 (UK).
Tel (1 866) 434 0320 (US).
W klm.com.tr

Pegasus Airlines
Tel (0845) 0848 980 (UK).
W flypgs.com

Qatar Airways
W qatarairways.com

Sunexpress
W sunexpress.com

Turkish Airlines (THY)
W turkishairlines.com

Airports

Atatürk Airport
Tel (0212) 444 08 49.
W ataturkairport.com

Sabiha Gökçen Airport
Tel (0216) 585 50 00.
W sgairport.com

Arriving by Rail

European Rail Ltd
W raileurope.com

The Man in Seat 61
W seat61.com

Arriving by Coach

Eurolines
Tel (08717) 818181 (UK).
W eurolines.com

Ulusoy
Tel (0212) 444 18 88.
W ulusoy.com.tr

Varan
Tel (0212) 444 89 99.
W varan.com.tr

The Bosphorus Bridge, one of two major road bridges

GETTING AROUND ISTANBUL

Central areas are generally well served by metro and tram lines. Buses and dolmuşes provide city-wide transport, but roads and vehicles can be extremely crowded at rush-hour times. Ferries and water taxis ply the Bosphorus and, to a lesser extent, the Golden Horn. The Bosphorus tunnel, which houses the Marmaray Metro line, opened in late 2013. It links the European and Asian parts of the city. On its completion, the Marmaray system, most of it under-gound, will cover a distance of almost 70 km (43 miles). See the map inside the back cover for more information on Istanbul's ever-expanding public transport network.

Visitors strolling in front of the serene Blue Mosque *(see pp80–81)*

Green Travel

It is possible to walk between many of Istanbul's major sights *(see below)*, and the vast majority of the further-flung points of interest can be easily reached by public transport. Sadly, due to traffic congestion and lack of cycle routes, few people brave the city by bicycle.

Some of the city's buses use natural gas, as do most taxis, and the Metrobuses *(see p239)* have fuel-efficient, environmentally friendly hybrid engines.

Walking

The development of semi-pedestrianized zones, such as İstiklâl Caddesi and central Sultanahmet, and walking/jogging routes on the shores of sections of the Sea of Marmara and Bosphorus, has made it possible to walk with ease around some parts of Istanbul. Quieter areas of the city, like Eyüp *(see pp122–3)* and parts of Fatih, Fener and Balat

(see pp112–15) have relatively little traffic. For specialist tour companies offering walking tours around the city see page 239.

Bear in mind that traffic only stops at pedestrian crossings controlled by lights, and always make use of pedestrian overpasses and underpasses on main roads.

Istanbul, like any city, has parts that should be avoided *(see p230)*. If you are planning to walk in areas off the usual tourist track seek local advice, take extra care and do not walk in unfamiliar streets after dark.

Taxis

Taxis are ubiquitous in Istanbul. Fares are cheap in relation to other major European cities

Sign for a pedestrian underpass

and cabs operate day and night. They can be hailed in the street or found at taxi ranks. Hotel and restaurant staff can always phone for a taxi.

Cabs are bright yellow, with the word "taksi" on a sign on the roof. They take up to four passengers. The fare is charged according to a meter. If you cross the Bosphorus Bridge the bridge toll will be added to the fare. The driver will not expect a tip unless he has helped you load luggage, but it is usual to round up the fare to the nearest convenient figure. Most taxi drivers speak little, or no, English. They may not be familiar with routes to lesser-known sights, so carry a map and have the name of your destination written down.

Taxis queueing for customers at a ferry port

A Plan Tours sightseeing bus

Dolmuşes

Dolmuşes are shared minibuses with fixed routes. The name derives from the Turkish word *dolmuş* ("stuffed" or "full"), and drivers usually wait until every seat is taken before setting off. Dolmuşes run throughout the day until mid-evening, and later on busy routes.

Points of origin and final destinations are displayed in the front windows. Fares generally range between ₺4 and ₺6, and you pay by handing your money to the driver or another passenger to pass forward. To stop the vehicle, simply say to the driver "*inecek* (pronounced eenejek) *var*" ("somebody wants to get out").

Dolmuş stops are marked by a blue sign with a black "D" on a white background. From Taksim, destinations include Aksaray, Beşiktaş, Kadıköy and Topkapı, and vehicles depart from the Taksim end of Tarlabaşı Bulvarı, and where İsmet İnönü Caddesi exits Taksim.

Getting around by Bus

Inner-city buses are operated by two companies, both under municipal jurisdiction. **IETT** (Istanbul Omnibus company) buses are red and the environmentally friendly ones (*yeşil motor*) are green and run on natural gas. Özel Halk (public) buses are mainly light blue and/or green. For a map of useful bus routes see the pull-out map.

IETT buses accept only the Istanbul Card travel pass (*see p241*). The pass can be purchased from main bus departure centres, newsagents, kiosks and private vendors near bus shelters.

You enter at the front of the bus and exit by the rear doors. Push the button above the door or attached to the railings to alert the driver that you wish to alight at the next stop. A list of stops is displayed on the side of buses or on a video screen. Most buses run from 6am until 10 or 11pm.

The large Metrobuses run on dedicated lanes. The first line completed is of little interest to visitors, but a line planned between Edirnekapı and Vezneciler will link the city walls with the Bazaar Quarter.

Useful Bus Routes

15 Üsküdar – Beykoz
15/A Beykoz – Anadolu Kavağı
22 Kabataş – İstinye
25/A Hacıosman Metro – Rumeli Kavağı
28 Edirnekapı – Beşiktaş
28/T Topkapı – Beşiktaş
37/E Eminönü – Edirnekapı
40 Taksim – Sarıyer
80 Eminönü – Yedikule
81 Eminönü – Yeşilköy
86/V Vezneciler – Edirnekapı

Guided Tours

Several tour operators run special-interest tours of Istanbul, as well as general guided tours of the city and further afield, including **Backpackers Travel**, **Fest Travel** and **Turista**. **Istanbul Tour Studio** has more offbeat tours, **Istanbul Walks** concentrates on walking tours and **Istanbul Eats** offers backstreet culinary tours. For more companies offering trips outside Istanbul see page 245.

If you are approached by people offering their services as tour guides, make sure you see their photo ID, make it clear what you want to see and agree a fee. If you have little time, or do not wish to travel by public transport, it may be worth negotiating a private tour or visit to a sight with a taxi driver. This is best done through your hotel. For a city tour on a double-decker, try **Big Bus City Tours**. Buses start outside Haghia Sophia and Taksim. There are two different routes, one of which includes Asia.

DIRECTORY

Getting around by Bus

IETT (Istanbul Omnibus Company)
Erkan-ı Harp Sok No. 4, Beyoğlu.
Map 7 D5.
Tel (0800) 211 60 68, (0800) 211 61 20. W **iett.gov.tr**

Guided Tours

Backpackers Travel
Yeni Akbıyık Cad 22, Sultanahmet.
Map 3 D4 (5 D3).
Tel (0212) 638 63 43.
W **backpackerstravel.net**

Big Bus City Tour
Aya Sofya Karşısı 1, Sultanahmet.
Tel (0212) 283 13 96.
W **bigbustours.com**

Fest Travel
Barbaros Bulvarı, 74/20, Beşiktaş.
Map 8 C2.
Tel (0212) 216 10 36.
W **festtravel.com.tr**

Istanbul Eats
W **istanbuleats.com.tr**

Istanbul Tour Studio
Halaskargazi Cad 6, Şişli.
Tel (0533) 355 30 49.
W **istanbultourstudio.com**

Istanbul Walks
Şifahamamı Sok, Sultanahmet.
Tel (0212) 516 63 00.
W **istanbulwalks.net**

Turista Travel
Divanyolu Cad 16, Sultanahmet.
Map 3 D4 (5 D4).
Tel (0212) 518 65 70.
W **turistatravel.com**

Getting around by Metro and Tram

Travelling in Istanbul by Metro and tram is surprisingly easy. A tunnel under the Bosphorus opened in 2013, making it possible to cross from the European side of the city to the Asian part by Metro. A new bridge across the Golden Horn links the Metro system in the Old City and its surroundings with the entertainment quarter of Beyoğlu and Taksim in the north. A modern tram runs through the heart of the Old City and across the Golden Horn to Karaköy and the ferry terminal at Kabataş.

A tram on Istanbul's modern tramway system

Tramway

Istanbul's tramway system is modern and efficient, but it can be very crowded at peak times. There are several tram lines in the city, run by the

Istanbul Transportation Co.

The most useful to visitors is the T1 tram line, which runs from Zeytinburnu (where it connects with the M1 Metro coming in from Atatürk Airport) through Aksaray and Sultanahmet. The line then crosses the Galata Bridge (see inside back cover) and continues to Kabataş, offering plenty of sightseeing spots along the way.

To access the tramway purchase a token (jeton), which operates the turnstile (these also accept the Istanbul Card travel pass).

Trams travel on the right-hand side of the street, so be sure to stand on the correct platform. Trams are frequent, running every 5 minutes between 6am and midnight.

It should be noted that during rush hours and on domestic holidays, the trams tend to get very crowded. Try not to sit or stand too far from the sliding doors, or you may find yourself pushing and shoving to get off at the right stop.

Metro

The M1 Metro runs east into the city centre from Atatürk Airport, with a few sections

Tram and Metro Route Map

The most useful Metro lines for visitors are M1 and M2. The Tramway is mainly an above-ground, electrified rail system.

Key
— Metro
— Lines under construction
--- Tramway
— Light railway
— Tramway
— Nostalgic Tram
— Funicular

Hacıosman
IV Levent
Levent
Gayrettepe
Şişli-Mecidiyeköy
Osmanbey
Taksim
Kabataş
Şişhane
Fındıklı
Tünel
Tophane
Üsküdar
Karaköy
Eminönü
Halıç
Topkapı-Ulubatlı
Vatan
Veznecİler
Sirkeci
Aksaray
Ayrılık Çeşmesi
Kartal
Emniyet-Fatih
Fetihkapı
Yusufpaşa
Haydarpaşa
Topkapı
Findizade
Cevizlibağ A.Ö.Y.
Merter
Merkez Efendi
Söğütlüçesme
Aksemsettin
Kadıköy
Gebze
Mithatpaşa
Zeytinburnu
Bağcılar
Davutpaşa Y.T.Ü.
Terazidere
Bayrampaşa-Maltepe
Edirnekapı
Esenler
Sağmalcılar
Sehitlik
Otogar
Demirkapı
Kartaltepe
Kirazlı
Habibler
Golden Horn
Bosphorus
Sea of Marmara
Airport

underground. It operates between 6am and midnight. The key stops are Zeytinburnu (for connecting to the T1 tramway) and Otogar, for the intercity bus station.

The Aksaray stop connects to the T1 tramway but it involves a short walk. This can be awkward with luggage because there is a bridge.

The M2 Metro runs from Yenikapı, across the Golden Horn to the Hacıosman station.

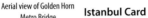

Aerial view of Golden Horn Metro Bridge

The Metro is clean, well-run and the cars are air-conditioned.

Many of the Metro stations are underground and passengers have to go through a series of moving stairs and ramps to get to or from the platform. Lifts are available but are often busy.

Journey tokens (*jeton*) purchased on entry, operate the turnstiles for both the tram and the Metro. Alternatively, you can use an Istanbul Card.

Cable Cars and Funiculars

A cable car connects the shores of the Golden Horn in Eyüp with the Eyüp cemetery and tea gardens, and runs between 8am and 10pm daily. There is also a cable car in Maçka Park, which is open from 8am to 8pm daily.

Inaugurated in 1875, the Tünel is a French-built underground railway. It climbs steeply from Karaköy to Tünel Square in Beyoğlu, where it connects with the period tram on İstiklâl Caddesi. The Karaköy station is set back from the main road just off the Galata Bridge *(see p91)*. The Tünel closes at 10:45pm. A useful modern funicular links Taksim Square with the ferry terminal at Kabataş from 6am to midnight.

The Nostalgic Tram

The Nostalgic Tram *(Nostaljik Tramvay)* covers a distance

of 1.5 km (just under 1 mile) along İstiklâl Caddesi from Tünel to Taksim Square. On the Asian side, the tram runs from Kadıköy along Bahariye Caddesi to Moda. Both run from 7am to 8pm. The trams are the original early 20th-century vehicles, taken out of service in 1966 but revived in 1989. The ticket collectors wear period costume. The Istanbul Card can be used on both.

Istanbul Card

The Istanbul Card *(Istanbulkart)* is a travel pass that can be used on the entire public transport system in Istanbul: tramway, Metro, city buses, ferries and sea buses. It is a prepaid and rechargeable contactless smartcard. The card can be bought from main bus stations and other public transport ticket offices or from vending machines at major stops, such as Atatürk Airport.

Istanbul Card

DIRECTORY

Tramway

Istanbul Transportation Co.
Tel (0212) 568 99 70.
W istanbul-ulasim.com.tr

When purchasing an Istanbul Card, you pay for a number of units in advance and a refundable ₺6 deposit for the card itself. The card can be topped up any time at kiosks or at distinctive orange vending/recharging machines located near transport stops.

To use, place the Istanbul Card in the proximity of a fare point, on a turnstile or boarding point, and the amount due will be automatically deducted. One card can be used for any number of passengers. An Istanbul Card saves passengers a considerable amount of money as each journey with a token (*jeton*) costs ₺4 but only ₺2.15 with the card. Fares come down even more on journeys made within 1.5 hours of each other.

A red tram travelling through crowded İstiklâl Caddesi

Getting around by Boat

The most pleasant and relaxing means of getting around Istanbul is by the innumerable waterborne craft which ply the Bosphorus between the European and Asian sides. These range from water taxis and small, privately operated ferries to larger ferries and high-speed catamarans. As well as being a relatively fast way to get around, a ride on a boat will also provide some great views of the city.

Passengers disembarking from a ferry, a popular mode of travel

Old ferries at Karaköy, from which ferries run to Haydarpaşa and Kadıköy

Ferries

A constant traffic of ferries crosses the Bosphorus and the Golden Horn, run by the **Istanbul Sea Bus Company (İDO)**. Private steam ferries, called *vapur*, are run by

Şehirhatları. The principal ferry terminus on the European side is at Eminönü *(see p89)*, just east of the Galata Bridge. Destinations served from here, clearly labelled on the relevant boarding halls at each pier, include Kadıköy, Haydarpaşa and Üsküdar on the Asian shore. There is also a pier marked "Boğaz Hattı" for the Bosphorus cruises *(see p243)*, and another labelled "Harem" for car ferries to Asian Istanbul. On the west side of the Galata Bridge is the pier for ferries up the Golden Horn (Haliç Hattı).

Another main terminus is Karaköy, opposite Eminönü, from which ferries run to

Haydarpaşa and Kadıköy. The international dock, where cruise liners berth, is also here.

There are ferries from Eminönü to Kadıköy between 7am and 9pm, and from Eminönü to Üsküdar between 6am and 11:30pm, every 15 minutes or so. Ferries from Karaköy to Kadıköy run daily between 6:30am and midnight. Other changes are less frequent. If you want to explore independently using ferries, especially to hop between the villages along the Bosphorus, you will need to arm yourself with a timetable (see below).

Sea Buses

The modern, Swedish-built catamarans which are known as sea buses (deniz otobüsü) are run by İDO. Their interiors resemble aircraft cabins, with long rows of reclining seats, piped music and air conditioning. Sea buses are considerably faster and more comfortable than ferries, but cost three times as much.

The most useful route is to the Princes' Islands (see p160), with 6–12 departures daily. For destinations outside Istanbul see pp244–5.

Motor Boats

A number of companies, including **Dentur** and **Turyol**, operate motor boats which cross the Bosphorus and Golden Horn at various points, and run up the Bosphorus. These routes are also served by Şehirhatları ferries and although cheaper, they are less frequent. Motor boats accept only the Istanbul Card travel pass or a jeton token.

Water Taxis

Water taxis are the latest addition to the city's waterborne transport scene. There are 27 designated docks across the city. To book a water taxi either phone or reserve online. They operate a shared rate system for

Water taxi on its way along on the Bosphorous

the 10-seater craft, and are very reasonably priced when shared.

The Bosphorus Trip

Şehirhatları runs daily ferry excursions up the Bosphorus (see pp138–51). Light refreshments are served but no meals. They

One of the many ferries operating on the Bosphorus

get crowded in the summer, especially at weekends, so arrive early to book your ticket and to ensure that you get a deck seat with a view. You should retain your ticket during the journey, as you must show it on the return trip. You can disembark at any pier along the way, boarding the next ferry that comes along with the same ticket; but if you make a second stop you will need to buy a new ticket to continue your journey. Şehirhatları also offers a trip from Kadıköy in summer at weekends only.

There are several alternatives to the official trip. The small private boats that leave Eminönü just after the Şehirhatları ferry sails in the summer months only go halfway up the straits and do not stop on the way. Alternatively, you can book a private cruise through a reputable company, such as **Hatsail Tourism**.

Tickets & Timetables

For ferries and sea buses, buy a flat-fare token (jeton) from the booth (gişe) at the pier or from one of the unofficial street vendors who sit nearby and sell them at slightly higher prices. Ferry fares cost ₺4, while those for sea buses to the Princes' Islands are ₺9. You can use jetons for all local trips. Better still, use an Istanbul Card,

which makes boarding quicker and offers a discounted fare. Tickets for the Bosphorus trip cost ₺25 and you cannot use the Istanbul Card for it.

To enter the pier, put the jeton into the slot beside the turnstile, and then wait in the boarding hall for a boat. A schedule of sailing times is on view at each pier and a copy of the timetable (tarife) can usually be bought at the ticket booth.

İDO İDO logo

DIRECTORY

Ferries and Sea Buses

Istanbul Sea Bus Co (İDO)
Tel (0212) 444 44 36.
W ido.com.tr

Şehirhatları
Tel (0212) 444 18 51.
W sehirhatlari.com.tr

Motor Boats

Dentur
Tel 444 63 36.
W denturavrasya.com

Turyol
Tel (0212) 251 44 21.
W turyol.com

Water Taxis

Deniz Taksi
Tel 444 44 98. W deniztaksi.com

Private Cruises

Hatsail Tourism
Tel (0212) 241 62 50.
W hatsail.com

Travelling Beyond Istanbul

The best way to reach nearby towns and cities from Istanbul is by coach. Further- flung destinations can be reached either by coach or air. A great number of coach companies operate in Turkey, but it is worth paying extra to travel with a reputable company. Many Turkish cities are served by domestic flights from both Atatürk and Sabiha Gökçen airports and fares are competitive. A high-speed train links Istanbul to Ankara. For destinations across the Sea of Marmara, ferries and sea buses are a relaxing means of transport.

High-speed sea bus on the Bosphorus

Intercity Coaches

The main coach station (otogar) for both domestic and international destinations is at Esenler, 14 km (9 miles) northwest of the city centre. There is another at Harem, on the Asian side of the Bosphorus. Both are scruffy and poorly maintained, but all coach companies have city centre branches where you can buy tickets, and they run shuttle services to collection points near the motorway, so you will probably not need to use them.

You must make a booking for all coach journeys. Most companies accept credit cards. Varan and Ulusoy (see p237), the two most reputable bus companies, take bookings and issue tickets from their city centre offices. They operate services between main centres such as Ankara, Antalya and İzmir, as well as to destinations along the Black Sea coast. **Kâmil Koç** has a service to Bursa. The journey goes via Gebze, boarding the ferry

to Yalova and takes about 4 hours. **Çanakkale Truva Seyahat** is the best company to use for getting to Gelibolu (Gallipoli), which takes about 5 hours, or Çanakkale, which takes about 6 hours. **Metro Turizm** is a large and reliable coach company that runs regular schedules to many destinations outside Istanbul. Single passengers will usually be seated next to someone of the same sex. Couples can sit together. Refreshments are served free of charge, and there are frequent rest and meal stops. The better companies have some buses with single seats, offer free Wi-Fi and have TVs in the back of the seats. As an example, the fare for the 450 km (280 mile) journey between Istanbul and Antalya is ₺75 with a premium company.

Air Travel

Flying makes sense in Turkey if you wish to visit distant cities such as Antalya, İzmir, Kayseri (for Cappadocia), Trabzon or

Van. Several companies compete on the same routes, so prices are very reasonable (starting from ₺90) if booked early. **Anadolujet** and **Sunexpress** fly only from Istanbul's Sabiha Gökçen Airport. **Atlas Jet** and **Onur Air** use Atatürk Airport, while **Pegasus** and **Turkish Airlines** use both. Turkish Airlines have flights to both Bursa and Çanakkale, if you are pressed for time. Although all domestic airlines have online booking systems, foreign cards are not always accepted. Use a domestic travel agent if you face trouble booking online.

Sea Buses and Ferries

High-speed ferries (hızlı feribot) and sea buses (deniz otobüsü) are a convenient means of travelling long distances from a city surrounded by water. Run by **İDO** and **Şehirhatları** (see p242), they are good value; cars are also carried on some high-speed ferry routes.

For Bursa, take the twice-daily high-speed ferry from Yenikapı to Güzelyalı (90 minutes), or the sea bus from Kabataş to Güzelyalı (2 hours via Kadıköy), then a bus into Bursa. Alternatively, take the high-speed ferry (seven daily; 1 hour 10 minutes) to Yalova, from where it is 1 hour by bus to Bursa. From Yalova, regular minibuses serve İznik (1 hour). Sea buses also travel to the Marmara Islands from Yenikapı.

Kâmil Koç minibus at a bus station in central İzmir

Car Hire and Road Travel

Turkey's comprehensive intercity coach and air network means that a car is not necessary for travelling to other cities. If you wish to drive, note that car hire companies including **Avis**, **Budget** and **Sixt** have both airport and city centre offices. You do not need an international driving licence, just your normal one. Turkish roads are hazardous because of fast, reckless driving. Traffic drives on and gives way to the right, even on roundabouts. The Turkish Touring and Automobile Club (Türkiye Turing ve Otomobil Kurumu, or **TTOK**), can give visiting motorists advice on driving in Turkey, as well as offering assistance with breakdowns, accidents and insurance. It has reciprocal agreements with the British AA and RAC.

Day Trip Tours

A number of companies offer day trips from Istanbul to the Princes' Islands, the Dardanelles, Bursa and villages on the Black Sea. These are often good value and offer an efficient and hassle-free method of simplifying your travel arrangements.

Reputable tour operators with English-speaking guides include **Plan Tours**, **Turista Travel** and **Türk Expres**. All offer classical, biblical and heritage tours in Istanbul as well as to regions throughout Turkey. Some companies offer personalized tours all over Turkey. **CARED** (Çanakkale Tour Guide Association) can provide tour guides who speak many languages.

Horse-drawn carriage (phaeton) on Büyükada

Car rental company logos

Local Transport Outside Istanbul

The main means of public transport in both Bursa and Edirne is the dolmuş. These are either minibuses or saloon cars, with the destination displayed on signs on the roof. If you stay in the centre of either city and are moderately fit, you will find that all of the major sights are within easy walking distance.

In Bursa city centre, Heykel, at the eastern end of Atatürk Caddesi, is the main dolmuş terminus. From there you can get dolmuşes to most other parts of the city. There is also an efficient bus service and a metro.

Edirne is much smaller than Bursa, and the public transport system is not as comprehensive. To get from the coach station to the town centre, a distance of 2 km (1 mile), take a Merkez–Garaj minibus dolmuş, or a taxi.

There are no motor vehicles on the Princes' Islands. On Büyükada and Heybeliada phaeton carriages can be hired.

DIRECTORY

Intercity Coaches

Çanakkale Truva Seyahat
Tel (0212) 444 00 17.
W truvaturizm.com

Kâmil Koç
Tel (0212) 444 05 62.
W kamilkoc.com.tr

Metro Turizm
Tel (0212) 444 34 55.
W metroturizm.com.tr

Air Travel

Anadolujet
Tel 444 25 38.
W anadolujet.com.tr

Atlas Jet
Tel (0850) 222 00 00.
W atlasjet.com

Onur Air
Tel (0850) 210 66 87.
W onurair.com.tr

Pegasus Airlines
Tel (0850) 260 07 37.
W flypgs.com

Sunexpress
Tel 444 07 97.
W sunexpress.com

Turkish Airlines (THY)
Tel 444 08 49.
W turkishairlines.com

Ferries

İDO
Tel (0212) 444 44 36.
W ido.com.tr

Şehirhatları
Tel (0212) 444 18 51.
W sehirhatlari.com.tr

Kabataş Pier
Tel (0212) 249 15 58.

Yenikapı Pier
Tel (0212) 516 12 12.

Car Hire and Road Travel

Avis
Tel 444 28 47.
W avis.com.tr

Budget
Tel (0212) 663 08 58.
W drivebudget.com

Sixt
Tel (0212) 215 24 19.
W sixt.com/car-rental/turkey

TTOK
I. Oto Sanayi Sitesi Yanı, Seyrantepe Yolu, IV Levent.
Tel (0212) 282 81 40.
W turing.org.tr

Day Trip Tours

CARED
Tel (0286) 213 90 40.
W cared.org.tr

Plan Tours
Cumhuriyet Cad 83/1, Elmadağ. Map 7 F3.
Tel (0212) 230 22 72.
W plantours.com

Turista Travel
Divanyolu Cad 16, Sultanahmet. Map 3 D4 (5 D4). Tel (0212) 518 65 70.
W turistatravel.com

Türk Expres
Cumhuriyet Cad 47/1, Taksim. Map 7 E3.
Tel (0212) 235 95 00.
W turkexpres.com.tr

STREET FINDER

The map references that are given throughout this guide refer to the maps on the following pages only. Some small streets referred to in the text may not be labelled on the map. References are given for hotels *(see pp182–9)*, restaurants *(see pp196–207)*, shops *(see pp210–19)* and entertainment venues *(see pp220–23)*.

The map below shows the area covered by the ten maps and the key lists the symbols used. The first figure of the reference tells you which map to turn to; the letter and number indicate the grid reference. For an overview of Greater Istanbul see pages 110–11. The map on the inside back cover shows public transport routes.

Key To Street Finder

- ▦ Major sight
- ▦ Place of interest
- ▢ Other building
- 🛳 Ferry boarding point
- 🛳 Sea bus boarding point
- 🚉 Railway station
- Ⓜ Metro / light rail station
- Underground funicular stop
- 🚊 Tram stop
- Cable car station
- 🚌 Main bus stop
- Ⓓ Dolmuş terminus
- ℹ Tourist information

- Police station
- Turkish baths
- 🅲 Mosque
- Synagogue
- ✝ Church
- ✚ Hospital
- === Railway line
- — Tram line
- Motorway
- Pedestrian tunnel
- — City walls

Scale of Maps 1–3 & 6–10

0 metres	250
0 yards	250

Scale of Maps 4 & 5

0 metres	200
0 yards	200

Street Finder Index

In Turkish, Ç, Ğ, İ, Ö, Ş and Ü are listed as separate letters in the alphabet, coming after C, G, I, O, S and U respectively. In this book, however, Ç is treated as C for the purposes of alphabetization and so on with the other letters. Hence Çiçek follows Cibinlik as if both names began with C. Following standard Turkish practice we have abbreviated Sokağı to Sok and Caddesi to Cad. References in brackets refer to the enlarged section of the Street Finder (maps 4 and 5).

General Index

Acknowledgments

Dorling Kindersley would like to thank the following people whose assistance contributed to the preparation of this book:

Main Contributors

Rosie Ayliffe lived in Turkey for three years, during which time she worked as a freelance writer in Istanbul for the English-language weekly *Dateline Turkey* and as a tour guide travelling all over western Turkey. She is one of the authors of the *Rough Guide to Turkey*, and has also contributed to the *Rough Guide to France* and to Time Out's London guides.

Rose Baring is a travel writer who has spent many months exploring Istanbul. She is the co-author of *Essential Istanbul* (AA) and has also contributed to guides to Tunisia, and Moscow and St Petersburg.

Barnaby Rogerson has travelled, written and lectured extensively in the countries of the eastern Mediterranean. He is, with Rose Baring, co-author of *Essential Istanbul* (AA), and has contributed to several other AA and Cadogan guides. He is the author of *A Traveller's History of North Africa*.

Canan Silay worked for many years as the editor-in-chief of the English-language magazine *Istanbul, The Guide*. Previously, she worked as a journalist with the Turkish daily newspaper *Hürriyet*. She has contributed to several books on Turkey, including Insight guides to Istanbul, Turkey and the Turkish coast.

Managing Editor Georgina Matthews
Managing Art Editor Annette Jacobs
Senior Managing Editor Vivien Crump
Deputy Art Director Gillian Allan

Additional Contributors

Ghillie Başan, Arzu Bolukbasi, Krysia Bereday Burnham, Professor Anthony A M Bryer, Jim Crow, José Luczyc-Wyhowska, Colin Nicholson, Venetia Porter, Dott. A Ricci, Professor J M Rogers, Sargasso Media Ltd, London, Suzanne Swan, Tina Walsh.

Additional Cartography

Robert Funnell, Emily Green, David Pugh, Lee Rowe (ESR Cartography Ltd).

Picture Research

Rachel Barber, Marta Bescos, Rhiannon Furbear, Susie Peachey, Ellen Root, Nikil Verma.

Revisions and Relaunch Team

Didem Mersin Alıcı, Gillian Andrews, Jasneet Arora, Lydia Baillie, Sonal Bhatt, Tessa Bindloss, Imogen Corke, Gary Cross, Mehmet Erdemgil, Alice Fewery, Isobel Finkel, Amy Harrison, Sally Hibbard, Susanne Hillen, Rupanki Kaushik, Hasan Kelepir, Sumita Khatwani, Batur Kızıltuğ, Priyanka Kumar, Maite Lantaron, Jude Ledger, Francesca Machiavelli, Hayley Maher, Alison McGill, Sam Merrell, Ella Milroy, Mary Ormandy, Catherine Palmi, Reetu Pandey, Marianne Petrou, Mani Ramaswamy, Lee Redmond, Lucy Richards, Terry Richardson, Nicola Rodway, Ankita Sharma, Azeem Siddique, Beverly Smart, Sands Publishing Solutions, Anna Streiffert, Rosalyn Thiro, Conrad Van Dyk, Nikhil Verma, Dutjapun Williams, Veronica Wood.

Proofreader

Stewart Wild.

Indexer

Hilary Bird.

Additional Photography

DK Studio/Steve Gorton, Lydia Evans, John Heseltine, Izzet Keriber, Dave King, Ian O'Leary, Fatih Mehmet Akdan, Rough Guides/Lydia Evans, Clive Streeter.

Artwork Reference

Kadir Kir, Remy Sow.

Special Assistance

The Publisher would like to thank staff at museums, mosques, churches, local government departments, shops, hotels, restaurants and other organizations in Istanbul for their invaluable help. Particular thanks are also due to: Feride Alpe; Halil Özek, Archaeological Museum, Istanbul; Hamdi Arabacıoğlu, Association of Mevlevis, Istanbul; Veli Yenisoğancı (Director), Aya Sofya Museum, Istanbul; Nicholas Barnard; Ahmet Kazokoğlu, Bel Bim A.Ş., Istanbul; Poppy Body; Banu Akkaya, British Consulate, Istanbul; Vatan Ercan and Mine Kaner, Bursa Tourist Office; Hanife Yenilmez, Central Bank of the Republic of Turkey, London; Reverend Father Ian Sherwood, Christ Church, Istanbul; Father Lorenzo, Church of SS Peter and Paul, Istanbul; Münevver Ek and Muazzez Pervan, Economic and Social History Foundation of Turkey, Istanbul; Edirne Müze Müdürlüğü; Emin Yıldız, Edirne Tourist Office; Tokay Gözütok, Eminönü Belediyesi, Istanbul; Mohammet Taşbent, Eminönü Zabıta Müdürlüğü, Istanbul; Orhan Gencer, Protocol Department, First Army HQ, Istanbul; Robert Graham; Cengiz Güngör, şevki Sırma and Mustafa Taşkan, Greater Istanbul Municipality; Hikmet Öztürk, İETT Genel Müdürlüğü, Istanbul; Bashir Ibrahim-Khan, Islamic Cultural Centre, London; İsmet Yalçın, İstanbul Balık Müstahsilleri Derneği; Nedim Akıner, İstanbul Koruma Kurulu; Sühela Ertürk Akdoğan and all staff of the Istanbul Tourist Offices; Abdurrahman Gündoğdu and Ömer Yıldız, İstanbul Ulaşım A.Ş.; Iznik Tourist Office; Mark Jackson; Sibel Koyluoğlu; Semra Karakaşlı, Milli Saraylar Daire Başkanlığı, Istanbul; Akın Bavur and Recep Öztop, Cultural Department, Ministry of Foreign Affairs, Ankara; staff at the Edirne Müftülüğü and Eyüp Müftülüğü; Mehmet Sağlam and staff at the İstanbul Müftülüğü; Professor Kemal İskender, Museum of Painting and Sculpture, Istanbul; Öcal Özerek, Museum of Turkish and Islamic Arts, Bursa; Dilek Elçin and Dr Celia Kerslake, Oriental Institute, Oxford University; Kadri Özen; Dr İffet Özgönül; Cevdat Bayındır, Public Relations Department, Pera Palace Hotel; Chris Harbard, RSPB; Rosamund Saunders; John Scott; Huseyin Özer, Sofra; Ahmet Mertez and Gülgün Tunç, Topkapı Palace, Istanbul; Doctor Tüncer, Marmara Island; Mr U Kenan İpek (First Secretary), Turkish Culture and Tourism Office in London and Istanbul, Turkish Embassy, London; Orhan Türker (Director of International Relations), Turkish Touring and Automobile Club, Istanbul; Peter Espley (Public Relations Counsellor) and all staff at the Turkish Tourist Office, London; Mustafa Coşkan, Türkiye Sakatlar Derneği, Istanbul; Dr Beyhan Erçağ, Vakıflar Bölge Müdürlüğü, Istanbul; Yalova Tourist Office; Zeynep Demir and Sabahattin Türkoğlu, Yıldız Palace, Istanbul.

Photography Permissions

Dorling Kindersley would like to thank the following for their kind permission to photograph at their establishments: the General Directorate of Monuments and Museums, the Ministry of Culture, the Ministry for Religious Affairs, İstanbul Valiliği İl Kültür Müdürlüğü, İstanbul Valiliği İl Müftülüğü, the Milli Saraylar Daire Başkanlığı and Edirne Valiliği İl Müftülüğü; also the many churches, restaurants, hotels, shops, transport services, and other sights and establishments too numerous to thank individually.

Picture Credits

a = above, b = below/bottom, c = centre, f = far, l = left, r = right, t = top

The publisher would like to thank the following individuals, companies, and picture libraries for their kind permission to reproduce their photographs:

360istanbul: 190cr, 204tr.

A Turızm Yayinlari: 160b; Archaeological Museum 44bl, 64bl, 65cra, 66cr, 66b, 67tl, 67c; *Aya Sofia from Fossart Album* 76tr; Topkapı Palace 58br; ABC Basin Ajansi A.ş.: 49clb, 46br, 215tr; The Advertising Archives: 104tr; Adahan Istanbul Hotel: 183tr Aisa Archivo Icongrafico, S.A., Barcelona: 22cb, 26c, 34tr, 35bc, 121tc, 173tr; Louvre Museum 23c; Topkapı Palace 57bl, 59cl; AKG, London: 33tl; Erich Lessing 32tl, Erich Lessing/Kunsthistoriches Museum, Vienna 34cb; Alamy

Images: Jon Arnold Images Ltd 81tl; blickwinkel 224–225, Mark Collinson 195crb, David Crossland 194br, Peter Forsberg 244br, Jeff Greenberg 109br; Chris Hellier 119br, Ali Kabas 193c; B. O'Kane 228tr; Justin Kase zninez 2bl; Justin Kase zsixz 231cla, 232bl, 235bc; Karl F. Schöfmann 202tl; John Stark 192cl, 193tl; **Ancient Art and Architecture Collection Ltd:** 22cr, 25tr; **Aquila Photographics:** Hanneand Jens Eriksen 171b; **Tahsın Aydoğmuş:** 4t, 19br, 23bl, 45b, 73cra, 74tr, 77bl, 80t, 88tr, 121ca, 146b, 172bl; **Jon Arnold Images:** Walter Bibikow 11tr; **Avis Budget Group:** 245cl, 245clb.

Baylo Suites: 182cr, 186bl; **Benaki Museum, Athens:** 27ca; **Bread and Butter:** 203br; **Bridgeman Art Library, London:** British Library *A Portrait of Süleyman the Magnificent* (1494–1566), Persian 34br; National Maritime Museum, London *Battle of Lepanto, 7th October, 1571*, Anonymous 29tr; Private Collection *Constantine the Great (c.274–337 AD, Roman Emperor 306–337AD)*, gold aureus 22tl; Stapleton Collection *Ibrahim from a Series of Portraits of the Emperors of Turkey, 1808*, John Young (1755–1825) 35tl; Victoria and Albert Museum, London *Sultan Mahmud II: Procession*, Anonymous 35tc, 163cl, 163crb; © **The Trustees of the British Museum:** 163cla; **Bunk Hostel:** 185tl; 188br

Cafe Mese: 196b; **Çalikoğlu Reklam Turızm Ve Tıcaret Ltd.:** 220br; **Jean Loup Charmet:** 31tr, 35crb; **Manuel Çıtak:** 48bl, 105cr, 143tr, 164bl; **Cok Cok Thai Restaurant and Bar:** 201br; **Corbis:** David Bathgate 238br; Atlantide Phototravel/Massimo Borchi 227tr; Paul Hardy 174cl; Robert Landau 237bl; Michael Nicholson 10br; Robert Harding World Imagery/Neil Farrin 8–9; Adam Woolfitt 10cla; Alison Wright 179tr; **Culinary Institute Restaurant:** 200tl.

Dreamstime.com: Steve Allen 96t; Murat Besler 64tr; Cylonphoto 241br, Enisu 138; Alexandre Fagundes De Fagundes 11c, 12bl; Ihsan Gercelman 152; Sadık Güleç 177br; Stefan Holm 206bl; Levent Karaoglu 36; Şebnem Köken 175ca; Aleksandra Lande 237tl; Daniël Leppens 96br; Yulia Makarova 136–7; Nexus7 102; Ewa Rejmer 194tr, 195br; Mario Savoia 110; Saiko3p 180–181; Softdreams 226bl; Nikolai Sorokin 50–51; Igor Stevanovic 143br; Muharrem Zengin 2–3, 18tr; Minyun Zhou 86.

Edition Hotels: 184br, 189tc; **ET Archive, London:** 20; Bibliotheque de L'Arsenal, Paris 26t; National Gallery 34bl.

Fes Café: 198bl; **First Army HQ, Istanbul:** 135br. .

Getty Images: 32crb, 34cla; Gary Yeowell 190–1; **Ara Güler:** 25bl, 28tl, 37br, 89br, 130c, 219tr; Mosaics Museum 79c; Topkapı Palace 1, 59tr, 59b, 83tr, 97bl, 163bl; **Şemsi Güner:** 45tl, 131cra, 142tr, 160tr.

Sonia Halliday Photographs: 30bc 129b; engraved by Thomas Allom, painted by Laura Lushington 25cr, 31br, 61tr; Bibliotheque Nationale, Madrid 23t; drawn by Miss Pardoe, painted by Laura Lushington 106cr; Topkapı Palace 35tr, 78br; **The House Cafe:** 205br; **The House Hotel Bosphorus:** 187tr.

İDO-Istanbul Sea Bus Company: 242tr, 243c, 243clb, 243tr, 244cla; **iStockphoto.com:** Anna Bryukhanova 241ca; **Istanbul**

Foundation for Culture and the Arts: 221cb; **Istanbul History Foundation:** 32br; **Istanbul Library:** 68br, 97cra; **Istanbul Metropolitan Municipality:** 231tr.

Gürol Kara:100cl, 117br, 148ca, 155tr, 171tl; **İzzet Kerıbar:** 5bl, 49cra, 54ca, 130tr, 140bc, 141tl, 148clb, 175br, 176tr, 176cl, 176b, 177tc, 179cr, 214br.

Lacivert: 207tl; **José Luczyc-Wyhowska:** 218tr, 219cl/cr/bl/blc/brc/br.

Magnum Photos Ltd: Topkapı Palace/Ara Güler 30bl, 35clb, 43b, 57tl; **Mary Evans Picture Library:** 144bc, 173bl; ES Collectionı/Vatican Library: 25tl.

Nar Lokanta Restaurant: 190bl, 199tr; **Nour Foundation, London:** The Nassar D Khalili Collection of Islamic Art Ferman (MSS801) 97tr, Mahmud II (CAL 334) 97cr, Leaf (CAL 165) 97cl; Burnisher (SC1210) 97bra, Knife (SC1297) 97brb.

Dick Osseman: 177clb; **Güngör Özsoy:** 62tr, 72b, 159tl, 159cra, 172c.

Park Şamdan: 191tl; **Paşabahçe Glassworks:** 148t; **Pera Museum:** 105cb; **Pera Palace Hotel Jumeirah:** 184tl, 188tl; **Photographie Giraudon, Paris:** 28crb; Bibliotheque Nationale, Paris 35bl; Lauros 31bl; Topkapı Palace 28br, 29c, 30cl, 30–31, 34ca; **Pictures Colour Library:** 46br, 215bl, 218cl; **Plan Tours:** 239tl; **Poseidon:** 190bl.

Robert Harding Picture Library: Robert Francis 37cla; Michael Jenner 1, 57br; Yadid Levy 211cr, Odyssey, Chicago/Robert Frerck 42bl, 170b; Ben Pipe 52; Adam Woolfitt 41clb, 93tr, 210bl.

Shutterstock: rm 178cla; **Sixt AG:** 245cla; **Antony Souter:** 55b; **Spectrum Colour Library:** 155br; **Star Gazete:** Murat Duzyol 227br; **The Stockmarket:** 132tl; **SuperStock:** age fotostock 70,72bl, 124tr; Tips Images 89tl.

Tatılya: 222b; **TAV Investment Holding Co.:** 236cla; **Travel Ink:** Abbie Enock 37bc; **Trip Photographic Library:** 156bc; Marc Dubin 47cra; **Turkish Information Office:** Ozan Sadık 47bc.

Peter Wilson: 58c, 77tr, 77cla, 120clb. **Erdal Yazici:** 46cla, 169bl, 171cr.

Front endpaper: Dreamstime.com: Enisu Rtc; Ihsan Gercelman Rtr; Levent Karaoglu Rbl; Mario Savoia Ltr; Nexus7 Rcr; Minyun Zhou Lcb; **SuperStock:** age fotostock Rbr.

Jacket
Front and Spine top – **AWL Images:** Alan Copson

Map Front Cover – **AWL Images:** Alan Copson

All other images © Dorling Kindersley.
For further information see: www.dkimages.com

Special Editions of DK Travel Guides

DK Travel Guides can be purchased in bulk quantities at discounted prices for use in promotions or as premiums. We are also able to offer special editions and personalized jackets, corporate imprints, and excerpts from all of our books, tailored specifically to meet your own needs.

To find out more, please contact:
in the US **specialsales@dk.com**
in the UK **travelguides@uk.dk.com**
in Canada **specialmarkets@dk.com**
in Australia **penguincorporatesales@penguinrandomhouse.com.au**

Phrase Book

Pronunciation

Turkish uses a Roman alphabet. It has 29 letters: 8 vowels and 21 consonants. Letters that differ from the English alphabet are: **c**, pronounced "j" as in "jolly"; **ç**, pronounced "ch" as in "church"; **ğ**, which lengthens the preceding vowel and is not pronounced; **ı**, pronounced "uh"; **ö**, pronounced "ur" (like the sound in "further"); **ş**, pronounced "sh" as in "ship"; **ü**, pronounced "ew" as in "few".

In an Emergency

Help!	**İmdat!**	eem-**dat**
Stop!	**Dur!**	door
Call a doctor!	**Bir doktor çağırın!**	beer dok-**tor chah**-ruhn
Call an ambulance!	**Bir ambulans çağırın!**	beer am-boo-**lans chah**-ruhn
Call the police!	**Polis çağırın!**	po-**lees chah**-ruhn
Fire!	**Yangın!**	yan-**guhn**
Where is the nearest telephone?	**En yakın telefon nerede?**	en ya-**kuhn** teh-leh-**fon neh**-reh-deh
Where is the nearest hospital?	**En yakın hastane nerede?**	en ya-**kuhn** has-ta-**neh neh**-reh-deh

Communication Essentials

Yes	**Evet**	eh-**vet**
No	**Hayır**	h-**'eye'**-uhr
Thank you	**Teşekkür ederim**	teh-shek-**kewr** eh-deh-reem
Please	**Lütfen**	**lewt**-fen
Excuse me	**Affedersiniz**	af-feh-der-see-neez
Hello	**Merhaba**	mer-ha-ba
Goodbye	**Hoşça kalın**	hosh-**cha ka**-luhn
Good morning	**Günaydın**	gewn-**eye'-duhn**
Good evening	**İyi akşamlar**	ee-**yee** ak-sham-**lar**
Morning	**Sabah**	sa-**bah**
Afternoon	**Öğleden sonra**	ur-leh-**den son**-ra
Evening	**Akşam**	ak-**sham**
Yesterday	**Dün**	dewn
Today	**Bugün**	boo-**gewn**
Tomorrow	**Yarın**	ya-**ruhn**
Here	**Burada**	boo-ra-da
There	**Şurada**	shoo-ra-da
Over there	**Orada**	o-ra-da
What?	**Ne?**	neh
When?	**Ne zaman?**	neh za-man
Why?	**Neden**	neh-den
Where?	**Nerede**	neh-reh-deh

Useful Phrases

How are you?	**Nasılsınız?**	na-suhl-suh-nuhz
I'm fine	**İyiyim**	ee-yee-yeem
Pleased to meet you	**Memnun oldum**	mem-**noon ol**-doom
See you soon	**Görüşmek üzere**	gur-rewsh-**mek** ew-zeh-reh
That's fine	**Tamam**	ta-mam
Where is/are …?	**… nerede?**	… neh-reh-deh
How far is it to…?	**… ne kadar uzakta?**	… neh ka-dar oo-zak-ta
I want to go to …	**… a/e gitmek istiyorum**	… a/eh geet-**mek** ees-tee-yo-room
Do you speak English?	**İngilizce biliyor musunuz?**	een-gee-**leez**-jeh bee-**lee**-yor moo-soo-nooz?
I don't understand	**Anlamıyorum**	an-**la**-muh-yo-room
Can you help me?	**Bana yardım edebilir misiniz?**	ba-**na** yar-**duhm** eh-deh-bee-**leer** mee -see-neez?

Useful Words

big	**büyük**	bew-**yewk**
small	**küçük**	kew-**chewk**
hot	**sıcak**	suh-**jak**
cold	**soğuk**	soh-**ook**
good/well	**iyi**	ee-yee
bad	**kötü**	kur-tew
enough	**yeter**	yeh-**ter**
open	**açık**	a-**chuhk**
closed	**kapalı**	ka-pa-luh
left	**sol**	sol
right	**sağ**	saa
straight on	**doğru**	doh-**roo**
near	**yakın**	ya-**kuhn**

far	**uzak**	oo-**zak**
up	**yukarı**	yoo-ka-ruh
down	**aşağı**	a-shah-**uh**
early	**erken**	er-**ken**
late	**geç**	gech
entrance	**giriş**	gee-**reesh**
exit	**çıkış**	chuh-**kuhsh**
toilets	**tuvaletler**	too-va-let-**ler**
push	**itiniz**	ee-tee-neez
pull	**çekiniz**	cheh-kee-neez
more	**daha fazla**	da-**ha faz**-la
less	**daha az**	da-**ha az**
very	**çok**	chok

Shopping

How much is this?	**Bu kaç lira?**	boo kach lee-ra
I would like …	**… istiyorum**	… ees-**tee**-yo-room
Do you have …?	**… var mı?**	… **var** muh?
Do you take credit cards?	**Kredi kartı kabul ediyor musunuz?**	kreh-dee **kar**-tuh ka-**bool** eh-dee-yor moo-soo-nooz?
What time do you open/ close?	**Saat kaçta açılıyor/ kapanıyor?**	Sa-**at** kach-**ta** a-chuh-**luh**-yor/ ka-pa-**nuh**-yor
this one	**bunu**	boo-**noo**
that one	**şunu**	shoo-**noo**
expensive	**pahalı**	pa-ha-**luh**
cheap	**ucuz**	oo-**jooz**
size (clothes)	**beden**	beh-**den**
size (shoes)	**numara**	noo-ma-**ra**
white	**beyaz**	bay-**yaz**
black	**siyah**	see-**yah**
red	**kırmızı**	kuhr-muh-**zuh**
yellow	**sarı**	sa-**ruh**
green	**yeşil**	yeh-**sheel**
blue	**mavi**	ma-**vee**
brown	**kahverengi**	kah-**veh**-ren-gee
shop	**dükkan**	dewk-**kan**
till	**kasa**	ka-**sa**
bargaining	**pazarlık**	pa-zar-**luhk**
That's my last offer	**Daha fazla veremem**	da-**ha faz**-la veh-**reh**-mem

Types of Shop

antiques shop	**antikacı**	an-**tee**-ka-juh
bakery	**fırın**	fuh-**ruhn**
bank	**banka**	ban-ka
bookshop	**kitapçı**	kee-tap-**chuh**
butcher's	**kasap**	ka-sap
cake shop	**pastane**	pas-ta-**neh**
chemist's/ pharmacy	**eczane**	ej-za-neh
fishmonger's	**balıkçı**	ba-luhk-**chuh**
greengrocer's	**manav**	ma-**nav**
grocery	**bakkal**	bak-**kal**
hairdresser's (ladies)	**kuaför**	kwaf-**fur**
(mens)	**berber**	ber-ber
leather shop	**derici**	deh-ree-jee
market/bazaar	**çarşı/pazar**	char-**shuh**/pa-zar
newsstand	**gazeteci**	ga-zeh-teh-jee
post office	**postane**	pos-ta-neh
shoe shop	**ayakkabıcı**	'eye'-yak-ka-buh-juh
stationer's	**kırtasiyeci**	kuhr-**ta**-see-yeh-jee
supermarket	**süpermarket**	sew-per-mar-**ket**
tailor	**terzi**	ter-zee
travel agency	**seyahat acentesi**	say-ya-**hat** a-jen-teh-**see**

Sightseeing

castle	**hisar**	hee-**sar**
church	**kilise**	kee-lee-seh
island	**ada**	a-**da**
mosque	**cami**	ja-mee
museum	**müze**	mew-zeh
palace	**saray**	sar-**eye'**
park	**park**	park
square	**meydan**	may-**dan**
theological college	**medrese**	med-**reh**-seh
tomb	**türbe**	tewr-**beh**
tourist information office	**turizm danışma bürosu**	too-reezm da-nuhsh-**mah** bew-ro-soo
tower	**kule**	koo-**leh**
town hall	**belediye sarayı**	beh-leh-dee-**yeh** sar-**eye'**-uh
Turkish bath	**hamam**	ha-**mam**

Transport

airport	**havalimanı**	ha-**va**-lee-ma-nuh
bus/coach	**otobüs**	o-to-**bewss**
bus stop	**otobüs durağı**	o-to-**bewss** doo-**ra**-uh
coach station	**otogar**	o-to-**gar**
dolmuş	**dolmuş**	dol-**moosh**
fare	**ücret**	ewj-**ret**
ferry	**vapur**	va-**poor**
sea bus	**deniz otobüsü**	deh-**neez** o-to-**bew**-sew
station	**istasyon**	ees-tas-**yon**
taxi	**taksi**	tak-**see**
ticket	**bilet**	bee-**let**
ticket office	**bilet gişesi**	bee-**let** gee-sheh-**see**
timetable	**tarife**	ta-ree-**feh**

Staying in a Hotel

Do you have a vacant room?	**Boş odanız var mı?**	bosh o-da-**nuhz** var muh?
double room	**iki kişilik bir oda**	ee-**kee** kee-shee-**leek** beer o-**da**
room with a double bed	**çift kişilik yataklı bir oda**	**cheeft** kee-shee-**leek** ya-**tak**-luh beer o-**da**
twin room	**çift yataklı bir oda**	**cheeft** ya-**tak**-luh beer o-**da**
for one person	**tek kişilik**	tek kee-shee-**leek**
room with a bath	**banyolu bir oda**	ban-yo-loo beer o-**da**
shower	**duş**	doosh
porter	**komi**	ko-**mee**
key	**anahtar**	a-nah-**tar**
room service	**oda servisi**	o-**da** ser-vee-**see**
I have a reservation	**Rezervasyonum var**	reh-zer-vas-yo-**noom** var
Does the price include breakfast?	**Fiyata kahvaltı dahil mi?**	fee-ya-**ta** kah-val-tuh da-**heel** mee?

Eating Out

A table for … please	**… kişilik bir masa lütfen**	… kee-shee-**leek** beer ma-sa lewt-fen
I want to reserve a table	**Bir masa ayırtmak istiyorum**	beer ma-sa 'eye'-uhrt-mak ees-**tee**-yo-room
The bill please	**Hesap lütfen**	heh-**sap** lewt-fen
I am a vegetarian	**Et yemiyorum**	et yeh-mee-yo-room
restaurant	**lokanta**	lo-**kan**-ta
waiter	**garson**	gar-**son**
menu	**yemek listesi**	ye-**mek** lees-teh-see
fixed-price menu	**fiks menü**	feeks meh-**new**
wine list	**şarap listesi**	sha-**rap** lees-teh-see
breakfast	**kahvaltı**	kah-val-**tuh**
lunch	**öğle yemeği**	ur-**leh** yeh-meh-**ee**
dinner	**akşam yemeği**	ak-**sham** yeh-meh-**ee**
starter	**meze**	**meh**-zeh
main course	**ana yemek**	a-na yeh-**mek**
dish of the day	**günün yemeği**	gewn-**ewn** yeh-meh-**ee**
dessert	**tatlı**	tat-**luh**
rare	**az pişmiş**	**az** peesh-meesh
well done	**iyi pişmiş**	ee-**yee** peesh-meesh
glass	**bardak**	bar-**dak**
bottle	**şişe**	shee-**sheh**
knife	**bıçak**	buh-**chak**
fork	**çatal**	cha-**tal**
spoon	**kaşık**	ka-**shuhk**

Menu Decoder

badem	ba-**dem**	almond
bal	bal	honey
balık	ba-**luhk**	fish
bira	**bee**-ra	beer
bonfile	**bon**-fee-leh	fillet steak
buz	booz	ice
çay	ch-'eye'	tea
çilek	chee-**lek**	strawberry
çorba	chor-**ba**	soup
dana eti	da-**na** eh-**tee**	veal
dondurma	don-door-**ma**	ice cream
ekmek	ek-**mek**	bread
elma	el-**ma**	apple
et	et	meat
fasulye	fa-**sool**-yeh	beans
fırında	fuh-ruhn-**da**	roast
fıstık	fuhs-**tuhk**	pistachio nuts
gazoz	ga-**zoz**	fizzy drink
hurma	hoor-**ma**	dates
içki	eech-**kee**	alcohol
incir	**een**-jeer	figs
ızgara	uhz-**ga**-ra	charcoal grilled
kahve	kah-**veh**	coffee
kara biber	ka-**ra** bee-**ber**	black pepper
karışık	ka-ruh-**shuhk**	mixed
karpuz	kar-**pooz**	water melon
kavun	ka-**voon**	melon
kayısı	k-'eye'-uh-**suh**	apricots
kaymak	k-'eye'-**mak**	cream
kıyma	kuhy-**ma**	minced meat
kızartma	kuh-zart-**ma**	fried
köfte	kurf-**teh**	meatballs
kuru	koo-**roo**	dried
kuzu eti	koo-**zoo** eh-**tee**	lamb
lokum	lo-**koom**	Turkish delight
maden suyu	ma-**den** soo-**yoo**	mineral water (fizzy)
meyve suyu	may-**veh** soo-**yoo**	fruit juice
midye	**meed**-yeh	mussels
muz	mooz	banana
patlıcan	pat-luh-**jan**	aubergine
peynir	pay-**neer**	cheese
pilav	pee-**lav**	rice
piliç	pee-**leech**	roast chicken
şarap	sha-**rap**	wine
sebze	seb-**zeh**	vegetables
şeftali	shef-ta-**lee**	peach
şeker	sheh-**ker**	sugar
su	soo	water
süt	sewt	milk
sütlü	sewt-**lew**	with milk
tavuk	ta-**vook**	chicken
tereyağı	teh-**reh**-yah-uh	butter
tuz	tooz	salt
üzüm	ew-**zewm**	grapes
vişne	**veesh**-neh	sour cherry
yoğurt	yoh-**urt**	yogurt
yumurta	yoo-moor-**ta**	egg
zeytin	zay-**teen**	olives
zeytinyağı	zay-**teen**-yah-uh	olive oil

Numbers

0	**sıfır**	**suh**-fuhr
1	**bir**	beer
2	**iki**	ee-**kee**
3	**üç**	ewch
4	**dört**	durt
5	**beş**	besh
6	**altı**	al-**tuh**
7	**yedi**	yeh-**dee**
8	**sekiz**	seh-**keez**
9	**dokuz**	doh-**kooz**
10	**on**	on
11	**on bir**	**on** beer
12	**on iki**	**on** ee-kee
13	**on üç**	**on** ewch
14	**on dört**	**on** durt
15	**on beş**	**on** besh
16	**on altı**	**on** al-tuh
17	**on yedi**	**on** yeh-dee
18	**on sekiz**	**on** seh-keez
19	**on dokuz**	**on** doh-kooz
20	**yirmi**	yeer-**mee**
21	**yirmi bir**	yeer-mee **beer**
30	**otuz**	o-**tooz**
40	**kırk**	kuhrk
50	**elli**	eh-**lee**
60	**altmış**	alt-**muhsh**
70	**yetmiş**	yet-**meesh**
80	**seksen**	sek-**sen**
90	**doksan**	dok-**san**
100	**yüz**	yewz
110	**yüz on**	yewz **on**
200	**iki yüz**	ee-**kee** yewz
1,000	**bin**	been
100,000	**yüz bin**	**yewz** been
1,000,000	**bir milyon**	**beer** meel-**yon**

Time

one minute	**bir dakika**	**beer** da-kee-ka
one hour	**bir saat**	**beer** sa-at
half an hour	**yarım saat**	ya-**ruhm** sa-at
day	**gün**	gewn
week	**hafta**	haf-**ta**
month	**ay**	'eye'
year	**yıl**	yuhl
Sunday	**pazar**	pa-**zar**
Monday	**pazartesi**	pa-**zar**-teh-see
Tuesday	**salı**	sa-**luh**
Wednesday	**çarşamba**	char-sham-**ba**
Thursday	**perşembe**	per-shem-**beh**
Friday	**cuma**	joo-**ma**
Saturday	**cumartesi**	joo-**mar**-teh-see

Istanbul Transit Map

Key

- Ferry boarding point
- Sea bus boarding point
- Ferry route
- Train station
- Railroad line
- Underground funicular stop
- Funicular route
- Metro station
- Tram route and stop
- Nostalgic tram route
- Cable car
- Bus route
- 56 Bus terminal
- City walls
- Major sight

0 metres 500
0 yards 500

47

Eyüp

Sütlüce

EYÜP

55T-99A

39

55T-99A

39

Ayvansaray

Hasköy

BALAT

55T-99A

Golden Horn

Kaşımpa

Şehitlik

Airport, Esenler Coach Station

39

Edirnekapı

28-87

Church of St Saviour in Chora

90-90B

910-91E

39-91O

28-87-91O

90-90B

CARŞAMBA

ABÜLEZEL PAŞA

46H-55T-61B-72T-80-83-87-90-91O-

93T-96T-99A

83-28T

Topkapı-Ulubatlı

39-91E

MAÇAR KARDEŞLER CADDESİ

90-90B

28-87-90-91O

ATATÜRK BULVARI

28-28T-96T

Halic

Topkapı

72T

FEVZİ PAŞA CADDESİ

VATAN CADDESİ

Pazartekke

Emniyet Fatih

908

Süleymaniye Mosque

47-80-81-90-91O-96T-9

93T

MİLLET CADDESİ

Çapa-Şehremini

FATİH

39-90B-91E

28-87-90-91O

28-28T-46H-61B-72T-80-83-87-90-91O-93T

BAZAAR QUART

Fındıkzade

28T-72T-83-93T

Aksaray

28T-46H-61B-72T-80-83-93T

Vezneciler

Grand Bazaa

Haseki

ORDU CADDESİ

39-46H-61B-90B-91E

Yusufpaşa

80

Aksaray

Laleli-Üniversite

Beyazıt

Çem

39-46H-61B-90B-91E

BELGRATKAPI DEMİRHANE YOLU

93T

KOCAMUSTAFAPAŞA

80

Yenikapı

KENNEDY CADDESİ

CADDESİ

81-96T

80

Yenikapı

KENNEDY CADDESİ

Airport

Marmara, Bandırma, Bursa

Yalova, Çınarcık, Gemlik